New Age Politics

Healing self and society

The emerging new alternative to Marxism and liberalism

MARK SATIN

$2.95

New Age Politics

Politics

HEALING SELF AND SOCIETY

The emerging new alternative to Marxism and liberalism

MARK SATIN

Whitecap Books

2229 Jefferson Avenue, West Vancouver, B.C. V7V 2A9
Telephone: (604) 926-0091

with

Fairweather Press
A Non-Profit Publishing Cooperative

revised, expanded and deepened edition

First printing, May, 1978 — 10,000 copies

Published by:
Whitecap Books Ltd.
2229 Jefferson Ave.
West Vancouver, B.C. V7V - 2A9
Canada

New Age Politics is available in bulk to individuals and groups and bookstores in the U.S. at the following rates (in U.S. currency — book rate
postage prepaid):
  5 - 99 copies, $1.75 each
  100 or more copies, $1.20 each

Mark Satin travels around North America giving workshops and talks on
New Age politics. For more information write Whitecap Books.

Figure on p. 12 and chart on p. 78 drawn by Suzanne Soldan of Seraphics
Artists' Guild (care of Ariel Women's Books, 2766 W. 4th, Vancouver).

Typing, typesetting and layout by M.S.

Portions of this book have appeared, in slightly different form, in the **New
Age Journal** and in **New Directions**.

~~~~~~

Canadian Shared Cataloguing in Publication Data

Satin, Mark Ivor, 1946-
    New age politics: healing self and society.

    1. Civilization, Modern - 1950 - 2. Social
values. 3. Radicalism - North America. I. Title

CB428.S385 1978   910'.03'09
ISBN 0 - 920422 - 01 - 2

Contents

Part V — New Age Society

Part VI — New Age Economics

Part VII — Healing Self and Society

Part VIII — Appendix

Chapter 1 — Introduction

This book is based on one very simple premise: the politics we need in North America today will not and cannot come from liberalism or Marxism, or even from 'just muddling through'. The situation we're in is so new — so unprecedented — that we need a whole new way of looking at the world. A whole new way of **seeing** things and thinking about things (especially 'political' things). One that comes out of our own experience. . . .

The point of this book is that a new way of seeing and a new politics is arising **already** in bits and pieces, here and there, across the continent; but that we (and especially our intellectuals) have been so desperately set on proving the new or improved applicability of: liberalism, Marxism, anarchism, etc. that we've missed the coming together of these pieces and trends, **right before our eyes**.

The new politics is arising out of the work and ideas of many of the people in many of the social movements of the 1970's: the spiritual, environmental, feminist, and 'men's liberation' movements; the human potential, simple living, appropriate-technology, and business-for-learning-and-pleasure movements; the humanistic-transformational education movement and the new nonviolent-action movement.

The new politics is also arising out of the work and ideas of a couple of hundred sympathetic economists and mystics, businesspeople and workers' self-management people, systems analysts and psychoanalysts, physicists and poets. . . .

Each of these movements and each of these writers has something to add to the new politics. Their contributions come together like the pieces of an intricate jigsaw puzzle.

More and more of us have, over the last 10 years or so, become deeply involved in one or more of the movements mentioned above. At the same time, though, the radical political movements of the 1960's seem to have collapsed.

Could there be a connection?

I believe that the radical political movements declined as soon as they began to promote a doctrine of us-against-them, of 'we have all the answers', of separation rather than healing. As soon as they began to promote a dogmatic Marxism that overstressed our need for **things** and tried to make us feel guilty about our deeper needs, which are emotional, psychological and spiritual (and which are what got us into the radical political movements in the first place). And I believe that the spiritual, feminist, environmental, etc., movements rose partly, at least, because they did contain a politics that did speak to our deeper needs. To all our needs.

But it was only an implicit politics, hard to see at first. And it was doubly hard to see just because it was so new and different from the politics that had gone before.

The purpose of this book is to make this politics explicit. To draw out, in some detail, its analysis of society (Parts I-III), its worldview (IV), its goals (V), its economics (VI), and its strategy (VII & Appendix).

Dozens of people have tried to give a name to the emerging new politics, or to aspects of the new politics. Here are some names that I liked enough to write down:

'Anarchic Capitalism' — William Irwin Thompson, cultural historian
'Cooperative Capitalism' — Joe Falk, community organizer
'Enlightened Humanism' — John Maher, organizer of ex-felons
'Global Humanism' — Richard Falk, professor of international law
'The New Localism' — David Morris and Karl Hess, political economists
'Participatory Divinity' — David Spangler, spiritual philosopher
'Personalism' — Nikolai Berdyaev, religious philosopher
'The Politics of the Person' — Theodore Roszak, cultural historian
'Radical Humanism' — Erich Fromm, psychologist
'Synergic Politics' — Jim Craig, management consultant, and Marge Craig, healer

I have begun to call this politics 'New Age politics'. Partly because so many members of the movements mentioned above have begun using the term 'New Age' themselves in their work. Partly because the term 'New Age' is broad enough to encompass all these other definitions — and flexible enough to be constantly open to redefinition. And partly because it suggests that the years since the Second World War represent the beginnings of a radical break with the past, or at least, with many aspects of that past. It implies that the world is being not just changed but transformed, and it implies that we had better see to it that it's transformed in a life-giving manner.

Aspects of the transformation can be grouped under five headings:

(1) **New technologies.** New means of transportation and communication have shrunk the Earth to such a degree that we're all united now, for better or worse, in a kind of 'planetary village'. For example, in 60 years we've gone from Kitty Hawk, North Carolina to the moon. Consider that since 1945 the atomic bomb, the neutron bomb, the 'electronic battlefield' and God knows how many military horrors have all been developed. Consider that between 1950 and 1970, world energy requirements rose from about 2560 million metric tons of coal equivalent to 6600 million metric tons — more than a 250 percent increase.

(2) **New problems**. The new weapons. Overpopulation. Our suicidal consumption levels (resources, energy) and the failure of other countries to learn from our mistakes. The new techniques of political repression and control. Our severance from the spirit, loss of the sense that we're of any ultimate value.

(3) **New possibilities**. Never before have we had the capacity to eliminate all hunger, disease, hard-core poverty, etc. — all physical manifestations of human suffering. In the affluent countries, meanwhile, as sociologist Laile Bartlett points out, for the first time we can consciously decide **what we are to become** as human beings. . . .

(4) **New consciousness**. Donald Keys, registrar of Planetary Citizens, thinks we can begin to speak about a 'new evolutionary step' for people in terms of their consciousness. People are becoming less egocentric, less dependent on science as the **one** way to truth, etc. What else, asks William Irwin Thompson, is behind the extraordinary recent interest in the mind of the primitive, the schizophrenic, the shaman, the child, the dolphin, and the 'extraterrestrial being'?

(5) **New energies**. Sensitive and spiritually oriented persons the world over have recently become aware of a subtle change in energies that the earth appears to be undergoing. The reason for this may be astrological — but at this point no one can really be sure. . . .

New Age Politics begins by saying that at the **root** of our troubles is a cultural complex whose six main elements make up a 'Six-Sided Prison' that traps us all.

In Part I I try to name and describe the six sides of the Prison: patriarchal attitudes, egocentricity, scientific single vision, the bureaucratic mentality, nationalism, and the big-city outlook. Capitalism and socialism are, I argue, both rooted in the Prison (which predates capitalism by hundreds of years) — though neither needs to be. (Racism, militarism, exploitation, ecocide, etc., are also rooted in the Prison.) I propose a method, 'tri-level analysis', for seeing all the way through to the Prison. And I look at history as if people mattered more than changes in governments or economic systems.

In Part II I argue that the Prison is institutionalized by the 'monolithic mode of production' which creates effective monopolies not for its brands but for its products (such as mass-produced white bread and rapid transit). I look at 16 representative monolithic institutions including: institutionalized medicine; the universal, compulsory school; compulsive heterosexuality; nuclear power plants; the 'monolithic state'; the large corporation; 'monolithic social roles'; and the 'monolithic mind'.

In Part III I argue that we're primarily self-developing persons, not economic people; and that we have to meet our needs on each of seven 'stages of self-development' before we can be self-reliant and whole. I look at what happens to us as persons in Prison society (i.e. as victims of the 'stroke economy'). And I propose a class analysis that sees us not as ruling-class, bourgeois or proletarian, but as life-, thing- or death-oriented.

In Part IV I try to show that the materialist and non-material worldviews are both inadequate — **neither** can give us the foundations for a wholistic new politics. I try to synthesize the emerging new 'trans-material' worldview which incorporates the 'material state of consciousness' but goes beyond it, too. And I suggest that the new worldview implies four 'primary' New Age ethics — the self-development, ecology, self reliance-cooperation and nonviolence ethics — which imply in turn a number of political and social values.

In Part V I try to suggest what 'New Age society' might be like. It would almost surely promote 'New Age feminist' attitudes rather than patriarchal attitudes; spirituality rather than egocentricity; and other life-oriented alternatives to the Prison. It would promote 'biolithic' rather than monolithic institutions — institutions that were largely or exclusively human scale and that offered us more choice in the ways we wanted to live. It would foster 'localization' — community and regional decentralization (to whatever extent the various communities wished). And it would foster 'planetization' — planetary cooperation and sharing.

In Part VI I say that there are at least four possible 'New Age economies': the crafts, service, leisure and 'household' economies. I try to suggest what a 'New Age capitalism' might be like. And I try to present some representative insights from the emerging 'New Age economic theory'.

In Part VII I argue against elections **and** revolution as strategies for getting us beyond the Prison and its institutions, and I argue for a strategy that would involve each of us assuming responsibility for (a) healing self, and (b) healing society. I argue that living a life of love in our culture of things and of death is an essential political act.

In the Appendix I argue that Marxism does not and cannot come up with the answers we need, in North America in the 1970's. And I include an annotated listing of 200 New Age books, 25 New Age periodicals, and 25 New Age groups that I hope you'll want to look into after you've finished with this book.

This isn't the first time that a political philosophy along the same general lines as New Age politics has begun to take shape in the world.

Prerevolutionary Russia: a collection of articles called **Landmarks**, published in 1909 and circulated widely, lashes out at the materialist worldview, at scientific single vision, and at all the old political 'ism's', and calls for a return to spiritual values as a precondition for social, cultural and political change. After the Revolution the book is banned, and its contributors, including the ex-Marxist philosopher Nikolai Berdyaev, flee the country.

Harlem and other black communities, U.S.A., 1920's: black people are beginning to work out a political alternative that puts special emphasis on culture and on ethnic group identity. But the black intellectuals are, according to black writer Harold Cruse, 'so overwhelmed at being "discovered" and courted' by white Marxists that they allow their insights to degenerate into a pampered cultural vogue (the Harlem Renaissance), meanwhile accepting political leadership from these same white Marxists.

India, 1920's - 40's: Mahatma Gandhi articulates a coherent new political philosophy under the slogan 'self-rule and self-restraint'. People are to lead simple lives, free of want and luxury; villages are to practice political and economic self-sufficiency as much as possible, and are to prefer human-scale technology to huge modern factories.

The 'self-rule' movement is successful — for India as a whole — but Gandhi is killed, and most of the rest of the independence leaders, good Marxists and liberals who are embarrassed by the rest of Gandhi's political programme, proceed to try to 'modernize' India in the best traditions of the industrial West.

France, 1930's - 1950's: a popular political movement called 'Personalism' arises that aspires to be genuinely different from Marxism and liberalism. Its leading journal, Emmanuel Mounier's **Esprit**, holds that the person is sacred; redefines 'bourgeois' to mean, he who has banished all mystery from life; speaks out against 'over-industrialism' and calls for a decentralised economy; and condemns the nation-state. The movement comes out of the second World War stronger than ever, with branches in many other European countries, but within five years of the Cold War it is effectively dead.

Roger Garaudy, dissident French Communist, claims that personalism died because it had failed to construct a genuinely different **worldview** for its politics — and so it had simply crumbled under the for-us-or-against-us kinds of pressures of the Cold War.

North America and to some extent Western Europe, 1960's: the new activism is proud, at first, of its refusal to rely on any known ideology, and of its first efforts to work out an 'independent' political programme based largely on its own actual experience of the world. The 'Triple Revolution' manifesto argues that the cybernetics, weapons and human rights revolutions are precipitating a 'historic break' with the past. Students for a Democratic Society, the leading radical student group, puts out a literature list that includes pamphlets by McLuhan, education reformers, neo-pacifists and therapists, as well as by Marxists and liberals. SDS activists attempt to identify a new, 'revolutionary' social class that would include some students and professionals. Nonviolence is 'discovered' (through Camus); the dangers of totalitarianism are stressed (Orwell). Books of spiritual concern are popular, especially those by J. Krishnamurti and Aldous Huxley, and are found to contain an underlying, and often enough a congenial, political dimension.

Liberals and Marxists alike are aghast at the unorthodox ideas and reading matter of the new activists, and regularly criticize their 'lifestyles' (a code word for their ideas) and their motives. Generally the activists respond on the same level as the criticisms. They laugh.

But then comes Vietnam, and most of them — most of us, me included — begin to want to come up with an analysis fast, an analysis that can tell us exactly what is happening and why and exactly 'what is to be done' about it. There is only one such analysis in town — Marxism — and so many of us become Marxists. But it is a decision that many of us are later to regret. For example: Julius Lester, who used to write the token black man's column for the Marxist weekly, the **Guardian**, has recently said that he'd always felt that 'real change was spiritual', but that his experiences in 'The Movement' had caused him to become self-righteous and hateful and ultimately to lose touch with himself. By 1969, he tells us, he felt himself to be 'a dummy for a revolutionary ventriloquist, an actor in a bad play'. Jerry Rubin, in his recent book, **Growing (Up) at** 37, says much the same thing — 'We activists in the 1960's eventually lost touch with ourselves' — and he adds: 'People out of touch with their bodies and souls cannot make positive change'.

By the early 1970's, most of us had begun to associate 'politics' with rhetoric and guilt, and had wisely left 'politics' behind.

If the experiences of the past can teach us anything, it is surely that we have got to learn to look at the world with fresh eyes and from our own point of view.

In North America, New Age political thinking is most advanced and may soon be in a position to capture the imagination of the general public . . . partly because we are the first people to learn-by-doing that the pursuit of affluence does **not** lead to happiness. But, significantly, New Age political ideas are surfacing today in many other places as well. For example:

In **Britain**, the environmental movement has published **A Blueprint for Survival** (1972) which argues that a decentralised society is not only **preferable** to what we have now, but may soon be **necessary** because of environmental and resource constraints. The **Blueprint** has recently become the basis for the 'Movement for Survival' whose aim is 'to influence governments into taking those measures most likely to lead to stabilization and hence the survival of our society'. The Movement has already gained a number of politically influential supporters in Britain and its **Blueprint** has been adopted as the platform of the new Values Party in New Zealand.

At the same time, a number of new political formations such as the Parallel Culture Group, and a number of independent scholars and activists such as Guy Dauncey, are speaking out against make-work projects; questioning the usefulness of economic class analysis; calling for political decentralisation; calling for 'social transformation' rather than revolution **or** reform; speaking out against urbanisation; and so on (see **Peace News**, 9 Jul. '76).

In **France**, many 'graduates of the streets' of May, 1968 have recently been turning **away** from Marxism and anarchism and **toward** a point of view, if not yet a politics, that looks very much like that of New Age politics. In at least 14 books, all published since 1975, these 'new philosophers' accuse the French left of 'intellectual betrayal' (for consistently lying about the events in the socialist countries); trace the Soviet labour camps back to Marx, rather than Lenin or Stalin; and attack the intellectual foundations of Marxism **and** liberalism, which they trace back to 'scientific rationalism' and the Western European enlightenment.

At the same time, a new, ecologically-oriented political party, 'The Greens', recently stunned the traditional political parties (liberal and Marxist) by receiving approx. 12 percent of the popular vote in the French municipal elections. Many of the Greens have been influenced deeply by the new philosophers' critique of socialism, and by a number of the authors listed in Chap. 24 below. Their rallying cry is 'auto-gestion' — decentralised self-government. As one of them explains it, auto-gestion is the political version of the 'auto-regulation' (self-regulation) of the ecosystems which owe their stability to their diversity.

Green activists include regional separatists, workers' self-management people, anti-nuclear activists, consumer activists, anarchists, non-violent activists, and various women's groups — a heterogenous lot that's fighting a decisive battle right now over whether or not to break with the rhetoric of the traditional anti-authoritarian Left (see **CoEvolution Quarterly**, Winter '77-'78).

With regard to **Russia**, Alexander Solzhenitsyn and half a dozen other Soviet dissidents have put together a book, **From Under the Rubble** (1975), that is consciously modelled on the old **Landmarks** of Berdyaev and company. In it, the spiritual wing of the dissident movement reveals itself as being totally committed to nonviolence — as an ethic as well as a tactic; speaks in the strongest terms about the material limits to growth; calls for political and economic decentralisation; and urges us to practice 'repentance and self-limitation' as individuals and as nations. 'Once understood and adopted, this principle diverts us — as individuals, in all forms of human association, societies and nations — from **outward** to **inward** development . . . '.

You can't say that New Age politics is 'left wing' or 'right wing'. It is perfectly compatible with public or private ownership of the means of production, and it speaks equally much to rich and poor, young and old, white collar and blue. Still, New Age politics does stand in a definite relation to the other political ideologies. From the perspective of New Age thinkers, there are two defining political choices that every society must make . . . and neither of them is covered by the old political categories 'left' and 'right'.

The first choice has to do with this. Do we want our society to encourage us to seek rich individual experience and to be of service to others — or do we want our society to encourage us to seek material riches in the form of possessions and status? Another way of putting this is: do we want our society to be based on the Prison, or do we want our society to be based on a complex of more life-giving ethics and values? (For more on the Prison, see Chaps. 3 & 13.)

The second choice has to do with this. Do we want our society to extend state and institutional control over our lives (for whatever reason) — or do we want our society to encourage us to be self-reliant and self-determining? Another way of putting this is: do we want our society to extend our 'monolithic' institutions, or do we want it to replace them with 'biolithic' institutions? (For more on our institutions, see Chaps. 7 & 14.)

In order to develop an accurate and telling substitute for the old left-right continuum and so better indicate the real political energies that are at work in the world and the choices that we really must make, I created two new continua based on the above, experience-versus-possessions and autonomy-versus-obedience, and crossed them at right angles, making the quadrant below:

(biolithic institutions)
individual autonomy;
community and/or regional
self-determination

	New Age politics	North America (in theory)	
individual experience and social service (Prison-free)	China	Soviet Union	individual possessions and social status (Prison-bound)

individual conformity;
state and/or institutional
domination
(monolithic institutions)

It seems to me that New Age politics might most comfortably fit into the upper left hand quadrant; North America, in the upper right in theory and the lower right in practice; the Soviet Union, in the lower right; and China, in the lower left (though whether the Chinese emphasis on being is meant to last or is only an expedient while it builds up a material base, is probably impossible now to say).

My last book was an autobiographical novel. I wanted to try to do for men what Violette Leduc, Kate Millett and others had done for women, to write as personal and honest a book as I could, and writing it made me cry, made me sick, made me swear that the air was 'thick with the dead', and made me cling to people as if I was drowning. So I looked forward to writing this book partly just because it would have to be 'objective' and almost formal, with lots of research, references, etc. (one version even has footnotes). But don't let that fool you: I feel passionately about every sentence in here, and every idea is rooted in my direct experience.

I was born in New York City in November, 1946 (double Scorpio, moon in Leo). I was brought up in small towns in the Midwest and in the South and for a long time I was a liberal too: civil rights worker, VISTA volunteer (domestic peace corps), good grades. All this changed with the war, and with my introduction to Marxism and (especially) to Marxists, who seemed to have all the answers I so desperately needed. In this phase of my life I was an underground journalist, president of an SDS chapter, and a draft resister — I started the Toronto Anti-Draft Programme and a hostel for resisters in Vancouver (When I was 'underground', in Oregon, I was a member of the Teamsters' Union — my name was 'Fred Wylie'. And I've also been a government bureaucrat!)

I broke with Marxism in the early 1970's when the 'revolutionary tide' receded enough for me to be able to admit to myself that Marxism didn't speak to my needs . . . or even to my everyday, common-sensical understandings of what was going on in North America.

For a year or two I felt guilty about this — Marxists have a way of making you feel that the struggle for socialism is, by definition, **the** struggle for truth and justice (but see Chap. 23 below). . . . Part of the process of my getting free from Marxism and, more generally, from the incredible self-righteousness of the 1960's, was beginning to get in touch with who I was and what I wanted from life . . . a kind of inner search that my 'revolutionary fervour' had obscured. One outcome of this inner search (which is still going on!) was my novel. Another part of this 'freeing' process was beginning to put together the emerging new non-Marxist, non-liberal ideas so that I could have a firm basis to engage in — no 'revolution' this time, but a deeper, more profound, and more **healing** kind of social transformation. One outcome of **this** process — my 'outer' search — has been **New Age Politics**.

This book couldn't have been written without the help of many people — far too many to even begin to list here. In fact, so many people have helped me in one way or another that I sometimes have a hard time thinking of this book as 'mine'. . . .

Part I — The Prison Within Us

Chapter 2 — A New Kind of Politics

Only a minority of New Agers call themselves capitalists or socialists, and even these tend to be deeply opposed to **liberal** capitalism, **Marxian** socialism. And they — we — tend to have important differences with anarchism as well. Here's why.

I. Liberalism

If our politics are liberal, we might say that people are having a hard time making ends meet financially. And that would be true enough. But it is also true that our average per person incomes are over $7,500 a year now, children included — and our average family incomes are over $18,000 a year. To a New Ager this is no small sum — many of us are living satisfying lives on a fraction of that income. It tends to suggest that our problems have a lot to do with the kinds of foods we eat (all that meat — all that packaged stuff); with the kinds of clothes we wear (chosen for fashion rather than comfort); with the kinds of living arrangements we make for our selves (which tend to encourage isolation and discourage sharing); with the kinds of cars we drive (their size) and the fact that we would **rather** drive cars than walk or even use the public transit (more families have two cars now than none); with the ways we entertain our selves ('nights on the town' rather than true intimacy); and so on. Many New Age writers have suggested that we tend to get our sense of worth from buying and owning things, rather than from, say, friendship and service. Many others have pointed out that, with six percent of the Earth's people we account for nearly 36 percent of the Earth's yearly resource use — about six times our fair share.

Or consider this: our incomes can buy over 60 percent more now than they could in the late 1940's, even after allowing for taxes and inflation (cited in Easterlin. **Note**: all books, authors, magazines, groups cited in the text are referred to in Chap. 24 below). To me this suggests that our material wants — including our desire to have others do **for** us what we once did for our selves — have also gone up by over 60 percent since the late 1940's, or even faster. And are we really as satisfied now, even on the material plane, as we were in the late 1940's? (Easterlin cites a number of studies that show that we are no happier now.) Consider that personal debt rises as we go on up the income scale. . . .

To a New Ager, all these facts suggest that our problems are only superficially economic, and that they have much more to do with culture: with who we are and what we want from life. (This translates itself in to the political arena in some amazingly self-destructive ways — e.g., in our reluctance to establish effective rent control.) Of course, it's not part of the accepted political wisdom to tell people that their values and priorities are doing them in: they won't vote for you if you do. But by encouraging people to feel that they need only more of the same — and, worse, that they can make use of top-down bureaucratic government to 'give it to them' — the liberals may only be adding to the problems that they say they hope to solve.

If our politics are liberal, we might also say that we are just not putting the 'right men' in office. (If we're liberal historians we'd say we've never really put our 'best men' in office. If we're liberal lawyers we might try putting our selves in office. And if we're militant liberals we might try putting black people in office, or women, or even black women!) But all these liberals are assuming that other people, 'men in office', can solve our problems **for** us.

And anyway, they're begging the question. Why **can't** we put the 'right' people in office?

Some liberals understand that our problems go deeper than 'more money' or 'bad politicians'. But they're at a loss to know how to define our deeper problems, let alone what to do about them.

Some of these liberals are willing to speak of a 'crisis in values'. But as Ruben Nelson, management consultant and theologian, points out — putting the problem in this way is implying that the crisis is happening 'out there', **to** us. And that it can therefore be 'patched up' by top-down government technicians ('the best and the brightest') through a kind of mass merchandising of newer and better values.

Others of these liberals have argued that our problems are too complicated to grasp — for now. Meanwhile, they think that pumping a lot of money into the problems might do some good. Unfortunately, however, as Nelson and many other New Agers point out, we not only need to try to do, but we must actually **do** the right things. Otherwise our projects may end up doing a lot more harm than good. Partly by reinforcing, inadvertently, some of the problems that we **most** need to solve, such as our overdependence on the top-down state and on our other 'monolithic institutions'. And partly by reinforcing and perpetuating the **consciousness that causes** these problems in the first place — what I like to call the Prison.

So the 'lessons of liberalism' are: (1) we can't do good until we understand what our problems really are; and (2) we can't do good until we understand and then redefine who **we** are, and what we want from life.

For a more thorough critique of liberalism, see Robert Ghelardi, **Economics, Society and Culture**.

II. Marxism

If our politics are Marxist, we would probably say that the problem is 'capitalism': a handful of bosses are 'ripping off' the workers. But most corporations have been averaging only 5-10 percent profit per year — and most of that is re-invested. (A socialist bureaucracy has to spend at least as much on extra administrative costs.) Economist William Nordhaus has recently shown that there's been an 'absence of "net" profitability in the corporate sector' since the late 1940's; 'that is, price was just sufficient to cover all costs including the cost of capital' (**New York Review of Books**, 17 Feb. '77). And Seymour Melman, a political scientist, and Harvey Leibenstein, an economist, have recently proposed different (but complementary) theories to show that corporations do not, generally speaking, minimize costs or maximize profits.

H. B. Wilson, who is a chartered accountant as well as an advocate of workers' self-management, has had what should be everybody's last word on the subject: '(Profit) is a word used by everyone but understood by very few because it is an abstract accounting concept having, at most, an incidental connection with cash. . . . What financial statements describe as "net income" (profit) is not really net income in the sense in which anyone but an accountant would understand the term. . . . It is neither a measure of success nor a measure of the extent of the exploitation of labour. . . . We may refer to the profit or loss figures to support our positions, but this is just a debating trick, or a rationalization, and is not what determines our opinions'.

If we are 'forward-looking' Marxists we might then say: 'It's not just the profits, it's that the goods are useless and the work degrading'. But people are still clamouring for all those 'useless' goods. And consider the fate of those politicians who have dared to call for 'meaningful' work or guaranteed incomes or reducing the work week. . . .

'But that's because of all the propaganda in the media, and because of all the advertising'.

But why do people believe the propaganda that they read? Why do they respond to ads for goods that will knowingly harm them? Are we to conclude that North Americans are brainwashed by the media — are suffering from 'false consciousness', as a Marxist might put it?

No. Social psychologist Daryl Bem has convincingly shown us that the media has only a very slight capacity to persuade us one way or the other. And he cites a number of recent studies that show that personal contacts, especially with friends, have a much greater capacity to affect our opinions and decisions. His conclusion: the media can help to persuade us (but not much) — but ultimately, we and our friends **decide**.

Moreover — if North Americans are suffering from 'false consciousness', then we must also conclude that North Americans **can't be held responsible** for the things they think and do. And then what can we say when a political party comes along that promises to force people to act 'in their own best interests', like in Russia or China?

For a more thorough critique of the Marxist analysis, see Chap. 23.

III. The Anarchist Alternative

The New Age position may seem closer to anarchism than to Marxism or liberalism, but it differs from anarchism too in many ways. For example:

(1) Most strains of anarchism are rooted in the socialist tradition. New Age politics is rooted in an amalgam of traditions of which feminism, ecology theory, Eastern philosophy and Western psychology are probably the most important.

(2) For anarchism our main enemies are capitalism and the state. For New Age politics the main obstacles to our development are 'monolithic institutions' — which are **common** to capitalism and socialism but not, strictly speaking, **necessary** to either — and the Six-Sided Prison, a 'cultural complex' of values and attitudes that make us **want to give up** our autonomy to our monolithic institutions . . . including the top-down state.

(3) Michael Albert, neoanarchist writer, notes (in **What Is To Be Undone**, 1974) that anarchism 'still lacks a "psychological model" that can be a basis for common collective tactical analyses'. New Age politics seeks to remedy

this lack with its seven stages of self-development, its theory of the 'stroke economy', and its psychocultural class analysis.

(4) Nikolai Berdyaev and many others have pointed out that anarchism definitely still shares in the 19th century, materialist worldview. New Age politics seeks to avoid falling into the opposite trap of the non-material worldview and is busily helping to articulate a new, trans-material worldview.

(5) Anarchist philosophy believes in the natural goodness of human beings. New Age politics is, I think, more realistic. It believes that 'defensive' aggression (aggression that aims at the removal of a threat) is an instinct in us, but that 'malignant' aggression (destructiveness and cruelty) is a **potential** in us — less than an instinct, but 'more than a learned pattern of behaviour that readily disappears when new patterns are introduced' (see esp. Erich Fromm, **The Anatomy of Human Destructiveness**). It is a potential that apparently 'actualizes' itself whenever our important psychic needs — for love, friendship, esteem, etc. — are not met. Whenever we fail to nourish our selves materially **or** emotionally **or** psychologically **or** spiritually.

(6) Anarchist philosophy believes that it is important to avoid structures and leaders as much as possible and that the ideal society could do without them altogether. New Age politics believes that — as Joreen expresses it in the anthology, **Radical Feminism** — there can be no such thing as a structureless group. Any group of people that comes together for any length of time will inevitably structure itself in **some** fashion. Therefore, while the idea of structurelessness may help to prevent the formation of formal or 'directive' structures, it cannot help to prevent the formation of informal or 'anarchic' ones that will be dominated by the strong or the charismatic or the manipulative. New Age politics has come up with the concept of 'synergic power' which can provide a genuine alternative to both 'directive' and 'anarchic' kinds of power; see Chap. 15, sect. II.

(7) Most strains of anarchism tend to believe in the 'ultimate necessity' of revolution and violence. New Age politics is uncompromisingly evolutionary and nonviolent, though it does believe that evolution can be speeded up and that nonviolence is at least potentially the most **effective** tactic as well as an ethical imperative.

IV. The Emerging New Alternative

So. Politically we seem to be in a next to impossible situation right now in North America. The anarchist alternative isn't thorough or realistic enough to speak for more than a temperamental minority. The liberal analysis leads to impotence and despair, or to a longing for a messiah (check out Jimmy Carter's campaign imagery sometime: it made masterful use of our longing for a messiah). And the Marxist analysis leads to bitterness and despair — to an anger that can, ultimately, only be directed back against 'the people' (who know not what they do) through a revolutionary 'vanguard' that claims to represent the people's 'true' consciousness as opposed to their false, or actual consciousness.

There are at least half a dozen **competing** revolutionary vanguards now in every major city.

And yet and yet. Any political theory should be able to tell us what's wrong with our society, and what we can do to heal it. If neither liberalism, nor Marxism, nor anarchism can do the trick, the point is not to give up in despair, and even less is it to return to other industrial-era political philosophies such as laissez-faire or Henry George-ism. It is, rather, to work out a new political theory that can help us get our bearings in the new age we are entering. Or, since new political theories always seem to come along just when they're most needed, the point is to look around and see if a new political theory isn't arising already among the supposedly 'apolitical' or 'semi-political' movements that many of us are involved in now.

As I suggested in Chap. 1, I believe that a new political theory — 'New Age politics' — is emerging out of the work of these movements.

It differs from liberalism and Marxism in many ways. With regard to the discussion above: it does not feel that the personnel of the system is the problem particularly; in free elections, people do tend to get the politicians they deserve. As Calif. State Assemblyperson John Vasconcellos puts it, 'We choose those people who most approximate our consciousness'.

Nor does New Age politics feel that the economic system is the problem. As economic systems, capitalism and socialism each have their strong points (freedom and security, respectively); a human-scale capitalism and a democratic socialism would appear to make the most of these strong points; but infected by the Prison and its institutions, socialism's 'security' tends to become regimentation, and capitalism's 'freedom' tends to become dog-eat-dog.

The New Age position suggests that the basic problem has partly to do with the **scale** of our society: the human scale **is** beautiful and nearly everything we have now is much too big (and powerful and speedy). And that has little to do with capitalism **per se**: Russia's SST is even bigger than ours would have been. Accordingly, the New Age solution does not call for top-down bureaucratic government, but for much more local autonomy than we have at present, with local cooperation on the regional and planetary levels. Similarly, the New Age solution does not call for socialism or capitalism (that kind of question would be decided on by the individual communities), but for an economy of life-oriented, mostly human-scale enterprises. Finally, the New Age solution would replace many of our 'monolithic institutions' with their 'biolithic' equivalents; see Chap. 14.

But even more than size and scale, the New Age position suggests that the problem is with 'the people' themselves: with **us**: with what we have become. And it holds that 'what we have become' goes back to a cultural complex — the Prison — whose six main elements predate capitalism by hundreds or thousands of years. . . .

Chapter 3 — The Six-Sided Prison

Many New Age writers and activists have pointed out that our social problems — war, exploitation, racism, environmental degradation — have their roots not so much in our institutions as in our 'mentality' or 'consciousness'. Wendell Berry, a writer on agriculture (and a farmer and poet), points out that it is the 'mentality of greed and exploitation' that is (ultimately) responsible for war, racism, and environmental degradation; Grace Stuart, a psychoanalyst, traces the fact of exploitation back to our 'hating and self-hate' which has, she reminds us, been with us for thousands of years; E.F. Schumacher, author of the book **Small Is Beautiful**, says it is the 'violence of greed, envy, hate and lust' in each of us that (ultimately) causes our problems; and so on.

Our institutional arrangements are, in this view, ultimately a reflection of our mentality or consciousness: we get back what we give out. Krishnamurti puts it well when he says, 'What you are within has been projected without, on to the world; what you are, what you think and what you feel, what you do in your everyday existence, is projected outwardly, and that constitutes the world'. Our institutions may **help** to determine the world — including our consciousness! (see Part II) — but our consciousness is ultimately, or as Marx might say, 'in the final analysis', the determining factor. (For more on this subject, see Chap. 23, sect. IV-2.)

What is there, then, that is most central to our mentality or consciousness? What is there that **defines** it? What are the beliefs, attitudes, values, myths, that are so important to us that they make up the taken-for-granted context of our lives?

Dozens of New Age writers and activists have been trying to define our most basic beliefs, and if you put their writings together, what you'll come up with is this. Our basic beliefs make up a 'cultural complex' whose six main elements are: patriarchal attitudes, egocentricity, scientific single vision, the bureaucratic mentality, nationalism, and the big-city outlook.

I like to think of these six elements as making up a 'Six-Sided Prison', partly because at least 12 authors in Chap. 24 have used the Prison metaphor in their own work, and partly because it is so apt. Calling the cultural elements a Prison implies that we're trapped not so much by the institutions of the society as by the culture of things and of death that we carry around in our **minds**. Michael Novak, political scientist, goes so far as to state, 'Institutions are what their perceivers wish them to be. Their life in the psyches of the community is their main source of power (and) stability. . . . When sufficient numbers of the community begin to think differently, those institutions lose their power (and) stability . . . '.

Basically the Prison is a way of **seeing** the world, a mental construct (as sociologists would put it) or an illusion (as Eastern philosophers would) that we create every day anew. And because we create it in our minds, we can undo it in our minds. We can change our consciousness individually and collectively so that we're not Prison-bound. (Carlos Castaneda's books, Ram Dass's books, Chogyam Trungpa's books, are about **seeing** the world differently, which is why they're more transformative, for our time and place, than the **Communist Manifesto.**)

And if enough of us do this — if enough of us can transcend and transform the Prison — then **and only then** would the institutions, goods and services that are set up to meet the needs of Prison-bound people lose (the Prison-bound aspects of) their appeal. We might still watch television, but not 28 hours a week (the national per adult average) and not because we weren't living as intensely as the people on the screen. We might still drive cars, but not to the corner store, and not because we needed to feel powerful and in charge. We might still get married, but not because we felt we had to, and not because we wanted to control our partner's growth. . . .

Once we were free of the Prison, all the propaganda and all the advertising in the world wouldn't be enough to make us want to lose our selves in our things; to make us want to give up our power and responsibility to our institutions. . . .

Then we could begin to really heal self and society.

(Some New Age writers have attempted to prove that **one** of the first three sides of the Prison has been the **really** determining one. For example, June Singer derives egocentricity from patriarchal attitudes — and Alan Watts derives patriarchal attitudes from egocentricity. The important point, to my mind, is that the origins of at least the first three sides of the Prison are lost in the mists of time . . . and are crucially and independently determining **today**.

(The second three sides appear to be more clearly connected to certain institutional forms — to bureaucracies, to the nation-state, and to big cities. Therefore, it's tempting to conclude that the second three sides can be done away with by 'breaking up' the bureaucracies and by reducing the size of our nations and cities. But the second three sides are reinforced and perpetuated by the first three sides — to such an extent that they would probably survive the physical break-up of the bureaucracies, nations and cities, and seek to stifle us in other ways ((and seek to re-create the bureaucracies, etc.)). They are also reinforced and perpetuated by many of our 'monolithic institutions' — see Part II.)

I. Patriarchal Attitudes

The patriarchy is a system of power in which men 'determine what part women shall or shall not play, and in which the female is everywhere subsumed under the male' (Adrienne Rich). It is the means by which men are able to get women to be their secretaries, make their beds, prop up their egos, and enjoy doing it. Aspects of the patriarchy may be enforced by law or through such venerable institutions as wife-beating; but mostly it's enforced by a series of 'patriarchal attitudes' that we don't even notice.

Patriarchal attitudes are the attitudes, values and beliefs that are supportive of the patriarchy. The patriarchy wouldn't exist for a moment without these attitudes, which are 'socialized' into us literally from the day we're born in the form of sex-role stereotypes. Hogie Wyckoff, a therapist, puts it this way (in Steiner): 'As women and men we are socialized to develop certain parts of our personalities while suppressing the development of other parts. This programming promotes a predetermined, stilted, and repetitive way of acting in life'.

For example. Men are taught to be aggressive, independent, rational, objective, intelligent, competent, ambitious, unemotional and detatched. And women are taught to be pretty much the opposite: passive, dependent, irrational. . . . Is it any wonder that men (want to) rule, or that (most) women obey?

It is important to understand that our sex role stereotypes are just that — stereotypes. In their book **The Psychology of Sex Differences**, Eleanor Maccoby and Carol Jacklin take a look at virtually all of the studies of sex differences that have been carried out in recent years. They are able to show conclusively that women are **not** 'naturally' passive, dependent, irrational, etc. (though they may be less malignantly aggressive than men). Their last lines: 'Social institutions and social practices are not biologically inevitable. . . . It is up to human beings to select those that foster the life styles they most value'.

We get our sex-role stereotypes mostly and most importantly from our parents. Our parents teach us their own sex-role stereotypes that have nothing to do with our own unique temperaments and interests but that lend themselves perfectly to the taken-for-granted patterns of submission and dominance. (They don't do most of this consciously, of course. They do it more by the raised eyebrow and the exasperated voice, and by the example they set as 'mommies' and 'daddies'.)

But where do our parents get these stereotypes from? Just how far back do they go? Only one thing is certain: they go back thousands of years before capitalism, and have survived all sorts of social and economic and political 'revolutions'. Anne Koedt, a founder of the radical feminist movement, makes the essential political point: 'The purpose of male chauvinism is primarily to obtain psychological ego satisfaction, and . . . only secondarily does this manifest itself in economic relationships'. For thousands of years the male identity has been sustained 'through its ability to have power over the female ego'. For thousands of years man has acquired his self-esteem 'in direct proportion to his ability to have his ego override woman's'.

Some anthropologists believe that societies have always been patriarchal in their power relationships. But many years ago Margaret Mead was able to prove that that is itself a patriarchal assumption. She went to New Guinea and reported on tribes that were patriarchal and matriarchal and even andro-gynous (**Sex and Temperament in Three Primitive Societies**, 1935). Neverthe-less, the overwhelming majority of societies over the centuries — over the millennia! — do appear to have been patriarchal.

There is some evidence that thousands of years ago the world was dotted with matriarchies. And these may have been more than just patriarchies spelled with an 'm'. According to Elizabeth Gould Davis, a feminist theorist, there is archaeological evidence that suggests that in some of them there had been no sacrifices of any living beings, no violent deaths, and — hard to believe! — no wars for a thousand years. According to Merlin Stone, a feminist historian, there is cultural evidence that suggests that some of them were societies of genuine political equality — e.g., 'the earliest Sumerian myths included both female and male deities in the decision-making assemblies of heaven'.

Nobody seems to know why the matriarchies ended. Predictably, Marx and Engels say that it happened because women lost control of the means of production. Not so, says cultural historian Helen Diner: we now know of matriarchies that existed in spite of that fact. Davis says that the matriar-chies were conquered by power-hungry males. Kate Millett, writer and sculptor, thinks that it might have had something to do with men figuring out how babies are started.

But even if the matriarchies never did exist, even if, as Adrienne Rich puts it, it is simply that 'we all carry in our earliest imprintings the memory of, or the longing for, an individual past relationship to . . . female warmth, nurture, and tenderness', it is impossible to deny these writers' main point: that fairly early on, women had lost whatever power they might have had in society.

Dworkin reminds us that, at different times and in different places, men have indulged in, for example, the practice of footbinding in China, an exceedingly painful practice that only began to end with Sun Yat-sen's revolu-tion of 1911; or, for example, the persecution of 'witches' in Europe and North America, especially from the 15th to the 18th centuries when possibly millions of women were slaughtered — and along with the women, their entire, separate culture.

Obviously, in North America today, patriarchal attitudes don't produce such horrors. But all things considered, women may not be 'better off today than ever before'. Davis, for one, contends that women have been rendered more and more useless over the centuries, with an ensuing loss in power and in self-esteem. And even if women are better off today in a material sense, and are 'allowed to do more', that doesn't mean that the patriarchy runs any less deep or that it does us less harm.

For in any society characterized by patriarchal attitudes, those of us who are women are made to feel powerless, inferior, incompetent and unattract-ive. Or, if we don't feel these things, then we've had to go through quite a struggle to free our selves from them. Partly just because — as Jean Baker

Miller, a psychologist, points out — women's psychological strengths are not recognized as such by men, nor by those women who want to 'make it' in 'the man's world'. Miller encourages women to recognize their strengths as strengths, and to add to them, not change them: (1) women are better able to admit to feelings of weakness and vulnerability than men; (2) women have a greater sense of the emotional dimensions of all human activity; (3) women have a greater sense of the pleasures of close connection with physical, emotional, and mental growth; (4) women have a greater recognition of the cooperative nature of human existence; and (5) women have a greater ability to create for themselves a new concept of personhood.

Many New Age writers have pointed out that patriarchal attitudes are harmful to those of us who are men. Patriarchal attitudes make it almost impossible for us to love or be emotional; turn us into success objects (as opposed to sex objects — though we can be that, too); keep us out of touch with our bodies; teach us to see women as inferior, and to hate women; and keep us from getting to know our children. Marc Feigen Fasteau puts it well when he says, 'The male machine is a special kind of being, different from women, children, and men who don't measure up. He is functional, designed mainly for work. He is programmed to tackle jobs, override obstacles, attack problems, overcome difficulties, and always seize the offensive. . . . His circuits are never scrambled or overrun by irrelevant personal signals. His relationship with other male machines is one of respect but not intimacy; it is difficult for him to connect his internal circuits to those of others. In fact, his internal circuitry is somewhat of a mystery to him, and is maintained primarily by humans of the opposite sex'.

If we try hard enough and know where to look, we can begin to change our patriarchal attitudes: men's and women's consciousness-changing groups are helping some of us do that right now (see Chap. 20, sect. I). But we can't change our patriarchal attitudes completely until we go on to change — not capitalism, necessarily — but the Prison as a whole. For each of the other sides of the Prison **reinforces and perpetuates** our patriarchal attitudes.

II. Egocentricity

In the tradition of Western psychology, 'egocentricity' refers to selfishness and false pride, and to the notion that the world exists for our own, personal benefit. In the tradition of Eastern philosophy, and in this book, egocentricity also refers to the notion that we are solid and isolated beings, sealed up in our skins like so many tin cans on a shelf.

In this view, egocentricity includes the notion that we are our bodies, period, or our social roles, period — the notion that we **only** exist in the material state of consciousness (see Chap. 11). It includes the notion that we are different from other people, period (as opposed to the idea that we can also and sometimes more **usefully** be seen as One, though we play the game of life in different ways). And it includes our fear of **losing** our egos, a fear that we try to avoid by constantly trying to extend our selves in the world — all those tall buildings, all those highways. (If we are adepts at Eastern philosophy, we tend to have the opposite fear, the fear of losing our egolessness!)

The notion that we are separate from trees, animals, stars, wind, rocks, minerals — from the life that is in all these things (which native North Americans have traditionally called the 'Great Spirit') — is a half-truth; and when we take it as the whole truth, it is reasonable to call it an illusion. It is an illusion that nearly all of us share: not only our separation from these things, but our domination of them, has been celebrated in our folklore for thousands of years, and is celebrated in Marxist economics (E. F. Schumacher: 'Even the great Dr. Marx fell into this devastating error ((of treating)) as valueless everything that we have not made ourselves').

But if our egocentricity doesn't come from capitalism — where does it come from?

Grace Stuart traces it back to the fact that we aren't constantly held and stroked and loved when we're young. This lack of happy and close physical intimacy with people makes it very difficult for us to love other people later on, and leaves us with a **generalized** fear of loving others and of expressing our love for them; and that makes it almost impossible for us to get out of our selves.

To Oscar Ichazo, founder of the Arica Institute, egocentricity is the limited mode of awareness, the distorted consciousness, that develops as a result of the socializing process (as we know it today). Between four and six years old 'the child begins to imitate (his or her) parents, tell lies, and pretend. . . . Personality forms a defensive layer over the essence (of the self), and so there is a split between the self and the world'.

To Joel Kramer, a meditation teacher, egocentricity is born of the fact that we seek pleasure — the pleasure of judging things, the pleasure of prolonging things. When we experience a landscape, an event, or whatever, at first there is no gap between the experiencer and the experience — it is one thing. But what always seems to happen is that we say to our selves, This is beautiful! or, How can I keep on with this? We separate our selves out from the experience in order to **retain** it — and as soon as we do this we have constructed a **barrier** between our selves and the experience.

Whatever their differences, Stuart, Ichazo and Kramer would agree that egocentricity is a very deep quality in us. But we shouldn't conclude that it's always been with us.

Until quite recently most Asiatics would have been baffled by the 'civilized' idea of self. So would many of those Europeans who, until modern times, stood outside of the Judeo-Christian tradition. Traditional North American native peoples are still baffled by it. Probably most people in the world have done without it. . . .

Theodore Roszak, Alan Watts, and many other New Age writers, have said that it goes back to the beginnings of the Judeo-Christian tradition, when God was first seen as being something apart from us. As Watts puts it: in most forms of Judeo-Christianity, 'the creature is as distinct from the Creator as the table from the carpenter'. Worse, the Creator is also the Boss, and 'the Boss notices; he loves and judges every creature separately, and his demands are stern'. Philip Slater, a psychotherapist, says that it began with the first kings. Acute self-consciousness engendered in kings an acute fear of death which led to their (and now our) desire to extend our selves into the environment, a desire that, according to Slater, 'constitutes the single greatest threat to our species'.

That is my real point: whichever theories about egocentricity turn out to be most accurate or useful, the fact is that for thousands of years our egocentricity has been doing us all great harm.

(1) It cuts us off from each other;

(2) It keeps us from realizing our obligation to love and respect our environment;

(3) It makes us keep wanting to go places, do things, have more. It makes us live in and for the future — or the past. As Ram Dass says, we can never really **be** where we are now;

(4) It causes us constantly to emphasize our separateness from others through craving, hate, anger, fear, jealousy;

(5) It keeps us from being able to reach any kind of common agreement about 'the world' — what it's all about, what life is **for**;

(6) It makes us terribly afraid of death.

We can try to get out of our egocentricity. Through Yoga, through Zen, and through many other Eastern traditions and disciplines, and through encounter and growth groups, many of us are beginning to lose at least the most destructive aspects of our egocentricity. But we'll never be able to really strip our selves of our egocentricity unless and until, having embarked on the process, we then also go on to change Prison society as a whole. For each of the other sides of the Prison reinforces and perpetuates our egocentricity.

Patriarchal attitudes encourage men to be arrogant and women, defensive. Scientific single vision encourages us to see our selves as the centre of the universe. The bureaucratic mentality encourages us not only to 'get ahead' but to trample on others in the process. Nationalism encourages us to 'get ahead' as a **nation** and to trample on other **nations**. And our big-city outlooks encourage us to loathe and fear other people and to separate our selves from them as much as we can.

III. Scientific Single Vision

'May God us keep, From Single vision and Newton's sleep' — William Blake. Scientific single vision (or the 'scientific outlook') is one way, our way, of **seeing** the world. It's the way that most of us think about things, including our selves, 'life in general', and the material in this book.

Scientific single vision is intellectual rather than sensuous, active rather than receptive, analytic rather than intuitive, verbal rather than spatial. It tends to be more interested in argument than in experience, more interested in understanding things sequentially (in terms of cause and effect) than as patterned wholes, more concerned with time than with eternity.

According to George Lodge, a New Age business theorist, scientific single vision is characterized by: specialization (and overspecialization); 'reductionism' (the way to understand whole things is to break them apart and examine the parts); 'objectivity' (knowledge must be quantifiable — if you can't count it, it doesn't really count); 'rationalism' (reason is all); and 'materialism' (what's real is what I can feel, touch, see — especially if I own it!).

In North America, scientific single vision is the outlook **par excellence** not only of scientists but of doctors and lawyers, politicians and revolutionaries, businessmen and scholars — of nearly everyone who's managed to 'make it big' outside of the arts. Which is, maybe, why most of us are convinced that it's the **only** way of seeing the world, of getting at 'the truth'. People who come up with other ways of seeing are usually called 'crazy' or worse. But are they?

Over the last 10 years or so, many of us have begun to discover whole **cultures** that share in an alternate way of seeing the world. Zen, Vedanta, Sufism, North American Indian culture — whatever their differences, each of them seems, in its way of seeing, to be the polar opposite of the scientific outlook: sensuous rather than intellectual, receptive rather than active, intuitive rather than analytic. . . .

At the same time, many recent investigators have begun to gather evidence that the two sides of the brain are specialized for different modes of consciousness. The left side of the brain is, apparently, specialized for analysis, verbal facility, linear time-orientation and the like; the right side of the brain for pattern recognition, spatial orientation, holistic thinking and the like (see Ornstein, Chap. 3, or Singer, Chap. 16).

So the reality would appear to be that, not only do different ways of seeing exist, not only do some of them go back thousands of years, but that these alternate ways of seeing are rooted in the workings of the right half of the brain just as much as scientific single vision is rooted in those of the left. Even in science's **own** terms, the alternate outlooks are as real and as valid as the scientific outlook.

The real question is, why is our **culture** so 'crazy' as to promote — to be partially based on! — an outlook that requires us to ignore the signals that are coming to us from the right side of our brains?

Theodore Roszak traces the scientific outlook back to the ancient Jewish belief that people who worshipped objects were being abusive of God (who was supposed to be invisible). According to Roszak, the Jews were simply suffering from a cultural misunderstanding; they didn't realize that for the peasants, God was manifest equally in all things. But the damage was done; from that point on, **things** began to lose their transcendent qualities and became merely objects to be manipulated.

And that was only the beginning. Later we would come to **actively dislike** the natural world. According to Joel Kovel, a psychohistorian, this dislike began when we learned to dislike our feces (for as we became more 'civilized' we learned to practice some pretty wicked versions of toilet-training); but it quickly and inevitably spread outward to all natural things.

Soon it was only a matter of time before we devised a system for subduing and punishing nature (as opposed to simply working with her), and cutting our selves off from her as much as possible. According to Roszak, the most important step here was taken by Galileo, for he did more than any other person to define the 'real' world as only what could be precisely defined in physical terms: if it couldn't be counted, it didn't really count. According to Lewis Mumford, a cultural philosopher, the turning point was Copernicus's discovery that the earth revolves around the sun (and not vice versa), for that appeared to give us the cultural authority to dominate everything everywhere.

Either way, the point is that the scientific outlook arose well before capitalism, and that, **because it was so narrow**, it's done us all great harm. (In North America, it's begun to do us more harm than good.)

(1) It has cut us off from other dimensions of reality besides the material;

(2) It has led to our worship of machines and of technique;

(3) It has led to a situation where the human scale is lost, and 'progress' means mostly destruction;

(4) It has helped us forget that after all the 'objective' facts are in, we still have to make moral choices and value judgements;

(5) It has led to a separation of means and ends in almost every human endeavour;

(6) It has led to a (society) (culture) of mostly unrelated specialties and specialists;

(7) It hasn't even delivered on what it promised in its **own** terms. We haven't understood the material world 'with absolute certainty' by ignoring our subjective experience of that world. We haven't understood human nature by describing it statistically. We haven't understood history by reading it 'scientifically'.

Many of us are trying to expand our scientific outlooks **now** by immersing our selves in Eastern disciplines or in encounter and growth groups or by working on our bodies — by getting back in touch with the sensuous, intuitive, holistic side of our selves. We're not going to be able to change our selves deeply, however, unless and until we also change the other sides of the Prison. For each of the other sides reinforces and perpetuates the scientific outlook. Patriarchal attitudes, for example, teach us that the traits that are accociated with the scientific outlook are **male** traits, and therefore the ones we'll need if we want to 'make it' in society. And the bureaucratic mentality has given that teaching the irresistible force of truth.

IV. The Bureaucratic Mentality

The bureaucratic mentality — or, more accurately, the 'functional' or 'rationalized' mentality — is an extremely important aspect of the Prison. According to sociologists Peter Berger and William Howton, some of its key elements are:

(1) Status-consciousness. Everybody has their place — 'above' or 'below' you.

(2) Depersonalization. Everybody comes to see themselves as things, objects, numbers.

(3) Predictability. Everything is done by means of 'regular procedures' that are known in advance.

(4) Orderliness. Everything is supposed to fit neatly into some category. If it doesn't fit neatly then it doesn't really exist for us, we put it out of our minds.

(5) Efficiency. This is not only the highest social value, it is the greatest metaphysical virtue.

(6) Arbitrariness. Rules and rituals are followed because they are supposed to be followed — because they are there.

(7) Discipline. Everybody is supposed to abide by the rules, or else.

The bureaucratic mentality is far from being a product of capitalism — it goes back thousands of years. It isn't even a product of mechanization, at least not originally. According to Mumford, 'the meticulous order that characterizes bureaucracy' probably derives from the ritual observances of the Temple; and even in the first organized wars 'we find remarkably early records, in definite figures, of prisoners captured, animals rounded up, loot taken'. Behind every later process of organization and mechanization Mumford is able to find 'primordial aptitudes . . . for ritualizing behaviour' and for finding satisfaction in repetitive order.

The bureaucratic mentality is, then, 'in the final analysis', responsible for bureaucracies, and not the other way around; but in the rich interplay of consciousness and society, bureaucracies have had a significant effect on the bureaucratic mentality, reinforcing and extending it at every turn.

Bureaucracies are organizations that are run from the top down and that see people, us, as **means** to the bureaucracies' own ends (above all that of self-preservation). According to Mumford they go back 5,000 years, to Egypt and Mesopotamia. According to Howton they go back 'only' 2,000 years, to Rome, because the Roman bureaucrats were the first to know that they owed their power to their offices, rather than to God. According to Simon Leys, a Sinologist, the Chinese bureaucracy had 10 distinct hierarchical classes in the sixth century B.C. (and it has 30 such classes today; see **New York Review of Books**, 26 May '77).

But bureaucracies have by no means managed to dominate society everywhere or at all times. Why, then, does bureaucracy become so determining in Prison society in our time?

According to Kenneth Boulding, the economist, it has little to do with our

need for large, hierarchical organizations. It has a lot more to do with the improvement in the skills of organizations and — even more important — in the ability of the organizations to grow, unchecked (after the 16th century or so) by any widely held ethics or values that were not Prison-bound. Possibly the only change in our demand for large, hierarchical organizations came as a result of the growth in strength of the other sides of the Prison: patriarchal attitudes caused us to become more domineering; egocentricity, more ambitious; and scientific single vision, more arrogant. And 'important', centralized and hierarchical organizations are nothing if not a means for allowing us to **be** domineering and ambitious and arrogant (in our different ways).

At any rate, the important point is that the bureaucracies — and the bureaucratic mentality — are 'here now', and that they are doing us all a great deal of harm.

(1) To begin with, take another look at those seven key elements of the bureaucratic mentality. **Every single one** of them encourages us to lose sight of our humanity in the interests of a 'higher' logic. Every single one of them encourages us to think of other people as a means — or, worse, as 'sand in the gears' — rather than as vulnerable, valuable and unique;

(2) The bureaucratic mentality causes us to fear and oppose all substantial change;

(3) The bureaucratic mentality makes it seem more interesting to manipulate the environment than to live in it, more rewarding to (try to) manage the world than to (try to) understand it;

(4) The fact that the bureaucratic mentality is depersonalized makes it seem objective — a cardinal value to Prisoners, as we saw in the section on scientific single vision — and so the public interest naturally comes to be redefined as part of the private interest of bureaucracies (look at our 'defence' policies!);

(5) Bureaucracies have become so big that they can't even deliver on some of their own values (efficiency, predictability, orderliness). Liberals and Marxists may rail against bureaucracy and call for increased and improved organization of services, but as Jacques Ellul points out, increased and improved organization would serve 'only to fortify the (bureaucratic) system and to improve its operation', making it more versatile, discriminating, intelligent — ultimately, more all-encompassing;

(6) To work well, says Boulding, bureaucracies seem to require what I later call Prison-bound personalities (see Chap. 9) — people who aren't able to have warm and open personal relationships, and who are therefore apt to translate their frustrations into personal ambition or into 'serving the people';

(7) But it isn't even a question of bad, or rather frustrated, individuals. No matter how life-loving we are, our consciences will be diminished at the point where we enter a bureaucratic structure. What happens is this: when we enter an authority system — or when we're living in one! — we no longer see our selves as autonomous, as acting on our own. We come to see our selves as

agents for carrying out the wishes of others. The psychologist Stanley Milgram calls this the 'agentic state of mind' (he could just as well have called it the 'bureaucratic mentality supreme'), and he argues that when we're in this state we no longer see our selves as responsible for our actions but as instruments for carrying out the wishes of others. 'An element of free choice determines whether the person defines (him- or herself) in this way or not', says Milgram (the bureaucratic mentality is **not** part of 'human nature'), 'but . . . the propensity to do so is exceedingly strong, and the shift (back to an autonomous state of mind) is not freely reversible'. This goes a long way towards explaining why so many of us are psychologically able to sell cars that are built to break down in five years (or is it three?), work strip mines, and murder each other.

V. Nationalism

The 'sense of identity with a small, earthbound "in-group" is extremely ancient', writes Mumford; 'the sentiment of nationality long antedates any conscious belief in nationalism'. Similarly, Vadim Borisov, a Russian historian — born in 1945, deprived of all employment — tells us (in Solzhenitsyn, ed.) that nationalism is 'above all an **ideology**, which directs the existing elemental national instincts into a particular channel'.

The 'sentiment of nationality' that predates nationalism — those 'elemental national instincts' — have nothing to do with the large nation-state, but are regional, even local in scope. Carlton Hayes, a well-known historian, has written several scholarly books whose message is that it's natural for us to love our own immediate surroundings — town, neighbourhood, countryside — but that it takes an artificial effort to make us love a whole nation (or at least, a geographically immense and socially-culturally diverse nation). It is natural for us to feel loyal to family and friends and to the people in our immediate communities, but it takes special civic training to make us feel loyal to all the people who are supposed to constitute our nation. It is natural for us to feel loyal to some ideas or ideals that are shared by our friends, but it takes systematic efforts to make us feel loyal to an entire national ideology.

So — localism is natural to us, regionalism is natural, but nationalism only **seems** natural because we're living in giant nation-states (and because of the Prison). In tribal society, our highest loyalties were to our friends and to our immediate communities. And even after tribal society was replaced by the great military empires, nationalism wasn't forced on us. All (all?) the Egyptians or Persians or Romans wanted from us was money and soldiers. They didn't want to weld us together into 'one people'.

Well into the 16th century, most of Europe was localistic or 'universalistic' — not nationalistic. The peasants, by virtue of the work they did and the community they enjoyed with each other, were loyal to lord and village. Many religious people and scholars, by virtue of the Christian religion and the Latin language, were 'cosmopolites', the kind of people that dedicated nationalists have always mistrusted — and mistreated.

In the 16th century, the triumph of Prison values plus new developments in military technology led to the 'emergence' — as they say in the polite history books — of the monarchical nation-state. And the nation-state was nationalist from the very beginning. It had to be and has to be, because it has to convince people to feel loyal to **it** rather than to their immediate or self-chosen surroundings. (This task was made easier because the Black Death and the schisms in the Christian Church had caused us to lose our faith and become afraid, and so we needed something to cling to and believe in.)

Even so, among all but the intelligentsia, the new nationalism spread slowly; it was given its first big boost by the French revolution. The revolutionary 'patriotes', nationalists, singers of the 'Marseillaise', short-sightedly identified the ideals of liberty and equality with the idea of nationalism. And so they crushed the peasants who tried to fight against the nationalization of the historic provinces of France and the elimination of provincial rights. Then they tried to export their revolution.

Nationalism continued to grow in the 19th century, but mostly in the cities, and mostly even there among those who were rootless (good soldiers but bad workers). It was **primarily** in order to foster our nationalism that our national governments introduced the system of universal, compulsory schooling. According to Hayes, universal schooling was intended primarily 'to unify a people by belittling their economic, social, (cultural), occupational and religious differences and by emphasizing their national language and the inculcation of a common national patriotism'. This strategy was fully justified during World Wars I and II, when there seemed to be a direct connection, in nearly every country on Earth, between the number of 'schooled' people and the degree of unquestioning national loyalty.

So nationalism has nothing to do with human nature — and nothing to do with political ideologies, either (by 1900 even communism had become a patriotic force). But just because it's been forced on us — has it really done us that much harm? Can we really speak of it as part of the Prison?

From the beginning, nationalism has served as a kind of **vulgarized religion** with its 'sacred' rituals and texts and its missionary zeal. And so we've come to believe that we are a chosen people; that our nation is eternal; that the deaths of its sons add to its glory; that we need to guard our selves against foreign 'devils'; and so on.

The nation-state has made us insufferably **chauvinistic**. If we are from big nation-states, we tend, inevitably, to feel that the world revolves around us and that other places, other ideas, other **peoples**, are of lesser importance. If we are from smaller nation-states, we tend to feel so defensive that often we shut our selves off from outside influences even more completely.

Nationalism compensates for feelings of inferiority or worthlessness in an extremely unproductive (and often downright dangerous) way. Krishnamurti says, 'Living in a little village or a big town or whatever it might be, I am nobody; but if I identify myself with the larger, with the country . . . it flatters my vanity'. Erich Fromm says that the degree of nationalism is 'commensurate with the lack of real satisfaction in life', is a function of material and cultural scarcity, of boredom. He says it's much more dangerous than personal narcissism, because 'an individual, unless he is mentally very sick, may have at least some doubts about his personal narcissistic image. The member of the (nation) has none, since his narcissism is shared by the majority'.

In other words, nationalism has encouraged us to live vicariously, through an abstraction called the nation-state. Even our self-esteem becomes dependent on what strangers think of our nation and its culture. As Richard Barnet points out — when foreign governments reject Coca-Cola, General Motors, Alcan, etc., we tend to feel **personally** rejected, personally attacked.

Many New Age writers have pointed out that the nation-state **system** leads almost inevitably to war. Margaret Mead points out that it is literally impossible for each and every nation to have a favourable balance of trade. Kenneth Boulding points out that the nation-state has **never** been a 'trading' organization so much as a 'fighting' one — that 'it is only a mild exaggeration to say that all states are the creations of their enemies' (the U.S. owes its existence to George III, Canada to the U.S., etc.).

Over the last few years, many of us have tried to change our loyalties — at least in our hearts and minds. Some of us have become 'planetary citizens' through constant travel or through exposure to other ways of **seeing** the world. Some of us have returned to a form of localism by doing intensive political work in our local communities or by starting community enterprises of one sort or another. Some of us have done both.

But we won't be able to lose our nationalism, really, until we leave the rest of the Prison behind. Because the rest of the Prison reinforces and perpetuates our nationalism and our nation-states. Egocentricity, for example, feeds Americans' sense that they are superior human beings, and Canadians' sense that they are morally superior to the Americans.

VI. The Big City Outlook

By a 'big city' I mean any place that has more than half a million inhabitants or so; and, yes, I mean 'big city' as a negative term. Because above that size, as E. F. Schumacher and many other New Age writers have told us, nothing is added to the value of a city, to its street life, its cultural offerings, its virtue. (It's a little-known fact, but 124 million North Americans — 54 percent of us — now live in urban areas of half a million or more. Seventy-one million of us — more than 31 percent — live in urban areas of **two million** or more!)

The 'big city outlook' is what happens inevitably to our outlook on life when we end up living in big cities no matter how 'nice' or 'cosmopolitan' they are. (What **has** happened and what **is** happening. Urban economist Elizabeth Bardwell speaks of an 'incubation period' of three generations for the effects of urban living to really begin taking their toll on people.) What happens is this: the very existence of the extra hundreds of thousands (or millions) of people, all crowded together, creates enormous problems that we can't get away from — and our big city outlooks are shaped by these problems.

(1) **Air pollution.** Big city air is four times as dirty as rural air, and particulates and other pollutants in the air are expected to increase from now on as population increases (Bardwell). Researchers have established significant connections between polluted air and bronchitis, asthma, pneumonia, lung cancer, eye allergies and mental depression.

(2) **Noise pollution.** Background noise has increased dramatically since World War II -- in fact, some experts estimate that background noise is now more responsible for 'impaired hearing' than industrial noise (Bardwell). Constant noise is known to produce annoyance, fright, irritability, tension and headaches in us.

(3) **Isolation.** 'There is a decrease of all-round trusted friends and neighbours who share the total process of living, and a resulting loss of emotional ties of affection and regard, and of a sense of social responsibility. Out of this lack comes a tendency to breakdown of ethical standards . . . ' (Arthur Morgan).

(4) **Lack of privacy.** The other side of the coin from isolation — made even worse because it often goes together with isolation.

(5) **Rootlessness.** The average North American moves every four years — the big city dweller more often than that. And can **anyone** feel rooted in a high-rise?

(6) **Anonymity.** In a big city, most of our transactions are carried on with strangers. 'Urban anonymity increases fear and suspicion, which in turn make people less mutually supporting members of the community' (Bardwell).

(7) **Overcrowding.** A considerable amount of research has demonstrated that density of living 'has definite negative effects on the behaviour and the body chemistry' of people (Bardwell). Not to mention on rats: when rats are allowed to multiply freely in a fixed space, catastrophe soon ensues. Mothers abandon their young; many rats withdraw from interaction, others wander about in a disoriented daze; still others become extremely aggressive. Of course, rats and people have nothing in common. . . .

(8) **Crime.** The crime rate is five and a half times as high in our big cities as it is in our rural areas. Or, more specifically: the crime rate per 100,000 people in rural areas was 985 in 1970; in cities pop. 50-100,000, 2,960; in cities pop. 500,000-1,000,000, 5,530. Significantly, the crime rate failed to rise (much) once the size of the city topped 500,000.

(9) **Danger.** Because of the crime rate, we become fearful and afraid. We expect trouble all the time — and that helps bring it about.

(10) **Hustle.** The only way to keep your head above water in these conditions!

(11) **Stress.** 'Diseases associated with stress, particularly ulcers, coronary disease, and high blood pressure, are . . . prevalent' in big cities (Ehrlich and Ehrlich).

(12) **Mental illness**. Anne and Paul Ehrlich, population experts and environmentalists, have suggested that 'the high numbers of contacts with individuals not part of one's circle of regular social acquaintances may lead to mental disturbance' — and they offer quite a bit of evidence to prove their point. In one study conducted in Manhattan on the effects of density on people, it was found that all but 18 percent of the people interviewed were suffering from some degree of neurotic or psychotic disturbance (this survey did not include the poorest neighbourhoods).

(13) **Higher death rates**. In New York State the death rates for both sexes are higher in metropolitan areas than in non-. The U.S. Public Health Service reports that coronary heart disease is 42 percent higher for people in metro areas. In Iowa, cancer is 40 percent more prevalent among urban dwellers than among non . . . (Ehrlich and Ehrlich).

(14) **Look out kid you better stay hid**. Even a generation or two ago big city children 'spent much of their time exploring and participating in the activities of the city, while today children are confined to dreary school rooms, their homes, and the local park (Ehrlich and Ehrlich). And even if they **are** allowed to roam, says Alison Stallibrass (in Holt, **Instead**), the environment **itself** is rapidly becoming one 'which they cannot become familiar with through the senses, cannot understand, and in which they cannot, therefore, use their own judgement'. Some children, finding that their 'tentative efforts towards independence or adventure and experiment' are (reasonably enough!) discouraged, may eventually conclude that 'passivity is the best policy'.

(15) **Materialism**. 'Urban anonymity' has contributed to our materialism — so say many sociologists. 'External appearance becomes important because so little is known about a person's character or ethical principles. The type of clothes, the cut of the hair, or the cost of an automobile or a home are often all one has to go on in sizing up people. In addition, the great variation in standards of living in (big) cities tends to heighten people's dissatisfaction with the quantity and quality of their own possessions' (Bardwell) — no matter what that quantity or quality might be!

(16) **Communications overload**. The big city dweller can't escape a constant bombardment of information and impressions. 'Excessive stimulation creates confusion and fatigue, sometimes to the point where the mind has to turn off' (Bardwell).

(17) **The tie that blinds**. 'The larger a city the more likely it is for people to get caught up in it', says Mike Nickerson, New Age author and activist. In other words: the more likely it is for us to get caught up in thinking that only urban technology, urban lifestyles, urban values, are natural to us, or at least, suitably 'modern'.

(18) **Skyrocketing costs**. Urban economist Richard Bradley, in a study done for a Colorado Springs, Colo., citizens group (**The Costs of Urban Growth**, 1973), concludes that 'all things considered, county areas having a population of about 25,000 people cost their residents the least amount of money per capita. Above this population size, per capita costs of all local

governments tend to increase'. Bardwell finds that total expenditures increase gradually with size in the 50-250,000 range but go up much more quickly after that — 'the law of diminishing returns sets in and produces significant diseconomies of scale'. In fact, a city of one million pop. costs **three times** as much to run, per capita, as a city of 100,000. I believe that the big city taxpayer learns a 'lesson' (usually subconscious) from these skyrocketing costs: (other) people cost us too much money — (other) people are burdensome. Therefore, (other) people are expendable.

(19) **Loss of the connection with life-as-a-whole-process**. In a big city, says Nickerson, 'where goods and food come from store shelves and end up in garbage cans or the sewage system, it is hard for people to be aware of the impact their lives have on the world around them'.

(20) **Loss of the connection with nature and with the spiritual and religious states of consciousness**. Walking Buffalo, a Stoney Indian from Alberta, says (in **The Mother Earth News**, May-June '77), 'Living in a city is an artificial existence. Lots of people hardly ever feel real soil under their feet, see plants grow except in flowerpots, or get far enough beyond the street lights to catch the enchantment of a night sky studded with stars'. And he adds: 'When people live far from scenes of the Great Spirit's making, it's easy for them to forget his laws'.

Because our big cities are so 'modern', so technologically advanced, it's tempting to conclude that the problems they pose for us are new and therefore traceable to 'capitalism' or 'technology'. But according to Lewis Mumford, nothing could be further from the truth. Huge, oversized cities ('megalopolises', the city planners call them) go all the way back to Egypt and Mesopotamia, where the first kings, eager to consolidate their new power, managed to replace the decentralized village economy with a highly centralized and therefore primarily urban one — 'centralized', that is, around the king's needs.

But big cities haven't always been dominant since then. According to Mumford, they tend to become really big only towards the end of a civilization — which tends to suggest that their overexpansion has less to do with economic forces than with cultural ones (the Prison). Certainly that is the case today: all over North America, the whole cultural structure of rural life has been collapsing, and people have been pouring into the biggest cities even with no prospects of finding decent work there. The **biggest** cities — because these provide us (or appear to provide us) with what rural life never seemed to be able to: 'excitement', (vicarious) pleasures, 'real life' — in a phrase, the consolations of the Prison.

A similar situation prevails in France: according to Schumacher, 'the French planners fight against France becoming "Paris surrounded by a desert" '. Similarly in the Soviet countries: Barbara Ward tells us that Moscow and Leningrad 'have continued to double in size after all policies likely to lead to further growth had been strictly banned', and she concludes that 'there must be evidence of some innate, forceful, and all but uncontrollable influences at work'. Mumford says much the same thing: 'The persistence of these overgrown containers (everywhere) would indicate that they are concrete manifestations of the dominant forces in our present civilization'.

I believe that they are manifestations of the Prison. And I also believe that they help to reinforce and perpetuate the Prison in us. For living in a place where endless streams of anonymous people pass us by every day, helps to convince us that human life is cheap (a **jailer**'s mentality). And living in a place where pollution, overspecialization, rootlessness, etc., appear to be unavoidable facts of life, helps to convince us that Prison values are necessary for our survival — that they are, in fact, natural and good.

Chapter 4 — Racism: A Product of Capitalism — or of the Six-Sided Prison?

Several times now I've said that the Prison, as distinct from capitalism or human nature, is ultimately responsible for racism, war, imperialism, ecological destruction. In this chapter I wanted to show **how** the Prison is responsible for one of these horrors. I drew straws (I really did!) and picked racism. To simplify things I'll focus on white racism in North America.

What is racism exactly? Most of us seem to think that it's a prejudice against people on biological grounds (as in 'they have low IQ's' or 'they smell funny') and that it can therefore be done away with by showing people that their prejudices have no basis in fact, or that 'the facts' are misleading. But if you actually sit down and talk with people who are 'racists' I think you'll find that their biological prejudices are really just rationales, excuses, that give a kind of scientific validity to a much deeper form of prejudice. (And people would have felt a need for scientific rationales only after the scientific outlook had begun to take hold, after the descent, that is, of the Six-Sided Prison.)

In this view, racism is not just a question of biologically mistaken beliefs, or economically convenient beliefs, or psychologically gratifying beliefs ('at least I'm better than **somebody**'), though all these things play a part. It is also, and more profoundly, a kind of cultural prejudice writ large, and with a scientific twist. And cultural prejudice goes back at least as far as the ancient Greeks. In fact, Roderic Gorney tells us that in the vast majority of cultures for which there are written records we can find some degree of connection between whiteness and truth, beauty, divinity, etc., and blackness and falsehood, ugliness, evil, etc.

So the question becomes, what is there about our **culture** that makes us prejudiced against blacks (and other dark-skinned peoples)? Why are we so culturally prejudiced that improvements in the economic and educational status of nonwhites may cause us to feel even more prejudiced against them? Why were we culturally prejudiced against nonwhites from the very beginnings of the settlement of North America?

The answer, I believe, lies in the workings of the Six-Sided Prison.

Patriarchal attitudes gave us a precedent for oppression, the oppression of women throughout history and in the family. As Shulamith Firestone points out, black and native and chicano oppression is modelled on the oppression of women — the parallels are exact and startling.

In addition, the patriarchy gives us an image of masculinity that leads inevitably to racism. For example, most white males are brought up to believe that the repression of emotion is normal, and so they come to look down on people like blacks and chicanos who are (supposedly) able to express their emotions more freely.

Egocentricity encourages us to build walls around our selves, and therefore contributes mightily to our tendency to see nonwhites as 'the other' . . . if not as 'the enemy'.

Scientific single vision causes us to think of the traits associated with the left side of our brains as 'light', and those with the right side of our brains as 'dark' (see Chap. 3, sect. III). And it causes us to be prejudiced against the traits that are associated with the right side of our brains. And so we think of darkskinned people as sensuous ('lazy'), receptive ('passive'), intuitive ('stupid'), etc.

In addition, scientific single vision led to our mistrust and eventual domination of natural things in the name of a 'higher rationality'; and this led in turn to our alienation from our bodies and to our culture's distortion of natural functions — in plainer words, to our love-hate relationship with feces. And in our culture, as any first-year psychology student can tell you, most of us subconsciously identify blackness with feces, and darkness with 'impurities' (see Joel Kovel, **White Racism**, for a thorough explanation of this point).

The **bureaucratic mentality** encourages us to feel that the world is **naturally** made up of powerful and powerless, winners and losers, jailers and jailed — whites and nonwhites.

Nationalism requires us to conform to the characteristics of the dominant cultural group. In North America, the dominant group is white, Anglo-Saxon and Protestant ('the WASP's'). Minorities that are obviously, even physically unlike this cultural group are automatically suspect.

In addition, the nation-state encourages us to think of other nation-states as 'weaker', 'poorer', 'menacing', etc. And these qualities naturally rub off — in our minds — on the people who are living in these other nation states.

Megalopolis, overlarge and overbearing, gives us an arena in which all our racial prejudices can be acted out in an appropriately vicious and satisfying manner.

I could go on — but by now I hope my point is made. Racism is a product of the Prison. It is not a 'part of human nature', and it isn't confined to capitalism, either. (Does anyone doubt that Stalin could have carried out the extermination of the Jews, which he'd planned, had he lived? Or that the Communist Party could convince the Chinese in a very short time to fear — and believe in — the 'white peril'?)

The conditions for cultural prejudice are deep-seated in all of us, for they were put there by the Prison. And if we don't change the Prison, changing our economic system or changing our schools won't do much to change our racist attitudes. It might even make us more subtly and deeply racist. For if we pass and enforce 'good laws' our racism might simply be driven underground, to live on in the fantasies an symbols that nourish the Prison. Moreover, if we pass 'good laws' and ignore the Prison we may only succeed in driving a wedge between our selves and our society. Barbara Amiel, a well-known Canadian journalist, tells us (in **Maclean's**, 4 Ap. '77) that Britain's liberal immigration laws have made a definite contribution to 'the growing alienation Britons feel from their society', that the presence of large numbers of black and brown immigrants 'may be one of the reasons for their indifference to its future'.

Chapter 5 — Tri-Level Analysis: How to See Through to the Prison

Because it's so pervasive and runs so deep, the Prison isn't immediately obvious to everyone. In order to see through to it, it helps to keep in mind a method that I call 'tri-level analysis'.

I call it that because it looks at the world on three levels at once. The first is concerned with the passing events of daily life; the second, with economic and political power; and the third, with the Prison itself (and with the worldview that the Prison spawns — see Chap. 11).

I didn't invent this method of analysis. It's been used under other names, or simply intuitively, by many New Age-oriented people over the years. In the field of psychology, for example, Daryl Bem has done a 'tri-level analysis' of the levels of belief — he calls them 'primitive', 'higher-order', and 'nonconscious'. In economics, Robert Theobald distinguishes among first-, second-, and third-order 'connections' that we make between phenomena. In sociology, Peter Berger distinguishes among ideas, ideologies and worldviews. In political theory, New Age authors and activists distinguish among 'reform', 'revolution' and 'transformation' (see Chap. 19, sect. VI). Willis Harman, of the Stanford Research Institute, says that there are three 'levels' on which we can 'view society's problems': (1) the level of symptoms — e.g., poverty, crime, racism, pollution, inflation; (2) the level of basic institutions — built-in distributions of economic and political power; and (3) the level of cultural premises, dominant values, and our **image** of our selves (i.e., our basic worldview).

To my mind, the greatest practitioner of tri-level analysis (he doesn't call it that, of course) is a French historian, Fernand Braudel. In his magnum opus, **The Mediterranean**, history moves on three levels at once.

On the first level, the most superficial, are the **events** that fill our daily newspaper — elections, murders, wage demands; 'surface disturbances', says Braudel, 'crests of foam that the tides of history carry on their strong backs'. This is the level that the liberals concentrate on, because it lends itself to irony and can be written about without challenging 'the system', any system.

On the second level is the history of **groups and groupings**, of changes in governmental and economic forms (monarchy to democracy, feudalism to capitalism and so on). This is the level that the Marxists concentrate on, in order to 'prove' that communism is inevitable.

On the third level, invisible to liberals and Marxists alike, is the history of **structures**. In **The Mediterranean** Braudel focuses mainly on changes in geography and climate, but many historians have pointed out that this level could — and should — also refer to **inner** structures; to deep-seated changes in states of mind, points of view, custom and routine, personality and consciousness (see, e.g., Hexter, listed under Braudel). Therefore, this is the level where the Prison can be found.

This third level of history isn't impossible to change; but it is the hardest to change. It's the level William Irwin Thompson is operating on, in **Passages About Earth**, when he sets out to describe a 'transformation of culture so large that it isn't an event any more'. No wonder most political activists have chosen to ignore it!

And yet — and yet — if it's true that governments and economic systems determine the nature of events, as the Marxists say, then it's also true that the third level of history determines the nature of governments and economic systems, and the context, the atmosphere, the quality of events. If we simply ignore the third level of analysis until 'later' we'll end up with no social evolution at all, in any deep sense. And we may end up with a stronger Prison.

Chapter 6 — History as if People Mattered: The Stages of Human Development

Tri-level analysis tells us that the minds and hearts of people were the determining factors in history, and that governments, economics, and so on, were not so determining. Does this make our history read any differently? Does our history make more **sense** when it's read in this way? And does it hold out hope for the future?

This chapter is an attempt to answer these questions. (It answers 'yes' to each of them.)

Before I begin though, I'd like to say something about what I think are the two main barriers to history-as-if-people-mattered: the idea that there are 'laws' in history, and the idea that we are primarily tool-making and tool-using beings (i.e., the idea that **who we are** must conform to material constraints).

The idea that history is governed by a series of unchangeable laws that are taking us from 'lower to higher', in Engels's phrase, or 'onward and upward', in Stalin's, obviously diminishes people's role in history — and provides a convenient excuse for authoritarian governments who would override the will of the people, or pay no heed to the views of dissenting minorities. For a critique of the currently most influential series of historical laws — Marxian 'dialectics' — see Chap. 23, sect. IV-4.

The other barrier is the idea that we are primarily tool users and tool makers ('man the maker'). A number of New Age-oriented people have recently pointed out that tool-making and tool-using are not our most characteristic activities.

Marshall Sahlins, an economic anthropologist, says that we're basically meaning-seeking beings and that we turn even the things we **need** to do into a vehicle for the expression of our search for meaning. In this view, culture is the sum total of our efforts to find out about our selves and to realize our selves — even when we're engaging in directly economic activities, our search for meaning remains primary. What is distinctive about human culture is not 'that it must conform to material constraints but that it does so according to a definite symbolic scheme which is never the only one possible' (see **Manas**, 21 Dec. '77).

Roderic Gorney, psychiatrist and social philosopher, says that 'the functional capacity that truly separates man from ape and all other animals is that of using **complex symbols**. . . . Tool-using and especially tool-making are manifestations of the symbolic process'.

Lewis Mumford says that we're not primarily tool-making, we're primarily 'mind-making, self-mastering, and self-designing', and so we've always been. For until we developed a culture (he says), our inner life must have been a madhouse — we wouldn't have been able to recognize a tool, let alone use one. Our first and greatest need wasn't to change the world but to change our selves, and the only instruments we had for doing this were our own gestures and sounds. The most important things tools did for us is that they helped us carry food, and freed our mouths for speech.

Speech, language, allowed us to create a symbolic culture, and (here Mumford's argument dovetails with the others) it's this that got us out of the animal world: not our tools. Many birds and mammals were more proficient with their tools. The unique human achievement was the **shaping of a self** by means of this symbolic culture; and from that point on, our main business was our own self-development.

The point is this, that in the last analysis we ourselves determine our consciousness. The material world helps, but **we're responsible**. Lawrence

LeShan, an experimental psychologist, puts it nicely when he says, 'A human being is an organizer of reality with a wide variety of options. The more (he or she) exercises those options, the more human and the less animal he or she is'.

If I had to choose one grand, global explanation as to why the Prison arose — one explanation as to how it achieved its 'leading role' — I would point to the finally uncontrollable desire for power **over** things (as distinct from the power to cooperate 'synergically' with people and with nature — see Chap. 15, sect. II).

Many New Age authors have imagined (or simply assumed) a history in which our growing fascination with (coercive) power and control is the dominant theme. In other words, in which our mentality or consciousness is the dominant theme: in which the Prison is the dominant theme. If you put their writings together I believe you'll come up with two main **stages of human development** — along with the notion that we're on the brink of a third stage, or on the brink of destruction.

The first stage is that of **Old Age people**, and it may be characterized by the fact that it was Prison-free.

By 'Old Age' I don't mean Europe before 1492, I mean the world as it existed until some time after we had begun to practice agriculture. For until that time our fascination with power — though definitely not absent — expressed itself only weakly and sporadically, and more often than not for the common good.

There is a difference between romanticizing the past and accepting that there are important things that we need to recover from the past. New Age people have been studying Old Age society not so much for models as for lessons, clues; what is it that we lack, what is it that we need to learn before we can break the Prison's grip on our society?

And they've come up with some suggestive 'finds'. Marshall Sahlins says that Old Age people formed the original affluent society. 'An affluent society is one in which all the people's material wants are easily satisfied', and in Old Age society our material wants were easily satisfied not because we could produce much but because we wanted little — because our material wants were 'finite and few'. Old Age people were **able** to temper their material wants largely because their worldview included a spiritual-religious and also a mythic-aesthetic dimension (largely because there was so much more **to** life, for them, than material things).

Certainly we worked hard in those days, says Mumford, but not any harder than we needed to. We didn't think of the world as a project (Illich), and we didn't feel a need to pour into our working lives the energy that could and did go into sex and play and rituals. (According to Sahlins, we may have worked as little as 15 hours a week!)

Sahlins finds it significant that the vast majority of our experience — and certainly our formative experience as a people — was not in complex 'civilization' (let alone huge cities) but rather in small-ish bands. Gary

Snyder, the poet, reports (in **East West Journal**, June '77) that these bands may have enjoyed 'the existence of a tremendous interest, exchange and sympathy between people and animals'.

Again: no one is suggesting that Old Age people lived in a 'golden age' or that we should imitate them in any way today. But it is impossible to confront the anthropology of the New Age and not begin to suspect that the following (at least) may represent deep-seated social needs that we can only ignore at our peril: the need for a concept of 'enough'; the need for a more sophisticated, more many-sided worldview than the materialist one; the need for a compelling series of ethics and values; the need for a (much closer) tie to nature and the 'natural world'; and the need for a much smaller **scale**, for many small societies rather than a few large ones. (These points will all be taken up in Parts IV-V).

The second 'stage of human development' is that of Prison or so-called **Civilized people**, and it has lasted from the beginnings of the agricultural era up to our own day. It is characterized by our growing fascination with (coercive) power; by the decline of all ethics and values that might have tempered this fascination; and by the birth and growth of the Prison.

Our quest for power **over** things (and eventually also over one another — whom we treat more and more like things) probably began as no more than a pragmatic and 'innocent' response to immediate dangers (e.g., traps for marauding animals). Unfortunately, however, the quest for power, once begun, seems to have no natural bounds. Our culture can restrain the power drive — primarily by subordinating it to a series of ethics and values — but if and when those ethics and values begin to disintegrate, the power drive becomes dominant . . . gets out of control.

New Age authors have isolated three historical events that seem to have been turning points with regard to the **strength** of our power drive — with regard to its significance as a force in history.

The first turning point came with the accumulation of our first agricultural surpluses, for these gave us our first real **opportunity** to exercise our coercive power — at least, on a grand and costly scale — and many of our first civilizations chose to do just that. The result was towns, ships, canals (but also war-chariots, pyramids, bureaucracies, empires, megalopolises . . .).

The second turning point came in the third century B.C. when Alexander the Great invented the concept of 'humanity' — the idea of the one-naturedness of people everywhere. What this idea did, says Ivan Illich (in **East West Journal**, Ap. '76), was to substitute the concept 'human nature', an abstraction, for the idea of a multiplicity of distinct, flesh-and-blood peoples, each with their own particular needs, wants, priorities. It implied that everybody had, or should have, the **same** priorities, and it gave (most of) us the notion that we knew — that we **could** know — what was best for everyone. In the long run it encouraged us to relinquish our responsibility for meeting our own needs, wants, priorities (because someone else could do it better, or more efficiently).

The third turning point was the Black Death and the schism(s) in the Christian Church — for these things made us feel fearful, and betrayed by our old ethics and values; and in response, we grasped at the sides of the Prison as if we were drowning.

Our new nations, our new cities, our new products and technologies, did manage to offset our loss of certainty; but they also took us farther away from the natural world and from the world of natural behaviour. They took us so far away that we began to love life less and love things more. In time we began to crave the Prison's products mainly because we could think of nothing better to do. And we tore up half the planet just to give our selves these false gifts. And we worked longer hours in the 20th century than we did in the 13th, and we enjoyed our selves less, both on and off the job (see, e.g., deGrazia). (How **could** Prison-bound people have enjoyed themselves more?)

The third 'stage of human development' is that of **New Age people**, and it's the alternative to the final triumph of the Prison — in other words, to spiritual suicide. A description of New Age people and New Age society is attempted in Part V, and here I just want to examine the historical evidence for signs that we may be moving in that direction. (Signs, not laws as in a Marxist reading of history. Giving up that 'certainty' is the price we have to pay for disbelieving in scientific single vision.)

First, following Braudel's lead (Chap. 5), some evidence from geography — from astronomy even. David Spangler puts it accurately enough: 'Earth moves through 12 ages during the course of 26,000 years as the equinoctial points revolve around the ecliptic through each of the 12 zodiacal signs or arcs. We are now leaving one age and entering another . . . (and it) is not far-fetched to assume that (this) may bring about the exposure of Earth and the life-strains upon it to differing energies from the cosmos'. If we can develop our selves enough to be open to these energies, we should be able to break out of the Prison — and go on to create something better.

My next two arguments are rooted more firmly in the history we've just been reviewing. They suggest that the Prison is **producing its own gravedig-gers** by going against deep-seated, third-level tendencies in our hearts and minds.

The first 'gravedigger' is the fact that the Prison has become a threat to our physical survival on earth (because of its 'ecocidal' tendencies and because of its system of military defence). Most psychologists believe that we have an innate, biological need to survive. Therefore, our need to survive may help to carry us out of the Prison and into a New Age where our desire to **have** more can be replaced by a desire to **be** more: by a desire to develop our selves and to relate to each other in a life-loving manner; and by a desire to serve others (but as a means of developing self rather than as a means of fighting self).

Well — we've always managed to make the right biological adaptations before.

The second 'gravedigger' is the fact that the Prison has taken away our rationale for the inevitable pain and sadness of life. (I don't mean the pain that comes from starving, I mean the pain that comes when, for instance, someone we love dies.) Peter Berger calls this rationale a 'theodicy', and he claims that having a theodicy is an inherent human need.

To provide us with a theodicy — to explain, without explaining away, our suffering — is what religion used to do, before we lost our faith and tried to replace it with the Prison's values. However, neither the scientific outlook nor any other side of the Prison has been able to generate an alternate theodicy. There are, of course, secular theodicies, such as national patriotism and Marxism. But while these might be comforting to those of us who face death on the barricades, they're not going to be very comforting to those of us who have heart attacks in the penny arcade — to those of us whose lives lack the (phony) grandeur of armed struggle. The Six-Sided Prison can't answer our need for a theodicy, and it's our search for a theodicy — for 'something to live for', in the watered-down popular phrase — that's carrying many of us out of the confines of the Prison, and beyond the materialist worldview.

Part II — Monolithic Institutions

Chapter 7 — The Monolithic Mode of Production: How the Prison is Institutionalized

The Prison doesn't exist only in our hearts and minds. It is institutionalized by means of what I call the 'monolithic mode of production'.

I'm sorry to have to introduce another cumbersome new term, but I couldn't see any way around it since it refers to something cumbersome and all too real. Marx used to speak of the 'capitalist mode of production', but the monolithic mode is common to both capitalism and socialism — it's a third-level concept if anything is. More recently, Kenneth Boulding has spoken of 'monolithic' and 'polylithic' organizations; Ivan Illich of the 'industrial mode of production'; Jacques Ellul of 'technique'; E. F. Schumacher of 'modern' versus 'appropriate' technologies; Lewis Mumford of 'poly-, mono-, and biotechnics' — in fact, at least 26 authors cited in Chap. 24 have spoken out against (what I am calling) monolithic institutions and technologies — and the 'monolithic mode of production' is a synthesis of their views.

I. Description

The monolithic mode of production makes it almost impossible for alternatives to exist to the products it creates. In North America some of its leading products are: institutionalized medical care, massproduced housing, compulsory schooling, organized religion, nuclear-family child care, and nuclear power. These products are produced by 'monolithic institutions': the medical profession, the housing industry, the compulsory school, the church, the nuclear family, the nuclear power-plant.

I call these institutions 'monolithic' because they establish a kind of monopoly over the production of goods and services. When we hear about monopolies it's usually Exxon's or Alcan's — some corporation's monopoly. That's a second-level monopoly, a **brand-name** monopoly. Monolithic institutions are third-level monopolies, more deep-seated, more profound, much harder to root out. Their monopolies are those of the **products** they create. Not the University of California but the university system of learning, not the American Medical Association but professional medicine, not the Catholic Church but church-centred religion, not the Atomic Energy Board of Canada but, if there are no serious accidents (fat chance), nuclear power — these are the kinds of monopolies that have been and are being produced by monolithic institutions.

It is, of course, theoretically possible for alternatives to many of these products to exist. And many of them do exist, at the edges and in the corners of society. But that is just my point: chances are good that if you've given birth at home, or built your own home, or taken your kids out of school, or put a solar heater up on your roof, then you're not really part of the mainstream of society.

In sect. III below I have listed and briefly described 16 **examples** of monolithic institutions, patterns, technologies. This is not meant to be a complete list, but it is meant to give some idea of the range of monolithic institutions — they are everywhere. But first, a little background. . . .

II. Origins

The monolithic mode of production creates a monopoly not only of products but of products that — when they are dominant in a society — reinforce and perpetuate Prison values (standardization, efficiency, hierarchy, order, etc.). In fact, to a great extent, the monolithic mode owes its origins to the Prison: is the natural and possibly inevitable institutional underpinning of a society whose members are Prison-bound.

Patriarchal attitudes have certainly contributed to our desire to have our institutions service us (and-or to devote our selves to serving our institutions). Philip Slater doubts that our monolithic institutions could exist without egocentric impulses having provided fuel for them in the first place. Theodore Roszak traces the roots of many of our monolithic institutions back to scientific single vision. And Lewis Mumford shows that the monolithic nature of our institutions would be impossible without the bureaucratic mentality.

According to Mumford (and to Jacques Ellul), the monolithic mode of production was dominant at least twice before in our history — at the time of the Pharaohs, and in ancient Rome. In its current form, the monolithic mode can be traced all the way back to the beginnings of modern culture. As we saw in Chap. 6, by the 15th century most people were in no mood to see that the old values (reverence, leisure, play, ritual) needed to be added to, not destroyed. After the Black Death and the splits in the Christian Church, they cast their old values aside and seized on Prison values with a vengeance. Spurred on, then, not by a desire to live more joyously, but by patriarchal fantasies of conquest, egocentric visions and desires, scientific arrogance, and bureaucratic-hierarchical notions of order, they managed not only to develop **but to abuse** standardization, prefabrication and mechanization centuries before the 'industrial revolution' (appropriately enough, these monolithic standbys were all first developed in the **state-organized military** arsenals in an early **megalopolis**, Venice).

It wasn't until the early 20th century that the monolithic mode actually triumphed. Alongside monolithic tendencies there had always been what Mumford calls the 'polylithic mode of production', which drew on a pool of tools, machines, materials and processes that went back hundreds or even thousands of years. This 'technological pool' was, in an important sense, our material heritage, and it had been passed on from generation to generation by skilled craftspeople and work teams. But when the jobs of these people were finally eliminated (by standardization, prefabrication and mechanization), the technological pool, and the polylithic mode of production that had depended on it, was of course eliminated too.

The triumph of the monolithic mode has taken place in three main stages, well described by Ivan Illich:

(1) **Each institution appears to earn the right to achieve a monopoly in its field**. In medicine, for example, around World War I medical school graduates became almost as good as herbalists at curing diseases. That was enough to convince us to identify healing with patriarchal, scientific, bureaucratic, professionalized health care. Professional medical associations were given the right to set standards and limit entry — and all other kinds of healers were prosecuted. Even self-care became more difficult.

(2) **Each institution comes to frustrate the end it was originally designed to serve**. In transportation, for example, the creation of faster and faster vehicles led to the creation of greater and greater distances within cities. Soon it was taking us longer to get to work than it ever had before. Or, for example, we spent an average of 1600 hours on our cars last year (driving them, earning money to pay for them, parking them etc.) and we drove them less than 7500 miles: less than five miles an hour!

(3) **Each institution becomes a threat to society**. Again in transportation, 64,000 North Americans were killed on the roads last year, and over four million were injured. Fewer North Americans were killed or injured in the War on Vietnam. But that was an easier threat to deal with, because it didn't involve changing our selves (or at least that's what we thought).

A dependence on monolithic institutions is transmitted to us in earliest childhood by our parents. Joseph Chilton Pearce has given us a fine description of this process: 'In the case of the injured child, for instance, the average parent (has) little capacity for responding to the needs of the situation. . . . Conditioned to surrender personal power and ability to the professional, the parent would have to rush the child to a hospital or doctor. . . . The child whose parent panics and rushes him-her to the professional (the person who stands between self and personal power) undergoes a deep and abiding learning. S-he learns that the parents do not have the personal power s-he believed them to have. S-he learns that the parents cannot act on his-her behalf, . . . that (power and possibility) must be bought from the professionals. . . . The parent who panics and shifts responsibility thus dispels the child's own sense of personal power and ability. The child learns that s-he is as impotent as the parents. The stage is then set for the child's own surrender of responsibility to the professional'.

Even if our upbringings were different, however, we would probably still be dependent on our monolithic institutions. Prison-bound people tend to be thing-oriented (see Chap. 10), and thing-oriented people tend to be driven by what social psychologist Michael Maccoby calls the 'fantasy of the mechanical womb'. Maccoby explains: 'Their goal is to live in a shelter in which modern technology gives them the possibility of pressing buttons to satisfy every need, whether it be for frozen foods, heat, exciting TV entertainment, electronic rock music, or effortless drug-induced ways of putting them to sleep and waking them up. When they leave the home, they feel secure only in a mobile mechanical womb that hurtles them to their destination . . . '.

III. Examples

(1) **The transportation industry** is an excellent example of a monolithic institution. Its product is the private automobile (and other speedy vehicles: planes, trucks, busses). Of course, auto manufacturers don't advertise their product as 'the automobile'. They tell us to 'buy GM instead of Chrysler' and so on. And there are always reformers who are telling us to 'break up GM' and so on. But on the third level of analysis, all the manufacturers, and all the reformers too, are telling us the same thing: without the private automobile, we are diminished as human beings. And our cities are designed and our society is run on the basis of, you might even say for the convenience of, the private automobile. (More than half of the ground space in our cities is taken up now by roadways, parking lots and gas stations; more than half of our urban air pollution comes from the automobile; more than three-quarters of

our noise pollution. . . .)

But — and this is my other crucial point — if the monolithic mode were changed to one that gave priority to bicyclists and walkers tomorrow, most of us would be very unhappy. For the Prison has made us feel that it's **important** to get where we're going as fast as possible and with as little exertion as possible and in as 'distinguished' or flashy a manner as possible. 'Dominant social values become embedded in the technology that they produce', says David Dickson, author of the book **The Politics of Alternative Technology**. Just so, the Prison is embedded in our monolithic institutions. (Barbara Ward tells us that Russia had attempted to 'delay' motorization but was forced to relent in the 1960's 'under consumer pressure'. You can't blame advertising for that.)

In this view, providing a 'good' system of rapid public transit (solution of the traditional 'ism's') would only be compounding the problem. For the problem isn't the domination of the private automobile so much as it is the Prison-bound notion that we've got to get to wherever it is we're going as quickly, smoothly, etc., as possible. It isn't even speed **per se** that's the problem but the fact that we can't escape from it, or from its effects, if we want to be a part of our society.

(2) **Professional, institutional medicine** depends on restricting our access to medical information and restricting the numbers of people who are allowed to practice 'medicine', formerly known as 'healing'. Like any other monopoly, its claims are inflated and its ill effects, understated.

As for its claims, Ivan Illich tells us that the great strides that we have, indeed, made over the last 100 years or so have come primarily from better nutrition, better housing and the like, rather than from doctors.

As for its ill effects, Illich mentions three: first, modern medical practice often **causes** illness by prescribing the wrong drugs, too many drugs, etc., or by allowing something to go wrong in hospital (there are more reported accidents in hospitals than in all industries but mines and high-rise construction!). Second, modern medical practice encourages us to become dependent on . . . modern medical practice . . . rather than to take any responsibility for our own healing (in Britain, one quarter of all visits to the doctor for free service are for the untreatable common cold!). Third, modern medical practice saps our will to master the arts of suffering and dying, and encourages instead merely an obsessive desire to 'kill' any kind of discomfort or pain. 'This progressive flattening out of personal, virtuous performance', writes Illich, 'constitutes a new goal which has never before been a guideline for social life'.

(3) **Universal, compulsory schooling** makes it nearly impossible for us to educate our selves outside of the school system. And partly for that very reason, universal compulsory schooling teaches us what educators John Holt and Ivan Illich call 'the hidden curriculum'.

The hidden curriculum, says Holt, consists of the things schools teach 'simply by the fact of being schools, of having the power to compel children to attend, to tell them what to learn, and to grade, rank, and label them'. The hidden curriculum consists of the things schools teach whether the curriculum is designed to make us good North Americans or good Communists or whether the teacher is strict or kind. . . .

The hidden curriculum consists of several interrelated 'messages'. Illich identifies them as follows: only through schooling can we prepare our selves for adulthood; what is not taught in school is of little value (and what is learned outside of school is not worth knowing); the degree of success we will enjoy in society depends on the amount of schooling we consume; learning **about** the world is more valuable than learning **from** the world.

Holt identifies many more 'messages', including: 'if we didn't make you come here you wouldn't learn anything, you'd . . . grow up to be a bum'; 'even if you could be trusted to find out about the world, you are too stupid to do it'; 'learning is separate from the rest of life'; 'your own questions are hardly ever worth asking or answering'; 'what is not rewarded is no good'; 'everything important about us can be measured'; 'there must be experts somewhere who know better than we do what is best for us'; and 'real life is a struggle, a zero-sum game, where no one can win without someone else, or everyone else, losing'.

All these messages can be seen as parts of a single message — 'learning is a commodity, it is not something that we do'.

(4) **The housing industry** has two purposes. The first is to build our housing for us. The second is to keep us from housing our selves simply and cheaply, and to keep us from building our own.

In 1945, Ivan Illich tells us, 32 percent of our homes were still self-built. By 1970 the proportion had gone down to 11 percent. We had actually grown more capable of producing tools and materials that fostered self-building, but unions, building codes, and mortgage rules — all of them reflecting the values and priorities of the Prison — had turned against self-building. And not only against self-building, but against **all** housing that was inexpensive and simple and easy to understand. To take but one example: Buckminster Fuller's 'dymaxion domes', three-bedroom homes with natural air conditioning that would have cost $1250 to put up in 1940, plumbing, wiring and furniture included, never got off the ground. Fuller's opposition came equally from three sources: from the building codes, from greedy investors, and from the plumbers' and electricians' unions. After five years or so, Fuller gave up in despair.

(5) **Church-centred religion** tells us — more or less bluntly — that we can only 'really' get to the spiritual and religious states of consciousness by means of the church. Church-centred religion tends to **cordon the spirit off** from the rest of life, and God becomes just another commodity to be purchased, along with the soap and the Wheaties. (Ironically, church-centred religion plays right into the hands of the materialists.)

(6) **The job economy** makes it hard for us to exist if we don't want to work at a regular, 40-hour-a-week job.

Advocates of the full-employment economy would guarantee 40-hour-a-week employment to all, thereby **strengthening** both the job economy and the Prison-bound rationale behind it ('if they don't wanna work let them starve'); for a critique of this proposal see Chap. 21, sect. III-1.

(7) **Monogamy, heterosexuality, marriage**, all become monolithic when they're seen as moral or cultural imperatives — as choices that we **must** make if we want to escape the feeling that we're unnatural, selfish, sick, immoral (not to mention the pain of our parents and the prejudice of our neighbours). In North America, most of us haven't even bothered to ask our selves whether or not we **want** to be monogamous, heterosexual, married — we simply **are**, or assume that we do. And if we do question these things, it is usually only an intellectual questioning.

Compulsive heterosexuality cuts us off from half the world as love partners and may diminish our overall enjoyment of people of our own sex. It also perpetuates sex-role stereotypes (partly by keeping us out of touch with the opposite-sex person **within** us, what Jung has called our 'anima' or 'animus'), and it perpetuates patriarchal attitudes — as Lucia Valeska puts it (in **Quest**, Fall '75), it is 'a mandate that all women be forever divided against each other through a compelling allegiance to one man at home and all men outside the home'.

Compulsive monogamy may have served some essential purpose two or three million years ago. But today, as Robert Thamm points out, compulsive monogamy tends to lead 'more to a dependent attachment than to a loving commitment'. And compulsive marriage tends to lead to 'mutual overdependence and restricted gratification'; tends to imply 'a more or less monotonous day-to-day living together'; and tends to change 'romantic love to dependent, possessive, and jealous love'. No wonder studies have found that the stability of marriage is a function of the couple's isolation from other important relationships, and that unhappiness tends to increase with the length of marriage — one recent study of middle-aged married couples (cited in LeMaster) found that the **typical** marriage 'represented a facade with no substantial marital relationship behind it'.

(8) **The nuclear family** can be devastating to parents and children alike — if it isn't consciously chosen, and if its inherent dangers are not then consciously dealt with.

For one thing, it tends to embody some — and usually all — of the monolithic institutions listed under no. 7 above. For another thing, it tends to embody the first four sides of the Prison in almost pure form — making it into a kind of transmission belt for the Prison. The patriarchy is embodied in the dominant male — 'husband' or 'father'; egocentricity is embodied in the isolated family's notion that it's 'us' against 'them'; the scientific outlook is embodied in the dualism this notion implies; and the bureaucratic mentality is embodied in the 'functional' hierarchy, pets-kids-Mommy-Daddy.

John Holt says that the relationships in the nuclear family are 'too intense', partly at least just because of its size; that 'too much is always at stake'. And the family 'is so dependent on these high-powered feelings, so shut in on itself, . . . so devoid of purposes outside of itself, that it is fragile, easily threatened by a quarrel'. Which is, perhaps, one reason why there's so much **suppression of feelings** in the nuclear family.

Finally, it's worth mentioning some of Thamm's objections to the nuclear family (he lists 44 objections in all!) — 'fails to provide an ongoing stability and security for members over generations'; 'friends take second place to relatives in the obligation hierarchy'; 'cannot function as a democracy when only two adults share the power'.

Some of the nuclear family's worst effects have to do with child-rearing. It gives the child a terrible model of adult and social life (typically — and this has been borne out by many studies — the father flops down on the easy chair after a hard day at work, and watches TV that night and for much of the weekend; the mother cooks food and cleans house). Then there's the fact that — starved for strokes, for friendship and esteem — we turn our children into objects for our own gratification, with ill effects for all concerned. We turn them into love objects, which we desperately need (Holt: 'It is very painful to have more love to give away that people to whom we can give it'). We turn them into help objects ('We value their dependency and helplessness'). And we turn them into hate objects, to work off the rage that we feel towards a world in which we can never get enough (**every year** in North America, 55,000 children die and 330,000 are permanently injured by maltreatment).

(9) **Monolithic technology** — generally known as 'modern' or 'industrial-era' or 'Western' technology — has come to dominate our society to such an extent that many of us are hardly aware that there **are** other technologies, other ways of doing things; or we think that the choice is between more of the same and 'going back to the Middle Ages'. All mass production technologies are by definition modern and 'good', or at least, 'functional'; all smaller-scale technologies are by definition backward and 'bad', or at least a little silly.

There is, however, nothing particularly modern about the **nature** of our large-scale technologies. Lewis Mumford has shown us that, 'Almost from the beginning of civilization, two disparate technologies have existed side by side: one 'democratic' and dispersed, the other totalitarian and centralized. . . . The large-scale organization of the proletariat in specialized workshops and factories, using what now seem like "modern" methods, is reasonably well developed for the Hellenic and Roman world but must have begun much earlier . . .'.

Moreover, there is nothing rhetorical about Mumford's use of the term 'totalitarian' — if we continue on our present course, our technology will make a totally planned, totally administered society all but inevitable. Consider these 'key' characteristics of monolithic technology: (1) grand in scale; (2) costly; (3) prodigious use of non-renewable resources; (4) considerable environmental damage; (5) difficult to maintain; (6) difficult if not impossible for most people to understand; (7) indifferent to its surroundings (could be anywhere). Clearly, some powerful central authority is going to have to be (is already) necessary to construct and pay for the technological apparatus;

to make sure that other governments or corporations don't muscle in on the needed resources; to train the 'keepers' of the system; and so on.

Monolithic technology is, then, neither particularly modern in nature nor particularly democratic in essence; but — and this 'but' is inevitable — doesn't it deliver the goods?

Well, up to now it has (for one-sixth of the globe perhaps) — but no New Ager would deny that, as Tom Bender puts it, 'The assumptions upon which present production processes have been built are no longer supportable'. Three of the most important assumptions are (a) continuously increasing the size of production facilities is the best way to maximize production and minimize costs; (b) we will continue to be able to buy more and more goods and services; (c) the economic effect of how we do things is more important than the political, environmental, or psychocultural effects.

Assumption (a) has been disproved by economists whose accounting practices figured in the 'secondary' and 'external' costs of goods (e.g., time lost in strikes; declining quality of goods) and who looked more closely at the so-called 'economies of scale'. Assumption (b) is obviously untrue — if the whole world 'enjoyed' the American standard of living we would run out of many crucial and irreplaceable raw materials by the end of the century. And assumption (c) is true only if people are held to be primarily economic beings, an assumption that's challenged — I think successfully — in Parts III and IV.

One of the advantages in seeing our technology as 'monolithic' is seeing that, as David Dickson puts it, our problems result 'as much from the nature of technology as from the way it is used'. In other words, technology is not neutral — it has a kind of life of its own. New Age writers like Theodore Roszak and William Irwin Thompson have gone so far as to claim that we've made our technology (and the science on which it is based) 'a culture in its own right — the **one** culture to be uniformly imitated or imposed everywhere'.

Peter Berger has recently shown us that our monolithic technology serves to **reinforce and perpetuate** the Prison in us. How does it do this? When we operate our machines, follow our bureaucratic regulations, etc., we learn the following 'lessons', among others: (1) reality consists of static self-contained units, it is not an ongoing flux; (2) reality consists of identical components, not unique entities; (3) there is no necessary connection between means and ends; (4) every action, however concrete, needs to be understood in an abstract frame of reference — abstractions are what count; (5) work is separate from private life; (6) it is functional to define other people as functionaries; (7) the self can only be expressed in a partial and segmented way.

(10) **Nuclear power** is, beyond some point that we may soon reach, an irreversible energy strategy. So it is important that we become aware of some of the dangers of nuclear power plants:

1. 'A single large nuclear reactor', says Dr. Patrick Moore, head of the Greenpeace Foundation (in **Greenpeace Report: 1976**), 'produces as much nuclear waste in one year as would result from the explosion of 100 Hiroshima-sized atomic bombs. . . . Due to the slow rate of decay of many of these poison-

ous nuclear wastes it is necessary that they be kept isolated from the environment for many thousands of years. . . . Thus we are confronted with the problem of trying to construct gigantic storage tanks that must not leak for thousands of years'.

2. An even more serious result of nuclear fission, according to Moore, is the production of a substance known as plutonium — 'aptly named after the Greek god of Hell. . . . Plutonium has a half-life of 25,000 years — this means that it takes 250,000 years for the total decay of this radioactive element. . . . Plutonium is the most toxic chemical known to (people). A piece of this element the size of a grapefruit is enough to poison every person on earth. . . . Plutonium is highly radioactive and the ingestion of even the most minute particle can cause cancer. . . . Plans for future nuclear powerplants call for the production of many hundreds of tons of plutonium. . . . It is inevitavle that some of this material will find its way into the environment'.

3. The **Clamshell Alliance News** (Oct.-Nov. '77) reports that Dr. Ernest Sternglass, of the University of Pittsburgh, has discovered evidence of 'exceptionally high cancer rates, infant mortality rates, and birth defects among people living near existing nuclear power plants'.

4. 'Accidents can happen', says a Clamshell Alliance pamphlet, 'causing release of radiation and possible contamination of lead and water for years, with thousands of deaths and injuries. There have been close calls already: at the Fermi plant in Michigan in 1966 and at Brown's Ferry, Alabama, where a fire in 1975 almost led to a "melt-down" and subsequent release of radiation'.

5. It is difficult to build a nuclear bomb from uranium — the construction of a plutonium bomb is, however, relatively simple. 'It is not difficult', says Dr. Moore, 'to separate the plutonium from the rest of the elements present in nuclear waste. Once their separation is made it is then possible, for a few thousand dollars, to construct a workable nuclear bomb'. Dr. Edward Teller — father of the H-bomb — has estimated that there are over 100,000 people today who have enough knowledge to build a nuclear bomb.

6. Even if all these things could be kept 'under control' — and they are already out of control — nuclear power would, as Gil Bailie puts it (in **Planet Drum** no. 4), 'limit the range of possible choices for future generations' more completely than anything else on the planet (this is what makes it a 'monolithic' institution, as well as a particularly dangerous one). 'Politically, centralization will be important for the required social control' — to oversee the transportation and storage of radioactive wastes, guard the storage tanks, regulate the producers, etc.

Amory Lovins, a well-known physicist, adds, 'Discouraging nuclear violence and coercion requires some abrogation of civil liberties; guarding long-lived wastes against geological or social contingencies implies some form of hierarchical social rigidity or homogeneity to insulate the (technocrats) from social turbulence; and making political decisions about nuclear hazards which are compulsory, . . . disputed, unknown, or unknowable, may tempt governments to bypass democratic decision in favour of elitist technocracy'.

Finally: if we **had** access to unlimited energy, all signs point to the fact that we would **use** it and create an almost inhumanly high-technology society (even compared to our present-day society which many people feel has already lost all sense of the human scale). As Bailie says, 'Maturity is the wisdom not to use all the power you have', and we have yet to demonstrate that we have that wisdom.

(11) Our **defence system** is totally dependent on monolithic institutions. Our tanks, our planes, our bombs, our military officers and so on, could only be produced by monolithic institutions and technologies. (And could our soldiers ever be free — really free — of the Prison?) If we want to transform our monolithic institutions, we're going to have to transform both the **scale** and the **nature** of our system of defence.

Marxists like to say that 'capitalism' is responsible for the military economy; and it's true that one out of every five jobs in the U.S. depends directly or indirectly on the Pentagon (Stavrianos). But it's also true that, as Seymour Melman puts it, there is no 'economic necessity inherent in capitalism which gives war economy such competence. That is a political choice'. Canada, Great Britain, Japan, and many other 'capitalist' countries have done without an undue amount of military spending. Nor is the military economy exclusive to capitalism — the Soviet Union is outspending even the U.S. Nor is the military economy particularly **good** for capitalism — on the contrary, as Melman has convincingly shown, what's good for the 'defence' industries is eroding the productivity of the rest of the U.S. economy.

(12) **The monolithic state** is a product of our wanting — and needing — the government to do things **for** us. By now it is, as Jacques Ellul puts it, 'the most important reality in our day. . . . We cannot conceive of society except as directed by a central omnipresent and omnipotent state'. And as we become more dependent on the state, the state continues to grow. 'The means through which the state can act are constantly growing. Its personnel and functions are constantly growing. Its responsibilities are growing. All this goes hand in hand with inevitable centralization and with the total organization of the society in the hands of the state'. In the U.S., expenditures directed by all levels of government increased from 15 percent of all expenditures in 1930 to 40 percent in 1973. The costs of government rose from three billion dollars in 1913 to 400 billion in the mid-1970's. Sixteen percent of the labour force now works for one or another governmental agency. . . . In proportion to our population, says George Lodge, government in North America is probably bigger than in those countries we call socialist.

'The nation-state is much more fundamental in our world than economic reality', says Ellul. 'Nowadays the state directs the economy'. This important point has been carefully documented by a number of New Age writers. Richard Barnet, for instance, has accumulated much evidence to show that World War II 'brought the federal bureaucracy to a new position of command over American society. . . . The corporations continue to exercise the dominant **influence** in the society, but the **power** keeps passing to the state'. Similarly, Seymour Melman holds that 'the traditional role of government in capitalism as the servant of business has been in transition. During the Cold War this relationship shifted toward collaboration, a partnership between government and big business. More recently, following the great institutional changes of the Kennedy-McNamara regime, a newer pattern emerged of business as the well-rewarded servant of government'. Melman points out that corporate taxes have risen about twice as fast as corporate profits since 1950 — proof positive that corporate decision-making power has declined vis-a-vis that of the state. 'I made a point of inquiring of officers of a few major firms, Why was such a reduction in decision power accepted. The typical reply was that the senior officers have been essentially "bought off" with handsome salaries and fringe benefits, not to mention occasional access to the highest places of power in the federal government'.

Ellul draws the essential political point: 'Marxist analysis was valid only in the 19th century, when the emergence of uncontrolled, explosive economic power relegated a weak, liberal, and unclearly delineated state to the shadows and subjugated it. But today the major social phenomenon is the state, becoming ever more extended, ever more assured . . . '.

(13) **The governing elite** monopolizes the key decisions — the policy decisions — and should therefore be classified as a 'monolithic institution' no matter how open to new members it is.

However — it is also true that, in North America today, policy is no longer 'imposed from the top' by 60 wealthy families (or whomever). In the U.S., Franz Schurmann, a well-known political scientist, has recently shown that policy emerges from an ongoing struggle between the 'realm of ideology' and the 'realm of interests'.

The realm of ideology consists primarily of the executive branch of the government — the President and his or her advisors. The realm of interests consists of all the different legislative, executive and military bureaucracies, as well as the pressure groups that feed them (this is where the corporations come in). The realm of ideology and the realm of interests are constantly at loggerheads, but the realm of ideology is also, generally, the stronger of the two (a point Schurmann makes with great skill in his long-drawn-out discussion of U.S. foreign policy).

This way of looking at the (divisions within) the governing elite suggests that there's a built-in, **structural** reason why the state is expanding. It is that the realm of ideology and the realm of interests would each like to expand their power vis-a-vis the other. And so private life, to whatever extent it remains independent of the state, **becomes a kind of 'disputed territory'** over which the various centralizing political ideologies and the various special interests try to exercise their sway.

The concept of the 'realm of ideology' and the fact that it's now the dominant realm raises an important point: that by our choice of President we may have much more power to affect the policy-making process than we think. 'All ideology springs from dominant social forces', writes Schurmann — a notion directly at variance with Marx'. For Marx, ideology was the belief system used by the rulers to delude the ruled. (Except for communism.) For Schurmann ideology is any kind of belief system 'deriving from social forces put to political use'. Fascism, nationalism, imperialism, socialism, Marxism, New Age politics, are all ideologies in this sense; and the President's role is, or can be, to represent one or more of these ideologies (as, e.g., Truman represented the imperialist ideology).

Why, then, if we have this power, is the governing elite still so obviously selfish, so obviously unjust? Primarily because we are our selves selfish and unjust; bound by the Prison. **We are not essentially different** from the President and his or her advisors, from the people we choose (allow) to govern us (if anything we're **less** tolerant and **less** humanitarian; see Monsma). According to Ferdinand Lundberg, we're not even different from the denizens of the 'realm of interests' — and Lundberg has spent at least one lifetime studying them. Our ethics are the same, our values the same, our attitudes the same, our motives the same; and what 'they' do in Vietnam, in Chile and elsewhere is what most of us would do too, if we were in their place. Condemning the governing class for its **deeds** is not unlike looking into a mirror — and then blaming the mirror.

As Lundberg puts it at the end of his book **The Rich and the Super-Rich**: 'The causes of (our) insufficiency . . . are political, not economic, or at least political before they are economic. Better put, they are cultural. Serious problems cannot be solved on the basis of a consensus of value-disoriented dolts'.

(14) **The large corporation** may or may not be monolithic by nature (New Agers disagree over whether the corporation needs to be 'broken up' or simply better controlled . . . by the communities themselves) — but there can be no doubt that our large corporations are monolithic today. We have permitted them to drive smaller enterprises systematically out of business (worse, we have encouraged them to do so: tax advantages for large corporations often make it impossible for small businesses to compete). We have permitted them to set prices. We have permitted them to impose a Prison-gratifying (and therefore profitable) culture of monolithic plastic sameness on our places and regions. At the moment, the 500 largest industrial corporations control nearly one **trillion** dollars in corporate assets (in North America); and the 600 largest multinational corporations will, us willing, control over 40 percent of **planetary** production by the end of the 1980's (and that's not counting the centrally planned nations where monolithic 'state enterprises' are even more powerful).

Taking their lead from George Lodge, a number of New Age people have argued that the **motive force** behind the large corporation has changed (or: is changing). Corporation managers and technical personnel are no longer primarily concerned with how much money they can make for their bosses; nor are they primarily concerned with how they can best extend their own power and privileges (though they're certainly not indifferent to these things!). Rather, a new breed of managers and technicians is emerging whose primary concern is, 'How can I further the (interests of the) **industry of which I am a part?**' Exxon and Texaco people are asking, how can I further the oil industry through my work; CBS and CBC people, the power-and-authority-of-the-media; and so on.

This makes a lot of psychological sense when you consider that the corporate managers and technical personnel are people who believe in 'the system' and in the basic goodness of their work. It might even be said to be a kind of idealism. Trouble is, it's a particularly monolithic kind of idealism.

(15) **Monolithic social roles** require us to say things, do things, and (inevitably) think and feel things, that we might not necessarily **feel** like doing or saying or thinking and feeling, but that are nevertheless deemed appropriate — by 'society' — to the occasion at hand. All social roles will, of course, require us to suppress certain parts of our personalities at certain times — there's nothing particularly harmful in that — but in North America many social roles require us to suppress our selves as a general rule, if we want to retain the role at all. Moreover, most of us are **more than willing** to repress our spontaneous selves on behalf of an easy social harmony and peace — what we like to call 'smooth personal relations'. Most of us are actually **more interested** in avoiding possible public embarrassment than in achieving any kind of genuine self-expression. (That's because we're trapped by the Prison — trapped and afraid to walk out.)

Nearly every possible role in North America today is, for most of us, a monolithic one: mother, son, wife, secretary, boss, factory worker, patient, friend. . . .

To some extent roles are useful and necessary — they give us a shape, an outer identity, and also a sense of inner continuity. The problem comes when the roles become monolithic — when there is no distance between our selves and our roles and when we fail to make a significant personal contribution to the way we see and live our roles.

1. We lose touch with our selves — the different parts of our selves do not mesh;

2. We tend to **become** our roles — we subordinate our personality to what we suppose to be the role's demands and 'a new creature replaces autonomous (humanity), unhindered by the limitations of individual morality, . . . mindful only of the sanctions of authority' (Stanley Milgram);

3. Roles represent institutions and, to a great extent, **are** institutions — 'roles make it possible for institutions to exist' (Peter Berger). Therefore, rigidly-defined, coercive roles **are** what keep all the monolithic institutions, above, going strong;

4. 'The life process itself renders (the) continuance (of roles) impossible; e.g., the aging of beautiful women; the loss of athletic strength; the disruption of the mother role through the maturity or death of her children. All these may produce very serious crises . . . ' (Roberto Assagioli).

(16) **The monolithic mind** races on and on endlessly, never giving us a chance to simply be, never giving us a chance to experience the world with

openness and vulnerability. As Luke Rhinehart puts it in his book about Erhard Seminars Training ('est'): 'Since the being inevitably identifies (his or her) being with (his or her) mind, the purpose of the mind becomes the survival of the mind: the survival of the tapes, the points of view, the decisions, the beliefs, the rightness of the mind. The mind thus seeks always for agreement and to avoid disagreement, always to be right and avoid being wrong, to dominate and avoid domination, to justify itself and avoid invalidation'.

The monolithic mind is more intent on being right than on seeing clearly; more intent on proving others wrong than on healing society.

IV. Effects

Summing up, New Age people have levelled three important criticisms at our monolithic institutions and technologies: they are counterproductive; they encourage us to become overly dependent on them; and they aren't natural to us, they do not suit.

(1) **Their Counterproductivity.** Our monolithic institutions are making it harder for us to get around, harder for us to care for our selves, harder for us to learn. Our jobs are less productive, or relationships less satisfying, our technologies less efficient. Every day the nation-state becomes more coercive; our roles more stereotyped. And every day our transportation systems, technologies, governments, etc., are costing us proportionately more: in money, in energy, in resources, in time; in wear and tear on the nerves.

(2) **The Overdependence That They Foster in Us.** 'Our industrial categories', says Ivan Illich, 'tend to define results as products of specialized institutions and instruments', rather than as products that we create using institutions and instruments as our tools. Doctors produce healing, schools produce learning, churches produce salvation, agribusiness produces food, armies produce defence, marriage produces intimacy, and so on. Meanwhile, we are encouraged to become **consumers** of these 'products', giving up in the process much of our capacity for personal responsibility and active choice. River, a rural self-builder, puts it this way: 'It all boils down to the desire of our security-centred culture for the illusion of painless, worry-free, and totally comfortable living. Conditioned to believe that Big Daddy will somehow make us safe, we have mistakenly looked to business and government to provide this impossibility'.

(3) **Their Un-Naturalness — The Fact That They Do Not Suit.** Because of our monolithic institutions, says Jacques Ellul, we must adapt our selves, 'as though the world were new, to a universe for which (we were) not created'. We were made to go 10 miles an hour and we go a thousand; we were made to follow the natural rhythms of the body and our psyches and of nature, and we go by the clock; we were made to share the earth with living things and we live in a world of stone.

'Biolithic' institutions — the New Age alternative to monolithic institutions — are described in Chap. 14.

Part III —
On the Prisoners Themselves
(On Our Selves)

Chapter 8 — Are We Economic People
— or Self-Developing Persons?

Liberals tend to believe that our need for material things is endless — a belief that obviously helps to justify the monolithic mode of production. Marxists tend to believe that our need for things will eventually be satiated, but they can't say when. . . . The Marxist psychologist, Wilhelm Reich, still seems terribly **avant-garde** to Marxists because of his suggestion that love should be thought of as a basic need.

What gives us the authority, what gives us the right, to ask people to live differently? What gives us the **gall** to ask people to live lives in which work and consumption would matter much less to them than love and play, spirituality and service?

(There is, of course, the ecological doomsday answer — if we **don't** cut down on our consumption, then . . . — and it is a powerful one; see, e.g., Ehrlich and Ehrlich. But I am looking for an answer that has more positive connotations.)

The question cuts deeply, I think, because those of us who do favour love, play and creativity — those of us who are oriented to life rather than things or death (see Chap. 10) — are in such a minority. It takes so much of our strength just to keep on believing in our own values and priorities (or even in our sanity. It doesn't occur to most of us that an entire society can be insane — but see, e.g., Fromm, **The Sane Society**, Chap. 2, or Maslow, **Farther Reaches**, Chap. 2). Certainly most of us don't try to push our values and priorities on to others.

Marxists, on the other hand, are only too eager to tell us what our values and priorities should be. That's because they're 'true believers' in a system of values handed down by an authority that transcends the individual. History, **Das Kapital** and the top-down state are common examples of such an authority.

The New Age approach is different from self-effacement **and** from 'I'm-right and you're-wrong'. It starts from one simple premise: that we can't help wanting to live. Many New Age writers have pointed out that it's our deepest inner nature to want to live, and it's this that defines us when all else fails.

But wanting to live — being alive — is a dynamic concept. It's the nature of all living organisms to develop or die, and people are no exception to that rule. If you want to live, you're not going to want to stand still or regress, you're going to want to evolve. Being alive and developing our potentialities are, then, one and the same thing.

So — to return to our original question — what gives us the right to ask people to live differently is the fact that **we aren't developing our potentialities** by working in order to work, and consuming in order to consume. Life is stagnant under these conditions, and the fact that nuclear or ecological disaster threatens simply bears out the rule that if we cease to evolve we die. Most of us have ceased to evolve. Therefore, all of us might die. And that's not fair.

Moreover, I want to be able to develop my potentialities no matter what the rest of us might want. And that means having some options in society — more than I do now. But I won't have those options until a lot more of us are turned off of the work ethic (work for work's sake) and turned on to love and play, spirituality and service.

Finally, though I don't want to sound like a good samaritan or anything, I'd like people to develop their potentialities because it's the only way they can get to know themselves and life. I think they'd like it better here if they did that. I know I would.

But what are our potentialities, exactly? And how do we develop them? Could there be any agreement here?

In the next section I'd like to show that, in the dynamic process of being alive, each of us goes through (or attempts to go through) a series of seven **stages of self-development**. Many New Agers have referred to the seven stages as a hierarchy of potentialities — a **hierarchy of human needs**. The idea is that we can't go on to the second stage until we've met our needs on the first, can't go on to the third stage until we've met our needs on the second, and so on.

(Some New Agers would disagree with the idea that the stages form a hierarchy. For example: Erich Fromm tells us that our strivings for love, freedom, truth, etc. 'are present from the very beginning of ((our)) existence, and often have even greater strength than ((our material)) drives'. Or, for example, in one of his posthumously-published essays Abraham Maslow says, 'I've found some degree of transcendence in many people other than self-actualizers'; and he adds, 'It is unfortunate that I can no longer be theoretically neat at this level'.

(Perhaps it is enough, for our purposes, to say that we have to ((at least begin to)) meet our needs at **each** of the seven stages before we can feel whole. If we fail to meet our needs at **any one** of the stages, then we'll leave that part of our selves undernourished and stunted. We'll feel frustrated and anxious, and we'll take our frustrations out on self, on others, and on society.)

The seven stages represent a synthesis of the work of ten very different persons: Roberto Assagioli, psychiatrist and founder of 'psychosynthesis'; Gopi Krishna, authority on Kundalini Yoga; Ken Keyes, healer and founder of the Cornucopia Institute; Lawrence Kohlberg, academic-experimental psychologist; Michio Kushi, Oriental philosopher and expert on macrobiotics; John Lilly, neurophysiologist and consciousness-explorer; Abraham Maslow, 'father of humanistic psychology', grandfather of transpersonal psychology; Ram Dass, formerly Richard Alpert of Harvard and now a well-known mystic; Carl Rogers, the first rogerian therapist; and Chogyam Trungpa, Tibetan Buddhist and director of the Naropa Institute.

I tried to combine the work of Easterners and Westerners, of academics and therapists and spiritual philosophers, because I wanted to come up with a series of stages that could apply to all of us regardless of our individual temperaments and personalities. . . .

I. The Seven Stages of Self-Development

Stage One: Physiological Needs. According to many different systems of Eastern philosophy, the invisible but very real 'psycho-physiological' energy for this stage is centred at the bottom of the spine, and no wonder: it's the stage where our physiological needs — for food, shelter, warmth, etc. — are most important (and also our need for sex, to the extent that our sex drive is physiologically motivated).

If we've met our needs at this stage and we **keep on** meeting them many times over without even trying to meet any of our other needs — then we tend to be unwilling to talk about our selves, close relationships tend to seem dangerous, we try hard not to pay attention to our feelings . . . and we don't want to change our selves, either. We tend to obey rules only to avoid punishment. . . .

Stage Two: Security Needs. Those of us who are able to gratify our physiological needs reasonably well come to be motivated by our security needs — for safety, order and so on. The energy centre is at the navel, naturally.

If we've met our basic needs at this stage and we 'go overboard' with them, meeting them many times over without even trying to meet any of our 'higher' needs — then we tend to speak only about things that don't concern us personally ('the weather'). When we do speak about our selves, we tend to speak in the past tense, and our feelings are described as objects and aren't described clearly. We tend to conform to authority to get rewards, have favours returned and so on. We tend to become concerned with dominating people and with increasing our wealth and our pride — with a million different forms of hierarchy, manipulation and control. We tend to become overly dependent on things that are safe and familiar — and tend to fear change. We can never quite get **enough** security — ironically, we tend to spend much of our time feeling bad.

Stage Three: Love Needs. At this stage, whose energy centre is in the heart region, we're motivated primarily by our love needs — for friendship, belongingness and affection, and also for sex, to the extent that our sexual feelings are motivated by love.

At this stage we tend to express our selves more freely . . . though if we never move beyond it we're never really willing to accept our feelings. And we still tend to think of them as shameful, bad or abnormal. We tend to conform to authority in order to avoid the disapproval or dislike of others. We tend to choose our food according to nutrition (books and charts). We mean well: we really do.

Stage Four: Need for Self-Esteem. The energy centre for this stage is also in the heart region, for here we're motivated by the need for self-esteem — for a sense of mastery and competence in the face of the world and for a sense of ego control.

We still tend to describe our feelings as objects, but as objects in the present. Sometimes our deeper feelings break through against our wishes, and then we try — not very successfully — to accept them. Mostly, though, our feelings centre around our fear that we should be 'doing more' — for anyone but our selves, usually. We tend to feel (genuine) compassion for all those 'caught up in the dramas of security, sensation and power' (Keyes). We tend to conform to authority to avoid censure and guilt. If we get stuck at this stage we tend to lose our selves in veritable orgies of self-condemnation.

Stage Five: Need for the Esteem of Others. At this point, some of us will pass directly on to stage six. But others of us will come to be motivated by a need for the esteem of others — for recognition and prestige that is honestly earned.

At this stage, whose energy centre is still at the heart, we tend to experience and express our feelings fully. There's still more fright than pleasure in this . . . but there's also a desire to **be** these feelings, to be the 'real me'. And as we become more loving and accepting, the world begins to seem more loving and accepting to us (up to a point of course). We tend to conform to authority to maintain the respect of an 'impartial spectator' judging in terms of community welfare — 'the law' (if it's fair) or 'the masses' will do. If we become stuck at this stage we tend to become obsessed with comparing our selves to others.

Stage Six: Need for Self-Actualization. At this stage, whose energy centre is at the throat, we're motivated by the need for self-actualization — by the need to be true to our own nature. We try to become what we can be . . . whatever that is. But as a matter of fact, our basic values and priorities at this stage are remarkably similar.

We tend to see reality clearly and to be at ease with it. We tend to be open to new ideas, new data, new experience. We tend to be spontaneous, simple and natural — to live fully in each moment. And we tend to work at some activity (it may or may not be our 'job') that allows us to feel competent and self-reliant. (We aren't waiting to have our needs met 'for' us by our husbands or wives or by other monolithic institutions.)

Emotionally, we allow our feelings to flow, and we experience them with great vividness. Our relationships are deep and profound. We obey authority — when we do — in order to avoid self-blame (which isn't the same as guilt); we operate by the morality of individual principles of conscience. Unlike stages three through five, this one is almost irreversible. The only drawback to remaining in it, and not going on to stage seven, is that we almost inevitably begin to feel superior when we find that we can live for mostly emotional or psychological rewards. . . .

Stage Seven: Need for Self-Transcendence. Not all of us who reach stage six feel impelled to go on to this stage. Those of us who do are motivated by the need for self-transcendence (or 'Self-realization') — the need to achieve a serene or contemplative state of being.

The energy for this stage is centred between the eyebrows or on top of the head, depending on the degree of transcendence. I like to distinguish three degrees. In the first we learn to impartially observe our social games 'from a place that is free from fear and vulnerability'. In the second we learn to activate and express **all** of our buried potentialities — self-less service, aesthetic creation, deep mystical love, access to the collective unconscious. In the third we learn to feel at one with everything — we **are** love, peace, energy, effectiveness, etc. In each case we've left dualism behind; in each case we're able to speak the language of poets and seers; in each case we're able not only to feel, but also to know, the sacredness in all things. If we have psychic abilities, they're likely to be activated at this stage. . . .

Like those of us at stage six, those of us at stage seven operate by the morality of individual conscience — but we also have a sense that our 'personal' morality fits a larger design. We're able to experience our feelings more vividly than before, and to see them more clearly, too. We come to experience life as a process, not as a series of structures that we've built up in our minds.

There are two disadvantages to being at this stage. First, many of us find it difficult to be at this stage and function competently in the material world. Second, many of us are prone to a kind of cosmic sadness. But it is always possible to return from this stage to stage six. In fact, six and seven may be thought of as complementary — as complementary dimensions of a whole self (see Chap. 11 for the **worldview** that comes naturally to those of us who are able to switch back and forth between six and seven).

II. Some Political Implications of the Seven Stages

(1) **Consciousness of wholeness vs. scarcity-consciousness**. Why is it so important for us to at least begin to meet **all** our needs? Why is it so important for us to feel whole?

A number of New Age people have recently shown that we think from a **ground** of scarcity or a **ground** of wholeness — and that that profoundly influences the way we see things, and the way we act.

If we're out of touch with our needs, or if we're not able to meet our needs, then we'll always think **from** what Werner Erhard (in Hunger Project) calls 'a condition of scarcity'. We'll act **as if** love is scarce, time is scarce, etc. (whether or not we actually **believe** these propositions). Our motto might be, 'I'm gonna get mine and to hell with everyone else'. Or, conversely, 'I'm a selfish, bourgeois oaf, and I've got to learn to forget about my self and "serve the people" '.

Erhard suggests, 'Pierce into your own system of beliefs and observe that you do believe in scarcity'. And he adds: 'While confronting this belief, get that it is not true that hunger and starvation persist on this planet because food is scarce'.

If we're not able to meet our needs , says David Spangler, 'if we despair of ever being fulfilled, if our consciousnesses have become wholly focussed on lack, then our attention and energy are not freed to help others'. In other words, 'We do not meet the needs of a hungry world because we are all hungry' . . . if not physically, then emotionally, psychologically and-or spiritually. On the other hand, 'There is a willingness to meet other people's needs if we feel our own needs are being met **or that the possibility of their being met exists and can be manifested if we choose**' (emphasis his).

The fact and the promise of wholeness, says Spangler, 'offers me a reason for self-development beyond personal needs: that I may become a source of nourishment for my world and a co-creator in the project of the Whole Earth'.

(2) **Guilt, coercion — or self-development?** One of the most important political questions of our time is, how can we get North America out of the Third World so that insufficiently developed countries can develop their own resources and industries, diversify their economies, and become self-sufficient?

Three answers have been offered.

Liberals would have us get out of the Third World by appealing to our **guilt**: to our feeling that we don't really **deserve** all those resources.

Marxists would have us get out of the Third World by **coercion**: by fomenting a violent revolution here in North America and then by insisting that we make do without the resources.

New Age people would have us approach self-development as — in part — a **political strategy**: the idea being that we would no longer **need or want** a disproportionate share of the world's resources if we were fully at home on all seven stages of self-development. We would simply have too many other things to do: love and friendship; arts and crafts; psychic activity, intellectual activity, political activity; spiritual and religious development, appreciation of the world, grounding of our selves in our bodies; community, regional and planetary service; sex, play, rituals. . . .

(3) **Why do we need more and more?** The reason we seem to be primarily 'economic people' has nothing to do with 'human nature', as the liberals would have it, or with the notion that we're 'economically deprived', as the Marxists would. Beyond a certain minimum point, beyond the hard-core poverty level, the feeling of economic deprivation is a relative thing and a subjective thing, and has a lot less to do with our economic assets than our emotional and psychological and spiritual ones. Some families can lead joyful and fulfilling

lives on $5000 a year and others feel deprived with five times as much.

The real political question in North America today isn't, How can we bring everyone up to a standard where no one feels economically deprived? Since the feeling of economic deprivation is relative and subjective, that's an impossible task by definition. The real political question is (or should be), Why do most people live in such luxury . . . and still feel economically deprived? An answer to that question is desperately needed because the world simply hasn't the resources to give everybody even a North American cat's standard of living (let alone a North American dog's).

The answer given by New Age politics is that in most cases the deprivation isn't really economic at all. In most cases the feeling of economic deprivation comes from the fact that the monolithic mode of production, and the Prison that's behind it, inevitably blocks our needs for love and esteem — the needs that are important at self-development stages three through five. And that throws us back onto stages one and two, onto our physiological and security needs, onto our needs for material things.

So the reason we need so many things — the reason we 'need' maybe 10 times more than we really need — is simple. It's that our needs for material things are the only needs that most of us are able to meet in Prison society.

And there's another thing. By blocking our needs for love and esteem, the Prison makes us feel lonely and worthless, weak and inferior. And so we produce more and more in order to win back our dignity, and consume more and more in order to buy back our humanity (see esp. Richard Sennett and Jonathan Cobb, **The Hidden Injuries of Class**, 1972).

Unfortunately (or maybe fortunately!), meeting our material needs isn't enough to keep us happy, or even healthy. For as we've seen, we need to meet our non-material needs if we want to feel whole, and if we want to do more harm than good.

Chapter 9 — Is Our Main Enemy
the Capitalist Economy — or the Stroke Economy?

That's quite a charge to bring to bear on Prison society — that it blocks our needs for love and esteem.

How does it do this exactly? How does it keep so many of us from being loving and self-respecting — from being **whole** — human beings? How does it give us all 'Prison-bound personalities'?

It does this by convincing us that there isn't enough affection to go around, by convincing us to make our contribution to what therapist Claude Steiner calls the 'stroke economy', a system of emotional control that's more devastating to most of us (in North America today) than the material economy.

In an efficient monolithic society like ours, few people die of material hunger — after all, there wouldn't be production and consumption if there weren't people. But in every monolithic society, and ours is the most 'advanced' in this regard, millions of us are dying slowly inside from emotional hunger — from lack of strokes.

A stroke is a unit of human recognition. A positive stroke is a unit of friendship or affection or esteem; a negative stroke, a unit of indifference or worse. Without strokes we couldn't survive, and when we feel we can't get or give positive strokes, we try to get or give negative strokes (see Steiner, Chap. 8).

Some of us have literally died from stroke hunger. Nearly all of us are unable to meet our needs for love and esteem because of the lack of freely-given positive strokes. It's an 'economic' scarcity — we are indeed living in a depression. And everyone knows that things are getting worse.

On the second level of analysis, there seems to be no reason why we can't give and receive strokes freely. (Liberals may point to 'human nature' with a sigh, and Marxists may point to 'capitalism', but these look more like rationalizations than reasons.) But on the third level of analysis we can see that the Six-Sided Prison **inevitably** makes us feel that there aren't enough strokes to go around. And so we withhold strokes from each other and even from our selves, even though each of us suffers from it.

Here's how the Prison causes and perpetuates the stroke economy:

Patriarchal attitudes convince men that they need to control women. The most effective way that men can do this isn't by physical or economic force but by withholding positive strokes from women. In response, women withhold positive strokes from men. (Men tend to win out anyway, since they tend to be able to withhold strokes longer; see Slater.) The withholding of strokes is a technique we learn when we're small and our parents use the 'withholding of love' technique to control us. (It's an even more prevalent technique in Russia; see Urie Bronfenbrenner, **Two Worlds of Childhood**, 1970.)

Egocentricity convinces us that we're separate, isolated beings, which makes us want to hoard our strokes. It also causes us to feel foolish and hurt when the strokes we offer are rejected, so much so that we can almost never dare to bring our selves to offer strokes freely.

Scientific single vision makes us see the world in hyper-rational terms, and it isn't 'rational' to give and receive strokes freely . . . is it? Scientific single vision also makes us see the world in quantitative terms, and so we suppose there's only a limited number of strokes we can give or receive.

The bureaucratic mentality encourages and even requires us to withhold strokes from 'rivals' (real and potential) and to give strokes in a calculating way.

Nationalism teaches us that there are lots of enemies in the world. And it teaches us that 'everyone wants what we've got' and that it's important not to give it to them.

Megalopolis surrounds us with dehumanized and dehumanizing structures and is disproportionately filled with people who are suffering from massive stroke hunger. It doesn't provide us with an atmosphere that's conducive to giving and receiving strokes freely! And so we tend to withdraw, psychically, from the world around us.

As the Prison clamps down on us more totally, it becomes harder and harder for us to give and receive positive strokes — love and esteem. And the consequences of this are all around us. Roderic Gorney puts it simply and well: 'We become destructive . . . when our love needs are severely frustrated'.

Sometimes when I'm feeling bad I think that the hippies were the last great flash of the dying flame of life (for six months or so there back in '66). But in my better moods I am aware that much of the aimlessness of modern life can be explained as a form of 'search behaviour' (searching for strokes) — a term coined by rat psychologists. I am able to see that much of the consumption in North America is an attempt to purchase substitute strokes. And I am able to believe that much of the hateful behaviour in the world is a way of getting negative but necessary strokes.

Certainly these things are true for me.

Chapter 10 — Should We Look to the Proletariat — or to All Those Who Love Life?

According to Marx, socialism would be fought for by 'the proletariat', by the working class, by all those whose basic needs were frustrated by predatory capitalism. In North America, most members of the working class weren't willing to fight for socialism. But they did change capitalism enough so that they could meet their material needs, their physiological and security needs (see Chap. 8).

The working class finds it incredibly hard to meet its non-material needs, but **so do the rest of us**. We're all in the same boat when it comes to these needs, when it comes to the Prison and its institutions.

But we can't expect all the classes to join together and work for New Age society. In fact, we can be almost certain that none of them will. For every social and economic class, **as a class** (as distinct from a collection of individuals), has a substantial stake in monolithic society. What would happen to the industrial proletariat if we wanted fewer goods? To the much-vaunted 'professionalism' of doctors if their professional organizations no longer had the power to keep competent 'nonprofessionals' from healing us?

No, New Age society won't be brought about by any particular class acting in its interests as a class. But it may be brought about by all those **individuals** who are able to see that Prison society is making it impossible for them to meet their needs **as individual human beings**.

Or, in more 'political' language: if revolution is defined on the third level of analysis, then the potentially transformative class is no longer the proletariat

— though it will certainly consist of **members** of the proletariat (and the bourgeoisie and the lumpenproletariat and — yes — even the ruling class!). It will consist of all those who want to change their lives and lifestyles in a way that is consistent with the New Age alternative (see Part V).

Or, in more 'religious' language: there are no good classes, there are only good people.

I. Economic Class Analysis — or Psychocultural Class Analysis?

To distinguish the proletariat from the bourgeoisie, Marx devised an **economic** class analysis. To distinguish those who are trying to become whole from those who are not, we need to make use of a **psychocultural** class analysis.

Marx asked, where do you work? We need to ask, Are you life-oriented, thing-oriented or death-oriented?

But can it be done? Of course it can! In our political work, we've just become so used to thinking of people in terms of their 'relationship to the means of production' (even liberals do this) that we've become blind to the fact that there are many other ways of thinking about people — and, in a society where most of us can afford to eat properly, many more useful ways.

For example: many researchers have found that, in North America today, race, religion, education, birthplace, sex, and-or ethnicity are more important than economic factors in determining our political preferences (see, e.g., David Segal and David Knoke, 'Political Partisanship', **American Journal of Economics and Sociology**, vol. 29, 1970). Joseph Scott, a black sociologist, has argued that economic class analysis tends to be misleading when it's applied to the black experience — and tends to strip that experience of much of its content and meaning (in Ladner, ed.). And Thelma McCormack, a social scientist, has shown that economic class variables 'are not as highly predictive for women as they are for men' (in Millman and Kanter, eds.).

Many New Agers have pointed out that there are now more **public bureaucrats** than there are industrial workers. . . .

Kenneth Boulding goes so far as to argue that there's no such thing as a working class in the West — 'there is a complex stratification of society with many vaguely defined classes'. In Boulding's view, the notion of two 'distinct and antagonistic classes' appeals just because it makes the modern world seem so much more simple, so much more cut-and-dried than it actually is. In other words, Marxist class analysis appeals not because it speaks to our political needs but because it speaks to our psychological ones.

Other New Agers have argued that there's a **kind** of economic class conflict in North America but that it has an overriding psychological dimension. Ivan Illich has spoken of it as a conflict between 'the prisoners of addiction and the prisoners of envy'.

'Status inconsistency theory' has recently made a much more sophisticated attempt to explain our behaviour than the old Marxist dichotomies ever could.

It examines people's status with regard to at least three socio-economic variables — often income, education, and occupational status. And it suggests that if a person's status is different ('inconsistent') in terms of the different variables, if a person has a lot of education, say, but little income, then he or she would be much more open to personal or social change than if his or her status was consistent across the board (consistently high or consistently low or consistently in-between — it doesn't really matter). This theory purports to explain why so many 'middle Americans' remain content with their lot — and also why so many underemployed B.A.'s turn out to be passionate advocates of violent revolution or self-and-social transformation (for more on this see Warren).

But as we saw in Chap. 8, we don't consist **primarily** of the social and economic roles (or 'games') that we play. We're **primarily** engaged in developing our selves (or in developing substitutes for our failure to do so), and the most important thing about us — the one that determines our behaviour more than any number of socio-economic 'variables' — is the relationship we have with life. Do we love it — or do we love death instead? Or are we somewhere in between, neither immersed in life nor 'attracted' to the dead, but drawn, more or less, to **things**?

The most meaningful class analysis that we can make today is one that distinguishes among life-, thing-, and death-oriented people. These psycho-cultural classes cut across traditional social and economic lines. At the same time, they appear to underlie many of the differences among people that we've noted in this book. Above all, perhaps, they underlie the context out of which we **see** things. For example: if we're life-oriented, walking through a slaughterhouse might make us wish we ate less meat. If we're thing-oriented we might complain about the smell, or worry about getting blood on our clothes, or wish we'd taken our cameras along. And if we're death-oriented we might find our selves smirking or smiling.

And these three class dimensions are **precise** — they're at least as precise (and therefore as practical to use) as the Marxist dimensions 'bourgeois' and 'proletariat'. They refer to distinct 'perceptual worlds' or 'universes of sensibility' that are no less real for being internal. What makes them appear less precise is just what makes them deeper and more significant: you can't tell just by **looking** at a person's collar, skin, hair, etc., whether or not he or she loves life. But in one sense this is an advantage, for it keeps us from making snap judgements about people. And in another sense it doesn't matter, since there are at least four clinically precise methods that can be used to find out whether a person loves life, things or death (see Fromm, **Anatomy**, Chap. 12).

Probably the simplest method is by means of a brief questionnaire devised by Erich Fromm, the psychologist, and Michael Maccoby, a social psychologist. This questionnaire has been included in Maccoby, 'Emotional Attitudes and Political Choices' (cited in Chap. 24 below), along with the scoring code he used and the results he got among several different groups of people.

Fromm and Maccoby broke people's responses down into two categories, life-loving and death-loving. These have the virtue of simplicity, but they're also poles of a duality, and dualistic thinking is Prison thinking nine times out of 10. In real life, people are oriented all up and down a **love-of-life spectrum**, which for convenience's sake I've divided into thirds: hence my life-, thing-, and death-oriented classes. Because they're segments of a spectrum (fluid) rather than poles of a duality (rigid), my three classes don't imply that anyone is **irrevocably** cut off from love of life — that anyone's 'class interests' are truly irreconcilable with another's (as the ruling class's were said to be with the proletariat's). Instead they're meant to suggest that it's in everyone's class interests to advance up the spectrum toward love of life. This is so because love of death isn't a biologically normal impulse, as Freud assumed. Love of life is biologically normal, but love of things and love of dead things is the result of a crippling process — is 'the outcome of unlived life' (Fromm), of the failure to progress beyond the physiological and security needs. However, love of things and love of death, like love of life, probably isn't completely absent in any of us. 'The dividing line cuts across the heart of every (person)' — Solzhenitsyn.

II. Life-, Thing-, and Death-Oriented Classes

Now for a description of the classes. It borrows from literally dozens of New Age writers and activists, many of whom tend to think in terms of life-, thing-, and death-oriented classes though they might never use the words.

Those of us who are (primarily) **life-oriented** tend to feel at one with life. We don't have a possessive attitude toward people or things; we enjoy people and things more because we're free from a need to cling to them. We want to **be** more rather than **have** more, we want to construct rather than destroy or retain. We don't **have** experiences, we **are** experience: the barriers between our selves and our experience begin to break down as we begin to forget about 'making an impression' and learn to rely on the fact that we **are** and that something good will be born if we're able to let our selves go.

We find it (relatively) easy to touch each other spontaneously and without sexual overtones; and the sex we have isn't goal-oriented. When we feel exploited we're capable of seeing our exploiter as a 'fellow victim of the same puppeteer' (Maya Angelou), namely, of the Prison and its institutions. . . . But what's more important than any of these traits is the attitude we have — a responsiveness to what's most alive and growing in our selves and in others.

It's pretty obvious who the life-lovers are in terms of this book. They're the ones who've managed to break free from the Six-Sided Prison; who aren't fooled by the false promises of the monolithic mode of production; and — since understanding isn't everything — who've **also** managed to reach self-development stages three through seven, or are definitely on their way there. In North America, probably no more than 10-15 percent of us are primarily life-loving at this point in time. 'Little pockets of humanity', in Tom Robbins's bittersweet phrase and in the mystique of the counter-culture; but the truth is, life-lovers can be found everywhere, in every social and occupational milieu, and in about the same proportions. LeMaster tells us that many of the construction workers he's interviewed have a more 'spontaneous', more 'free-flowing' approach to life than a great many middle-class strivers he's known.

If we're (primarily) **thing-oriented**, we tend to see everything as a commodity — not only all things but all people, not least of all our selves. We tend to feel, 'I am what I have'; and we collect injustices done to us (and, if we have a political conscience, to exploited groups) as if these injustices were valuable possessions.

We dream of romance and of power. If we're men we lavish a great deal of affection on our cars and other shiny devices; if we're women we lavish our affections more on our 'appearance'. But we feel more comfortable touching objects than we do touching each other — especially objects that we own. And we tend to feel proud of our sexual prowess, or obsessed with our 'performance' in bed. Our bodies tend to be somewhat constricted, as if we're keeping them from getting out of control.

Those of us who are thing-oriented are trapped by the Prison, though we're capable of seeing that at least some of its sides are neither necessary nor desirable. We're taken in by monolithic institutions, so much so that we don't think the world could go on without them, but we're willing to admit the desirability of alternatives ('if it wasn't for human nature', etc.), especially after sexual intercourse. We tend to be incapable of meeting our needs at self-development stages three through five (which is why we dream about romance and power).

The great majority of us (probably 70-80 percent of us) are largely thing-oriented, and being able to see this is being able to see where the political left has made one of its greatest errors. For Old Leftists have always insisted that most of us are life-oriented, and many New Leftists have countered with the assertion that most of us are death-oriented. **Both** positions can be used to justify dictatorship (to save us from the supposedly death-oriented ruling class or to save us from our selves).

Those of us who are primarily **death-oriented** tend to be fascinated by the not-alive — not only, or even necessarily by corpses and decay, but also by the many mechanical artifacts that abound in megalopolis. There is, for example, the salesperson who will always add up even two or three small items on the calculating machine, or the person who will always take the car to the corner store. It's like being thing-oriented only many times more so; our feelings aren't so much repressed as withered. Often they'll take the form of crude passions, such as the passion to win (at other people's expense) or the passion to destroy.

We tend to avoid experience as much as possible, finding it messy or threatening, a 'time-waster'. We tend to carry our bodies stiffly, like corpses, and we use sex mostly as a tension-reducing device. We tend to feel exploited by nearly everyone, and in response, we project a free-floating **ressentiment** (resentment coupled with anger and envy) out onto the world that would deny everyone — especially the powerless — the right to be happy.

When we're death-oriented, we tend to be so caught up in the Prison that it's hard to even tell us about it. (Try it and see.) We're so wrapped up in monolithic institutions that we aren't capable of thinking up — or even thinking about — alternatives to them. We're stuck at self-development stages one and two, so we think of work as a duty and pleasure as an immorality. Often we're quite 'successful', but we're hell to have to live with. Maccoby finds that about 10-15 percent of us are largely death-oriented.

In 1848, Marx saw capitalist society as a battleground between the bourgeoisie and the proletariat. I'd like to suggest (along with Erich Fromm, anthropologist Jules Henry, and many other New Age-oriented writers) that monolithic society is a battleground between those who love life and those who don't.

Unfortunately for the scientific pretentions of tri-level analysis (i.e., unfortunately for its value as myth), there appears to be nothing 'inevitable' about the outcome of this battle. As we've seen, the Six-Sided Prison is gaining in depth and strength, and the Prison and its institutions are making it harder and harder for us to meet our needs for love and esteem, without which we cannot develop our selves — we cannot **be** our selves — we cannot truly live. In this view, it's only a matter of time before the world becomes unlivable, for one reason or another. But as we've also seen, many of us are managing to escape from the Prison by means of the attack on predefined sex-roles, the rediscovery of the spirit, and so on. And many of us are becoming aware of the perverse effects of monolithic institutions because they're getting so much more monolithic — and so much worse.

If many of us can begin to look at the world in a different, more multifaceted way (Part IV); if a desirable and workable alternative to the Prison and its institutions can be forged out of the ideas that many of us have been coming up with over the last 10 years or so (Parts V-VI); and if many of us who are thing-oriented can meet our needs for love and esteem by taking part in the rich and life-giving experience of self-and-social transformation (Part VII) — then, perhaps, the forces of life will triumph.

Part IV —
The Trans-Material Worldview

Chapter 11 — The Trans-Material Worldview: Foundation for a New Age Society

The Prison and its institutions are compatible with two different ways of looking at the world. Both of these ways are so partial as to be dangerous. The first of them, the one we're used to, is so taken-for-granted that probably most of us don't even notice that it's **there**.

This first way of looking at the world can be called the 'materialist worldview'. From the materialist point of view, the only way we can know things is by the evidence of our senses (if we can't see it touch it smell it, etc., it isn't real). 'Reality' is independent of our mental processes. We end at our skins. Our behaviour is a product of stimulus-response type conditioning (some liberals may give more weight to genetics). 'Man', so called, is the 'king of the universe', and the rest of the universe exists to serve 'man'. And so on . . . and so on.

A second way of seeing the world can be called the 'non-material worldview'. It can be seen as a kind of protest against the materialist worldview, and, like all protests, it tends to claim just the opposite of what the 'official version' claims. The only way we can know things is by looking within. The material world is dependent on our mental processes. We are all One. Our behaviour is a manifestation of God's will. And so on. . . .

Marxism and liberalism are political expressions of the materialist worldview. That is why they are based on the ideas of unending economic 'growth', unlimited technical 'progress', and unceasing personal or social 'achievement'. On the other hand, in North America today, the non-material worldview is essentially a reaction against the materialist worldview. It may not be Prison-bound, but it is bound up in a love-hate relationship with the Prison. So it can't really generate a coherent new politics of its own. In fact, many of its advocates pride themselves on being 'apolitical', or only conventionally political.

Many New Age writers understand how important it is to work out a **new** worldview. A worldview that can serve as the 'metaphysical basis' for New Age society and New Age politics. At least 40 books listed in Chap. 24 touch on this theme. Economist E. F. Schumacher sums up their thrust succinctly when he says, 'We are suffering from a metaphysical disease, and the cure must therefore be metaphysical'. Lewis Mumford — a person not given to overstatement — says, 'The achievement of a new personality, a new attitude toward (people) and nature and the cosmos, are matters of life and death'.

Some New Age people believe that the new worldview is arising already and that the kinds of insights and understandings that were reported on in Parts I-III are early political expressions of that worldview. This chapter is an attempt to (drastically) condense and synthesize the efforts that New Age writers have recently been making to set this worldview down on paper. I like to call it the 'trans-material' worldview because it includes materialism but goes beyond it, too.

Sections I-II take a look at some of the weaknesses of the materialist and non-material worldviews. Sects. III-IV contend that we can more usefully look at 'the world' (or 'life') in terms of at least four equally valid and equally necessary states of consciousness — material, spiritual, religious and mythic. Sects. V-VI look at two of the important implications of the trans-material worldview: the 'space beyond conditioning' and the notion of personal responsibility.

I. The Materialist Worldview

Even in its **own** terms, the materialist worldview is finding it a lot harder to pose as the 'one, true way' to understand Reality. Facts keep turning up that suggest that there's more to 'the world' than meets the eye — let alone the materialists' eye. Research findings keep turning up that show very clearly that the materialist worldview is not so much 'wrong' as narrow — partial — incomplete.

(1) **Psychic research.** Research into such phenomena as telepathy (extra-sensory communication), clairvoyance ('seeing' distant events), and precognition ('seeing' future events), is now being carried out at 'respectable' universities and institutes all over North America. (This research is reported on at length in Edgar Mitchell, **Psychic Exploration.**) Evidence is mounting that, as Willis Harman puts it, 'These sorts of preternormal knowings and abilities are latent in all persons but are typically highly repressed'.

Psychic research has been defined as 'the scientific study of impossible facts' — those things that **cannot** happen, but do. What are we to do with these facts?

(2) **Life after death.** A number of studies have recently been published that point to the survival of consciousness after death. Dr. Elisabeth Kubler-Ross, a leading psychiatrist, has studied nearly 200 cases of people who had been declared dead and later spontaneously revived — people of all ages and economic backgrounds, religious and nonreligious alike — and according to her, 'All experienced the same thing. They virtually shed their physical bodies, as a butterfly comes out of a cocoon. They describe a feeling of peace, beautiful, indescribable peace, no pain, no anxiety. . . . They were so content that they resented, somewhat bitterly, the attempts to bring them back to life'. And she adds: 'Not one of them was afraid to die again'.

(3) **The new physics.** It is often said that the materialist worldview is based on the worldview of the sciences and especially that of the 'queen' of the sciences, physics. If so, then the least we can say is that the materialist worldview is badly out of date.

For example. According to classical physics, mass is associated with what physicist Fritjof Capra calls an 'indestructible material substance'. However, contemporary physics tells us that mass is 'nothing but a form of energy' which, far from being indestructible, 'can be transformed into other forms of energy'. The conclusion seems obvious, and has been stated by many: there is no true physical matter ('true' in the sense of being indestructible); there is only energy in motion.

Another example. According to materialist physics, 'the fundamental building blocks of matter' are supposed to be solid. But quantum theory has shown us that — as Capra puts it — 'the subatomic units of matter are very abstract entities which have a dual aspect. Depending on how we look at them, they appear sometimes as particles, sometimes as waves; and this dual nature is also exhibited by light which can take the form of electromagnetic waves or particles'.

And a final example. Classical physics assumes that the world is 'out there' and that it's our task to observe it . . . to make reconnaissance raids on it. But a central insight of atomic physics is that observer and observed are not so distinct. We can only take certain factors into account at any one time. Our beliefs and desires will colour our data. And the very act of observing will affect what we observe. Physicist John Wheeler concludes that we live in a 'participating' universe, and David Spangler concludes, 'Reality is a joint creation or product of the participation of observer and observed'.

Where are these discoveries taking late 20th-century physics? Sir James Jeans sums it up: 'Today there is a wide measure of agreement, which on the physical side of sciences approaches almost to unanimity, that the stream of knowledge is heading towards a non-mechanical reality; the universe begins to look more like a great thought than like a great machine'.

My point, remember, is not that the materialist worldview is 'wrong', but that it's incomplete; that it doesn't fit with what we know about the universe. Unfortunately, it's become so universally accepted as the 'one, true way' (to the truth) that the answers it cannot give us are often assumed **not to exist**. And I don't want to have to live with the results. I think of the man from the International Commission on North Atlantic Fisheries, who told the Greenpeace Foundation's harp seal campaign, 'These seals should be eliminated because they eat too damn many fish — and what use are they, anyway?' And I think of an article in the prestigious **Journal of Biosocial Science** (vol. 4, July '72) which states: 'Why should publicly financed resources be devoted to preventing infant mortality when the economic worth of such marginal infants is negative? The economy would be better off without them'.

We need a trans-material worldview to give us a basis for answering these questions.

II. The Non-Material Worldview

Sensing the inadequacies of the materialist worldview for our time and place, and appalled by some of its moral and political implications, some New Age writers have begun to promote a **non**-material worldview that's the mirror image of the materialist worldview.

The non-material worldview certainly has its advantages. We do need to be reminded that there's more to life than our jobs and our possessions. And the non-material worldview opens up vast spiritual horizons that materialism has ignored or ridiculed for centuries. But I just don't believe that the non-material worldview, by itself alone, can give us a basis for healing our selves and transforming our society. Like the materialist worldview, it is simply too narrow.

As John Amodeo, a hatha yoga teacher, puts it (**Yoga Journal**, July-Aug. '77): just as the Marxists and liberals 'tend to identify with one aspect of their being while neglecting the self-growth aspect, so does one who seeks psycho-spiritual growth tend to overidentify with the sub-personality which seeks spiritual growth, deeper awareness and psychological fulfillment. One example of this is the prevailing myth that we are totally responsible for the reality we have created for ourselves, a point of view which perhaps keeps many Blacks and Third World people away from the growth movement'.

The materialist worldview encourages us to talk with a straight face about 'the economic worth of marginal infants'. But the non-material worldview doesn't do much better. I've heard non-materialists say that the Jews were responsible for the concentration camps. Or, when a small child drowned because her daycare centre didn't supervise the swimming hole, 'Well, that was her karma'. The non-material worldview allows us to look at human atrocities like concentration camps with total acceptance and without the feeling that 'something should be done' about a world that allows them.

III. The Trans-Material Worldview

Many New Age writers believe that both old worldviews are inadequate, that neither of them can give us a basis for a wholistic new politics. Some of these writers are trying to work out a new, 'trans-material' worldview that reflects more accurately what psychic research, 20th century physics, etc, are telling us about reality.

If you try to put together what these New Age writers are saying, you'll come up with this: there are at least four 'valid' states of consciousness (or 'modes of being' or 'separate realities' or dimensions or aspects or levels of reality). One of them is, indeed, the material state of consciousness. But another of them is the spiritual (non-material) state. And there are two other states, the religious and the mythic states. **Each** of them is valid or 'true' when used for its own special purposes. And each of them is equally necessary for us. We need each of them to be healthy, to feel whole: experiential proof that reality is trans-material.

Three New Age writers have been consciously trying to create a trans-material worldview for us, and the following section relies heavily on their work: Lawrence LeShan, **Alternate Realities** (1976); Huston Smith, **Forgotten Truth** (1975); Charles Tart, **States of Consciousness** (1976). (LeShan is an experimental psychologist, Smith a religious writer, and Tart an experimental psychologist at the University of California at Davis.) But they're only trying to systematize what many New Age writers and activists have been saying (or simply assuming!). For example: Jane Roberts, originator of 'aspect psychology' as well as a noted medium, says that 'the physical senses present one unique version of reality, in which being is perceived in a particular dimensionalized sequence . . . and is the result of one kind of neurological focus. There are alternate neurological routes, biologically acceptible, and other sequences so far not chosen'. And David Spangler, a spiritual teacher, says that his own particular tradition, the 'esoteric' tradition, 'is simply one container that we have discovered to catch the outpouring of reality. It is undoubtedly more useful than some containers in certain situations and not so useful in others, but no container . . . should be expected to catch all of a limitless truth'.

I should also mention that the notion of states of consciousness (or aspects of reality) is a familiar one to many peoples. Sri Aurobindo says that East Indian philosophy speaks of a single Reality with four discrete levels: Matter, Life, Mind, and Superconsciousness. And John Mbiti says that African religion speaks of four 'levels of order' in the universe: (1) 'order in the laws of nature', (2) 'moral order', (3) 'religious order', and (4) 'mystical order'.

Each of the states of consciousness (or aspects of reality, modes of being, etc.) has the following characteristics (according to LeShan):

1. Each is 'a way of structuring what is out there and in here';

2. Each has a 'clearly defined set of laws', each is 'self-consistent', and 'nothing can occur while using it that is contrary to these laws';

3. Each can help us to 'accomplish certain goals and answer certain questions. Each is irrelevant to certain other questions and goals';

4. 'Each has room within it for a great deal of individual variation in the interpretation of (reality)';

5. Each is discrete (Tart), though there may be some overlap (LeShan, Smith);

6. 'Each satisfies certain parts of our needs, and when (we don't) use one of them with a whole heart, fully accepting its validity and reality, that part of (our selves) remains undernourished and (our) whole being is stunted in its development'.

We should also note this, that when we're very young we're taught that the material state of consciousness is the **only** 'true' or useful state. In fact, in Prison society, the 'growing up' process consists of our learning **precisely** this! So it's not going to be easy for us to learn to return to the other states and-or to feel at home in them. It's going to take conscious effort.

We should also note this, that when we're very young we're taught that the material state of consciousness is the **only** 'true' or useful state. In fact, in Prison society, the 'growing up' process consists of our learning **precisely** this! So it's not going to be easy for us to learn to return to other states and-or to feel at home in them. It's going to take conscious effort.

States of Consciousness	Objects, Events, Self	Distinctive Categories	Appropriate to	Critical Stage of Development	Essential Need It Fills
Material	...are clearly separate from one another	space/time matter brain	crossing the street, etc. 'normal' science	to age 7	gives us techniques for living
Spiritual	..... are seen as One.	the One spirit	yoga meditation body therapy	age 14 & up	gives us reasons for living
Religious	..... are seen as separate but flowing into a larger One.	God spirit	prayer re-sourcement attunement	age 14 & up	gives us ethics & moral structures for living
Mythic	..... can have all the characteristics of the whole.	symbol archetype soul	play art dream	ages 7-14	keeps us alive to the wonder of our being

The Trans-Material Worldview: Four Self-Consistent and Necessary States of Consciousness

IV. The Four States of Consciousness

(1) **The material state of consciousness.** When we're in this state, objects, events and self are clearly separate from one another. We think in terms of concepts such as space, time, matter, number. All information comes from the senses, everything has a cause, all objects are made up of parts that can be understood and-or improved separately, and so on. The material state of consciousness is similar to the materialist worldview, but because it exists in conscious awareness of the other states, it is far less rigid, far more modest in its claims.

As LeShan points out, this state is 'ideally adapted to asking and answering questions such as "how" and "how to" '. But it's 'completely irrlevant to questions starting with "why" or to questions of value and moral judgement'. It can tell us how to kill and cure, but not which is right, moral, good (and it can't tell us how to **heal**). . . . We need the material state in order to know what Le Shan calls the 'techniques for living', but we need access to the other states in order to know why and how to live — and if we want to treasure life.

(2) **The spiritual state of consciousness.** This state and the next one, the religious state, are lumped together by Smith (as the 'infinite' state) and in popular thought, but there are some important differences between them.

When we're in the spiritual state, everything merges into one great unity: the unity of the cosmos. The senses can't be trusted; events don't 'happen', they 'are'; all desires and beliefs must be given up, because they separate us from the One; all categories must be given up, even the categories of 'good' and 'bad', for the same reason; and so on.

Within its frame of reference, the spiritual state of consciousness is just as valid or 'true' as the material state. And it enables us to meet needs that are equally vital. LeShan states, 'It is our need for a sense, a knowledge, of our solid connectedness with the totality of whatever is. . . . Without this, there is always somewhere a sense of alienation and a need to somehow act to strengthen and cement our anchor ropes to the world'. If we can't achieve a sense of oneness with nature, or the human race, or the cosmos, then chances are good that we'll try to 'leave a mark on history' by following the path of least resistance to growth, or by advocating violent revolution, or by having lots and lots of children.

When we're in the spiritual state we're in touch with feelings of joy and of deep inner peace. We feel much less inclined to try to come out 'on top' in our social lives; much less paranoid about other people and groups wanting to come out 'on top' of us.

(3) **The religious state of consciousness.** In this state, objects, events and self are neither separate, as in the material state, nor identical, as in the spiritual. Objects, events and self are seen as separate **and** as flowing into a larger unity. As David Spangler puts it, difference is seen 'as really an enriching manifestation of this unity rather than a fragmentation of it'. Universal forces and energies can sometimes be called upon, and knowledge

can come from sense impressions **and** from 'being a part of the whole and so perceiving other parts through the whole' (LeShan).

One way of getting in touch with the religious state is through prayer. Another way, reported on by Sally Gearhart (in **WomanSpirit**, Winter '76), is through the process of 'energy re-sourcement'. In this process, women get together for substantial periods of time — often in the country, but also in quiet and sheltered places in the city — 'to re-touch their inner channels of energy and to join those channels with those of other women'. A third way is through the process of 'attunement' as developed by the Findhorn community in Scotland. Here people try to get in touch with the energies that are said to emanate from devas, nature spirits, and greater Beings. There are many forms that attunement can take. . . .

The religious state of consciousness is as valid as the others and as necessary to us, for without it we would have no ethics, no morals, no guidelines for living. In the material state, ethics and morals are meaningless. An action works or it doesn't work, and that's that. In the spiritual state, ethics and morals are impossible; if you wish for something for your self, even guidelines or principles, you've already separated your self out from the one (and besides, everything is as it should be). But in the religious state, an ethical principle is inherent in the universe, since **whatever is done to one part affects the whole**. As LeShan puts it, 'if one part moves another toward greater harmony with the whole, all of the whole — including the part that took the action — benefits'; and the reverse is also true. Therefore, 'anything that moves a part toward its fullest development and fullest integration with the whole is good', any anything that does the reverse is evil.

(4) **The mythic state of consciousness**. In this state, objects, events and self 'can become identical with anything else or stand for anything once the two have been connected. . . . If you treat the flag of a country reverently, you are treating the country reverently. . . . If you were born at a particular time, that time and you are permanently associated . . . '.

Thy mythic state is expressed in play, art, dream. In play — real play — anything can be anything and new combinations are always being arrived at; similarly in poetry and in the dream. The mythic state is reflected in the myths and legends of a culture, and in his book **Festivals in the New Age**, David Spangler urges that we begin to re-infuse the seasons with rich symbolic meanings. Winter, for example, might be given over to celebrations of identity, celebrations of renewal, celebrations of the birth of Jesus (rather than Christmas).

The mythic state is a valid way to construe reality — as valid as the others. LeShan sums up its special usefulness very nicely when he says, 'As the material (states of consciousness) tend always to the general, to the understanding of the general laws that underlie each separate event, the mythic (states) tend toward the individual. Each thing and each event is charged with meaning, is unique and important. The world is full of specialness and newness due to this uniqueness. The child's eye is filled with wonder and possibility as long as this (state) is perceived to be as valid as any other. When we teach the child that play is inferior to work, that the mythic (states) are invalid, (he or she) becomes blase, the shining newness goes out of things, and the colour and possibilities that underlie (his or her) creativity are lost'.

The mythic state is a kind of 'psychological adrenalin' for us. Without it we run the risk of becoming bored with our selves and with life. Without it we can undergo serious psychological deterioration (in laboratory experiments, when people are prevented from dreaming, most of them undergo profound negative personality changes and become psychologically quite ill). Without our psychological adrenalin we're liable to look for a 'fix' in the endless buying of things or in the 'high' we get from one-upping other people.

V. We Are More Than Our Conditioning

According to the materialist worldview we are completely determined by our social conditioning. According to the non-material worldview, only our most superficial characteristics are determined by our conditioning. The trans-material worldview is able to give us a much more rounded sense of who we are than either of our old worldviews. It sees us as existing in both material and non-material dimensions — therefore, it sees us as made up of both matter and spirit; part socialized, and part spirit. (And the point, say many New Agers, is to infuse our socialized selves with spirit. . . .)

Even in the material dimension there's now much evidence to show that awareness can't be reduced to brain functioning (the implication being that we aren't completely determined by our conditioning, that there's a 'space beyond conditioning'). Some of this evidence comes from neurophysiology: there is no brain-spot which, if electrically stimulated, will induce (people) to believe or to decide' (Smith). Other evidence comes from people's experiences in altered states of consciousness: 'experiences of feeling that one's mind leaves one's body, of supernormal knowledge directly given, (etc.), fit more comfortably into schemes that do not assume that awareness is only a function of the brain' (Tart). Still other evidence comes from psychic research (see sect. I above).

The fact that there is in each of us a 'space beyond conditioning' has tremendous political importance. For one thing, it means that there is, or at least, there can be 'freedom of choice' — and so it gives the lie to all those Marxists (and Skinners and Delgados) who find it convenient to deny that there is such a thing. For another thing, since the space exists **within** us, it follows that the individual is to be treasured — not suppressed — in New Age society. If we have another violent revolution in which the person is 'compressed into being a unit in the mass', says William Irwin Thompson, 'we will lose the unique opening to the universal that is contained in the self'.

VI. Personal Responsibility

The materialist worldview says that we're totally determined by our genes and social conditioning; therefore, we lack free will (not to mention personal identity!); therefore, we can't be held responsible for our actions and situations. The non-material worldview says that we bring our social conditioning (and even our genes) on to our selves and are therefore totally responsible for our actions and situations. The trans-material worldview is careful to distinguish between what we can and can't be held responsible for **in the different states of consciousness**.

New Age people disagree over how responsible we should consider each other to be in the material state of consciousness. Probably most New Agers would consider us to be partly responsible for our situations — for who and what we are — and ultimately responsible for what we do. Edgar Z. Friedenberg, educator and gay activist, says, 'However pitiable their own lots may be, the poor whites of Texas and the blue collar workers of Detroit must be held responsible, by anyone who defends the democratic state in principle, for what was done to the peasants of Indochina. To refuse to hold them responsible for what they have endorsed is to deny them exactly the dignity as persons that citizenship in a democracy is supposed to confer'.

Still in terms of the material state, many New Age activists choose to go further — not for philosophical reasons but for political ones, in order to get **results**. Mimi Silbert, counsellor at the Delancey Street Foundation (for ex-felons), puts it this way: 'If someone has been blaming the system all their lives, you have to say to that person, "No — it's **your** fault". Whether or not that is empirically correct, it is the correct **antidote** for his chronic dependence. It is by going to the "extreme" of self-determination that he breaks the chain'.

In the **spiritual** state of consciousness, New Age people find it useful to go further still. We recognize that we're responsible for choosing everything — our parents, our personalities, everything. We even experience events as if we've created or willed them in some way. In the **material** state of consciousness this experience is of course not 'true', it is only a way of experiencing the world; but it's often an extremely valuable and stimulating one. It takes us out of the powerless feeling of being 'done to' since, no matter how disastrous a situation may be, we also look for what we can gain from it. (We might ask: **Why** is this happening to me, at this particular point in my life? What is it trying to teach me ((meant to teach me))? Or we might ask: Why am I **causing** this to happen to me?) It's kind of like confronting every situation with the old pragmatic North American question, 'What's in it for me?' — except we're looking not for material benefits but for consciousness-and-growth benefits.

Jerry Rubin says, 'Whenever I come into any situation in my life, whether it's an auto accident, an upset, anything externally oriented that causes me pain, if immediately I choose it and act as if I was responsible for it, all of a sudden I have increased power'. Where does this power come from? According to Patricia Sun, a healer, it is our **own** power, freed at last from the shackles of the 'anger and grief and remorse and hatred and sadness' that we feel when we **don't** experience the world from a position of total responsibility.

Marx used to say that the most dynamic 'contradiction' we faced was the one between our new productive technologies and our old productive forces (capitalism). But Marx was wrong: in practice, capitalism has been enamoured of the new, capital-intensive, ever-more-monolithic technologies (the ones Marx meant); and in theory, capitalism, like socialism, is compatible with any kind of production technology. Maybe it would be more useful for us to say that the most dynamic contradiction we face is the one between the new, multi-dimensional picture of our selves, and our old self-understandings.

Chapter 12 — New Age Ethics and Values

The trans-material worldview is more than a satisfying intellectual construct. It implies a whole new way of looking at people; and a whole new set of ethics, values, goals, priorities. And since the trans-material worldview is **natural** to us when we've begun to transcend the Prison . . . New Age society would be based on the ethics and values that are embedded in the trans-material worldview.

Section I of this chapter says that four 'primary' ethics — the self-development, ecology, self reliance-cooperation, and nonviolence ethics — are embedded in the trans-material worldview. Sect. II says that these ethics imply six 'primary' political values. Sect. III looks at some social values and goals that are consistent with the New Age ethics and political values.

I. The Four New Age Ethics

(1) **The self-development ethic.** The trans-material worldview says that there are at least four valid and self-consistent 'states of consciousness' and that each state satisfies certain parts of our needs. If we're not able to get in touch with one or more of these states, then we'll be dangerously out of balance. And we'll be sure to compensate by doing harm to our selves and-or to others (see Chap. 11, sect. IV).

In order to get in touch with all four states — in order to be at least **comfortable** in each of them — we are going to have to develop our selves. We are going to have to go beyond our obsession with material things and learn to desire the non-material 'things' that the spiritual, religious and mythic states of consciousness can give us. We are going to have to come un-stuck from self-development stages one and two.

So. Getting in touch with our selves would appear to be, not just 'fun' (though it can be that), and not self-indulgence at all, but an imperative for survival that's built right in to the structure of the universe. (Maybe even an evolutionary imperative.)

(2) **The ecology ethic**. Each state of consciousness speaks to us here. In the material state, scientists of wildly different political persuasions have been urging us to learn to work **with** nature's resources rather than merely to use them up. The consequences, if we don't learn this, are too terrible to contemplate (in the material state). More mundanely, one of our commonest adages is the one about not fouling your nest; and you don't need the least bit of 'non-material' awareness to grasp that the nest is now our planet (and always has been really).

The spiritual and mythic states of consciousness both suggest the interdependence and interpenetration of all things. And the religious dimension has its own built-in ecological principle in that it implies that 'if one part moves another toward greater harmony with the whole, all of the whole — including the part that took the action — benefits' (and vice-versa).

The self-development and ecology ethics are closely connected. Willis Harman says, 'These two ethics, one emphasizing the total community of (people) in nature and the oneness of the human race, and the other placing the highest value on developing one's own self, are not conflicting but complementary — two sides of the same coin. . . . Each is a corrective against excesses or misapplications of the other'. Stephen Gaskin, founder and spiritual leader of The Farm, in Tennessee, speaks to the politics of the two ethics: 'We have it within our power to voluntarily assume a simpler lifestyle which can be so graceful and so much fun that it will just naturally spread of its own accord. . . . Whether we like it or not, we're all going to have to assume that simpler lifestyle anyway (for environmental reasons — M.S.). . . . It's just that some of us are going to be dragged into it kicking and screaming, and some of us are going to adopt it beforehand, on purpose, and enjoy it and make it a nice way to live'.

Two corollaries of the self-development and ecology ethics are so important that they should stand as ethics in their own right.

(3) **The self reliance-cooperation ethic**. Self-development makes it possible for us to be self-sufficient and cooperative at the same time, and makes us **want** to be both at once. Individually, and as communities or regions. (Really self-reliant behaviour would be impossible without our ability to act cooperatively in many ways, and really cooperative behaviour would be impossible if one of us was leaning on the other. See sect. III - 'Autonomy and Community' below.)

(4) **The nonviolence ethic**. 'If one part moves another toward greater harmony with the whole, all of the whole — including the part that took the action — benefits'. Is there any need to show, at this late date, that only nonviolent and noncoercive behaviour is harmonious with the whole? (In fact, violence can be defined **as** disharmony at its most extreme; though nonviolence should never be confused with lifelessness or indifference.)

The self reliance-cooperation and nonviolence ethics are connected. Richard Gregg, nonviolent strategist and activist, has found that only those of us who are self reliant **and** cooperative can practice nonviolence successfully. And it's obvious that violence or the threat of violence would make 'cooperation' pretty shallow.

If the trans-material worldview is the emerging shared worldview for the New Age; and if the four New Age ethics are implicit in the trans-material worldview; then quite a few of us should be discovering and acting according to the four New Age ethics.

And it's happening. For example, the Stanford Research Institute recently completed a report on the 'Changing Images of Man' (sic) — see **Renaissance Universal Journal**, Summer & Fall '76 — and **their** findings were that (1) a 'new image' of the person is definitely arising, an image that 'reinstates the transcendental, spiritual side of (people) . . . (while denying) none of the conclusions of science in its contemporary form'; in other words, an image based on the trans-material worldview; and (2) the 'ecology' and 'self-realization' ethics are inherent in the new image.

But we don't really need the Stanford Research Institute to tell us that the worldview and its ethics have arrived! Consider, e.g., that there are now literally dozens of groups and magazines whose purpose is to promote one or more of the New Age ethics. Some examples (all from Chap. 24):

1. **Self-development ethic**: Actualizations; Cold Mountain Institute; **Journal of Transpersonal Psychology**; **Yoga Journal**;

2. **Ecology ethic**: Friends of the Earth; New Alchemy Institute; **Environment Action Bulletin**; **Natural Life**;

3. **Self reliance-cooperation ethic**: Institute for Liberty and Community; Institute for Local Self-Reliance; **Communities**; **Seriatim**;

4. **Nonviolence ethic**: Clamshell Alliance; Greenpeace Foundation; **Green Revolution**; **Rain** ('nonviolent technology').

II. The Six New Age Political Values

The four New Age ethics translate themselves fairly easily into six basic political values — like this:

To maximize the **self-development** ethic we need (1) maximization of social and economic well-being. We need (2) maximization of social and political justice — prevention of genocide; elimination of colonial regimes; elimination of torture and cruelty; equality of treatment for people of all ages, races, sexes, religions. . . . And we need (3) maximization of cultural, intellectual and spiritual freedom.

To maximize the **ecology** ethic we need (4) maximization of environmental quality — including maximization of the well-being of all creatures.

To maximize the **self reliance-cooperation** ethic we need (5a) maximization of self-reliance of communities, regions, and nation-states, and (5b) maximization of the cooperative **potential** of communities, regions and states (which they can choose to take advantage of if they wish).

To maximize the **nonviolence** ethic we need (6) minimization of violence between individuals, groups and governments.

In the short run, some of these values may conflict with one another (e.g., 1 and 4); in these cases people and politicians should — as Richard Falk advises — judge proposals according to what they think might be their **net** effects. In the long run I suspect that all six political values are interconnected and interdependent.

Some 'radicals' have argued that 'maximization of cultural, intellectual and spiritual freedom' is a Western cultural value and not a 'primary' political value at all. But in the New Age perspective, with its stress on self-development, we are able to recognize this value as a **precondition** for all genuine culture and for the life of the mind and spirit; just as 'minimization of violence' is a precondition for the continuation of physical life.

III. Some New Age Social Values

New Age ethics and political values are suggestive of a great many other values that New Age communities might want to 'operationalize' in some way. The Synergic Power Centre (see Chap. 24, sect. III) has recently drawn up a list of 30 'New Age values' that are consistent with the New Age ethics and political values as I've described them. Among these values are: 'security (survival necessities assured for everyone)'; 'respect for people, their ideas, and their feelings'; and 'joy and pleasure'. The Twin Oaks community is trying to operationalize its own 'core values' which are also consistent with the New Age ethics and political values: 'cooperation', 'sharing', 'treat people in a kind, caring, honest and fair manner . . . '.

What follows is far from being a complete list of New Age social values — even the Synergic Power Centre's list is less than complete — but it is meant to be representative and suggestive.

ENOUGHNESS. In Prison society we usually think of 'enough' in a negative sense — as in 'That's enough of that!' And 'more' is usually considered 'better'. But in New Age society we would be free of the Prison, and so we would find that our needs for things were actually quite limited. (Many of the goods we would need would actually be **tools** we could use to make our own goods with. That's the point of the **Whole Earth Catalog**, whose subtitle is 'Access to Tools', and of Ivan Illich's book **Tools for Conviviality**.)

We are learning', says Tom Bender, 'that too much of a good thing is not a good thing, and that we would often be wiser to determine what is enough rather than how much is possible. . . . The fewer our wants, the greater our freedom from having to serve them'.

STEWARDSHIP. 'Progress', says Tom Bender, 'assumes that the future will be better — which at the same time creates dissatisfactions with the present. . . . As a result, we are prompted to work harder to get what the future can offer, but lose our ability to enjoy what we now have. We also lose our sense that we ourselves, and what we have to do, are really good. . . . Stewardship, in contrast to progress, elicits attentive care and concern for the present

— for understanding its nature and for best developing, nurturing, and protecting its possibilities. Such actions unavoidably insure the best possible future as a byproduct of enjoyment and satisfaction from the present'.

AUTONOMY AND COMMUNITY. Marxism stresses community at the expense of autonomy, and liberalism does just the reverse. But each of these values requires the other, and is the logical extension of the other, like the light and dark sides of the moon. By stressing the one and repressing the other, we don't come to know either, since the one that's stressed gets exaggerated and distorted: autonomy becomes isolation and community becomes conformity. In New Age society we would learn to make our own decisions and not to hang on others. But that wouldn't isolate us from others; as Claude Steiner points out, it would make us more attractive to others and more confident about being in community with them.

DIVERSITY. New Age people aren't interested in creating a 'perfect' or 'utopian' society run according to the 'correct' political principles. Instead, **diversity** would be treasured — partly as a safeguard against authoritarianism, and partly as an enrichment of life.

The Twin Oaks community is run along these lines. Vince, who lives there, writes (in **New Directions** no. 21) that at Twin Oaks there are people 'with endless interests and paths and approaches to what is best for each. This is one of my reasons for being here. . . . In the process of close cooperation with people of varying attitudes, it is important to be open to many approaches and points of view regarding decision-making, priorities, resolving conflicts, and ways to express our growth. . . . The ego is constantly being tested. What a wonderful opportunity for expansion of consciousness!'

MANY-SIDEDNESS. Diversity would reach in to our inner lives. Maslow tells us that self-developed people 'are simultaneously selfish and unselfish, Dionysian and Apollonian, individual and social, rational and irrational, fused with others and detached from others . . . '. Michael Rossman figures that most of us would choose to lead 'a way of life which cycles harmoniously between travel and indwelling, between city and country, between community and isolation . . . (between) the polarities of engagement-retreat, creation-reception, etc.'. Probably more of us would — most of the time — be more receptive than active, since the world would no longer be seen as a project, and a receptive attitude would allow us to see the world more clearly.

DESIRELESS LOVE. Today we often love because we need something from the other, praise, approval, vindication of our being, whatever. In New Age society we would love other beings in a desireless way, not because we needed something (some thing) from them but because — out of our fulness — we wanted to share our time with them. Anne Koedt writes, 'In reality there can be no genuine love until the need to **control** the growth of another is replaced by love **for** the growth of another'.

REVERENCE FOR LIFE. This has two aspects, equally important. To Erich Fromm it means, 'Valuable or good is all that which contributes to the greater unfolding of (our) faculties and furthers life. Negative or bad is everything that strangles life and paralyzes (our) activeness'. On the other hand, here is Wendell Berry on the poet Gary Snyder: 'His realization of the smallness and shortness of his life in relation to the world's life is of such intensity as to make him virtually absent from the place and from his own sense of things. He is present in the poem finally only as another creature, along with moon and rock and juniper and the wild animals. And in proportion as he withdraws himself and his human claims, his sense of it grows whole and grand'.

SPECIES MODESTY. If we felt the kind of oneness with nature that Snyder and Berry describe, we would find it hard to think of our selves as 'kings' of the universe. Black Elk teaches that we 'two leggeds' are **sharing** in life 'with the four leggeds and the wings of the air and all green things . . . '. John Lilly notes (in **Seriatim**, Spring '77) that whales, dolphins and porpoises have 'shown a hell of a lot better survival record than we are showing today', and he asks, 'What kind of interpersonal relations, ethics, philosophy has led to their survival over the last 15-million-year period? What is this mysterious business that they can do and we can't?'

QUALITY. Many good people feel that reverence for life is the highest New Age value; however, I feel that beneath it and beneath all things lies what Robert Pirsig calls 'Quality'.

Quality is both a noun and an adjective. As an adjective — as quality behaviour (or 'high-quality behaviour') — it refers to what Esalen's George Leonard calls the 'Zen strategy of seeing equal "religious" significance in every aspect of life, not holding ceremonial meditation to be any more or less crucial than eating or sleeping or building a wall'. In Pirsig's book **Zen and the Art of Motorcycle Maintenance**, fixing a motorcycle turns out to be a higher-quality activity — for Pirsig — than attending the University of Chicago.

As a noun, Quality is much harder to define — exactly; and according to Pirsig, it can't and shouldn't be defined. It is whatever **feels** right and good to us when we're at self-development stages six or seven. If, as Erich Fromm says, reverence for life is the basis for the art of loving, then reverence for the Good is the basis for the art of living, for the art of self-development.

For thousands of years people felt no need to define Quality, it was so natural a concept. But in Civilized society, in order to defend the concept from the Prison (which had begun to descend), the philosopher Phaedrus did try to define it. And then Aristotle redefined it as being less important than reason. And from that time on, we have been willing to do things that are 'reasonable' even when they aren't any good.

Does anyone doubt that in New Age society, Quality — our intuitive, Stage Six and Seven ideas about the Good — would temper and guide all our other values, reason included?

BE KIND TO YOUR SELF. Some people like to say (usually sanctimoniously), 'I won't get a massage until every single person can afford one'. Or they'll say that people who take yoga classes are being 'self-indulgent'. But if you say, 'I've had a rotten week, I need a stiff drink', you probably won't be criticized. Same if you say, 'Thank God it's Friday, tomorrow I can go to the football game'.

The implication is that if you spend your dollars on booze, that's okay; but if you spend them trying to feel better in a healthy way, like with massage, that's not okay. If you spend your dollars sitting passively in a stadium, watching football, that's 'relief'; but if you spend them on a yoga class, trying to get in touch with the non-material states of consciousness, that's 'self-indulgence'.

In Prison society we practically consider self-abuse to be a moral virtue. And a virtue that somehow makes us 'one of the folks'. (Philip Slater goes so far as to suggest that we **collect** tokens of suffering — because they make us feel so good.) In New Age society, kindness to self would follow naturally from the self-development ethic. It is, or was, already the basis for one of our most profound religious truths, 'Love thy neighbour as thyself'; the idea being that you **can't** love your neighbour if you don't love your self. . . .

Part V — New Age Society

This Part is about the way we might want to live after we've begun to get free of the Prison and its institutions, after we've begun to **use** (and not just intellectually understand) the trans-material worldview, after we've begun to live by the New Age ethics and values. It covers quite a bit of ground: alternatives to the Prison, 'biolithic' institutions, community autonomy and regional cooperation, planetary consciousness and the planetary guidance system (the New Age economy — and the emerging New Age economic theory — are dealt with in Part VI).

Some of the alternatives proposed here could be implemented tomorrow (some are being implemented now, if you know where to look), others not for a hundred years or more. But all of them have this in common: **all of them are rooted in present trends**, are extrapolations based on present trends. Minority trends, to be sure, but we **could** go in the direction set forth below — that's my point. It is not a 'utopian dream'.

Chapter 13 — New Age Alternatives to the Prison

I. Androgynous Attitudes — and New Age Feminism:
The New Age Alternative to Patriarchal Attitudes

In Chap. 3, sect. I, we saw that patriarchal attitudes turn us into half-people — into 'men' or 'women'. In New Age society, our attitudes, values and beliefs wouldn't be based on our sexual identities. They would be sex-free, or 'androgynous'.

Androgynous attitudes can't be typed. They are simply the attitudes that are natural to us (to our temperaments and personalities) when we're free of sex-roles and when we're at self-development stages six and seven. Certainly men would learn to be more in touch with their feelings and their bodies, to be less aggressive, and so on; and women would learn to feel more independent, more assertive. But beyond that, our androgynous attitudes would be as varied and as protean as New Age society itself.

June Singer, a Jungian psychologist, puts it nicely when she says, 'We need to think of ourselves as no longer exclusively "masculine" or exclusively "feminine" but rather as whole beings in whom the opposite qualities are ever-present'. The power of androgyny 'lies in the openness to the opposites within oneself — not by an effort to integrate that which is strange or foreign, but by awakening to the reality that the opposites have been there all along, and would coexist in harmony if only we did not drive a wedge between them'. Singer's conclusion: 'We do not become androgynous; we already are. It is necessary only to let ourselves be ourselves. . . . This may seem like the easiest thing in the world, but . . . there may be much to **unlearn** in the process'.

Why is it important to become androgynous? Why is it a New Age goal? Simply because we can't become whole without becoming androgynous. If we want to become whole, then we're going to have to get back in touch with that part of our selves that has been lost to us through sex-role training and patriarchal attitudes. . . .

Matriarchal attitudes are occasionally proposed as the New Age alternative to patriarchal attitudes (see, e.g., Jane Alpert, 'Mother Right', **Ms.**, Aug. '73). Androgynous attitudes would — or could — include many traditionally matriarchal attitudes (among them compassion, unconditional love, supportiveness and generosity), but they would — or could — include much else besides. The point is simply that they be free of patriarchal attitudes (and that they embody Quality, that is, the Good as we perceive it at self-development stages six and seven). For example: many religious mythologies provided a 'primal androgyne' that managed to combine male and female energies in a synthesis that was greater than the sum of its parts; even the symbols of Yin and Yang were united at one time in the holy woman T'ai Yuan, who was an androgyne; and I am sure that many of us would try for such a synthesis in our own lives.

A number of feminists have begun to articulate a feminism that incorporates many 'New Age' insights and understandings. For example:

Robin Morgan, editor of the well-known anthology **Sisterhood Is Powerful**, recently said (**Sojourner**, July-Aug. '77), 'I thirst for more feminist theory.

But I mean really theory, not what masquerades for that. I do not mean accusation and counter-accusation; ... I do not mean rehashing of the old Marxist and capitalist theories. I mean really pulling up from the depths of one's terror some honest thoughts about one's experiential reality and then hazarding an analysis on that ...'.

Her newest analysis centres on what she calls 'metaphysical feminism'. She explains, 'My point is ... that what the definition of the metaphysical poets has been is an excellent definition of modern feminism, radical feminism. ... The metaphysical poets engaged in "passionate thinking" — the unification of opposites, ... the refusal to bifurcate, to separate, to settle for either-or. ... (Metaphysical feminism) is very difficult to simplify. ... I can say it's about the basic demands that go beyond the physical ones — the spiritual, the emotional, the sexual, as well as the economic and the right of self-determination and so on ...'.

Bonnie Kreps, feminist writer and filmmaker, recently gave a talk called 'New Age Feminism' (Women's Resources Centre, Vancouver, 2 Mar. '77) in which she said, in part:

'The trouble with the fight for "equal rights" is that, if it is not seen in the context of the need to abolish sex-roles, we are liable to end up in yet another power struggle. The **real** fight is to abolish the notions of masculinity and femininity which have divided our world against itself. Equal rights for women will be a natural outcome of such a fight. ...

'This is not to suggest in any way that the fight for, say, equal pay for equal work is not a worthy one. ... My point is merely that we must not lose sight of our ultimate objectives and be sidetracked, once again, into a struggle which will ultimately get us nothing better than an "equal" position in the male world. ...

'I think one of the reasons people think the women's movement is dying is that we are looking for "success" in the wrong place. The changes which the movement is bringing about are so profound that they are not easily visible in the usual way. What we are about is changing consciousness — meaning changing people's heads so that they see the world differently and therefore are able to live differently — ... and in our society people don't usually advertise the fact that they might have had a wholly new insight. I mean, you don't exactly put a sign on yourself to that effect, even if it may be an important event to you. ...

'It is my opinion that feminism is an integral part of "new age consciousness". In fact, I think we have had the roots of new age thinking all along, but we have also forgotten about some of these roots. ... The roots are spiritual — they're about a way of seeing the world, of changing consciousness on the deepest level of our being. ...

'New Age thinking can help lift feminist thinking beyond the quest for coercive power and into its true home. ... And feminism is absolutely essential to the New Age movement. Because without it, we will merely have yet another version of sexist thinking — only this time in terms of yin and yang, anima and animus, and so forth. . . .

'In order to break out of (the) Prison, we have to come to grips with at least one of its six sides — and feminism is the surest tool I know of to understand and therefore change the major side of the Prison: patriarchal attitudes'.

II. Spirituality: The New Age Alternative to Egocentricity

At least 12 people in Chap. 24 — community organizers and political scientists among them — have called for the creation of a new spirituality. We need a new spirituality if we want to get beyond the isolation, pride and guilt that egocentricity imposes (see Chap. 3, sect. II) and if we want to have a foundation for constructing a new theodicy, a new and more believable rationale for life's suffering that can give us back our sense that life is worth living for — and worth preserving (see end of Chap. 6). We need a new spirituality if we want to get in touch with the spiritual and religious states of consciousness.

But why do New Age writers and activists speak of a 'new' spirituality? Surely the Judeo-Christian tradition isn't 'dead'?

Wendell Berry has found in John Collis's **The Triumph of the Tree** an almost perfect statement of what is 'new' about New Age spirituality: 'Both polytheism and monotheism have done their work. The images are broken, the idols are all overthrown. This is now regarded as a very irreligious age. But perhaps it only means that the mind is moving from one state to another.

'The next stage is not a belief in many gods. It is not a belief in one god. It is not a belief at all — not a conception in the intellect. It is an extension of consciousness so that we may **feel** God, or, if you will, an experience of harmony, an intimation of the Divine, which will link us again with **animism**, the experience of unity lost at the in-break of self-consciousness'.

It is of course that 'experience of unity' that can break down our egocentricity. And introduce us to the spiritual and religious states of consciousness.

There are a number of paths that can help us return to that experience of unity, that can help us feel at home again in the spiritual and religious states of consciousness. In **Unfinished Animal** Theodore Roszak lists over 150 such paths (!), and here I just want to mention eight general **kinds** of paths — and make one general observation. A spiritual path is valid **for us** if it is appropriate to **our** needs as **we our selves** define them. Whether or not it seems 'glamourous' or 'sophisticated' to others is not the point at all. (In this sense, a spiritual path is just like any other 'appropriate technology'!) Still, Collier is right, for most of us the old images **are** broken, forever. And so most of us are going to have to follow a path that is — for North Americans, at least — genuinely new.

For example:

(1) **Judeo-Christian revivals**. Chassidic Judaism; contemplative Christianity; 'charismatic' or 'evangelical' congregations in mainstream churches. . . .

(2) **The Eastern philosophies and religions**. Zen, Tibetan Buddhism,

Tantrism, Vedanta, Yoga, Sufism, Subud, Baha'i, Taoism, Sikhism. . . .

(3) **Mass movements.** Transcendental meditation ('TM'), Happy-Healthy-Holy Organization ('3HO'), Krishna Consciousness, Integral Yoga, Ananda Marga Yoga. . . .

(4) **Spiritual teachers and healers.** Rabbi Shlomo Carlebach, Sri Chinmoy, Bubba Free John, Kirpal Singh, J. Krishnamurti, Bhagwan Shree Rajneesh, Ram Dass, Jane Roberts, David Spangler, Patricia Sun, Vimala Thakar, Chogyam Trungpa. . . .

(5) **The trans-material therapies.** Jungian psychiatry Psychosynthesis, est, Arica, Mind Dynamics, the Living Love Way, Actualizations. . . .

(6) **The body therapies.** Many of us have found that shiatsu massage, ta'i chi, 'sensory awareness', rolfing, etc., can put us in touch with the spiritual and religious states of consciousness. Stanley Keleman, a teacher of 'bioenergetics', writes, 'I understand spirituality as a heightening of the excitatory processes of the human animal. The religious experience . . . is our vivid experiencing, and it is the vividness of what we experience. Its depth and intensity correspond with how deep and intense our (bodily) streamings are. . . . To experience our streamings is the spiritual experience'.

(7) **Native people's religion.** North American Indian spirituality has inspired many of us and has a lot to teach us. Doug Boyd, who has studied the Hindu mystic Swami Rama and the Shoshone medicine man Rolling Thunder, reports that 'Swami Rama's method is to work internally, to withdraw the mind's attention from external perceptions. . . . Rolling Thunder's way is to work externally, to sharpen the senses, to embrace the world. . . . Through interaction with his environment (Rolling Thunder) learns about the natural world and then comes to understand his own nature. He becomes one with nature, one with himself, one with the Great Spirit'. Vine Deloria, Jr., well-known native writer and activist, has argued that Christianity, like Marxism and liberalism, is a European import, and that North Americans must seek God here, within their own land. All true religions, he says, are intimately connected with the land of their people, and the North American religion should be no exception. 'It is the spirit of the continent . . . that shines through the Indian anthologies and glimmers in the Indian communities in grotesque and tortured forms . . . '.

(8) **The new paganism.** Deloria calls Christianity a European religion; Tom Robbins calls it an **Eastern** religion, and argues that it was imposed on Western Europe by the Church — imposed on our own, natural, pagan religion which we had been celebrating for thousands of years.

'The Old Religion', says Andrea Dworkin, 'celebrated sexuality, fertility, nature and women's place in it . . . '. Its central figure, says Robbins, was 'a hairy, merry deity who loved music and dancing and good food'. It was nature-centred and woman-centred. There were priestesses, wise women, midwives, goddesses, sorceresses. 'There was no dogma; each priestess interpreted the religion in her own fashion'.

The Old Religion couldn't be re-established in New Age society, but we **could** adapt its nature- and woman-centredness to our own new priorities and concerns. In fact, both these things are already happening.

Nature-centredness has an obvious parallel in our growing recognition that the quality of our connection to the environment — both natural and people-made — has a lot to do with our spiritual health and spiritual growth. Tom Bender would have us 'spiritualize' our surroundings by building things that are in harmony with nature and with natural forces. In his novel about a New Age society (which he calls 'Ecotopia'), Ernest Callenbach has his narrator see 'a quite ordinary-looking young man, not visibly drugged, lean against a large oak and mutter, "Brother Tree!"'.

Significantly, among those of us at self-development stages six and seven, religious worship has already begun to rely less on the tradition of the sky god and more on the tradition of the earth goddess. As sociologist Robert Bellah sees it, 'The sky religions emphasize the paternal, hierarchical, legalistic and ascetic, whereas the earth tradition emphasizes the maternal, communal, expressive and joyful aspects of existence. . . . The earth tradition is tuned to cosmic harmonies, vibrations and astrological influences . . . (and it) expresses itself not through impersonal bureaucracy or the isolated nuclear family but through collectives, communes, tribes and large extended families'.

Mary Daly, a Boston feminist, believes that the new spirituality can learn even more from the feminist movement, that the current 'unfolding of woman-consciousness is an intimation of the endless unfolding of God'. In this view, God isn't a noun (let alone a gender) but a verb, an endless Being; and those of us who are trying to develop our selves are at One with God, because we are challenging our own non-'Being' in Prison society and actively participating in God the Verb.

III. Multiple Vision: The New Age Alternative to Scientific Single Vision

In Chap. 3, sect. III, we saw that our narrowly scientific way of 'seeing' the world requires us to ignore many of the insights of the Eastern philosophies, and many of the signals that are coming to us from the right side of our brains. And in Chap. 11 we saw that the emerging new 'trans-material worldview' recognizes that there are at least three other **essential** states of consciousness besides the material (and that the material state itself is far too narrowly understood). In light of all this, it isn't going too far to say — as many Eastern philosophers do — that the 'reality' that scientific single vision reveals to us is so narrow as to be an illusion.

In New Age society, scientific single vision would be replaced by 'multiple vision' — by a way of seeing the world that takes all four states of consciousness into account. Different New Age thinkers have proposed different versions of this 'multiple vision' science, but all of them would agree on the main point: that we need to learn to combine the functions of the left and right sides of the brain. We **desperately** need to learn to be intellectual **and** intuitive, analytic **and** holistic, active **and** receptive, etc.

Beyond that, there seems to be a wide measure of agreement with some other points, recently summed up succinctly by Robert Ornstein and George Lodge. Ornstein says that we need to recognize 'the importance of consciousness itself as an object of inquiry'; that we are 'sensitive and permeable to subtle sources of energy from geophysical and human forces'; and that we need to greatly expand our conception of the normal (it was, for instance, until recently considered 'paranormal' to be able to control our nervous systems, despite the fact that yogis had been doing it for thousands of years).

Lodge makes the following points: (1) 'everything must be considered in relation to everything else'; (2) 'wholes cannot necessarily be understood solely by the analysis of their parts'; (3) 'subjectivity must complicate objectivity' — we must recognize that all observation and all experience is necessarily subjective; (4) 'the subjective and the irrational (must be) granted status as real' (I think this is what Charles Reich is getting at in his new book when he calls for 'a new epistemology . . . which declares that our feelings are factual truth'); and (5) materialism must be complemented and to some extent replaced by 'a new tenderness for the value of the human being'.

But beyond these points there are some important differences of opinion, and they seem to be rooted in this: Fritjof Capra believes that there can be no synthesis between science and what he insists on calling mysticism, that science and mysticism are 'two complementary manifestations of the human mind. . . . Science does not need mysticism and mysticism does not need science; but (people) need both'. On the other hand, Theodore Roszak, Willis Harman, and many other New Age thinkers, would change the scientific enterprise itself: would change its **purposes**, its **methods**, and its **scope**. Multiple vision, says Roszak, 'can never be achieved . . . by processing young scientists through an additional course of study in Taoist nature mysticism. It's a matter of changing the fundamental sensibility of scientific thought . . .'.

Purposes. The task, says Roszak, is to 'deepen the personality of the knower' rather than merely or primarily to 'increase what is known'. Harman adds that multiple vision science 'would aim to . . . guide individuals and society in their efforts to discover new realms of experience and potentiality and to foster actively the growth and evolution of society and individuals'.

Methods. According to Harman, multiple vision science 'would foster open, participative inquiry; it would diminish the dichotomy between observer and observed, investigator and subject. Investigations of subjective experience would be based on collaborative trust and "exploring together", rather than on the sort of manipulative deception that has characterized much past research in the social sciences'. According to Roszak, multiple vision science 'would surely end some lines of research entirely out of repugnance for their reductionism, insensitivity and social risk'.

Scope. To Harman, multiple vision science would encompass 'objective experience', 'religion', and 'philosophy, literature and the arts'. To William Irwin Thompson, it would encompass 'math', 'spirituality', and 'music'. To Robert Pirsig it would encompass 'conventional science', 'religion' and 'art'.

To each of these writers, then, multiple vision science would be based on a fusion of the material, spiritual-religious, and mythic states of consciousness.

There has already been at least one detailed proposal for a multiple vision science — Dr. Charles Tart's proposal for what he calls 'state-specific sciences'. According to Tart, single-vision science is a state-specific science, specific to our ordinary state of consciousness; and each of the other states of consciousness would require its own 'state-specific' science! 'Scientists might want to investigate . . . internal phenomena of the particular (state), the interaction of people in that (state), the interaction of that (state) with other (states), and so on . . . '.

What might our new multiple-vision science produce in the way of insight? Thompson summarizes what might be called the conventional wisdom of multiple-vision science: (1) 'There is intelligent life in the universe beyond earth'; (2) 'The Gods do not talk to us, they play through us with our history'; (3) 'Our religious myths are the detritus of the lost history of earth'; and (4) 'Matter, energy and consciousness form a continuum' (as in the worldview of the Hopi Indians). Alyce and Elmer Green, a pair of psychologists who have come as close as anyone to working in this new mode, hypothesize (in Boyd) that a 'unique energy field, a "field of mind", must surround the planet'; that 'each individual mind with its extension, the body, must have the inherent capability of focussing energy for manipulation' of both internal and external 'events'; and that 'the individual mind and the general "field of mind" meet in the unconscious'.

IV. The Cooperative Mentality: The New Age Alternative to the Bureaucratic Mentality

In Chap. 3, sect. IV, we saw that our bureaucratic mentalities and our large, bureaucratic-hierarchical organizations are doing us all a lot of harm. It should not be surprising, then, that New Age thinkers and activists have been experimenting with a number of attitudes and organizational forms that can take us 'beyond bureaucracy'.

(1) **I-You Attitudes**. In Prison society most of our relationships are of the I-It type: the other person becomes an object, a means, a number. This is especially true in the work-world (and helps to explain why some New Age people are in favour of replacing, e.g., supermarket tellers with computers — a supermarket teller could probably never escape being treated like an object.) The anarchist alternative to this situation is to convert as many relationships as possible to the I-Thou type: relationships of intimate friendship. In the 'real world', however, as Ruben Nelson points out, 'there simply is not enough time to develop, test, and sustain friendships with the large number of people whom we know and with whom we deal'. Therefore, Nelson and many other New Age writers have suggested that we convert most of our relationships with people to the 'I-You' type. In I-You relationships, says Nelson, 'we acknowledge that the other is a person and potentially a friend, although for a variety of reasons, he-she will not be so with us'.

David Spangler would have us learn to share 'a **spirit** of familiarity, a **spirit** of shared personhood, a **spirit** of the presence (and the potential) of connections and bonds beyond the functional' (emphases added). And he'd have us learn 'to see the "personhood", the divine potential, of things, thus seeing things as persons rather than persons as things'.

(2) **The Win-Win Model.** In Prison society we assume that those who disagree with us must necessarily be in conflict with us, and we spend a great deal of time arguing with them in order to show that 'we're right' and 'they're wrong'. In New Age society we would acknowledge that, as economist Robert Theobald puts it, 'It is possible for everybody to gain from an interaction rather than for some people to win and others to lose'. We would develop 'an inclusionary, win-win model, where we recognize that those who are not against us are for us. We need to understand that all of us can be better off if we share our divergent perspectives. 'People are rarely wrong; rather, each person focusses on different parts of the truth, which can then be pieced together to produce a larger vision of reality. Once one understands that subjective diversity is inevitable, then one can consider differences of opinion as healthy and productive and a way of learning more rapidly'.

(3) **Synergic Principles**. 'Synergic' principles are those that make it possible for us to produce **more and better** when we're working together than when we're working apart — and to enjoy our selves more — and to grow. The Synergic Power Centre has recently drawn up a list of 18 basic synergic principles that all New Age organizations might want to follow (and build on). Some examples:

1. Embrace a set of (New Age) values agreed upon by members;
2. Give equal attention to the organization's external mission and to the fulfillment and growth of its members;
3. Involve affected persons from the larger society in designing the organization's external mission;
4. Design your organization's impact (products, services, education, etc.) upon the larger society so as to make it more receptive to New Age transformation;
5. Make policy changes only after involving or at least consulting **everyone** who might be affected;
6. Resist any tendency for power and decision-making to become concentrated in one or a few hands;
7. When conflict arises, substitute 'joint problem-solving' for adversary negotiatons and aim for **full satisfaction for all parties** rather than compromise.

(4) **Synergic Interactions**. New Age organizations would introduce into their day-to-day functioning many of the techniques that are currently being used in the human potential movement. According to the Synergic Power Centre, members of New Age organizations would 'share power and build trust by regularly and openly sharing information, feelings, desires, intentions, reservations, objections, fears, options and choices'. And members would 'employ rituals and-or other activities to build cohesion and intimacy

within the organization'.

Jim and Marge Craig, co-directors of the Centre, tell us that human potential techniques would have many advantages. Partly for our selves alone — e.g., they would help to put us in touch with our selves — but partly for our organizations as well as for our selves. For example, members of New Age organizations would learn to expand their awareness and understanding of all the needs and desires and fears that are at work in any group process; and the efficiency of the group would — in the long run — definitely increase.

(5) **Sapiential authority.** The bureaucratic mentality holds that only certain people are capable of making the decisions. The cooperative mentality holds that, not only are most people capable of making the decisions, but that we should be held responsible for those decisions that we do make — and even for those decisions that we 'merely' carry out (no more 'I was only following orders'). Therefore, in New Age society, we would have to create institutions in which we could **refuse** to 'follow orders'; in which we could exercise what Robert Theobald calls 'sapiential authority'.

Sapiential authority as I understand it would hold us **personally and legally responsible** for our actions in an organization — its effect would be to keep us from falling into the 'agentic state of mind' that was reported on in Chap. 3, sect. IV. At the same time, it would give us the right to refuse to follow orders, rules, guidelines, standards, whatever — not on a whim, but if they didn't seem good and right to us (if they didn't seem like **Quality** orders, rules, etc.).

Theobald points out that we've already begun changing over to a system of sapiential authority here and there — e.g., a soldier is now told that he or she should refuse to obey an order 'when on the basis of (his or her) own judgement, (he or she) believes it to be unlawful'. He also points out that the (first glimmerings of the) transition to sapiential authority has made many of us fear, wrongly, that we're experiencing the end of **all** authority.

Still, that fear makes a lot more sense when it's put this way: if New Age institutions really did give us the 'right to say no', how could a New Age society **survive**?

New Age institutions would have to agree not to fire or otherwise punish their members for exercising their sapiential authority. Their only alternative, then, would be to accommodate themselves to the special needs and perspectives of their dissident members. For their part, members would have to be willing to engage in 'give and take' with their institutions; to share their views and change their views; to feel responsible not only for their own development, but for that of their institutions as well.

There can be no doubt that this is a very tall order — and a delicate one. But if we were at self-development stages six and seven, we wouldn't want it any other way.

(6) **An Easy Death.** As organizations get older, Kenneth Boulding observes, they tend to 'harden' no matter how democratic or open-ended they might have been in the beginning. He sees only one remedy for this, the 'constant death of the old. . . . The less existing organizations are protected and the

easier it is for them to die', the more likely it is that the old will give way to the new, to new organizations that are sapiential and synergic and humane.

V. Localization and Planetization: The New Age Alternative to Nationalism

In Chap. 3, sect. V we saw that it's natural for us to identify with our local communities and-or with the planet as a whole, **not** with the nation-state; and we mentioned some of the harm that's come to us because of our nationalism and our bigger nation-states. In New Age society, towns, rural districts and big city neighbourhoods would be able to achieve as much autonomy as they wished (and would be encouraged to cooperate on a regional basis). And governments, **all** governments, would be encouraged to cooperate on a planetary basis — to cooperate in a kind of 'planetary guidance system' whose purpose would be to implement the New Age ethics and political values. See Chaps. 15-16 below.

VI. The Human-Scale Outlook: The New Age Alternative to the Big City Outlook

In Chap. 3, sect. VI, we saw that our big cities — cities of maybe half a million people or more — are destructive to those of us who live in them (a **majority** of us) by their very **nature**. And we saw that our big cities generate a 'big city outlook' in us, a fearful and withdraw-ful way of looking at the world. In New Age society, therefore, we would want our big cities to be drastically reduced in size — and to be utterly transformed as places to live in.

This would be easily possible for two reasons. First, our big cities no longer serve any **necessary** purpose (Buckminster Fuller points out that big cities have been our warehouses and our factories, and neither of these functions needs to be centralized any more — if indeed they ever did). Second, in New Age society we would no longer be Prison-bound, and so we'd no longer be driven to big cities for psychocultural reasons.

There would, of course, still be cities of half a million people or slightly fewer. New Age society would be nothing if not diverse, and merchants, drifters and intellectuals would probably always prefer large cities to small ones. But most of the rest of us would probably not choose to live in cities of even this size (except for brief periods), since self-development can take many forms, and most of them require not the passionate anonymity of city life but the rootedness and warmth of human scale community.

There would be no standard city size — though many New Age writers have said that the 'ideal' city size is around 100,000 people. Partly for negative reasons (the crime rate tends to take a big jump around 100,000 pop.) and partly for positive ones — e.g., Barbara Ward tells us that a community that's much smaller than 50-100,000 wouldn't be able to sustain the 'shops, schools, entertainment, recreation and special events' that are necessary to attract visitors from elsewhere (to keep the place lively) or to satisfy the less or **more** mobile members of the local society. 'It is also the scale needed to allow for

smaller cultural groupings . . . to join (together) in a shared (subculture)'.
Still, there's nothing magical about the 100,000 figure — for example, cities
don't become conspiculously more expensive, per person, until they've
reached a pop. of 250,000 or so.

The more important question is, what would our new Prison-free dwelling
places **be** like? And the answer is simple: they would take on every form
under the sun — and I mean that literally. Just so long as the form was able to
foster the New Age ethics and values. Here are some of the most talked about
proposals:

(1) **Intentional communities.** Some of them, certainly many more than
today, would be 'intentional communities' — country communes and the like
— dwelling places whose purpose was to demonstrate a particular truth, reveal a particular vision.

(2) **Anthropopolis.** Probably most of our New Age communities would try
to break down the distinction between city and country altogether. Constantinos Doxiadis, the Greek city planner, has proposed a number of 'extended
cities' that would blend farms and factories, gardens and homes. Extended
cities would be made up of many different-sized and independent (or
semi-independent) communities strung together by rapid public transit.
Communities would be multi-dimensional and human-scale (few or no high-
rises; few or no cars), but beyond that, as diverse as possible: 'continuous
streams of fairly intense neighbourhoods of the human scale' is how Doxiadis
likes to put it. The point is that the extended city would then truly be an
anthropopolis — 'city of all the people' — and we could enjoy an environment
of maximum community **and** maximum contact with other communities,
other cultural groupings. Marharet Mead, an advocate of this approach,
adds, 'We rebuilt (North America) after World War II, and we can rebuild it
again very easily'.

(3) **Arcologies.** Paolo Soleri, an Italian architect and student of the evolutionary thinker Teilhard de Chardin, believes that human evolution is characterized by (a) increasing 'complexification', and (b) increasing 'miniaturization'. His 'arcologies' (literally, architecture plus ecology) are designed to
help us in our evolutionary journey; they are, therefore, cities in which everything contracts, intensifies (miniaturization, Soleri explains, isn't a 'scaling
down' or 'piling up' of things so much as it is 'the expulsion of those elements
that go for the chastening of the urban landscape and the punishment of its
dwellers. . . . By expelling, for instance, the car and the paraphernalia of its
demands, 50-60 percent of the urban topography' could be 'miniaturized' out of
existence).

'The bridge between matter and spirit', says Soleri, 'is matter becoming
spirit' — becoming more complex, more condensed, more dense.

In practice, Soleri's arcologies would be medium-sized (pop. 3,000 and up),
multi-levelled 'cities in the image of (people)'; cities that were physically,
ecologically, and to some extent economically self-contained . . . and carefully
designed to promote face-to-face encounters. **Too** carefully designed, **too** to-

tally planned, say some New Agers. At any rate, you owe your self a couple of hours paging through Soleri's lovingly intricate designs for these arcologies (**Arcology**, 1969). Or for $270 a month you can work as a labourer-apprentice with Soleri in Arizona, where he's building the first arcology.

(4) **Tetrahedronal cities**. Buckminster Fuller has proposed building floating 'tetrahedronal cities', pyramid-like structures that could be 'symmetrically growable as are biological systems'. They may start with a thousand occupants and grow to hold (hundreds of thousands) without changing overall shape though always providing each (household) with 2,000 sq. ft. of floor space' — including 1,000 sq. ft. for a garden. 'Withdrawal of materials from obsolete buildings on the land (could) permit the production of (many) of these floating cities'.

(5) **The small community reborn**. The movement out of our biggest cities has already begun, and surveys have shown that many more people would leave if they (felt they) had the chance. But New Age people hope to do more than **return** to smaller places. As Arthur Morgan, founder of Community Service, Inc., puts it, 'The small community of the future will be . . . a new creation, uniting the values of both (the small town and the city), and largely avoiding their limitations'.

(6) **Coherent neighbourhoods**. Neighbourhoods would become more physically coherent (Leopold Kohr would have us **focus** our neighbourhoods on a central plaza or square).

Chapter 14 — New Age Alternatives to Our Monolithic Institutions

In Part II we saw that the Prison is institutionalized by means of 'monolithic' institutions that establish a monopoly not of brands but of products and processes: in healing there's a monopoly of 'professionalized' medical care; in transportation, of rapid transit; in education, of universal and compulsory schooling; and so on. In New Age society, we would be free of the Prison, and so we would want to replace our monolithic institutions with what I call 'biolithic' institutions.

Biolithic institutions would not **require** us to 'do things their way', would allow for the existence of institutional and technological alternatives — we would enjoy, as Ivan Illich puts it, 'freedom from monopoly in the satisfaction of any basic need'. Biolithic institutions would offer us the **widest possible choice** of goods and services, information and technology. They would allow us — Illich again — 'the freedom to make things among which (we) can live, to give shape to them according to (our) own tastes'.

Biolithic institutions wouldn't do away with professional medical care, cars, etc. (not necessarily, anyway), but in a biolithic society these things —

because they tend to be monolithic — would have to be definitely subordinate to products and processes that fostered diversity (by fostering self-reliance, say, or by being ecologically more sane). Each New Age society would have to determine its own **point of maximum synergy** between industrial-era institutions and technologies and those institutions and technologies that fostered individual autonomy and self-reliance (for an introduction to the concept of 'synergy', see Chap. 15, sect. II).

Biolithic institutions would increase our ability to develop our selves and our self-reliance, would encourage our capacity to cooperate with others, would be ecologically more sane and would only be compatible with a non-nuclear defence. Biolithic institutions are obviously necessary if we hope to live by the New Age ethics and values! Necessary but not sufficient: for we would also have to want to **use** the opportunities that our biolithic institutions would give us. And no institutional arrangement, no matter how life-oriented, can ever give us that.

---

(1) **Biolithic transport** wouldn't eliminate cars altogether (though some **communities** might). But if we wanted a diverse society we would have to devise a form (or forms) of transportation in which the car was definitely secondary. These might be as diverse as the communities that adopted them. Probably one alternative form would be a much-improved system of rapid transit — but as we saw in Chap. 7, rapid transit doesn't really get us away from the Prison-bound needs for speed and efficiency. So I would suspect that a more popular substitute for reliance on the automobile would be a system of bicycles and pedicabs, complemented perhaps by a system of busses to bring people in from beyond the city limits.

According to Barbara Ward, a telecommunications system would make it possible for us to do away with much of our transport — including most long-distance transport. A telecommunications system would also make it possible for us to radically decentralize our work-places — again, making it more possible for us to come to work on foot or by bicycle. (If we were free of the Prison, it wouldn't much matter if we came to work with wind-blown hair, or rain-spattered pants — we might even enjoy bicycling through the rain and cold.)

I also suspect that a maximum speed limit would be set on travel between cities (say, 35 mph) — partly to save on energy, but mostly to get the pace of life back under control. In his new book Charles Reich writes, 'I learned that if I slowed down, things in my immediate surroundings became more interesting, more capable of giving me good feelings'; and Ivan Illich writes, 'Beyond a critical speed, no one can save time without forcing another to lose it. . . . Beyond a certain velocity, passengers become consumers of other people's time, and accelerating vehicles become the means for affecting a net transfer of life-time'.

(2) **Biolithic healing** wouldn't do away with professional, institutional care, but basic medical information would be made available to all of us — and so

would the tools that we might need to care for our selves and to cure our selves of most diseases. Paramedics might be trained to make house calls or to set up shop in local communities (possibly through neighbourhood 'health centres'). Oriental and herbal medical practices would be fostered and encouraged (for the extraordinary possibilities of these, see — respectively — Naboru Muramoto, **Healing Ourselves**, 1973, and Jethro Kloss, **Back to Eden**, 1971).

Just as important, health would be **redefined**. Toward the end of his life, Abraham Maslow spoke of 'full humanness' rather than health, and recently Eric Utne (in **New Age Journal**, Sept. '74) stated, 'Health lies in the presence of something rather than in the **lack** of physical disease or pain'. What is this something? To Utne it's our ability to be fully in touch with body, heart and mind — with all four states of consciousness. To Philip Slater it's our ability to connect with others. Utne says that 'we are all healers', that we should look to see what's right with self and others and give it recognition. Elisabeth Kubler-Ross would have us redefine tragedies as 'gifts, virtual gifts, which help you understand the meaning of life'.

(3) **Biolithic learning** wouldn't do away with all schools — but their **nature** and their **purposes** would be totally transformed.

New Age schools wouldn't be compulsory, wouldn't rank students, and wouldn't lock students into, as John Holt puts it, 'a prescribed sequence of learning determined in advance'. Moreover, laws would have to be passed stating that no one would be denied an available job solely on the basis of school credentials, and whenever a credential was needed for a job there would have to be a way to get this credential without going to school. (One way might be by extending the idea of apprenticeship; another, by extending the idea of the equivalency exam.) Finally, our notion of the 'student' would have to change — Ivan Illich warns us against the 'immigrant syndrome', which 'impels us to treat all (students) as if they were newcomers who must go through a naturalizing process'.

At the same time, the **curriculum** of our schools would have to be transformed. Monolithic schools, true to the materialist worldview, focus on what they like to call 'the basics' — the three R's. Biolithic schools, true to the trans-material worldview, would focus on **their** basics: would focus on the development of the personality as a whole (body, emotions, imagination, intuition, will, **as well as** mind) and would help us get in touch with what Roberto Assagioli has called our 'transpersonal essence' and I earlier (Chap. 11) called our 'space beyond conditioning'.

According to Jack Canfield and Paula Klinek, co-directors of the Institute for Humanistic and Transpersonal Education, our schools could nurture the whole self by making systematic use of 'humanistic' and 'transpersonal' methods of teaching that are already in use here and there.

The field of humanistic education has developed techniques 'to help people validate themselves, to communicate more effectively with others, to enhance their self-concepts, to ask directly for what they want, to clarify their values, to express their feelings, to celebrate their bodies, to use their will, and to take responsibility for their lives'. The newer field of transpersonal education acknowledges and fosters our non-material states of consciousness through working with forms such as dreams, meditation, 'guided imagery', chanting, centering, and fantasy literature. Canfield and Klinek state, 'Now is the time to combine both of these focuses, for the New Age means integrating the soul and the personality' (see **New Age Journal**, Feb. '78).

Despite these transformations, many New Age people would rely primarily on self-motivated learning — New Age families would, after all, themselves be producing well-developed and spiritually aware young people. At different times in their lives, whenever it felt right (made sense) to them, many New Age people might choose to enter into what Ivan Illich calls a 'learning web' — a series of community-based educational networks that could help us gain access to information and understandings **outside** of the regular school system. Networks might be run at one-hundredth the cost of public schools and universities if they consisted simply of (a) bulletins that would allow us to describe the learning activities we wanted to engage in (would help us find partners); (b) bulletins that would allow us to list our skills and experience and the conditions under which we were willing to share our skills; and (c) bulletins that would allow us to find the things we were interested in — things stored in museums, laboratories, etc. (Call it premature, but The Learning Exchange, P.O. Box 920, Evanston, Ill. 60204, has been running something similar to Illich's learning web since 1972.)

According to Michael Rossman, some of us might go so far as to create 'learning families', supportive groups 'flexible enough to be seminar, action group, economic collective, playground and hospital'.

(4) **Biolithic housing** would be characterized, above all, by its diversity. Yes, some buildings might still be put up by 'developers' (following stringent community guidelines). But those of us who wanted to make our own homes would be encouraged, not hounded — Ivan Illich suggests that all self-builders be given 'access to some minimum of physical space, to water, some basic building elements, some convivial tools ranging from power drills to mechanized push-carts, and, probably, to some limited credit'. 'Making our own' would come to be seen as a process of healing and growth — and the home would come to be seen 'as a natural extension of the creative vision . . . of those who will live within its walls' (among some New Agers this is already happening — see River's remarkable book, **Dwelling**, 1974).

At the same time, **community** building would take on a life of its own. New Age architect Hassan Fathy has proposed a system of cooperative design and construction that would cut present-day construction costs by up to 85 percent (and have many other advantages besides!). Architects would be trained to help people design their own structures; contractors, subcontractors and imported labour would be replaced by community labour at the standard minimum wage; buildings would be made of cheap, readily available local materials; and emphasis would be placed on intuitive decision-making rather than on 'rationalization' of the building process, and on the creation of beauty.

An elementary school was recently built along these lines in northern California (despite stiff opposition from the construction and teamsters' unions). According to Colin Kowal (in **Seriatim**, Spring '77), 'The actual construction of the school was an epic story of community participation. . . . Hundreds of people with a great diversity of skills worked on the school and taught others their know-how. . . . Children dug ditches, planted flowers and fruit trees, and seeded and mulched the grass. . . . Highlights of the building include . . . stained glass windows, hand-crafted tiles, hand-carved beams . . . and a massive stone fireplace'. Cost of the building? Twenty percent **less** than the next lowest bid received by the school board.

(5) **Biolithic religion** would retain our churches — but most of them would be community- rather than denomination-based, far less powerful and 'efficient' than they are today. And most New Agers would supplement or even replace their church-going with many other religious and spiritual activities.

Ivan Illich foresees 'the face-to-face meeting of families around a table, rather than the impersonal attendance of a crowd around an altar', and would have many, possibly millions of laypeople be ordained for this purpose. The Findhorn community has developed a spiritual practice called 'attunement', and the people around **WomanSpirit** Magazine, a practice called 'energy re-sourcement'; both these practices would probably become common. Most important of all, perhaps, our surroundings would become 'spiritualized' as we learned to see things through the trans-material worldview — the world would once again be seen as a sacred place (but not, this time, **only** as a sacred place!).

(6) **The biolithic economy** would provide alternatives for those of us who wanted to do things that could not be structured into jobs. Some New Age economies might provide free essentials for all, or nearly-free essentials along with easily obtainable day-a-week-type employment; other New Age economies might provide free access to land and easy access to tools; still other New Age economies might provide a guaranteed subsistence income.

(7) **Biolithic sexual relationships and commitments** would be incredibly diverse. Monogamy, heterosexuality, and two-person marriage would remain — but no longer as the only 'normal' relationships, or even (in some communities, anyway) the most common ones.

Compulsive heterosexuality would give way to androgyny, and so there would be room for a wide range of love-sex relationships — finding a good person (or persons) would be all that mattered. **Compulsive monogamy** would give way to many different kinds of sexual patternings — the one(s) we chose for our selves would depend entirely on our own needs and wants (which would probably vary over time). Conscious monogamy would remain, as one choice among many. Similarly, **compulsive marriage** would give way to many different kinds of union between (or among) people, some permanent, some temporary; some exclusive, others 'open' — but all would be consciously chosen (and all would be in keeping with the New Age ethics and values!).

Formal marriage might remain, but its content would change substantially. For example: Anais Nin says that men and women would stop struggling against each other for power, and learn, instead, 'the subtle art of oscillation. . . . Neither strength nor weakness is a fixed quality. We all have our days of strength and our days of weakness'.

At one point on the New Age spectrum, Ananda Cooperative Village has been developing 'spiritual marriage'. In open marriage, says Nalini (in **Communities**, Nov.-Dec. '75), growth is defined as the process of learning to relate to more and more people; in spiritual marriage growth 'is defined inwardly, in terms of **depth** — the depth of one's relationship with one other person and with (his or her) higher Self, or God'.

Other unions among people might dispense with 'marital ties' altogether (some communities might not even issue marriage licenses). Robert Thamm believes that, in the long run, the communal or cooperative family is the only real alternative to the 'ultimate fragmentation of the nuclear system', that is, to living alone. (It's already happening — between 1960 and 1971 the number of people living in unrelated groups jumped by over 40 percent.) 'As the importance of our marital ties diminishes', says Thamm, 'groups of adults and children will form living units based upon friendship ties. These ties may or may not include sexual involvement'.

The cooperative (or 'polycentric') family would have many advantages, according to Thamm. 'Total sexual-emotional involvement between two people will be modified to partial involvement among a few. This pattern will prevent both our restricted gratification and our overdependence on one person. . . . and jealous possessiveness will evolve into a loving concern'. Sex and age roles would (or at least, could) be completely broken down. And if we wanted to leave for some reason, whether temporarily or permanently, the stability of the family wouldn't be threatened — its continuity could be maintained.

The Kerista group, in San Francisco, is setting up experimental 'superfamilies' of 24 adults each. In their introductory booklet they write, 'The adult members of a superfamily have equally deep relationships with each of their 23 partners' — 23 primary relationships! (For more information write: Storefront Classroom Community, P.O. Box 1174, San Francisco 94101.)

(8) **The biolithic family** would be very different from the monolithic family, as you can see from no. 7 above. And so would its 'product', our children.

If the **quality** of the nuclear bond were altered in a New Age direction, we would be better models for our kids, and we wouldn't need to use them as love or help or hate objects. Better yet, we would feel good about giving them as many 'adult' responsibilities as they wanted — about giving them the opportunity to explore the world on their own (see Chap. 21, sect. III-7). At the very least, we would be willing to hold them and to openly express our affections for them . . . partly to keep them from falling into the 'stroke economy'.

If the **bond itself** were altered — expanded — so that there were many nurturers, not just one or two, then we would have an even greater opportunity to give our young people Prison-free and stroke-economy-free upbringings. If we felt unhappy or upset, our young people would have many other sources of love to turn to — so they wouldn't grow up fearing the loss of love (according to Philip Slater, that fear leads directly to the stroke economy). And if we were sharing our nurturing duties, we would find it relatively easy to offer **unconditional love and respect** to our young people — and that would make it even more possible for them to grow up free of the fear of the loss of love — free of the 'withdrawal of love' technique of child-rearing. (Psychologists like Abraham Maslow and Carl Rogers are convinced that unconditional love and respect are the absolutely necessary **prerequisites** for self-development.)

(9) **Biolithic technology** wouldn't necessarily do away with all large-scale, complex, capital- and resource-intensive technologies. 'Biolithic' means 'oriented to life', and biolithic technologies would be all those ways of doing things that were able to help New Age communities meet what they consider-ed to be their life needs. Some New Age communities might define their life needs in such a way as to exclude all large-scale production. But probably most communities would hold, with Ivan Illich, that small-scale production can be 'supplemented by industrial outputs that will have to be designed and often manufactured beyond direct community control. Autonomous activity can be rendered both more effective and more decentralized by using such in-dustrially-made tools as bicycles, printing presses, (tape) recorders, or X-ray equipment . . . '. Not to mention computer typesetters!

Biolithic technology would, then, most usually be a balance (or 'synergy') between certain kinds of 'high' technology and what is currently known as 'appropriate' or 'alternative' technology ('A.T.' for short). There have been a number of attempts to list the central characteristics of A.T., and my attempt, below, is based on previous lists by: Tom Bender (co-editor of **Rain**), David Dickson, William Ellis (editor of **Tranet**), Amory Lovins (of Friends of the Earth), E. F. Schumacher, and John Todd (of the New Alchemists) — my ninth point is Peter van Dresser's.

Appropriate technology should:
1. be small scale;
2. be low cost;
3. be simple, and easy to understand;
4. be inexpensive, or easily accessible;
5. be easily maintained;
6. be non-violent — not even potentially dangerous to people;
7. be sustainable with renewable energy resources and material recycling;
8. be in harmony with nature;
9. be closely adapted to local and regional topography and biotic patterns;
10. reduce dependency among individuals, communities, regions, nations;
11. substitute human resources for energy and material ones;
12. generate meaningful employment;
13. be designed on the basis of ecological and social considerations rather than those of economic efficiency;

14. do away with the alienation and exploitation of people;

15. provide support for our social, emotional, psychological and spiritual growth;

16. be diverse.

This list represents something less than a perfect synthesis, since the six writers manage to contradict each other in various ways — some of them might even claim that my definition of biolithic technology is the 'real' definition of A.T. Certainly there's no difference in the sense that, as David Dickson puts it, 'The main importance of (A.T.) does not lie in the particular solutions which may be offered to certain problems. Rather it is in the approach that they represent, that technology should be designed to meet human needs and resources — and not the other way around'.

New Age communities would be responsible for choosing their own particular mix of technologies according to what they felt were their own needs and priorities — but always in the context of the New Age ethics and political values. Specifically, if a community wanted to charter or develop a 'high' technology industry, it would also have to (a) adopt an extremely frugal lifestyle, to cut down on energy and resource use, or (b) pay a special tax to an appropriate planetary body for using up more than its fair share of the world's energy or resources. The tax might be paid in the form of a certain percentage of whatever the energy- and resource-intensive industry produced — thereby helping to make it possible for other communities to obtain the printing presses, tape recorders, X-ray machines, etc., referred to above (the planetary guidance system might oversee, coordinate and even suggest such transactions; see Chap. 16, sect. III).

(10) **Biolithic energy** could **not** include nuclear, which would unavoidably threaten both the ecology and the nonviolence ethics (see Chap. 7, sect. III-10). Nor could it involve anything more than a transitional dependence on fossil fuels (consultant physicist Amory Lovins states that the commitment to a long-term coal economy would make 'the doubling of atmospheric carbon dioxide concentration early in the next century virtually unavoidable, with the prospect then or soon thereafter of substantial or perhaps irreversible changes in global climate').

There is, however, one energy strategy that is not only **consistent** with the New Age ethics and values but is in some ways **dependent** on them, on our learning to live by them. That is what Amory Lovins calls the 'soft technology' energy strategy, combining rapid development of renewable energy sources (especially solar), special transitional fossil-fuel technologies, use of thriftier technologies ('technical fixes'), and a much greater commitment to 'simple living' — to car pooling, walking, opening windows, dressing to suit the weather, recycling materials, etc. (see Chap. 20, sects. III-IV). Lovins suggests that in the long term, technical fixes alone — thermal insulation, more efficient furnaces, less overlighting in commercial buildings and the like — could improve our energy efficiency **by up to 80 percent**, and that even by the turn of the century we could nearly double the efficiency with which we use energy.

If we cut our energy consumption in half by becoming (even slightly) more New Age in our living habits, then we could construct a largely or wholly solar economy in North America by the year 2025 — using only those technologies that are now economic (or nearly economic). And, according to Lovins, a solar economy would have many advantages over a nuclear or fossil fuel economy (or combination of the two). For example: (1) a solar economy would cost less because of its technical simplicity, small unit size, scope for mass production and so on; (2) its environmental impacts — unlike those of nuclear energy or coal — are relatively small, and reversible; (3) coal and-or nuclear energy relies on a very few high technologies whose success is by no means assured; solar distributes the technical risk among many diverse small-scale technologies, most of which are already known to work well; and (4) unilateral adoption of solar energy by North America could help to control nuclear proliferation — the power of the North American example is still very great.

(11) **Biolithic defence** would have to be compatible with New Age society: with the New Age ethics and values (including the nonviolence ethic!), with other biolithic institutions, and with people who were oriented to life rather than things or death. And it would have to be accessible to communities and regions that wanted to put some distance between themselves and the national government (i.e. it would have to be cheap and decentralist).

New Age defence strategists have come up with at least two schemes that fit these criteria — and that promise to be at least as effective as our current 'defence' strategy.

Gene Sharp, a Boston-area defence strategist, and many other New Age activists, have proposed what they call a 'civilian' (not 'civil') defence strategy — 'civilian' because it relies on people's own sense of responsibility and worth rather than on guns. I like to call it a system of 'cooperative nonviolent defence' because it relies on our ability to work together as well as responsibly, and because it would be completely useless if we were to engage in any kind of interpersonal violence.

The first thing to realize is that civilian defence does **not** mean the reduction of defence capacity. Instead, as Sharp puts it, 'the changeover to civilian defence is **transarmament** — the substitution of a new defence capacity that provides deterrence and defence without conventional and nuclear military power. It also contributes to world peace, since unlike military means civilian defence cannot be used for, or be misperceived as intended for, international aggression'. Mulford Sibley, a well-known exponent of 'nonviolent resistance', adds that a government committed to civilian defence would, indeed, 'surrender' some things — 'would surrender everything likely to incite others to violence or apparently defensible only by violence. Thus, grossly disproportionate economic power, military bases and threats, . . . and imperialist control of other peoples would have to go'.

What would civilian defence look like in action? If a New Age community were invaded, we could wear mourning bands, stay home, defy curfews, etc. All these actions would let the invader know that we meant to resist the occupation of our community — forever if need be. The invader's soldiers could be told that the resistance wasn't being directed against them personally, but against their attempt to take control. (That might encourage them to be less brutal than they would be if they thought they might be killed.)

Eventually there might have to be more substantial forms of noncooperation. For example, we might simply refuse to carry out the invader's orders. Or, for example, attempts to exploit our (relatively paltry!) economic capacities might be met with limited strikes, the 'disappearance' of New Agers who were in positions of authority, etc.

Sharp acknowledges that, in the long run, injuries and deaths in retaliation for such behaviour might be common. But he is convinced that they would be less common than if we were to take up arms our selves.

The main point would be to keep the invader from getting control of our institutions. For in civilian defence, keeping a free press, or keeping the invader's propaganda out of our educational networks, would be a more important strategic objective than the possession of, say, a given mountain. And since our institutions would be biolithic — incredibly diverse — getting control of them would be an almost impossible task in the first place.

In civilian defence, then, even under the worst of circumstances, we could still hang on to a measure of autonomy for our community and its institutions. And as the invader failed to break the resistance down totally — because he failed to break us down totally — there would be unrest within his country, and international pressures would mount. Even the invader's soldiers would begin to wonder what they were fighting for (or rather, not fighting for).

A second 'biolithic' defence strategy has recently been proposed by Adam Roberts, a British strategist and a convinced civilian-defencer until the Russian invasion of Czechoslovakia. That event (the Czechs made a heroic, but largely futile attempt to defend their country nonviolently) caused him to think twice: and he has since worked out (or rather, systematized) a possibly more effective system of defence which he calls 'territorial defence'.

Territorial defence is a method of defending a community or region (not a large country) by force of arms — but with a difference. First, the arms would be small — too small to use effectively for offensive purposes, and cheap enough to give to everyone ('only by democratizing the distribution of armed force within a state can the danger of domination by a small military clique be overcome'). Second, there might or might not be professional soldiers, but the bulk of the defence would rely on a citizen army, including local units of a militia type (these could be easily run on a volunteer basis — if the militia were purely for defence, many New Age people would want to join). Third, the militia might make a tactical defence of the borders of the community or region, but the larger strategy would be to allow the invader to enter — and to harass him-her continually while he-she was there. In part this harasment might consist of the kinds of noncooperation Gene Sharp talks about above (the militia might train people in this). In part it might consist of military retaliation (which might be carried out by specially-designated forces, to keep the invader from feeling threatened by the population-at-large).

Territorial defence is, then, a kind of synthesis of the neo-pacifism of Sharp and the various guerrilla movements that have been so successful in so much of the third world. (It does have some precedents though — for example, something very much like it was used by the Iroquois Indians.) It could be used not only for defence against invasion, but for defence against any undemocratic regime. And it could be used as a transitional strategy — as a kind of bridge **between** nuclear and civilian defence. It would be compatible with the New Age ethics and values in communities where nonviolent behaviour was defined in such a way as to include defensive violence (for more on this point see Chap. 21, sect. IV).

(12) **The biolithic state** would allow — encourage — communities to determine how 'decentralized', how powerful, how autonomous they wanted to be (see Chap. 15). At the same time — as Jacques Ellul emphasizes — faith would be restored in other avenues of human effectiveness than the traditionally 'political'. As a result, we would no longer **want or need** the monolithic state.

(13) **The biolithic governing elite** — a contradiction in terms. In most New Age communities, policy decisions would be made by a series of self-selecting, task-oriented work groups, from the bottom up; see Chap. 15, sect. III. (And yet, there would probably be some people who were much more active than others. According to social planner John Friedmann, no more than one-third of the adult population has **ever** been willing to involve itself in the decision-making process. But a self-selecting 33 percent of the population is not a governing elite. It is a governing people.)

(14) **The biolithic corporation** wouldn't necessarily **have** to be small, but if it weren't small it might end up being **completely frozen out** of some New Age communities and regions. (Loss of some critical markets might force all large corporations to reduce their size.) Other communities and regions might insist that corporations adhere to strict **community and regional charters** on pain of expropriation (see Chap. 17, sect. II). At the same time, many New Age communities and regions, worker collectives, and local businesspeople might be starting their own small corporations — and communities and regions could obtain the authority to tax all competing corporate 'goods' at the border.

(15) **Self-images** would, to a great extent, replace roles in biolithic society. 'Self-images', says Stanley Keleman, 'grow out of our individual living process. Our unique livingness initiates each of our self-images. Each self-image reflects our own unique self-forming'.

We would probably continue to have **some** expectations about how we should act as, e.g., parents, lovers, workers; but our expectations would come primarily from our own sense of our selves, from our own understanding of our wants and needs, and from the New Age ethics and values as our communities and regions and we our selves defined them. Keleman states, 'I do not have a fixed role, nor am I everybody in the world (as someone who was only concerned with the spiritual state of consciousness might think — M.S.). I don't have to be a fixed thing and I don't have to be everything. I'm always forming, expressing that which shapes me, that which gives me an identity'.

At the very least we would strive to put some distance between our selves and our roles. Peter Berger reminds us that in ancient Greece the word 'ecstasy' referred to 'the act of standing or stepping outside the taken-for-granted routines of society', and he says, 'As soon as a given role is played without inner commitment, deliberately and deceptively, the actor is in an ecstatic state with regard to (his or her) "world-taken-for-granted". What others regard as fate, (he or she) looks upon as a set of factors to reckon with in (his or her) operations. . . . In other words, "ecstasy" transforms one's awareness of society in such a way that **givenness** becomes **possibility**'. (A well-known technique in psychosynthesis called 'dis-identification' has helped some New Agers move from an overidentification with their socially assigned roles to the recognition that we are, each of us, 'a centre of awareness and of power'.)

(16) **The biolithic mind** would rather see clearly than be right; would rather heal society than prove others wrong; would rather help the person 'experience experience' than go on and on endlessly with its positions, points of view, beliefs, attitudes, justifications. . . .

The mind is not, however, 'naturally' biolithic — its natural tendency is to forever try to escape from what Krishnamurti calls 'that fear of emptiness, that fear of loneliness, that fear of stagnation, of not arriving, not succeeding, not achieving, not being something, not becoming something . . . '. The biolithic mind is a product of the kinds of 'spiritual therapies' that are reported on throughout this book and in the **Journal of Transpersonal Psychology**.

II. Some Other New Age Alternatives

(1) **Freedom to Give All We Wanted to Give: The New Age Alternative to the Stroke Economy.** In Chap. 9, we saw that the Prison gives us 'Prison-bound personalities' by convincing us that there aren't enough positive strokes to go around (positive strokes are units of friendship or affection or esteem). As a result, we are fearful of giving or even receiving strokes. In New Age society, the Prison and its institutions would be collapsed by their New Age alternatives, and as a result, we would find it much, much easier to give (positive) strokes if we had them to give; to ask for strokes if we needed them; to feel free to accept them if we wanted them; to feel free to reject them if we didn't want them; and to feel free to give our **selves** strokes (see Steiner, Chap. 8).

If we were more willing to give each other 'strokes', we would probably also be willing to touch each other more (as the term implies). Many New Age people have argued that touching not only makes us **feel** better but that it might actually be **necessary** to us — to our physical and emotional well-being and to our intellectual development. Joseph Chilton Pearce reports that Kenyan and Ugandan babies are the happiest in the world — and are more **cognitively** advanced than North American babies — primarily because their mothers stroke and 'stroke' them constantly.

The fear that a society of 'touchers and feelers' (as we put it so priggishly) might be oppressive and forced, is a fear that comes right from the 'stroke economy': from our assumption that we'd have to give **more** than we wanted to give. As one woman puts it (in **The Hite Report**), 'Perhaps if we all had more people we related to with physical affection and touching, . . . we wouldn't necessarily feel that every contact points in the direction of intercourse so that you don't feel free to take Step A unless you are willing to take Step B, C, D, etc. . . . (Perhaps) we'd have a generally more loving atmosphere in which to dwell'.

(2) **Decentralization and 'Decriminalization': The New Age Solution to Most Criminal Behaviour.** New Age politics believes that most crime is caused by our lack of shared culture and common purpose. (It is definitely not caused by economic deprivation. Several studies have shown that crime and delinquency do not vary significantly from one socio-economic group to another — only the **kinds** of crimes change. The poor steal, the rich 'embezzle'.)

The lack of a common bond among us is not only the leading **cause** of crime, it has also made us **need** a criminal population in our midst. Eugene Doleschal and Nora Klapmuts (in Dodge, ed.) argue that the identification of acts as criminal 'allows a harmless channelling of aggressions, while at the same time reinforcing group solidarity', and that the public denunciation of criminal acts helps to reinforce the norms on which the society is based.

New Age politics has no illusions that a New Age society would do away with all crime, but New Age society could certainly do away with say 90 percent of all crime. George Leonard points out that half of it — literally, 50 percent — could be done away with tomorrow by eliminating all laws against 'non-victim' behaviour — gambling, drunkenness, vagrancy, drug use, sex 'deviancy' and the like. And most of the rest of it could be eliminated by the kind of drastic decentralization of our society envisaged in Chap. 15. If communities became coherent, self-reliant, human-scale; if communities were based on the New Age ethics and values and were allowed to interpret them in their own way; if communities were encouraged to be as open or as exclusive, as fluid or as purposive as they liked; if it were possible for us to **choose to live in a community that suited** our particular temperament and interests — then we would no longer suffer from a 'lack of shared culture and common purpose'. And society would no longer need the 'social glue' that a criminal element provides.

How realistic is this? As Klapmuts points out (in Dodge, ed.), **most** post-1960's criminology theory 'views crime and delinquency as symptoms of disorganization of the community as much as of individual personalities — **or even as a product of an inadequate mesh between the two**' (emphasis mine).

As for those of us who were still driven to criminal behaviour: the traditional prison or training school is ineffective (in fact there's now much evidence to show that the prison does more harm than good — to all concerned), not to mention that it costs upwards of $15,000 a year to keep one criminal in jail! On the other hand, a New Age community setting — human-scale, life-oriented — would make 'community-based alternatives' to prison far more likely to succeed than they are at present. Even in Prison society, numerous studies have shown that community-based alternatives can handle the offender at least as effectively as prison and at a fraction of the cost.

(3) **Truth in Service to Wholeness: The New Age Alternative to Truth in Service to Power.** What is 'objectivity'? Usually it is defined as the separation of facts and values in the service of 'truth'. But why do we adhere to the separation of facts and values? What makes 'truth for its own sake' such a compelling goal? It must be that 'truth' refers to something more than 'reliability' or 'validity', that the notion of objective truth is what sociologist Alvin Gouldner calls a 'crypto-ethic' concealing certain compelling **values**.

In Prison society it is, in fact, easy to see what these values are. Underlying the quest for objectivity has long been the hope of asserting our selves **over** one another and over nature; in Prison society, 'objective' truth is truth that serves the purposes of coercive power. But it is possible, as Gouldner points out, to see another meaning in 'objectivity', even today, and that is the longing for wholeness — the desire to tell the whole story, the desire to transcend or embrace the differences that divide us both within and without.

In New Age society, objectivity would serve the purposes of wholeness rather than coercive power, and 'objective' truth would be truth that served the purposes of human unity both within and without: (a) it would recognize the reality and validity of our non-material needs (for love and esteem, for self-actualization, for spiritual development); (b) it would recognize the reality and validity of all four states of consciousness (i.e. of the trans-material worldview); and (c) it would recognize the validity of the New Age ethics and political values, which are implicit in the trans-material worldview.

(4) **Human Growth as a Social Value: The New Age Alternative to All Social Hierarchies.** In Chap. 10 I argued that in New Age society we would be oriented to life (rather than things or death) and that we would, therefore, necessarily be off of the production-consumption merry-go-round. Unfortunately, however, for hundreds of years — ever since the Prison came down in full force — most of us have been able to meet our needs for esteem (and self-esteem) only in the world of production and consumption — only by 'making it' in terms of some status hierarchy or other, only by making a lot of money, say, or by running a handsome home. So how could we meet our needs for esteem in New Age society?

Every society has what sociologists call a 'central project'. In our society (characterized as it is by the Prison and its institutions, and by the materialist worldview), our central project has been **material growth**. Little wonder, then, that we've only been able to meet our esteem needs in the world of production-consumption! In New Age society we would be free of the Prison and its institutions, and so our central project would be shaped by the trans-material worldview (which is natural to us) and by the New Age ethics and political values that it implies. The various New Age communities and regions might define their central projects somewhat differently from one another, but if it had to be summed up in a phrase I think it would everywhere be stated as: **human growth**. (Willis Harman would state it more precisely, as follows: (1) promoting individual growth in awareness, creativeness, love, etc.; (2) evolving social institutions to foster such growth; and (3) participating with nature in the further evolution of the species.)

Where does this leave us in terms of esteem? It leaves us with this: we would obtain our esteem in New Age society not so much for **what we did** in the world of production-consumption, but for **who we were** as human beings. We would be able to meet our needs for esteem if and when we were meeting our personal growth needs (or trying to meet them).

There is a built-in safeguard here against new kinds of status hierarchies. For anyone who took pride in the fact that he or she felt 'more evolved' than another would only be demonstrating how **little** he or she had grown: how little he or she had emancipated him- or herself from the pride nexus (father of the cash nexus). And would be told so, in no uncertain terms!

If there were any such thing as a system of social ranking in New Age society (probably impossible to avoid, at least for the next couple of generations), it would consist of this: that people would be more highly esteemed if there were not only trying to meet their own growth needs, but were trying to help other people meet their growth needs as well (and remember, our basic material needs are included among our growth needs; see Chap. 8).

Chapter 15 — Localization: Celebration of Diversity

Localization is 'decentralization' with a positive focus. Localization is decentralization as seen from the perspective of the New Age. Let me attempt a formal definition: **Localization** is the process of the continent evolving in the direction of its natural diversity by means of the spread of community consciousness and the evolution of various forms of community and regional self-reliance.

As we become more self-reliant, it makes sense that we'd want our dwelling places to become more self-reliant too. As we become more cooperative, it follows that we'd want our communities to cooperate with other places consciously and voluntarily, rather than because they had to (as they have to in the traditional nation-state).

Most New Age people believe that the most important unit of government should be, not the nation, and not the state or province, but the 'community district'. Community district is a New Age term for: rural districts, 'intentional communities', cities, and big-city neighbourhoods (or any self-chosen combination of same). On the other hand, most New Age people also believe that you don't make non-viable people viable simply by splitting a nation into a number of community-districts. The initiative has to come from the district itself. (Otherwise the district is in danger of being controlled by a tiny minority of 'true believers', or a smaller, more competent, and so less vulnerable bureaucracy.)

As New Age society evolves, New Age people would want community districts to have the right to redefine their relationship to the nation-state. Some community districts might opt for complete independence. Still, probably most community districts would choose to retain some kind of formal association with the nation-state (economic common market, open borders, etc.). Community districts might redefine their association in such a way as to obtain full power to decide on such things as: levels of taxation (if any), kinds of social services (if any), kinds of institutions, housing and employment policies, income distribution, foreign policy, defence policy (the Quebec independence movement has coined a name for this: 'sovereignty-association'). Community districts might also seek out new relationships with other community districts (not necessarily neighbouring ones); some community districts might get together to form autonomous or semi-autonomous regions.

Under this plan (which is emerging now among many New Age thinkers), much of the U.S. and Canada might remain at least formally intact. And the life-giving diversity of the society might be increased a hundredfold.

Just as the American colonies felt it was necessary to separate from England at the end of the 18th century — partly for economic reasons and partly, I would say primarily, in order to become themselves — so many community districts that prized the New Age ethics and values might want to enter into a different relationship with the nation-state. Partly to eliminate a number of monolithic institutions, and partly to become themselves, to become more specific manifestations of themselves (of the collective identity of their residents).

Furthermore:

(1) Community power would make it possible for us to take real responsibility for the decisions that affected our lives — to replace our monolithic institutions with biolithic ones;

(2) Self-governing communities would have less need for bureaucracies and hierarchies than centralized governments do;

(3) 'Until the community knows what it wants and what it can do on its own, it is in no position to bargain effectively with global corporations' or with anyone (Barnet and Muller);

(4) Community power would encourage us to get to know our communities, at least as well as we now 'know about' Manhattan and L.A. from our television screens. Without a substantial degree of autonomy and self-sufficiency, there would be no reason for community to be 'aware of itself' (Wendell Berry's definition of community);

(5) 'Everything that pertains to the feeling of belonging to a place has almost nothing to do with county, state, province, and national boundaries' (Peter Berg, in **Planet-Drum** no. 4). Community and regional autonomy would allow us to establish boundaries that made more geo-cultural sense.

(6) Community power would make our immediate surroundings central and interesting and vital. Therefore, it would help make us central and interesting and vital **to each other**.

It is, of course, impossible for a district to obtain any kind of political autonomy without also — and first — acquiring a considerable degree of economic self-sufficiency; and in Chap. 21, sect. I-9, I look at some of the groups, some of the ideas, some of the tactics, that can help us to increase a community's self-sufficiency. But in this chapter my purposes are somewhat different. Sect. I is about our need for community; sect. II introduces the New Age concept of 'synergic' power (as distinct from coercive or anarchic power); sect. III attempts to bring the New Age concepts of community and power together; and sect. IV says something about the role of the regions.

I. Community

Most North Americans have **lost** their sense of community, and no wonder. The average North American moves once every four years, and those of us who are under 40 tend to move more often than that. With predictable results: on the one hand, the transient society encourages a concern with narrowly-defined property values. We buy and keep our homes, etc., with an eye to their expected resale value rather than with a desire to turn them into really unique (not **Better Homes and Gardens** unique) and interesting expressions of who we are. Our neighbourhoods are equally 'unsullied': equally bland. On the other hand, we are more prone to abuse and eventually destroy our living places, because the transient society leaves us without what Wendell Berry calls 'the comfort and the discipline' of old memories and associations. 'Without a complex knowledge of one's place', he warns, and without the 'faithfulness to one's place' on which such knowledge depends, 'it is inevitable that the place will be used carelessly, and eventually destroyed'.

Many of us feel that our 'networks' have been able to replace community. Network is Philip Slater's term for a group of people who think like we do, who have common interests, and who have no territory. There can be networks of friends, political activists, poker players, professionals. By contrast, a community has people — many people — who don't think like we do; who we may think of as boring or prejudiced or even slightly crazy; who may remind us of those parts of our selves that we don't like. 'But it is community that heals', says Lee Swenson (in **Simple Living** no. 7), 'while a network cannot sustain us for long. We are healed by the fresh air of life diversity brings us — others who are different from us can help us fill out, round out ourselves. We need both network and community, but we would do well to know the difference, and get on with living in our community as well as our network'.

Community heals — that is the point. Community tells us things about our selves that we could never learn in any other way. Community nourishes many parts of our selves that need to be nourished. When Konrad Lorenz separated a flock of ducklings from their mother, they became 'imprinted' on Lorenz and followed him around. According to Philip Slater, 'Humans deprived of community can become in a sense "imprinted" on rules, machines, ideologies and bureaucratic structures'. Rene Dubos goes so far as to suggest that we have a 'biological need . . . to be identified with a place'.

What is this 'community' exactly? As a physical place it could be a rural district, a small town, an 'intentional community', a city, or a big-city neighbourhood. David Morris and Karl Hess say that their 'homeliest test' for a big-city neighbourhood is whether or not a person 'can easily walk its boundaries'. But even these hard-nosed political economists recognize that a neighbourhood is more than the sum of its physical parts. 'You or we probably would be hard pressed to define any neighbourhood. Yet, once in one, we would know it'. (In **Planet-Drum** no. 4, Eric Bookhardt and others discuss a New Age science called 'geopsychics' whose subject is the 'phenomena that may be seen as an expression of the consciousness of a locale in its most unique . . . manifestations'.)

To New Age people, community has to do above all with people's **experience** of a place. According to Wendell Berry, community is 'local life aware of itself'. According to David Spangler, community is 'a spirit of the presence (and the potential) of connections and bonds beyond the functional'. According to Arthur Morgan, community is a 'quality of society' present when (many of) its members have such 'traits of mutuality' as 'intimate acquaintance', 'mutual confidence', and a 'feeling of oneness'. (**Zen and the Art of Motorcycle Maintenance** might say: community is Quality-in-a-community-district.)

II. Power

To many of us, says Kat Kinkade of the East Wind Community in Missouri, 'power is a dirty word'. And no wonder. If asked to define the word 'power', most of us would probably say something like 'being able to tell other people what to do'.

We are all familiar with that kind of power. It is what the boss has; it's what our parents had before the boss took over; for women, it's all too often what their husbands have. Most of us are locked into power struggles at home and at work and, if we have strength left over for it, in society, too. The Biblical injunction to 'do unto others as you would have them do unto you' has become translated to 'do unto others before they do unto you'.

The choice seems to be either to be power-full or power-less — and nobody likes to feel powerless. At best we hope for some kind of uneasy truce where the power is 'equalized'.

New Age people have begun to realize that there are a number of different **kinds** of power, and that power doesn't necessarily mean coercion or manipulation. To Jean Baker Miller, feminist psychologist, power is basically 'the capacity to implement'. To Leroy Pelton, psychologist of nonviolence, it's 'potential social influence'. To David Spangler it's 'the capacity to act'.

What's wrong with that? Nothing. The more we're capable of **doing** something, the better.

In their book **Synergic Power**, which is an attempt to synthesize many New Age ideas about power, Jim and Marge Craig call our commonly-accepted notions of power, 'directive power'. According to the Craigs, directive power 'includes any form (of power) in which the initiator intentionally makes people act against their will, their judgement, their interests, or leads them to act blindly without considering their interests and those of others'.

In response to this obviously Prison-bound notion of power, quite a few of us have decided that it's wrong to try to affect the behaviour of others. And that the good society would be a totally permissive and anarchic one (within the limits of the psychologically acceptable). This attitude toward power may not be Prison-bound, but since it's merely a reaction **against** the Prison it's not very likely to change things. The same attitude was common on many communes and in many political groups in the 1960's, and the result was that power was wielded indirectly or 'unofficially' by the charismatic or the energetic or the lucky.

The emerging New Age definition of power, according to the Craigs and others, would mix the concept of 'synergy' with the concept of power-as-the-capacity-to-act. Synergy is another awkward but indispensible New Age word; to the Craigs it means 'working together to benefit myself and others at the same time' or 'the working together of unlike elements to create desirable results unobtainable from any combination of independent efforts'.

Synergic power, then, according to the Craigs, means 'the capacity of an individual or group to increase the satisfactions of all participants by intentionally generating increased energy and creativity'. And they add: 'Synergic power differs radically from directive power in the concern it expresses for other people and the roles it affords them. Any application of synergic power accords with the will, the judgement, and the interests of the other human beings, and it is fully effective only when no energy or creativity is wasted in domination and resistance to domination. For example, we will have exercised synergic power if other people's behaviour becomes more in tune with ours after we have shared information and feelings with them in non-manipulative, non-coercive ways, and have creatively cooperated with them to discover new solutions to problems or conflicts. . . . The more synergic we observe (a person's) power to be, the more fully does (he or she) seem to display the same positive attitudes toward his adversaries as he does toward his followers and allies'.

That's probably the key to seeing if a person is wielding (trying to wield) directive or synergic power. Watch how he or she handles those who disagree.

The Craigs give a nice example of using synergic power. If I want to plant a vegetable garden and you want to plant a flower garden on the same plot of land, how do we settle the matter? The 'fair' way, according to the directive power approach, would be to split the land 50-50 between us. But that wouldn't really satisfy either of us. From a synergic power perspective, say the Craigs, 'every initial request or demand is seen as a proposed solution to a usually unstated problem'. And the point is to explore that deeper level. . . .

With regard to the garden, we might find that behind my desire to plant vegetables is really a desire to do **anything** creative, and-or that behind yours is a desire to grow the most luxuriant flowers possible. So I might end up writing **New Age Politics** and shopping at the local health food store. Or you might end up growing even more luxuriant flowers in a greenhouse on the roof. Or we might find a neighbour who might let one of us plant our garden in his or her yard (because he or she liked flowers, or in exchange for some of the vegetables). As the Craigs put it, 'The search for new solutions becomes an adventure in openness and creativity that is far more satisfying than attacking or resisting each other's initial proposals'.

The concept of 'synergic power' has some extremely far-reaching political implications. Especially, it means that our traditional ways of deciding things — by voting and by collective bargaining — may be less constructive than the small-group decision-making process, so long as the small groups are (1) open and representative, and (2) based on synergic power. For in voting, however 'fair', the winners, ostensibly the majority, are able to force the minority to give in to their wishes, thereby making them 'losers'. And in collective bargaining (which is not confined to the conference table but goes on all the time between lovers, friends, and political associates), two or more 'adversaries' face each other, each of them claiming to be 'right', each of them unwilling to 'give an inch' . . . until the process of bargaining begins; and this is often a swapping of point for point without regard for the rightness or wrongness of the individual points.

Most New Age thinkers would put small, synergic groups at the heart of the decision-making process. For example, Frederick Thayer, a political scientist, has worked out a 'theory of extended face-to-face discussion within an almost infinite number of small groups'. Similarly, John Friedmann, a sociologist, would organize communities according to the principle of 'cellular structure'. Communities would have as their smallest unit the 'task-oriented working group' of maybe 50 members each, temporary, voluntary, and relatively autonomous, and these groups would come together in 'working group assemblies' to exchange information and set policy.

III. Community Power

So far we've seen that New Age people would want to make the important decisions at the community district level (rather than at the national level). And we've seen that they'd want to make these decisions through the use of 'synergic' power — which means, through the use of the 'small group' decision-making process. We're now about ready to see how New Age communities might choose to govern themselves. Only one more thing needs to be added. In most socialist and anarchist scenarios, the new society would be run by 'workers' councils'. But in New Age communities we would each have a right to a say in things, whether or not we were able to structure our activities into 'jobs', for the simple reason that we are all alive and therefore equally valuable; equally One; and equally **responsible** for planetary stewardship.

So. How could we structure the decision-making process so that all of us could have a say — a real say — in the decisions that were made?

New Age activists believe that we should be able to do more than just advise decision-makers of our views (at public meetings, say). This type of 'citizen participation', which is common now in North America as well as in the socialist countries, still puts us in the role of petitioners (for the redress of grievances), of people asking someone **else** to solve our problems **for** us. It doesn't allow us to assume any real responsibility.

On the other hand, most New Age activists believe that we shouldn't **all** get to decide on **all** issues through a kind of continuing referendum system (a scheme advocated by many 'futurists' and anarchists). As Robert Theobald points out, it simply isn't true that all of us are equally able to make decisions on all issues or that all of us are willing to spend a great deal of time in thinking about each issue. Probably most of us will always be oriented to private life, not to public life, at least for the greater part of our lives; after a while even Castro recognized that the revolutionary is a personality-type, not a valid model for the new 'Socialist Man'. In New Age society, socially committed people would also be regarded as a personality-type — a necessary type, but no more noble a type than the others.

It isn't hard to see that the choices we've been considering, no-final-decisions-by-us and all-final-decisions-by-all-of-us, are products of the Prison (of its tendency to dichotomize). New Age activists believe that everyone should have the opportunity to make decisions but that our commitment to an issue and to the decision-making process itself should carry some weight. Therefore, most New Age activists believe that those of us who are informed about (or concerned about) a particular issue should have the opportunity to take part in the decision-making process — maybe even the final decision-making process — on that issue.

The 'typical' New Age community, then, if I can even speak of such a thing, might be organized as follows. Decision-making units would be made up of Groups of all those people who were informed and-or concerned about an area, problem, issue, crisis, etc. One Group might be in charge of housing policy, a second Group in charge of medicare policy, a third Group in charge of New Age festivals, and so on. And there could be 'ad hoc' Groups formed around passing issues, and Groups formed to **prevent** issues from arising. . . . The point is that the Groups themselves, and not their (or our!) elected representatives, would be making the actual decisions about housing policy, the rites of spring, etc.

If a Group felt it was becoming too big, it could, among other things, divide into sections and have sectional representatives come to a final decision.

Some New Age communities might choose to have these Groups present their decisions to an elected governing body or to a general assembly. Other communities might choose to have Group leaders come together in community congress. Still other communities might allow final decision-making power to rest with the Groups — though a governing body would have to decide how much money to give each Group. All kinds of variations could be worked out.

It hardly needs to be added, though, that this form of government could only work if we were committed to using synergic power rather than power based on the force of money or numbers. Without a firm commitment to discovering and then meeting each other's deepest needs, there could be no open discussion in Groups, and we wouldn't be able to learn and grow and change through the process of Group discussion. Without synergic power, there would be a multitude of hostile and competing Groups.

On the other hand, the fact that we were free of the Prison would make the success of this genuinely democratic form of government a real possibility. Versions of it are being used successfully **now** at Findhorn, at Twin Oaks, and at several other intentional communities.

IV. 'Watershed Politics'

Today, regional development calls for the formation of an 'infrastructure' of multimillion-dollar dams, power networks, and superhighways. This infrastructure then leads (hopefully!) to the development of extractive industries, huge farms or ranches, a tourist industry, and 'urban areas', as well as to the establishment or 'uplevelling' of all the monolithic institutions that I dealt with in Chap. 7. You don't have to be a committed New Age activist to see that this process displaces many people (often to the urban slums), consumes terrible quantities of energy, minerals, water, and land, makes us almost completely dependent on faraway markets, imported necessities, mass transportation and the like, and destroys the integrity of the regional culture.

Fortunately, there is an alternative.

Those of us who take the New Age ethics seriously are more and more coming to believe in what has been called 'watershed politics'. Watershed politics, says Lee Swenson (in **Simple Living** no. 7), 'could be seen as linking the size and scale of your political and cultural community to the biology of the place. It means adopting a bioregional process of working from the ground up, letting the culture flow from the natural base. When this happened organically, all over the world, it was what gave us the rich, rich diversity of culture' that we're now in danger of losing, thanks to the descent of the Prison and its institutions.

The clearest and most practical single expression of watershed politics to date has come from Peter van Dresser, economist, tax refuser, and lifelong simple liver. Van Dresser's thesis is that the essential infrastructure for a region isn't dams, power-plants and superhighways but 'a thriving permanent population sustaining a way of life ecologically adapted to the regional environment'.

Central to van Dresser's argument (and to the watershed politics philosophy) is a redefinition of the concept of 'natural resources'. The monolithic mode of development defines natural resources as anything that can be sold on the continental market for a profit. Peter van Dresser defines natural resources differently, as all those resources that can 'fill the bulk of human needs'. And he claims that most of our bioeconomic regions contain enough arable land to raise a region's food; enough timber and minerals to construct a region's buildings, equipment and tools; enough plant and animal life for meat and fuel and textiles. 'Out of such taken-for-granted factors', he says, 'an ingenious and intelligent people can fabricate most of the necessities and many of the embellishments of a good society'.

Obviously, watershed politics is the regional equivalent of the drive for **community** autonomy and self-sufficiency that we examined above. The goals of the two movements are substantially the same. And even though the people involved are, by and large, not the same, I think that most of them would agree that the two movements reinforce each other and are going to grow into each other over time.

Chapter 16 — Planetization: Celebration of Unity

'Planetization' is a process that's complementary to localization — and necessary to it (since if communities and regions and nation-states want to be more self-reliant, then they're going to have to learn to cooperate together in an effective way). Here is a formal definition: **planetization** is the process of our species evolving in the direction of its natural unity by means of the spread and deepening of what many New Agers have begun to call 'planetary consciousness' and the evolution of an effective system of 'planetary guidance'. (But don't forget, 'union differentiates' — Teilhard de Chardin.)

Or, more simply: planetization is the (effective) application of the New Age ethics and political values to planetary problems.

Section I takes a brief look at nine planetary problems that most of us consider to be basically insoluble, or soluble only by force of arms. Sect. II introduces the concept of planetary consciousness. Sect. III introduces the concept of planetary guidance, the New Age alternative to Prison-generated ideas such as world government and Prison-generated realities such as the growing political power of the multinational corporations. Finally, sect. IV suggests some New Age solutions to the nine planetary problems cited in sect.

I — solutions that planetary consciousness and a planetary guidance system might make possible.

(New Age people prefer to say 'planetary' rather than 'world' for a number of reasons. 'World' implies a system of nation-states, 'planetary' implies a kaleidoscope ((calliope?)) of communities, regions and nations. 'World' implies a place where people dominate the ecosphere and dominate each other, 'planetary' implies a place where people cooperate with the ecosphere and cooperate with each other. 'World' implies that the Earth is the centre of the cosmos, 'planetary' that the Earth is an integral part of the cosmos.)

Monolithically developed countries will be referred to as 'MDC's' and insufficiently developed countries, the 'Third World', as 'IDC's'. Biolithically developed countries would be referred to as 'BDC's', but there aren't any.

I. Welcome to the World!

(1) **Food**. One-quarter of the human race experiences severe hunger or famine during some part of every year (Shurtleff and Aoyagi). Seventy percent of children in the IDC's are suffering from malnutrition (Tinbergen). Between 10 and 20 million deaths a year — about 40,000 a day — are directly or indirectly attributable to starvation or malnutrition: diseases that are only nuisances to most of us are devastating to the malnourished (Ehrlich and Ehrlich).

(2) **Population**. The earth's population is doubling now every 35 years (Shurtleff and Aoyagi), and what is now being discussed with **hope** is the achievementof a 'reasonably stationary population' somewhere in the middle or latter half of the 21st century, at a level of **12 to 20 billion** (Tinbergen). (Today we are 'only' four billion.)

(3) **Income distribution**. Today about a billion human beings (try to) live on an **annual per capita income of $75 or less** (Ward). Over the next 50 years, the average income gap between the market economy MDC's and Latin America is expected to **increase** from 5:1 to about 8:1. The gap between the MDC's and South Asia and Tropical Africa will, however, remain about the same: 20 to 1 (Mesarovic and Pestel).

(4) **Trade**. With 71 percent of the world's population, the IDC's account for only seven percent of world industrial production. Therefore, their annual deficits are going up at an astronomical rate, and their share of world trade is actually decreasing due to deteriorating terms of trade (in 1974 the IDC's paid 65 percent more for their imports, though they only bought 20 percent more goods) (Tinbergen).

(5) **Aid**. In 1961, the market economy MDC's agreed to target one percent of their Gross National Product (GNP) to the poor nations, with 0.7 percent to be spent in the form of 'development assistance' (outright grants). By 1975 the flow of development assistance from the MDC's had **fallen to less than half** that figure, and was expected to fall to 0.28 percent by the end of the decade (Tinbergen).

(6) **Resources**. 'To raise all the 3.6 billion people of the world of 1970 to the American standard of living would mean . . . the extraction of some 75 times as much iron as is now extracted annually, 100 times as much copper, 200 times as much lead, 75 times as much zinc, and 250 times as much tin. The needed iron is theoretically available, . . . but a serious limit could be imposed by a shortage of molybdenum, which is needed to convert iron to steel. Needed quantities of the other materials far exceed all known or inferred reserves. . . . Of course, to raise the standard of living of the projected world population of the year 2000 to today's American standard would require doubling all of the above figures . . . ' (Ehrlich and Ehrlich).

(7) **Multinational corporations**. The multinational corporation doesn't train people in entrepreneurial skills (which the IDC's need badly), and the much-vaunted 'transfer of technology' is often minimized because research and development is generally carried out by the parent company, and because the technology itself is often closely held (Falk). Net foreign direct investment into the IDC's tends to be **one-third or less of the investment income outflow** — so much for the much-vaunted 'transfer of capital' (U.N. report).

Without changes in present trends, multinational corporations will control more than 40 percent of planetary production by the end of the 1980's (Tinbergen).

(8) **Arms**. In 1948, worldwide expenditures on 'defence' budgets totalled $65 billion in constant (1970) dollars. In 1976 they totalled $334 billion (Robert Anson, in **New Times**, 5 Aug. '77). That's about 25 times the amount that's spent each year by everyone, everywhere, on development assistance (Inge Thorsson, in Tinbergen).

Between 1965 and 1974, the IDC's increased their share of world military spending from six percent to 17 percent. There was no increase in their share of world financial resources during that time (Tinbergen).

The MDC's spend about $20 billion annually on military research. Close to **half a million scientists and engineers** are involved in this research (Donald Neff, in **New Times**, ibid.). One of the promising new fruits of this research is the 'neutron bomb'. Technically speaking it is an 'enhanced radiation warhead', not a nuclear weapon, so it's much more likely to be used in the next war. It is designed to kill people slowly, over days or weeks (your cuts won't heal, your hair will fall out, your breathing will become heavier and heavier, you'll begin to spit blood, you'll fall into a coma) but buildings, **things**, will be left intact (Anson).

(9) **Human Rights**. In Indonesia there are 100,000 political prisoners (people who've been imprisoned for their race, religion or beliefs). Most of them have never been tried. And most of them have been in detention for 10 years or more (Amnesty International; International League for Human Rights). In China, possibly 16 million people are in 'reform through labour' camps where people are kept indefinitely or until they're considered to be 'remould-

ed'; and an indeterminate number are in 'education through labour' camps where sentences are at least set (Jean Pasqualini, **Prisoner of Mao** — a book that's not unsympathetic to Mao, despite its title). In Uruguay, one out of every 500 persons is a political prisoner, and Amnesty International has documented evidence of literally hundreds of cases of death by torture there. Many Uruguayan officers volunteer to work even on their days off so they can witness the 'interrogation' of women prisoners (AI). In the Soviet Union political prisoners are often sent to 'mental hospitals' where patients are regularly terrorized by 'orderlies' and given unwarranted treatment with drugs (AI; ILHR).

II. Planetary Consciousness

What can we say to facts like these? Our most characteristic response, I suppose, is to look away; and our second most characteristic response is to throw up our hands in despair. Those of us who've tried to confront these facts in some way can be divided up into two broad groups, which I like to call the 'internationalists' and the 'planetarians'.

International consciousness sees the world whole, but from the perspective of a particular nation-state or ideology, whose interests are held to be **separate from** and **prior to** those of the whole. International consciousness believes very strongly that the Prison and its institutions represent 'modern' consciousness and institutions (a hundred years ago it might have said: 'civilization itself') and that 'progress' or even 'survival' depends on spreading the Prison and its institutions as fast and as far as possible.

Planetary consciousness recognizes that the world is full of dread and danger — but also promise and possibility. (Both recognitions — danger and possibility — are inherent in the often repeated planetary perception that, as Margaret Mead puts it, 'Our technology has increased the size of interdependent units to include the entire planet'.)

Planetary consciousness recognizes our oneness with all humanity and in fact with all life, everywhere, and with the planet as a whole.

Planetary consciousness recognizes the interdependence of all humanity, of all life, and of all our nation-states.

Planetary consciousness sees each of us as 'cells in the body of humanity', as Planetary Citizens puts it — with all the obligations that implies. (Rolling Thunder conceives of the Earth as a body, 'a gigantic body of a conscious, struggling, living being', and says that we 'have to learn to be within it — like cells'.)

For some of us, planetary consciousness may come as the direct result of an experience, even so simple an experience as stalking the halls of the U.N. or canvassing a neighbourhood for a community project. For others of us it may come from a simple intuitive understanding of all people as brothers and sisters with a common destiny. Margaret Mead says that it comes from being a part of a multigenerational community — 'All you need is your child, grandchild, or someone in front of you that you care about and a little bit of imagination'. I think it's obvious that it comes (or can come) from the trans-material worldview, from learning to be at home in all four states of consciousness.

Planetary events are, in a sense, **conspiring to inspire** us to recognize our oneness and interdependence. Our modern means of transportation and communication have recently put us in touch with each other — continuously and totally — for the very first time. Then there was the race to the moon, which for all its surface irrationality, did cause us — for the first time ever — to see our planet from outer space. 'In an instant of space exploration', says a Planetary Citizens publication, 'we became increasingly aware that life is precious in the universe. And somehow, we began to see the inhabitants of the earth as one family — no longer "we and they" — but interdependent'. The feeling of oneness and interdependence had some obvious political implications. 'Almost spontaneously, the need was recognized by concerned people in many countries: the human family must find a way to work together if human life on earth is to be preserved and improved'.

III. The Planetary Guidance System

Internationalists tend to believe that our problems can best be solved by a strong world government, by a kind of nation-state writ large. (One that would be based on their own political philosophies.) Many planetarians have begun to speak out **against** the concept of world government as it has been traditionally understood. Ervin Laszlo, a systems analyst who is running the Club of Rome study on 'Goals for a Global Society', notes that even the large nation-states are too richly diverse to govern by a single political philosophy, 'yet diversity on the global level is incomparably richer still. If a kind of world government would head it which we now know from national political experience, it would almost certainly need to exercise highly coercive policies to stay in power'. Richard Falk, professor of international law and a member of the World Order Models Project, adds, 'There is nothing intrinsic about the idea of world government that precludes elitism, mass poverty, ecological decay, or even large-scale violence'.

Many other planetarians have made the point that our problems aren't really institutional at all, but are problems of will (and therefore ultimately of ethics and values). Barbara Ward, for example, claims that we would have no difficulty in working out a 'just political framework' **if we wanted to** — 'What is lacking is political will'. Similarly, Donald Keys, President and Registrar of Planetary Citizens, says that there's 'no dearth of possible blueprints (for world order), and that the logic in most of them is impeccable', but that the real or at least the deeper problems have to do with the lack of a shared set of values on the **basis** of which we could solve our problems.

In response to these understandings, some New Age people have begun to argue for the polar opposite of a 'world government'. In their view, all we really need is a 'maximally functioning communications system'; once we devise an adequate set of values and an adequate philosophical basis for them, access to relevant information should be enough; and setting up a world 'authority' that could wield any kind of power would almost certainly do more harm than good.

I believe that the New Age ethics and political values imply some commitment to working in the world as we know it. And I have no trouble agreeing with Laszlo that it 'appears unreasonable to assume that a dependable form of mutual accomodation could evolve among the world's peoples' without some form of institutional guidance — especially since our situation is so unprecedented (planetary constraints have never limited growth before) and so dangerous and urgent.

So what we need to evolve is a kind of institutional system that falls between the extremes of monolithic world government and power-less communications. An institutional system that would (a) allow us to deal with the nine world problems listed above (among others!); (b) have as its main, acknowledged purpose the furthering of the New Age ethics and political values (however these might be described); and (c) allow us to plug into it gradually and voluntarily. Following Laszlo and others, I'll call it a system of 'planetary guidance' (it would, after all, seek to be the 'central guidance mechanism' for Spaceship Earth).

A planetary guidance system, as opposed to a 'world government', could exercise some control over global processes without having to deny different ideological systems the right of existence. As Laszlo points out, a guidance system would recognize that different political and economic structures may have the same **effects** on the environment — for example, a socialist steel mill pollutes neither more nor less than a capitalist one — and it would focus its attention on those effects.

In other words, the planetary guidance system would **regulate** society, not **organize** it. It would inform governments and corporations of the potentially harmful effects of their activities (especially with regard to the New Age ethics and political values) and make recommendations to them. If the harmful behaviour continued, the regulation system would have the power to impose political and economic sanctions — sanctions that, in an increasingly interdependent and cooperative world, would probably be decisive.

Planetarians tend to be extremely pragmatic about the shape of the future guidance system. Probably most planetarians see it as an outgrowth of the U.N. The U.N. doesn't really fail in conception, says Donald Keys, 'it fails from lack of support by the member states who are so reluctant to allow any world organization to assume rival authority, rival jurisdiction to what they wish to retain for themselves even if it means the death of humanity'. Certainly few planetarians would deny that the U.N. mirrors the actual state of the world's readiness to cooperate — that it is a 'reality-mirror', as Planetary Citizens puts it — and that our main task must therefore be, not to change the mirror, but to change the values and priorities that the mirror reflects.

Richard Falk would like to see the planetary guidance system evolve in the direction of a 'wide dispersion of authority and distribution of power'. Similarly, Margaret Mead says, 'For the planet to work as a whole system, you need a series of systems, not just one system. Any one system can crack'. According to Keys, these views are more or less shared by the U.N., which has for some time now been establishing a series of 'departments of planetary management' in the fields of, for example, health, education, agriculture, (atomic) energy, economic development, population and environment. 'Almost without public awareness, a pattern has emerged: There will not be a unitary "world state" with centralized powers. Instead there will be a system of interrelated departments each with its own area of competence and mechanisms for governance, as well as a system of representation from the world community. They will remain ultimately responsible to the main Organs of the United Nations — the General Assembly and Security Council'.

Despite these positive changes, nearly all planetarians are hopeful that the U.N. will evolve more speedily than it has so far; and many have their own ideas of where it should go. For example, Falk would like to see the U.N. evolve into or be replaced by a 'World Assembly' made up of three chambers: an Assembly of Governments (roughly equivalent to the present General Assembly); an Assembly of Peoples (kind of like the American House of Representatives or the Canadian Parliament); and an Assembly of Organizations and Associations. Mead would like to see the guidance system work without reference to the system of nation-states. And Frederick Thayer and John Friedmann would have their small, synergic, face-to-face groups at the community level, send representatives to similar groups at the regional level, and so on up to the planetary level.

IV. Planetary Solutions

With planetary consciousness and a planetary guidance system, we could make a lot of headway against the nine problems that I mentioned in sect. I. Here are some ideas that planetary thinkers and activists have been coming up with — ideas that are rooted in the New Age ethics and political values.

(1) **Food.** Every society should try to be self-sufficient in food production. Rather than going abroad for luxury produce, societies should seek to improve the quantity and quality of their own produce. 'A native rice-bean-fish standard would become a better rice-bean-fish, not a foreign and dearer meat-carrot-pea' (Kohr).

For the IDC's to become self-sufficient food producers, they are going to have to carry out thorough-going programmes of agrarian reform. At the same time, we — the MDC's — are going to have to agree 'not to strengthen the powerful vested interests that have been delaying, distracting, or stopping those reforms' (Myrdal).

(2) **Population.** Theoretically, the planet can feed many more people than it does today, and materialists often use this fact to 'prove' that we are not

overpopulated. I think most planetarians would define overpopulation some-what differently, would say that it has to do with how many people we feel comfortable sharing the Earth with, and how many people the Earth can safely carry. I agree with the Ehrlichs that our rapidly expanding population has already begun to have disastrous, if subconscious, psychological effects on us, leading to the cheapening of life everywhere; I believe that the 'material limits to growth' argument is more than a 'capitalist plot'; and I believe that an enormous population would require an enormously high degree of social organization. Therefore, I believe that our planetary guidance system should strive to bring the planet down to about half its present population — 'down' to about two billion people. Since there are at least **eight times** as many people on earth today as there were in 1800, I don't think two billion represents an 'unnaturally' low figure. (At the same time, I think that many other endangered species should be encouraged to multiply — cougars, wolverines, osprey, linxes, whooping cranes, polar bears and grizzly bears, prairie dogs and prairie chickens, walruses, bison, antelope. . . .)

The most important step that our planetary guidance system can take with regard to population control is to help make economic conditions more secure in the IDC's. The most important step that we can take is to set a good example. . . .

(3) **Income distribution**. In the short run, there should be an increased transfer of wealth from rich to poor countries, and, just as important, an increased transfer of income and resources from the rich minority in the IDC's to the poor majority. (Development strategies in the IDC's should be designed **first of all** to meet people's basic and immediate needs in the areas of food, shelter, clothing and health.) In the longer run, but as soon as possible, a kind of Planetary Treasury should be set up whose purpose would be to promote planetary equity and eliminate planetary poverty. An internationally recognized definition of (degrees of) poverty would have to be worked out.

(4) **Trade**. The IDC's should be encouraged to be more than hewers of wood and drawers of water for the MDC's; to be more self-reliant industrially as well as agriculturally; to be BDC's, in effect. Nations should join together to work out a planetary industrial strategy that could help them in formulating their own self-chosen industrial policies within the limits of planetary energy and resource capacities. These strategies could serve as a basis for negotiation with other parties, for example, with multinational corporations.

(5) **Aid**. Aid is no substitute for the social and economic reforms that can only be carried out by the IDC's themselves. Therefore, aid should **not** be given to regimes that are resisting important reforms (except in emergencies, for humanitarian purposes). Also, aid should not be given 'bilaterally', from one country to another; instead it should be channeled through the guidance system. This would have the effect of restricting the role of national interests in decisions on aid. . . .

(6) **Resources**. 'Mineral resources (should) be viewed as a common heritage of mankind. This concept implies . . . a system of world taxation (on

resource use)' (Tinbergen). Also, a Planetary Energy Authority should be set up to stimulate research on solar and geothermal energy and to make this research available in the form of technical assistance to all governments.

(7) **Multinational corporations.** Multinationals can be useful **under certain circumstances.** For example, a foreign multinational could contract with the government of an IDC 'to set up and manage a new plant for a limited period, say 10 years. The foreign concern could either make a direct investment for the period agreed upon, or could make it a joint project with the state or an indigenous firm. . . . In any case, the contract should assure the foreign concerr a management fee and, in the end, the return at fixed dates of any capital provided, as well as a normal profit on it until then. On its side, it should provide the needed technology and management, but undertake to train and gradually employ personnel from the country itself' (Myrdal).

As a result, the IDC 'would be assured of an industrial start and the needed skills' and would eventually get the plant itself (to manage or pass on to a group of its nationals, or the community, or the employees). And the multinational corporation would make a 'fair' profit.

(8) **Arms.** Complete military disarmament is the final goal. But there can be little real progress along these lines until people are free of the Prison. As we work against the Prison and its institutions, we should also be trying to establish a negotiated time-table for reductions in military budgets; regulate and then prevent altogether the enormous and expanding trade in arms (a $20-billion-a-year business); ban the use of 'unnecessarily' cruel conventional weapons and of chemical weapons; and begin genuine nuclear disarmament.

(9) **Human Rights.** The planetary guidance system should withhold (some agreed-upon percentage of) funds from governments that are abusive of human rights. (Like poverty, human rights would have to be very clearly defined.) Priority should be given to human rights abuses that involve actual physical violence or coercion or are clearly unacceptible to a majority of people in the country concerned. At the very least, the planetary guidance system should make its facilities and a part of its budget to human rights organizations such as Amnesty International and the International League for Human Rights.

Part VI — New Age Economics

Chapter 17 — The New Age Economy

The New Age economy is compatible with either capitalism or socialism (i.e. with private or public ownership of the means of production). Probably most New Age communities would favour some mixture of the two, since New Age society would favour diversity more than purity; and probably some New Age communities would, over time, evolve several new economic 'ism's'. But every New Age economy would — by definition — organize its production and exchange according to some very definite criteria:

1. Community and-or regional self-sufficiency to be promoted;
2. Planetary cooperation and sharing to be promoted;
3. National economic ties to be sought neither more nor less than other planetary ties;
4. New Age ethics and values to be institutionalized ('operationalized');
5. Life oriented behaviour to be promoted (rewarded);
6. Biolithic institutions to be preferred to monolithic institutions;
7. An alternative to the 'job economy' to be provided, possibly in the form of a guaranteed subsistence income or guaranteed access to basic goods and services.

Within the limits of these criteria (which are based on what has been said so far in this book), there is plenty of room for diversity. The purpose of this chapter is to explore (some of) the contours of this diversity. . . .

I. Four Possible Economies

Within the limits of these criteria, there are at least four ways that New Age communities or regions could organize their economies. (Some of these ways overlap; and in practice, I'm sure that New Age communities would develop a hundred hundred variations on these ways.)

(1) **The crafts economy**. 'The human being', says economist E.F. Schumacher, 'enjoys nothing more than to be creatively, usefully, productively engaged with both (his or her) hands and (his or her) brains'. The result of this process he calls 'real production' (to distinguish it from, e.g., planning and paperwork). Monolithic technology has reduced the amount of 'real production' time down to about 3½ percent of all our time, and Schumacher's New Age economy would seek to increase 'real production time' sixfold, partly by reducing the scale (though not necessarily the sophistication) of our technology. 'An incredible thought!' he says. 'Even children would be allowed to make themselves useful, even old people. . . . There would be six times as much time for any piece of work we choose to undertake — enough to make

a really good job of it, to enjoy oneself, to produce real quality, even to make things beautiful. Think of the therapeutic value of real work; think of its educational value'.

The purpose of the crafts economy, then, would be to offer maximum opportunities for life-oriented productive work for all. By 'life-oriented' I think crafts people might mean: the work would take place in workshops of a human scale, rather than in factories; would be performed with tools that people could understand; would proceed at a pace set by the rhythms and needs of human beings; would be deemed socially desirable and necessary by a majority of the members of the community; and would often take place in a cooperative or collective context. A substantial minority of the people in a crafts society would be farmers.

Schumacher says that the crafts economy would not mean 'an enormous extension of working hours', and he gives four reasons why: (1) many paper-pushing jobs, jobs that are a result of our monolithic technology, would disappear; (2) 'there would be little need for mindless entertainment or other drugs, and unquestionably much less illness'; (3) we would no longer make a hard-and-fast distinction between 'working hours' and leisure; and (4) everyone or nearly everyone would **choose** to work.

(Economist Hazel Henderson has said that we could hire a million new postal workers **right now** if we'd 'put them to work handling the mail carefully and lovingly by hand' and if we'd go 'back . . . to the twice-a-day mail service which our forefathers used to take for granted'.)

(2) **The service economy.** 'Instead of devising employment policies aimed at putting people back into precisely the same jobs they have left behind', says futurologist Alvin Toffler, 'it would be far more intelligent to design selective re-employment policies that continue our conversion to a service-oriented society'.

Millions of socially necessary jobs — 20-hour-a-week jobs, 40-hour jobs, or unspecified-number-of-hour jobs (you do what you can, when you can) — could be created **right now** in a variety of fields: reforestation, rat control, work with the mentally ill, work with convicts, work with alcoholics, child care, community health, and so on. All of these jobs could conceivably be carried out in biolithic institutions (even though some service economy advocates, such as Toffler himself, would retain some of our monolithic institutions). Policy analyst Michael Marien (in **Futures**, Oct. '77) says that a service-oriented economy could do away with monolithic institutions so long as (a) we were willing to reduce our workweeks and live simple lifestyles, and (b) 10-20 percent of us were willing to become small-scale farmers.

A service economy would have two great advantages, Toffler explains. First, it could 'help us solve many accumulated social, community, and environmental problems' bequeathed to us by our 'unrestrained economic growth policies'; and, second, 'a service-oriented society is less dependent on high inputs of energy and resources than is a traditional industrial society'.

(3) **The leisure economy.** Political scientist Sebastian de Grazia argues

forcefully and, to some New Agers, convincingly, that the 40-hour work week is debilitating to us (partly just because it's no longer necessary) and that only an economy that maximized leisure would allow us to live 'lives of quality' (Quality). 'Tomorrow's city', he writes, 'slightly mad, not too neat, human, will become a place to stroll, to buy and sell and talk of many things, to eat and drink well, to see beauty and light around. . . . Work, we know, may make a (person) stoop-shouldered or rich. It may even ennoble (him or her). Leisure perfects (him or her)'.

The problem with the leisure economy is that it would — to some extent — have to be based on an energy- and resource-intensive technology. And North America is already using six times more than its fair share of the world's energy and resources. However, this problem would disappear if a New Age community wanted to live at a subsistence level. In their book **Communities**, Paul and Percival Goodman point out that we are actually producing **10 times more than we need** to survive at a reasonable subsistence level (recently that figure has been revised upward, to 14 times). Therefore, if we cut back on production by a factor of 10 or more we'd be able to live in a leisure society **without** being abusive of the New Age ethics and values. Or the leisure society could pay a certain agreed-upon percentage of its mass produced goods to the planetary guidance system, as a kind of resource tax. Everyone could then benefit. (And it's possible that we'll be able to automate our factories someday using renewable energy resources. It **may** be possible — depends on who you read.)

There are so many ways that our jobs could be reduced in **scope** and therefore in time. For example: rather than being hand-delivered, our mail could be put into neighbourhood post-office boxes. If the neighbourhood post offices had lounges and coffee shops, picking up our mail could be an enjoyable social experience. Like going to the well in the old days.

(4) **The household economy.** Economist Scott Burns estimates that we could meet 70-80 percent of our needs **in our homes** by learning to do our own carpentry work, gardening, sewing, etc. and by making use of small-scale, often quite sophisticated technologies that we could share with other members of the community. Burns further estimates that if everyone in the community agreed to work two or three years at jobs that went beyond the scope of what he calls the household economy — for example, if the community instituted a kind of labour-draft — we could then sustain our selves through household work, voluntary work, sharing, and barter for the rest of our lives. (For more on the household economy, see Chap. 18, sect. P.)

The household economy differs from the crafts economy mainly in that the latter would create workshops and factories to do many of the things that we could do for our selves, or that we could obtain for our selves through barter. The household and crafts economies differ from the service economy mainly in that the former are convinced that, as policy analyst John McKnight puts it (in **CoEvolution Quarterly**, Fall '77), 'there is a hidden dilemma in the growth of our services. In order to provide universal work by serving each other, we will need **more** clients who need help, or clients who need **more** help. . . . To develop a serving economy we depend upon more crooked teeth, family disarray, collapsing automobiles, psychic malaise, educational failure, litigious conflict and underdeveloped human potential. . . . A service economy needs people in need'. The household economy differs from the leisure economy mainly in that the latter would remain dependent on many more of our mass production facilities.

II. The Participatory Economy

Many New Age people are critical of our big corporations — for basically two reasons (apart from their size). First, their behaviour is often considered to be irresponsible. Second, they're losing their sense of legitimacy as more and more of us are asking, what gives them the **right** to do what they do?

Socialists and anarchists aren't stumped by these difficulties. At least as a first step, they would have the government take over ('nationalize') the corporations. New Age writers and activists are more inclined to see government ownership as a false solution to these problems, false because it fails to address what New Age business theorist George Lodge sees as the real or underlying question. That question is, as Lodge puts it, 'What are to be the criteria for and means of controlling large bureaucratic entities, whether corporate or governmental?' In Lodge's view, nationalization 'merely pushes our problems from one inadequately controlled bureaucracy to another' and can all too easily become a substitute for our **really figuring out what we want** from our corporations.

In a similar vein, but from a different point of view, New Age economist Jaroslav Vanek — a specialist in workers' self-management — says that the question, 'Who owns the capital?' isn't nearly so important as the question, 'Who controls and manages the firm?' The first question implies that the difference between public and private ownership is the really important one. But the second question is able to take us beyond the second-level differences between capitalism and socialism. After all, a community- or worker-controlled firm is possible under capitalism **or** socialism — and is maybe even more genuinely possible under capitalism, since there aren't any central economic planners under capitalism to tell firms what to do.

The New Age economy would have its own ways of dealing with the problems of corporate responsibility and legitimacy.

Corporate responsibility. New Age communities and regions would (could) acquire the power to **charter** all businesses and industries operating within their territory. These charters would be as general or as detailed, as restrictive or as permissive, as the various communities chose to make them. Probably most charters would say something specific about such questions as: the amount of money that investors would be allowed to make on their investments; the maximum size of firms; the number of community representatives that would sit on each firm's board of directors; and the kinds of corporate issues that would have to be submitted to the board (a crucial point, according to Barnet and Muller). Most charters would undoubtedly allow communities to start their own competing businesses and industries and to engage in joint investments with private or outside investors.

Corporate legitimacy. In the 19th century, corporations derived their authority from the notion of property rights. In the New Age, corporations would derive their authority from the people, or more precisely, from the consent of **all of the people involved** in an enterprise. Therefore, I am sure that most community charters would insist that 'all the people involved in an enterprise' should have the right to **at least participate in some of the decisions** that were made.

Recently some North American firms have been experimenting with limited degrees of worker participation in management. A number of studies of these experiments have been carried out, and are summarized by Frederick Thayer as follows: 'If the objective is to increase productivity, participation helps; if the objective is to increase quality, participation helps; if the objective is to transform work into something which does not alienate the individual performing it, participation helps'.

Men's liberationist Marc Fasteau is particularly excited by the achievements of a new General Foods plant near Topeka, Kansas. This plant had been divided into 'self-governing' work teams of 8-12 members each; and each of these work teams had been given collective responsibility for large parts of the productive process. Individual assignments were made by the teams themselves. Pay increases were geared to the number of jobs a worker could master — in effect, workers were paid for learning about their work. 'No plant rules were laid down by management; instead a commitment was made to let rules evolve through collective experience'.

Even without profit sharing, the results were impressive. Industrial engineers had estimated that 110 workers would be needed to run the plant, but only 70 were needed; greater productivity, minimized waste and avoidance of shutdowns brought major cost savings; and outside the plant an unusually high percentage of workers became involved in community projects.

Some community charters might go so far as to insist that **all** community businesses (or at least, large businesses) be **fully participatory**. The fully evolved 'participatory economy' would have five defining characteristics, according to Vanek (who sees it as an alternative to 'capitalism' and 'socialism'):

(1) **Genuine participation.** Everyone would have the right to participate in management, on the basis of 'one person - one vote'. Some work groups might choose to make all decisions collectively; others might choose to let the 'owners' structure the decision-making process; still others (Vanek feels this might be the norm) might elect officers and a body of representatives and hire an outside manager.

(2) **Income sharing.** All participants would share in the income of the enter-

prise. Workers would have to agree on an income distribution scale. 'A collectively agreed-on share (could) be used for reserve funds, and various types of collective consumption, or investment'.

(3) **Ownership separate from control.** The working community would have the right to control and manage the firm, but only in rare cases would it own the capital assets. The working community might pay a contractual fee to investors, or an agreed-upon percentage of the net income, or rental-and-interest plus — some scheme would have to be worked out.

(4) **Genuine decentralization.** All decision-making units — firms, households, associations, and the 'public sector' — would decide freely on their actions. (This defining characteristic is meant to ward off the possibility of an authoritarian socialism with its top-down economic planning.)

(5) **Freedom of employment.** A person would be free to take, not to take, or to leave a particular job.

(6) **Latitude.** (A sixth 'defining characteristic', not on Vanek's list.) New Age enterprises would give a lot of freedom to those of us who worked in them. We would be able to work in many capacities and at many levels of responsibility. We would be able to rotate our tasks. We would be able to decide how many hours we wanted to work each week. And we would be able to share our jobs with friends.

Some people are already working this way. Susan Steinberg, who has begun to share a teaching job with a friend, says (in **Simple Living**, Winter '77), 'It's remarkable how much more space I feel in my life. . . . The difference, I think, is that my job is no longer my whole life. I can become absorbed in the people in my life and so my life has many more dimensions. . . . Of course, I do have less money and that has taken adjusting to. I've especially had to cut back on the money I spent to entertain myself and to ease the pain: less movies, less eating out, less buying new clothes to counteract my depression. But I also need all those things less'.

III. New Age Capitalism

Especially in North America, many New Age communities might want their economies to be 'based on capitalism'. But it would be a very different capitalism from the one we know today. The capitalism of the New Age — a capitalism that's evolving already in the cracks and on the margins of our society — would reflect the values of a human-scale, life-oriented society, just as today's capitalism reflects the values of a monolithic, thing- and death-oriented society.

But why 'capitalism' at all? Isn't 'socialism' (or 'post-socialism') the aim of radicals everywhere?

Not at all. Many New Agers are more drawn to capitalism (as a theory) than to socialism (as a theory). Three of our main reasons are:

1.) There's been a historical connection between the economic market and political democracy — between economic and political choices. Precisely **because** of capitalism's greater economic competitiveness, it tends to have 'a strong pluralistic thrust' while socialism tends to have 'a built in tendency to contain plurality' (Peter Berger). Which isn't to say that competition is absent from socialism, only that it's expected to take a different (and less open) form. In socialism, the competition is 'an endless maneuvering for position within the bureaucratic hierarchies'.

2.) Capitalism is often spoken of as a way of concentrating economic and political power. But New Age entrepreneur Robert Schwartz states, 'Capitalism is a method of spreading the power, not concentrating it. Private property and individual production are **systems for the dispersal of power**. The absence of private property almost universally leads to the concentration of power in the state — with an attendant deadening of individuality. . . . The principal pay-off of capitalism is not that it produces goods but that it produces islands of independence'. Schwartz concludes, 'Capitalism, for all its faults, creates a feisty, independent citizenry with private personal, property and local power bases'.

3.) Socialism is often said to be more **moral** than capitalism, because socialism is supposed to make it harder for people to take advantage of one another. But according to Nikolai Berdyaev, the greater degree of constraint in socialism represents no moral victory. Instead it suggests that socialism has a rather pessimistic view of human nature, even a cynical one; whereas the optimism behind the assumptions of free-market capitalism is great indeed.

Basically, capitalism can work well in a society where people are free of the psychological need to control and exploit one another. So we might expect that many New Age communities will move from a kind of socialism to a kind of New Age capitalism as their members get more and more free of the Prison — thus reversing the 'dialectical movement' that Marx felt was taking us 'inevitably' to communism.

So — back to New Age capitalism.

Robert Schwartz believes that the emerging New Age entrepreneur — a species that his School for Entrepreneurs is helping to bring about — may be 'the ultimate agent of change in making the transition to a new way of living'. (Just as a different kind of entrepreneur was the 'ultimate agent' in bringing the present society about.) The new entrepreneurs differ from the old in at least three ways, according to Schwartz: in their motivation, in the kind of product they offer, and in their relationship to the market.

The new entrepreneurs are motivated not only or even primarily by a desire for money, but by a desire to express themselves in some creative and healing way. 'Right livelihood', says a pamphlet put out by the School for Entrepreneurs, 'means that work should not only provide a living but also develop selfhood, foster companionship and nourish the earth. If a business makes money but alienates its members from one another, from themselves and from nature, it is a livelihood — but it is not a Right Livelihood . . . '.

The new entrepreneurs want to produce a new kind of product, not 'services' in the traditional sense so much as what Schwartz calls 'problem-solving things of a subtler nature'. Transactional analysis and Actualizations and recreation-learning packages, for example, are 'products in a sense, but they actually are problem-solving or growth services. They're part of a new kind of education . . . '.

Finally, the new entrepreneurs want to establish a new relationship to the market. In capitalism today, money is the primary thing; then the idea; then the entrepreneur. It's like businessman Carl Frederick says in his book about Erhard Seminars Training: as it is today, first you have, then you do, then you are. In New Age society, this sequence would be reversed. As Frederick says, first you are, then you do, then you have. If what you are is **really you**, the rest will follow.

Similarly, Schwartz says that 'the quality of the person, the integrity of the idea, and the person's relationship to it' will determine which entrepreneurs are successful in the future. Even today, 'Nothing is as irresistably attractive to a potential investor as a person with conviction about (his or her) vision'. Michael Phillips goes so far as to advise, 'Do it! Money comes to you when you are doing the right thing'. (But also: 'Money has its own rules: records, budgets, saving, borrowing'.) Be, do, have.

In the San Francisco Bay area, many New Age entrepreneurs and busines-ses — 180 at last count — have joined together to share ideas, services, exper-iences in a network called the Briarpatch. Briars define themselves as 'posi-tively oriented' raccoons, groundhogs, and rabbits who hope to make a living (not a killing) by doing exactly what they want to: stuffing chairs, teaching yoga, fixing trucks, reconing chairs, healing animals, making windmills, run-ning health resorts. . . . Their lifestyles and political outlooks are incredibly diverse, but despite or even because of this, they are working out many of the principles of the emerging New Age capitalism. In practice!

Some of these principles are:

(1) **Social purpose rather than profit**. 'When I went to the bank', says Paul Hawken (in **New Age Journal**), 'I had to pretend that I was really in it (his natural foods company) for the money or they would have jumped out of their shoes for fright. We simply wanted to "stay" in business in order to accom-plish our goals. That was reward enough'. What were their goals? 'We were all motivated', says Hawken, 'by the vision of growing and distributing natu-ral foods, rather than by profit'.

(2) **Sharing rather than greed**. 'Greed', says Hawken, 'is condemned not for moral but for practical reasons: it doesn't work. . . . Briars have decided to abandon that game in favour of a new game, an open-ended game, a game which is evolutionary and noncompetitive'. This 'game' is called sharing. 'We can't imagine . . . Coke cheerfully sharing with Pepsi, but Briars can because they don't see size as a goal, nor sales as a ranking'.

(3) **Learning rather than acquiring**. 'If a Briar business fails economical-ly', says Hawken, 'but the people involved have learned a great deal, then that

is seen as success enough. . . . (I)f we are a learning-based society and think of our roles as a continuous learning process, we will naturally have a sound economy as a result'.

(4) **Openness rather than secrecy.** In a long article in the **Briarpatch Review** (Spring '77), Kristin Anundsen and Michael Phillips say that openness of books — and openness in general — 'is a keystone of Briarpatch operations, for it promotes community and learning, two other Briarpatch values. Openness leads to trust, responsibility, new ideas, greater awareness . . . '. Anundsen and Phillips argue that the value of information 'increases with its abundance' and 'if I give information to you, both of us are better off. . . . Sharing of information often leads also to sharing of material things such as trucks, houses, and tools'. Briars are expected to share information even if it means giving help to a potential 'competitor'.

(5) **Networking rather than separateness.** Briars keep in touch with each other with two full-time coordinators, an excellent quarterly magazine, and lots of personal contact — especially at parties. (At the same time, most Briars have deep mistrust of anything more formal than networking.)

(6) **Fun rather than solemnity.** Anundsen and Phillips state that 'historically, in cultures not so specialized as ours, fun has been an important part of the business scene' — in Africa, for example, the marketplace is the 'one place to come for fun', with clowns, jugglers, singers, and comedians — and in the Briarpatch, they say, this tradition has resurfaced. Partly because Briars hope to integrate their lives ('business with pleasure') and partly because fun is 'part of the way we learn'. You can see their sense of fun in the names they choose: Raskinflakkers Divinely United Ice Cream Organization, Lifestyle Restructurers, Rare Earth Real Estate Brokers of Remote Retreats, etc. The slow pace and unpretentious quarters of most Briar businesses actually gets people talking to one another. . . . 'If you take "making a lot of money" off the list of reasons for being in business you can pretty easily replace it with "fun", since you then have time to enjoy yourself by interacting with others'.

IV. Money

Some New Age people believe that money is a product of the Prison and should be gradually done away with in New Age society. One New Age editor writes, 'The existence of money implies centralization, competition, theft, bureaucracy . . . '. Other New Age people believe that money is essentially a mirror and that our relationship to money tells us not so much what money is but who and what we are. Michael Phillips, a co-founder of the Briarpatch, says that we'll always want to exchange our services and that 'keeping score with currency' is the simplest and the **cleanest** way we have for doing this.

We can expect, then, that New Age communities will take many different approaches to money and to the question of economic exchange.

Lee Swenson, an editor of **Simple Living**, takes a representative position. He writes (in **Simple Living**, Summer '76) that money is not **intrinsically** destructive so much as it is **simplistic**. 'If the only tool you have is a hammer, you tend to treat everything as if it were a nail. Money is a dense tool, limiting our vision of the way we can exchange with one another. . . . It cuts down relationships to a narrow exchange. It's a lean way to deal with one another'.

Swenson believes that the transition to a New Age society is going to have to involve a transition to a 'more mixed economy', mixed in the sense of the money economy being mixed with other systems of economic exchange. With a system of labour credits, for example, and with a system of barter.

Barter is what happens when people exchange their goods and skills directly, tit for tat — without money. I'll fix your sink if you'll paint my room. I'll help you build your house if you'll help me edit my manuscript. There's really nothing to stop us from bartering with each other right now, except for the Prison and its institutions — above all perhaps, the incredible amount of time and energy that we put into working for money in the job economy. (This is one of the ways that the job economy keeps the other economies from blooming.)

Lee Swenson recently helped organize a 'barter group' of 30 people. On their first day they formed a circle and each person said what he or she wanted or had to offer. 'At first women seemed to say, "I can't do anything", while men responded, "I don't need anything". But that melted down as one idea of a skill or need set off another'. And people were amazed to discover just how many skills they shared, once everything was added up. 'Each of us has skills', says Swenson, 'often certified skills, that cannot be used in an autonomous manner'. In other words, you can't make a 40-hour-a-week job out of it, but you **can** barter it.

Barter, like money, has its drawbacks. But it has its advantages too. You can make friends through bartering — especially when it involves you in something like helping someone build a house or edit a manuscript. And it encourages us to 'use more of ourselves'. For example, Swenson is a 'professional' writer and teacher, but he couldn't use those skills in the group he organized to barter for basic necessities. Instead he had to make use of some of the other things he could do: 'do carpentry, make good yoghurt on a volume basis, care for children . . . '.

Some New Age communities might decide to 'institutionalize' barter, to base their systems of economic exchange partly or even largely on a barter basis. There are a number of ways that this could be done.

V. Planning

Suddenly, national economic planning has become as North American as maple syrup. Liberals (most of them) and Marxists alike are in favour of it, and according to George Lodge, the biggest corporations are in favour of it too. Even the Movement for a New Society advocates an overall planning system (though they stress that at various points the Plan would be 're-submitted to the local unit for approval'. Like in China?).

The New Age position is that national economic planning is undesirable, period. Only the New Age position recognizes the truth in E. F. Schumacher's assertion that 'genuine planning is coextensive with power' (meaning: the more planning you have, the less control of your life you'll have). Only the New Age position recognizes that a planned society — exactly to the extent that it was planned — would 'imply the end of freedom'. (The planned economy implies the 'necessity for consensus on major economic decisions', says Kenneth Boulding ((in **CoEvolution Quarterly**, Summer '77)) — and that, he says, would make 'political liberty and democratic institutions' all but unworkable.)

In the New Age view, planning represents the ultimate technocratic-bureaucratic solution to our problems. But since our problems are, to a great extent, rooted in the technocratic-bureaucratic mentality (the Prison), a technocratic-bureaucratic 'solution' represents no solution at all. Certainly it has no right to present itself as a 'radical' solution ('radical' in the sense of going to the root).

Economist Eugen Loebl has made an extensive survey of the planned economies, and one of his main conclusions is that 'in most cases target figures express quantity whereas qualitative aspects cannot be, as a rule, expressed in target figures. Consequently, . . . the primary concern of both management and labour is quantity rather than quality'. Another conclusion is that 'no one would dare take responsibility for something that was not explicitly assigned to (him or her) by the target figures'. Finally, and ominously, Loebl concludes that if you plan what is produced you are also — necessarily — planning what is consumed; therefore, 'planning cannot involve just the planning of materials and energy; it necessitates that (people), too, must become an object of planning'.

A different kind of critique of planning has been expressed by Tom Bender. 'Planning', says Bender, 'prevents us from experiencing, enjoying, and acting rightly in the present, as we attempt to keep events in line with our projections of the future'.

New Age people do have some alternatives to planning. Robert Theobald and Jeanne Scott would like to see everyone have 'access to relevant information' — who has what, who needs what, etc. — information that could easily be computerized and made available to all people and groups, community districts and regions, and (of course) to the planetary guidance system which might take the responsibility for collecting this information. Schumacher would like to see 'the fullest possible statement of intentions by all people (and groups) wielding substantial economic power, such statements being collected and collated by some central agency. The very inconsistencies of such a composite "plan" might give valuable pointers'. And Bender gets to the **root** of the matter when he says, 'There is no need to plan or to attempt to control future events if we believe that persons involved in those events will have an ability equal to our own to understand the situation and act rightly. . . . We plan today only because we are incapable of acting rightly and continuing to act rightly with each changing moment'. In New Age society, 'acting rightly' would mean: acting according to the New Age ethics and values. Therefore, a lot of the energy that a socialist society might put into economic planning, a New Age society would put into fostering and refining those ethics and values.

Chapter 18 —
The ABC's of New Age Economic Theory

When most New Agers talk about economics they usually confine themselves to two main points: (1) small is beautiful, and (2) an environmentally benign economy might mean more jobs. For the rest, New Agers tend to assume that they can get all the economic theory they need from the old political 'ism's'; an assumption that may save us a lot of trouble in the short run, but that will keep us from becoming a political presence in the long.

The purpose of this chapter is to show that a New Age economic theory is arising that borrows from — but is substantially different from — what can be found in Marx and Kropotkin and Keynes. The reason that this economics is not well known is partly that it's very new (12 of the 16 sections below are based on material published in 1975 or later) and partly that it tends to be found in writers who are professional and technical rather than 'popular' (for the long term, this is a good sign). Mostly, though, it's that no one has ever bothered to bring these ideas together and to suggest that they're on the verge of melding into a coherent whole.

Another purpose of this chapter is to show that 'New Age' insights and understandings are emerging among people (in this case, economists) who **don't** consider themselves to be standing at the beginnings of a 'New Age' political-economic tradition and who've probably never even heard of the term. New Age economic insights are emerging simply from the effort to **look** at our problems in a fresh and relevant way.

I should add two things. First, some of the ABC's are meant to apply to one or more of the possible New Age economies, not to all of them (Chap. 17, sect. I). And, second, the ABC's aren't meant to be comprehensive — that's why I stop at P. They're meant to give a sense of the quality and scope of a new direction in economics — some of the basics of that new direction.

(A) WEALTH. Economics is the study of wealth. But what is wealth? I think John Ruskin, 19th century cultural historian and political economist, had it right: 'There is no Wealth but Life. Life, including all its powers of love, of joy, and of admiration'. In this view, goods and services are 'wealth' to the extent that they promote life, 'illth' (Ruskin's term) to the extent that they do not. And 'the real science of political economy . . . is that which teaches nations to desire and labour for the things that lead to life'.

But what is 'life'? you might well ask; for Ruskin is obviously using the word in a special, ethical sense. New Age economics would say: life in this sense is behaviour that is compatible with the four New Age ethics and the six New Age political values. Therefore, goods and services are wealth to the extent that they promote these ethics and values, illth to the extent that they do not.

(B) **SCARCE RESOURCES?** Economics is often defined as the 'study of scarce resources'. But economist Eugen Loebl argues (in **Humanomics**) that 'the "allocation of scarce resources" is only one element of many factors economics needs to study'. After all, 'with the same allocation of scarce resources, the economic results can differ according to the design (of enterprises), the level on which the enterprises operate, macroeconomic decisions, and a multitude of other factors'.

The reason economics tends to define itself as the study of scarce resources, says Loebl, is that it is still based on the mechanistic worldview of 19th century physics. 'The view that the economy is part of the determined world on the same order as (Newtonian) physics tends to narrow down our angle of vision to that which is quantifiable', and scarce resources are quantifiable. 'But what really matters — applied science, organization, the intellectual and technical infrastructure, and other essential factors . . . — are not at all quantifiable'.

(C) **GROSS NATIONAL COST; SPIRITUAL PRICE; AVAILABLE SATIS-FACTIONS AND UNFULFILLED DESIRES.** The Gross National Product (GNP) is the standard measure of economic well-being, not only in North America but in many other places all over the world and even (ominously) at the U.N. Basically, the GNP is a measure of the production of all marketable goods and services in the course of a year. North America's GNP is now over 1.1 trillion dollars a year; in 1950 it was around half a trillion.

Obviously, GNP is an extremely misleading measure of economic well-being — are we really twice as well off today as we were in 1950?

Tom Bender states (in **Sharing Smaller Pies**), 'The more we must spend for transportation, for education, or for medical services; the farther we must go for oil, wood, and food; the more our GNP grows. And the more it appears that our quality of life is improved. This focus on production has effectively ignored the reality that most production and consumption (90 percent, according to Bender) is actually the COST of replacing and maintaining our stocks of goods and services rather than a measure of our wealth'.

Anne and Paul Ehrlich report that economist Edwin Dolan 'would rename GNP the Gross National Cost (GNC). More importantly, he would distinguish between Type I GNC and Type II GNC. Type I GNC would measure that fraction of GNC produced with renewable resources. . . . Type II GNC would be that depending on the depletion of nonrenewable resources. . . . As Dolan says, "Politicians and economists would then design their policies to maximize Type I and minimize Type II" '.

Another problem with GNP is what it leaves out. Economist Scott Burns says, 'Virtually all work that is not rewarded with wages is excluded from conventional accounts of the national income. While the household economy is, by far, the largest omission (see P below), the volunteer economy and the cooperative economy are also excluded. The common denominator of these forms of economic activity, beyond their failure to use money, is that they are organized around the idea of giving, of mutual need, and of cooperation rather than competition. . . . Perversely, our system of economic accounts excludes all motives but the competitive desire for money'.

Just as important, GNP fails to measure what Gary Snyder (in **East West**

Journal, June '77) calls the 'real values', those that are found 'within nature, family, mind'. He says we should develop a form of national cost accounting that would ask, ' "What is the natural-spiritual price we pay for this particular piece of affluence, comfort, pleasure, or labour saving?" "Spiritual price" means the time at home, time with your family, time that you can meditate, the difference between what comes to your body and mind by walking a mile as against driving (plus the cost of the gas). There's an accounting that no one has figured out how to do'.

True. But it is already possible to devise economic measures that can point us in the right direction. In **Environmental Design Primer**, Tom Bender suggests a number of such measures: 'a Gross National Service (index) — measuring amounts of service rendered rather than dollars of products consumed; an Available Satisfactions Index — similar to census information on plumbing, etc., which would measure who or how many people have what available to use; an Unfulfilled Desires Index — which would be a more helpful measure of the success of the productive ability of a society in serving that society . . . '.

(D) RATIONAL SELF-INTEREST? Capitalism is supposed to be built on the principle of 'rational self-interest'. Ethics and values aren't supposed to have any place in economics, everyone is supposed to be out for what they can get for themselves, and everything is supposed to be regulated by an 'invisible hand' that's somehow capable of turning our amoral behaviour into behaviour that works for the common good.

Most 'radical' economists like to point to these widely-accepted assumptions to show that the market economies are amoral (or immoral). Economist Fred Hirsch (in **Social Limits to Growth**) doubts that these assumptions are true. Consider, he says, that whenever we find out that a politician — a controller of the market system — has been 'out for him- or herself' we are instantly inclined to throw him or her out of office. Consider that a society whose members regularly lied, cheated, stole, and used violence, simply would not work.

The reason that most of us don't resort to such tactics, says Hirsch, even though they may be in our 'rational self-interest', is that we're still caught up in vestiges of a genuinely religious morality. 'The market system (is), at bottom, more dependent on religious bindings than the feudal system, having abandoned direct social ties maintained by the obligations of custom and status'.

Unfortunately for us all, the Prison and its institutions are steadily eroding the vestiges of our old religious morality. And 'we may be near the limit of explicit social organization possible without a supporting social morality'.

(E) MATERIAL GOODS, POSITIONAL GOODS, AND EXPERIENTIAL GOODS. 'Material goods' is economist Fred Hirsch's term for products that can be enjoyed no matter how many other people are consuming them. For example, my enjoyment of a meal or a TV set should in no way lessen your enjoyment of a similar meal or TV. 'Positional goods' is Hirsch's term for products that can't be enjoyed if a substantial number of people are also enjoying them. The pleasure that I get from a house in the country is diminished if too many other people have houses in the country. The advantages of a college diploma on the job market would vanish if everybody had diplomas. Hirsch likes to say that having a positional good is like standing tiptoe in a crowd: 'If everyone stands on tiptoe, no one sees better'.

So long as people are trying to meet their basic physiological and security needs (self-development needs one and two), getting 'enough' material goods is their dominant concern. But once people have met their basic material needs, 'demands for goods and facilities with a public (social) character' — in other words, demands for positional goods — 'become increasingly active'.

In this view, our economic problems are a product of our economic **success** and can't be cured by 'priming the economic pump' in the traditional way. Our economic problems come from the fact that most of us have **already met** our basic material needs and are busily acquiring positional goods, thereby making it harder and harder for us to **enjoy** our positional goods: cottages, diplomas, cars, etc. Our economic problems also come from the fact that none of our political ideologies are able to see this, and so the 'solutions' they propose only make things worse by holding out false expectations. For example, schools are too expensive so we turn to the state to foster equality of educational opportunity, only to see our diplomas lose even more of their value on the job market'.

New Age economic theory must recognize two things. First, it must recognize that positional goods are inherently abusive of New Age political value (1), 'maximization of social and economic well-being', because they tend to require a considerable degree of social and economic inequality for their enjoyment. And, second, it must concede that material goods as defined above are not enough to keep most of us happy — not, at any rate, after we've begun to take our material goods for granted (which has begun to happen in the Soviet Union but not yet in, e.g., China). Therefore, New Age political-economic practice must (1) seek to replace positional with material goods, generally by replacing monolithic with biolithic institutions — shared cabins for private cottages, bicycles for automobiles, 'alternatives to compulsory schooling' for the universal compulsory school, etc.; and (2) seek to replace the desire to acquire positional goods with the desire to acquire 'experiential goods'. ('Experiential goods' is my term for experiences that can be enjoyed no matter how many other people are having them. Appreciation of the world, psychic research, intellectual or artistic activity, and interpersonal relationships are examples of such experiences.)

(F) **DIRECT VERSUS TRANSFERRED ECONOMY.** 'A native economy is a direct economy', says the Frisco Bay Mussel Group in their pamphlet 'Living Here' (available for $1.50 from **Planet-Drum**). A direct economy 'places value on what is already there. Values are complex; oaks are tree-presence as well as bearers of acorns, tule reeds are both singing spirits and basket material, salmon are annual visitors and smoked winter supplies. They are both personally direct for each person and direct to the place. It is an economy of seasons and migrations rather than accounts. . . .

'Non-natives imposed a transferred economy. Transferred in were foods, materials, and cultural ideas that were familiar to the new occupiers before they came. Transferred out were things from the region that had some value elsewhere. . . . Subsequent waves of regional immigrants have accumulated so much, put up so many buildings, imported so many devices to "succeed" here, and transferred so much out that the region has been transformed into an enormous junkyard. . . .

'Empty cans for holding Japanese oysters thrown into the Bay spoil nesting beds for native oysters. Housing tracts cover up topsoil that is essential for feeding people. Miles of pavement prevent the natural flow and seepage of water actually causing floods . . .'.

At the end of their pamphlet the Mussel Group urges that we 'begin un-doing the damage invader society has done', and it asks: 'Considering how much has already been changed . . . how can we become native to what is here now?'

(G) THE STEADY STATE. According to economist Herman Daly (in **Toward a Steady-State Economy**), if we want to create an environmentally benign economy we basically have to create a 'steady-state' economy. 'By "steady-state" is meant a constant stock of physical wealth (capital), and a constant stock of people (population)'.

Naturally, these stocks don't actually remain constant; people die, and 'wealth' — goods — are consumed. 'Therefore the stocks must be maintained by a rate of inflow (birth, production) equal to the rate of outflow (death, consumption)'.

But there can be a high rate of throughput or a low. The steady state concept additionally means that the rate of throughput should be as low as possible. 'For the population a low rate of throughput (a low birth rate and an equally low death rate) means a high life expectancy. . . . For the stock of wealth (sic) a low rate of throughput (low production and equally low consumption) means greater life expectancy or durability of goods and less time sacrificed to production'.

('The existence of new and open frontiers', says Richard Falk, 'may be very crucial in a steady-state economy to avoid a collective mood of depression, even psychosis'. It is very important, therefore, to re-define 'growth' in emotional, psychological and spiritual terms.)

(H) SPILLOVER EFFECTS. Economists tend to pay little or no attention to what economist E. J. Mishan (in **The Costs of Economic Growth**) calls the 'spillover effects' of goods and services. Spillover effects are **disservices** that are produced by industries and institutions in the course of providing us with goods and services. Spillover effects are rarely figured into the cost of goods and services and are therefore absent from the price of goods and services.

Some spillover effects take concrete form (e.g., plutonium from a nuclear reactor). Others are less tangible, having to do with such things as privacy, quiet, and clean air. In either case, Mishan believes that individually or collectively we should have the right to **sue for compensation** from individuals or groups that are persistently responsible for spillover effects. 'The extent of the compensatory payments that would perforce accompany the operation of industries, of motorized traffic and airlines, would constrain many of them to close down — or else to operate at levels far below those that would (otherwise) prevail — or else to discover 'inexpensive ways of controlling their own noxious by-products'. Owners of power lawn mowers might be required to pay a set fee to the community. . . .

(I) SOCIAL TRANSACTION COST. The fastest-growing single cost in monolithic society is the cost of trying to keep things **hanging together** a bit longer. Economist Hazel Henderson calls this cost the 'social transaction cost', and she says (in Toffler), 'The proportion of gross national product that must be spent in mediating conflicts, controlling crime, protecting consumers and the environment, providing ever more comprehensive bureaucratic coordination, and generally trying to maintain "social homeostasis" begins to grow exponentially'.

Elsewhere (**Humanizing City Life**, May '77) Henderson speaks of transaction costs as 'the social costs of the old way of doing business, whether it's automobile accidents, or workman's compensation, or industrial safety requirements or the whole cost of the regulatory structure. . . . All of those are social costs, **very necessary** social costs that we, as taxpayers, have to incur to clean up and deal with the system that we have created'. And she adds, 'I would say that the only fraction of the GNP that is growing at this point is the "social costs" fraction'.

(J) LAW OF THE DISAPPEARING MIDDLE. When technological development takes place outside of a system of ethics and values, or in **terms** of a system of ethics and values that celebrates growth and size and power, 'all ambition and talent **goes to the frontier**', says economist E. F. Schumacher (in **Rain**, Jan. '77), 'the only place considered prestigious and exciting. Development proceeds from Stage 1 to Stage 2, and when it moves on to Stage 3, Stage 2 drops out; when it moves on to Stage 4, Stage 3 drops out, and so on'. In this process, 'The "better" is the enemy of the good and makes the good disappear even if most people cannot afford the better, for reasons of Money, Market, Management, or whatever it might be. Those who cannot afford to keep pace drop out and are left with nothing but Stage 1 technology'.

In Schumacher's example: if you want to farm, and you can't afford a tractor or a combine harvester (Stage 3 technology), you're not going to be able to find efficient animal-drawn equipment anywhere (Stage 2) — and so you're not going to be able to farm. (Stage 1 technology — in this case, the hoe and sickle — does tend to remain available. For the 'nostalgia' market.)

Julius Lester puts it well when he says, 'We're given two choices only: A shack, or a house that looks like it came in a cereal box. . . . I do not want to retain the shack, but there is something about its spirit which it may be fatal to lose. "I was made by a person", it says, standing shakily at the edge of a cotton field . . . '.

(K) THE PERSON BEFORE THE FIRM. Conventional economics begins by making assumptions about firms and households. Two commonly-made assumptions about firms are that they maximize profits and that they tend to be extremely rational economic actors.

A New Age economics would begin — as economist Harvey Leibenstein suggests (in **Beyond Economic Man**) — with the individual person. It would recognize that firms and households do not, strictly speaking, make decisions or have objectives; that all decisions are made by individuals. And so it would ask: on what basis do individuals make decisions in a particular society? What are their values, motives, goals? And how are individuals related to the economic decision units that operate as a group? Only then would it ask, how do the 'highly complex groups we call firms and households' behave? (As it is now, we simply assume that groups behave like individuals!)

(L) MARGINAL RATIONALITY. Economists of all political hues tend to believe in something called 'economic man'. Economic man is a totally rational creature whose aim in life, says Leibenstein, 'is to do as well as he can. Hence he is presumed to maximize profits, or income, or utility, or something like that'. Economists tend tc make this assumption because the apparent alternative — that people are 'irrational' — seems absurd (and also, perhaps, because it would detract from the 'predictive value' of economics).

New Age economics would recognize that, as Leibenstein puts it, 'there is an important sense in which non-maximizing behaviour is not at all irrational'. To demonstrate this proposition (which is obvious to many New Agers), Leibenstein develops a series of 'dimensions of rationality'. One dimension of rationality is 'calculatedness', but there are a number of other dimensions as well. For example: our assessment of a situation can range from completely emotional to completely 'dispassionate'. Or, for example, we can learn nothing from past experience or we can learn an almost infinite amount.

Leibenstein's point is that we tend to find a spot on each of these dimensions (eight in all) that 'feels right' to us depending on our personalities and values — that it is, in fact, absurd to assume that we will try to 'maximize our behaviour' in terms of each dimension or that different people won't give different weight to different dimensions at different times in their lives. 'Sensible behaviour requires only marginal rationality, not rationality at every point in time. There is no need to assume that people need to stretch themselves along every dimension at each point in time to gain every advantage open to them. It may indeed go against their psychological makeup to do so. They need only do so from time to time when the results seem important'.

(M) X-INEFFICIENCY. When mainstream economists criticize the economy, the inefficiencies are all of a kind, what economist Harvey Leibenstein calls 'allocational efficiencies'. These are the inefficiencies that arise from how societies organize their production and trade; these are the inefficiencies that are the standard topics of political discussion today. However, Leibenstein summarizes a number of studies that show that 'the problem of allocational inefficiency is trivial'. The benefits from eliminating monopoly, for example, would raise national income by no more than one-thirteenth of one percent. Eliminating trade restrictions would raise national income by less than one percent.

The reason the 'welfare effects of reallocation' are so small is that firms are **shot through** with inefficiencies, and the most important kind of inefficiency has to do with what Leibenstein calls 'factor-x inefficiency'. It might also be called 'motivational inefficiency'. As Leibenstein puts it, 'Individuals who are members of production (or consumption) groups, and act in part as agents for these groups, have split loyalties (or split motivations) — loyalties to their own ends as well as loyalties to what they see as the group's objectives'. To the extent that the members of a firm act on their own personal loyalties or motives (as opposed to those of the firm) — to that extent a firm is 'x-inefficient'.

One important implication of this view is that 'except in extreme cases firms do not minimize costs, maximize profits, or optimize the rate of technological change'. These may be the ostensible objectives of the firm; but 'the firm' is a collection of individuals, and those individuals will be motivated not only by the firm's objectives but by their own, multiple and more or less conscious objectives as well. From the owner(s) on down.

Another important implication is that a firm can increase its output without increasing its expenditures by organizing itself **around** people's motivational needs rather than against or apart from them. It can, for example, reduce its size; reduce the length of the working day; attempt to introduce 'synergic principles and practices' (see Chap. 13, sect. IV-3 & 4); and be owned and-or run by all of the people involved with it. These kinds of changes, says Leibenstein, leading to a reduction in 'x-inefficiency', would increase GNP by up to six percent. In North America that would be by up to $66 **billion** a year.

(N) INCOME A FUNCTION OF FELT CONSUMPTION NEEDS. Traditional economists tend to assume that consumption is a function of income. In other words, that the amount of money we spend is dependent on the amount of money we make. But economist George Katona suggests (in **Psychological Economics**) that for most of us, the **opposite** may be closer to the truth. The amount of money we make depends on the amount we feel we need to spend.

Katona suggests that the amount we feel we need is a function of (1) the kind of lifestyle we want to lead, and (2) the kind(s) of consumption we want to go in for. He says, 'Neglecting the constraint supplied by absence of opportunities, there is . . . justification to reverse the traditional equation: Instead of expenditures being a function of income, income becomes a function of consumption'.

'Be, do, have' (Chap. 17, sect. III). According to Katona, we're living by this philosophy already. It's **who we are** that has to change. . . .

(O) INFLATION: ITS SOCIAL AND PSYCHOCULTURAL ROOTS. Marxists and anarchists tend to blame inflation primarily on the capitalists; liberals, on the unions and their wage demands. New Age economics isn't interested in making debating points along these lines, possibly because it isn't interested in winning social classes — as distinct from individuals — over to its way of seeing. New Age economics tends to give more weight to the social and psychocultural factors behind the inflationary spiral, factors that appear to be traceable to all of us, and in about the same proportions.

Social factors. New Age economics sees no point in denying the fact that a large number of people — people whom E. F. Schumacher (in **Rain**, Nov. '75) refers to as 'groups of essential producers', garbage collectors, airline pilots, coal miners, etc. — have recently 'discovered that they can successfully insist on much higher incomes than society . . . had hitherto granted them. They can insist because by withholding their goods and services they can bring the whole of society, or essential parts of it, to a standstill'. They are, in short, demanding a larger piece of the economic pie — but the rest of us aren't prepared to give it to them. The rest of us are determined to defend our own incomes 'by passing on higher costs and insisting on the maintenance of previously established relativities'.

It isn't really a matter of employers gouging workers. Profit levels have — if anything — fallen since the 1940's and after-tax profits range from three to seven percent. It's more a matter of white-collar workers refusing to let their income levels fall below blue-, beginning university instructors refusing to let their levels fall below garbage collectors' levels, and so on. Obviously, says Schumacher, no substantial group can obtain a bigger piece of the pie if the rest refuse to be content with a smaller piece. And so wages (and prices) are pushed up endlessly. . . .

The reason society continues to accede to **all** these groups' demands is that we no longer have a commonly shared system of ethics and values that can tell us what a fair system of income distribution might be. Until we have such a system, each group will feel that it has the right to decide on its own fair share, government will have no basis on which to intervene (without calling down the wrath of the electorate), and inflation will continue. In fact it will continue to get worse, for as society becomes more complexly dependent it becomes more vulnerable to the demands of its 'essential producers'.

(New Age economics would graduate incomes on the basis of the New Age ethics and political values — ethics and values that are rooted in the trans-material worldview. These values might be differently manifested by the different New Age communities, but the **context** would clearly be one that sought to ((1)) maximize equity, and ((2)) give higher pay to groups whose work was least pleasant — since non-material 'wealth' would be seen to come more easily to those whose jobs were most pleasant.)

Psychocultural factors. The very fact that we **expect** inflation to continue, says economist E. J. Mishan, causes us to ask for greater wage benefits and raise prices higher than we ordinarily might. To some extent, inflation is a **self-fulfilling prophecy.**

(P) THE HOUSEHOLD ECONOMY. We have not one but three economies; economist Scott Burns (in **Home, Inc.**) calls them the 'market', the 'collective', and the 'household' economies. Marxist and liberal economists probably wouldn't even recognize the existence of the 'household economy', but Burns is able to show that it's our **biggest** economy now. And if we want to break our dependence on our monolithic institutions, it's going to have to keep on growing.

The market economy, says Burns, is the sum of all the goods and services produced in all our privately-owned businesses and industries. The collective economy is the sum of all the goods and services produced in all our publicly-owned businesses and industries. And the household economy 'is the sum of all the goods and services produced within all (our) households. . . . This includes, among other things, the value of shelter, home-cooked meals, . . . weekend-built patios, . . . home sewing, laundering, child-care, home repairs, voluntary services to community and to friends, the produce of the home garden, and the transportation services of the private automobile'.

The reason that the household economy is invisible to most economists is simple. They don't consider that it **produces** anything. Which is true in the sense that nearly everything it produces comes without a price tag on it. But if people were paid for working in the household economy, the payments would amount to nearly a third of the Gross National Product (GNP) and about half of disposable consumer income!

The **imputed income** of household capital (how much we save by not paying for people to wash our dishes, build our patios or grow our vegetables) was over $50 billion in 1970. This sum is slightly larger than the after-tax profits of **all the corporations in North America**. (Burns concludes from this that household returns on investments are now superior to market returns — which augurs well for the future of the household economy.)

Moreover, the household economy is amassing **physical wealth** faster than the corporate economy. Radical economists are fond of telling us that the 100 largest industrial corporations control an ever-larger share of corporate assets. But we never hear from them that the corporate share of total national wealth has decreased substantially since 1929, and is continuing to decrease. In fact, by 1976, for the first time since the 1700's, the household economy was expected to contain **as great a percentage** of the U.S. national wealth as the market economy (roughly 41 percent), with the collective economy, at 16 percent, bringing up the rear (but up from 12 percent in 1929).

The growth of the household economy implies that people are taking over from the monolithic institutions many of the tasks that they can do more cheaply or more efficiently or more satisfyingly by themselves. Consider, says Burns, that it is now possible to rent almost anything, from medical equipment to cement mixers. Consider that our new small-scale technology is making it possible for us to produce many goods more cheaply by the home than by the marketplace (a $12 tofu maker, for example, can give us an incredibly cheap source of protein). 'The most significant aspect of the rise of rented objects and equipment is the fact that the labour usually employed in this equipment has been displaced from the marketplace to the household'.

Burns estimates that, just like a household in the 18th century, a diligent household today can 'internalize' **70-80 percent of its needs**.

Burns concludes that the household economy is in a 'no-lose' situation. If a full employment economy is our social goal, 'traditional economic forces will work to push ever more labour out of the market economy and into the household economy, which obviously will continue to grow'. On the other hand, if we adopt a guaranteed annual income, 'that would allow millions of people to become full-time "employees" of the household economy'.

I feel less optimistic than Burns; I think the major threat to the household economy will come not from the market but from the collective economy. Like the household economy, the collective economy has gained about five percent of the national wealth (excluding land) since 1929; and unlike the household economy, the collective economy has many powerful advocates in

Congress and in Parliament. The advocates of the collective economy, in their push for full 40-hour-a-week employment for all, are calling for a massive programme of public works that would create many 'jobs' that would, in effect, be **competitive with jobs in the household economy**. For example, some environmentalists have recently called for an energy package that would give people jobs putting storm windows on our houses and insulation in our attics. At public expense.

I don't find it too far-fetched to imagine that, in the near future, people will feel a lot of pressure **not** to do much work in the household economy (recycle your own wastes and you'll be doing garbage collectors out of their jobs, etc.). And that would make the concept of biolithic institutions (which allow us to **do for our selves**) about as realizable as the Marxists' 'withering away of the state'.

Part VII — Healing Self and Society

Chapter 19 — Some Guidelines

So far in this book, we've seen that Prison society cripples us in many ways — in so many ways that we tend to become our own best jailers. We have also seen that a genuine alternative to Prison society is at least possible for us now. What we've yet to see is whether we can **get** from here to there. And, just as important, whether we can do it without becoming like the liberals and Marxists in the process.

One thing is sure, it is important to do **something**. For as we've repeatedly seen, the Prison is growing in depth and strength, and we're becoming ever more dependent on our monolithic institutions (rather than on our selves). Unless this process is reversed, and soon, there will be no escaping from it, and life will become as comfortable, as regimented, and as flat as is life in a real prison. Then there are all the disasters, nuclear and ecological, that are waiting for us if we can't learn to love life more than things (according to Robert Heilbroner, a well-known economist, many of us are already subconsciously thinking, 'let the drama proceed to its finale, let mankind suffer the end it deserves').

But what can we do? And where to begin?

The rest of this book is designed to (help you) answer these questions. Chap.

20 is about healing self (how to). Chap. 21 is about healing society (how to). Chap. 23 comes to grips with the Marxist analysis and shows — I think successfully — why it's less useful for us than the emerging New Age analysis. And Chap. 24 directs you to a representative sampling of New Age books, magazines and groups.

In this chapter my purposes are more general. Sect. I argues that we should at least **begin** to change our selves (our values and goals) **before** we begin to change society; sect. II is about the New Age theory of political power (where political power comes from, and how to manifest it); sect. III tries to de-fuse the 'working from within' controversy; sect. IV says that, yes, we can change society without a 51 percent majority **and** without violence; and sect. V introduces the concept of 'evolutionary transformation' (as distinct from 'revolutionary change').

I. Inner Before Outer

Traditionally, 'political' people have believed that we needed to change the outer forms of society before we could — or should — begin to seriously change our selves. And in countries where millions of us are starving, who would disagree?

In North America today, however, the problem isn't that millions of us are starving (in fact, one symptom of the problem is that millions of us are over-eating). The problem is that most of us are trapped by the Prison and its institutions and are therefore **suffocating** — starved for strokes, starved for affection and esteem. Thrown back on self-development needs one and two. Always in need of **things** to ease our (boredom) (pain).

In North America today, our problems are different from those of most other countries, and it follows that our strategy must also be different. In North America our institutions are a fairly accurate reflection of our consciousness. If anything our institutions are better than we deserve — surveys have consistently shown that our politicians are **more** knowledgeable, **more** concerned about civil rights and civil liberties, and **more** concerned about social justice than most of the rest of us. If we did begin by changing our institutions — if that was our strategy — then what kinds of changes would we try to bring about? Inevitably, I think we'd try to make our institutions even more monolithic than they are. I think we'd choose to give up even more of our power and responsibility to our institutions — including the top-down state.

If we want to change North America in a New Age direction, then we're going to have to begin with our selves: with the Prison, with our way of looking at the world, with our ethics and values. If we're able to begin to change these things then our demands on our institutions will change. Instead of wanting them to do more **for** us, we'd simply want them to make it possible for us to do what we need to — for our **selves**. We'd change them the better to allow us to lead lives of simple (and genuine) pleasures such as friendship and creative activity and service to others.

Werner Erhard and The Hunger Project have drawn our attention to a very important point. Every attempt to change society takes place in a particular atmosphere, or **context**. The context is our way of **seeing** the world, and it determines, in large part, the meaning, the quality, the 'content' of what we see and do. In North America today, I think it's fair to say that the context — for most of us — is the Prison. Therefore, when we try to 'change the world' we almost inevitably project the content of the Prison out **onto** the world. For example, those of us who recognize poverty as a problem inevitably end up proposing 'solutions' that would render us **more** dependent on the federal bureaucracy and **less** capable of caring for our selves. Those of us who recognize transportation as a problem end up proposing 'solutions' that would speed the tempo of our society up even faster.

Before we can change society deeply — before we can change it on the third level of analysis — we're going to have to transform the context out of which we see. Specifically, we're going to have to transform the Prison. And that means transforming our selves (see Chap. 20, sect. I).

Another reason why it's important to **begin** with self has to do with this: personal growth that's undertaken as **part** of a political movement tends to become something else, something very different from personal growth. People begin to treat themselves as means rather than ends, try to become 'good communists' or 'good Findhornians' (or whatever) rather than **who** they really are. People begin to subordinate their personalities and energies to group goals and group standards and may end up even more out of touch with themselves than when they started.

If we aren't clear about our own purposes and motives, those purposes and motives will return to confound us and corrupt our political work. In the late 1960's I think that many of us felt too guilty and-or too beset by urgency to begin with our selves — and it's **because** of this that our movements so quickly lost touch with North American reality.

Personal growth must be priority number one for racial and ethnic minorities, for ex-felons, for addicts . . . for everyone. John Maher, head of the Delancey Street Foundation and an ex-felon himself, says (in Hampden-Turner), 'People have gotta understand that society is all screwed up. We're going to change it. . . . But **before** we do that, we gotta understand that we ain't nice guys either. Social victims are generally pretty dangerous, nasty characters because we're pretty twisted, and we gotta untwist ourselves, so we're human beings . . . '.

And remember: healing one's self leads almost inevitably to a sense of oneness with other beings and to a desire to heal society. But ignoring one's self often leads either to apathy or to a desire to submerge one's self in a movement that gives one a counterfeit sense of identity and power.

J. Krishnamurti says somewhere that, after you become a whole human being, anything you do will be appropriate. However, until you become a whole human being, nothing you do will be quite appropriate.

I love that quote, but I think it's too extreme (product of the non-material worldview). There's no reason for us to wait until we've healed our selves completely (and thanks to our monolithic institutions, how can we — completely?). But there is reason to wait until we've at least got some perspective on our selves (that is to say: some humility) and some perspective on the Prison. Until we've at least **begun** to deal with our selves.

II. The Ballot, the Bullet — or the New Age Strategy?

Some of us believe that elections, all by themselves, can usher us in to the New Age. Others of us believe that a violent revolution will be necessary — at least at some point. However, I believe that there's an emerging consensus among New Age people that sees serious flaws in both these solutions, and that calls, instead, for each of us to (a) begin to get in touch with our selves and simplify our life styles, and (b) begin to work against our monolithic institutions in whatever way seems to flow most naturally from out of our own life situations.

Liberals hope to bring about social change by the ballot — by voting. It is true that many first- and second-level (see Chap. 5) reforms have been voted in, and it's obviously worth our while to continue to vote them in. But we can't change society on the third level of analysis — we can't break out of the Prison — through the electoral process.

For one thing, election speeches, door-to-door campaign workers, etc., can rarely if ever change people's underlying ethics and values. (Our attitudes maybe — but the Prison is a matter of our nonconscious ideologies, not of our attitudes.)

For another thing, elections aren't designed to encourage us to make our own decisions or in any way to take responsibility for our lives; instead they're designed to encourage us to give our responsibility away to somebody else who promises to make our decisions for us.

The Marxist solution, on the other hand, and often also the anarchist solution, is to call for the bullet — to call for a violent revolution. But if voting helps keep us passive, taking up the gun helps keep us death- and thing-oriented . . . obviously.

According to Richard Falk, the record of history shows that 'drastic strategies of change are virtually doomed to produce bloodshed, excess, and a new reign of oppression'. Jan Tinbergen reminds us that the resolution of conflict through violence opens the way to nuclear war, 'a possibility unknown to the fathers of revolutionary thinking'.

Violence could never, in any event, lead to a New Age society, since violence would drive most life-oriented people out of the revolutionary camp. (It always has — which is one reason why violent revolutions turn totalitarian.)

Another problem here, well made by Gene Sharp, is that violence leads to the centralization of power. For one thing, violent revolutionary organizations require hierarchy and centralization in order to survive police repression; and once begun, this is a process that can never be stopped . . . even 'After the Revolution'. For another thing, a regime that's born out of violence and centralization will require continued violence and centralization to defend itself against internal and external 'enemies'. Finally, the violent struggle for power always weakens the independent revolutionary institutions and social groups that grew up before the violence started . . . leaving the new state that much more powerful, that much more of a monolithic institution.

But if the ballot and the bullet are both false options — where then can we turn?

On the second level of analysis, voting and violence do appear to represent all of our options. But on the third level of analysis, we can see that voting and violence are based on the **same false assumptions** about political power. The New Age perspective is based on different assumptions. And so it can lead to a different strategy for change.

On the third level, we can see that both liberals and Marxists assume that political power is **ultimately in the hands of an elite** — of competing elites or 'countervailing powers' (a favourite liberal term) or of a 'ruling class'. And so both assume that in order to change society, we've got to change elites — by voting in a different elite, or by killing off the ruling class and setting up a 'dictatorship of the proletariat', that is, a dictatorship.

Gene Sharp calls this the 'monolith theory' of power. He states, 'The "monolith theory" of power assumes that the power of a government is a relatively fixed **quantum** (i.e., 'a discrete unit quantity of energy'), a "given", a strong, independent, durable (if not indestructible), self-reinforcing, and self-perpetuating force. . . . If it were true that political power possesses the durability of a solid stone pyramid, then it would also be true that such power could only be controlled by the voluntary self-restraint of rulers, by changes in the "ownership" of the monolith (the State) — whether with regular procedures (such as elections) or with irregular ones, or by destructive violence'.

The problem with the monolith theory of power is that it is factually not true — 'all governments are dependent on the society they rule' — and 'even a regime which believes itself to be a monolith, and **appears** to be one, can be weakened and shattered . . . when people act upon (a more accurate) theory of power'.

Following Sharp (and others), New Age politics has been developing what I like to call the 'biolithic theory' of political power. The biolithic theory holds that governments — all governments — **depend ultimately on people**, and that political power is therefore fragile, very un-stone-pyramid-like, because it depends ultimately on the (continuing) cooperation of many different groups of people. In this view, as Julius Lester puts it, 'Power does not come from the barrel of a gun. Only bullets'. Negative sanctions, including violence, may help to maintain a ruler's political power, but even the ability to impose sanctions depends on the obedience and cooperation of at least some of us. And the rest of us would have to fear the sanctions — more than we valued our freedom — for the sanctions to work.

Political power depends, then, ultimately on our consent. And in North America we give that consent for the most part freely. We give it for many reasons besides fear of sanctions: habit, self-interest, apathy . . . we feel that we should, we identify with our rulers, we know things could be worse, we are lacking in self-confidence . . . our very belief in the monolith theory of power is a tacit way of giving our consent to the powers-that-be. Above all, though, is the fact that the American and Canadian governments are governments of, by and for the Prison-bound. They are based on, and they foster, all the Prison values. Is it any wonder that most of us are loyal?

In order to change Prison society, then, we are first going to have to withdraw our consent from the Prison within us. Otherwise we wouldn't **want** to change things on the third level of analysis, and all our elections, all our violence, would only help to produce societies that were more comfortable and more efficient Prisons.

At the same time, though, we can see that changing the Prison within us would not be enough to change Prison society. For the Prison has generated monolithic institutions that are self-perpetuating and that help to perpetuate the Prison within us. Our national governments are, themselves, monolithic institutions.

So we are going to have to withdraw our consent from our monolithic institutions — including our national governments (at least to some extent) — as well as from the Prison itself.

Withdrawing our consent on these two levels (inner and outer) **is the beginning of 'New Age politics'**.

III. On Working from Within

Political people have tended to disagree — often quite bitterly — over the question of whether it's 'better' to work from within the system or outside it. Even some New Age people are at odds on this issue. For example: Donald Keys, of Planetary Citizens, feels there's a real need for 'planetary-conscious' people to run for political office, while Stephen Gaskin, of The Farm, urges, 'Don't take over the government. Take over the government's function'.

There is, however, an emerging consensus (among New Age people) that suggests that the question is being posed in the wrong way. The point, they say, is first to get in touch with your self, and then to begin to simplify your personal life and life style in a way that can reflect and deepen your new understandings. From there, each of us 'should go where our hearts tell us to go', as David Spangler puts it, 'hopefully without prejudgement . . . '.

Some of us will break away from the mainstream of society; others of us will work from within. Still others of us will find some kind of middle ground. **If we've begun to transcend** the Prison and our dependence on its institutions, if we've begun to see things in terms of the trans-material worldview and the New Age ethics and political values, then virtually **anything we did** would contribute to the healing of society. Mike Nickerson goes so far as to say, 'An individual deciding to take a walk in the park rather than drive somewhere inclines the culture in a (New Age) direction . . . '.

IV. Critical Mass

It's true. There isn't time to wait for 51 percent of us to embark on our own personal journeys. . . . And even if there were time — how **could** the rest of us wait?

Fortunately, the transition to the New Age doesn't have to wait with baited breath for the formation of a 51 percent majority. A 'critical mass' will do the job.

A 'critical mass' is the number of concerned and committed people it would take to move the continent — democratically — in a New Age direction. Estimates of what makes a critical mass range all the way from two percent (Transcendental Meditation) to 25 percent. The implication is that commitment and concern has a certain political weight of its own and that a minority of concerned people can and **should** affect the democratic process more strongly than a larger number of apathetic people.

If a critical mass is to develop around New Age issues and concerns it would have to be made up of people who are both free (or becoming free) of the Prison and who are willing to act. (To Werner Erhard the critical mass would consist of people 'who are willing to take responsibility for themselves. To Robert Theobald the critical mass would consist of people who are prepared to act cooperatively around a particular issue.)

Some New Age groups have already had impacts way beyond their size. The Clamshell Alliance and the Greenpeace Foundation have demonstrated that life-oriented people united in nonviolent action can generate a lot of sympathetic attention.

Erich Fromm has suggested that 20 percent of the people could successfully use the threat of a consumer strike as a way of forcing major concessions from the corporations and the national government. If 20 percent of us were to decide not to buy or use private automobiles — even for a year — we could have an enormous impact, not only on the automobile industry but on the economy as a whole.

The New Age can be brought about by a concerned and concerted minority acting on behalf of the New Age ethics and political values.

V. Revolutionary Change — or Evolutionary Transformation?

On the first level of analysis, we can speak of reform; on the second level, of revolutionary change. But on the third level I think we can only speak of evolution, unfolding, process — of changes so deep and thorough that they have to go by another name (see Chap. 5). Moreover, changes of that magnitude couldn't be forced on us — we'd have to grow into them. And that could only be an evolutionary process.

But just because it would have to be evolutionary doesn't mean that it would have to be **slow**. Tom Robbins uses the term 'evolutionary outburst' to describe what is happening to our religious beliefs. Theodore Roszak anticipates 'an evolution of consciousness that will unfold with the sweep and depth of revolution'. Even Buckminster Fuller, who disagrees with proponents of the human scale on so many things, is able to speak of our impending 'evolutionary transformation' without batting an eye. New Age politics is, in part, **about** how to speed up the social evolutionary process.

Many New Age people have begun to speak of the (evolutionary) changes they'd like to see as 'transformative', as distinct from 'mere change', 'revolutionary change' and the like. David Spangler says, 'Change I will describe as alterations of forms or behaviours within a given system which alter the arrangement and even the structure of its contents, . . . but which leave the fundamental nature of the system unaltered. On the other hand, transformation I define as a higher order change which alters the fundamental nature of the system itself, creating a new system'. Changing the ownership of the means of production or even the structure of factory management would, in this view, be simple change. But changing our lifestyles, ethics and values in such a way that less was produced (because we were more interested in 'experiential goods') would be transformative.

Willis Harman distinguishes transformation 'from other changes that are revolutionary in a social or political sense but do not involve a significant change in the basic, implicit, unchallenged, taken-as-given metaphysic of the society'. Changing over from liberalism to Marxism would, in this view, be revolutionary change. But changing over from the materialist to the transmaterial way of **seeing** the world would be transformative.

(Note: no one is saying that third level transformation would **preclude** first- or second-level change. In fact, it would **encourage** such changes; see Chaps. 20-21.)

In his new book, Charles Reich speaks of transformation as 'not the sudden acceptance of some foreign and external teaching, but an awakening — the release of some life-force already within'.

Chapter 20 — Healing Self

This chapter is about how New Age people are trying to heal themselves. Sect. I is about how many of us have begun to break out of the Prison. Sect. II is about further steps that many of us have felt it was important to take in the spiritual and human potential movements. Sect. III is about the kind of simplified, more life-oriented lifestyle that people who've begun to get free of the Prison and its institutions are almost inevitably drawn to. Sect. IV lists a couple of dozen steps that we can begin to take **right now** in the direction of a lifestyle of voluntary simplicity. (Until we've begun to learn to live together self-reliantly and cooperatively and with life- rather than thing-oriented pleasures, our political work cannot reflect the ethics and values in this book.)

I. Breaking Out of the Prison

In order to **begin** to change our selves deeply, we are going to have to try to break out of at least one side of the Prison. (If we can begin to break out of one side, we can begin to see the rest of the Prison for what it is.)

(A) Many of us who've chosen to focus on our **patriarchal attitudes** have joined men's and women's consciousness-raising groups (which I prefer to call consciousness-changing groups, for reasons given in Chap. 23, sect. IV-7). Many women have found a good brief introduction to consciousness-raising (concept and issues) to be Koedt, Levine and Rapone, eds., **Radical Feminism**, Part IV (first four articles); the whole anthology is an excellent introduction to feminist issues from a 'radical feminist' perspective (as distinct from a Marxist feminist perspective). (Reminder: this book and most of the other books, magazines and groups referred to in this section are listed more fully in Chap. 24 below.) Current issues of interest to feminists are discussed in feminist community newspapers such as **Plexus** (San Francisco) and **Sojourner** (Boston).

Many women who've gone through the initial stages of consciousness-raising are, as Terri Poppe explains it (in **off our backs**, March '77), 'breaking from a central mass into more specific interest-action groups. For some of us that means . . . organizing around political groups . . . (or working in) communications — newspapers, journals, records, radio networks, coffeehouses, bookstores, restaurants' (the **Feminist Art Journal** gives a good indication of the new feminist **sensibility** that's arising out of many of these endeavours). 'For others of us it means being separatist to varying degrees — from living in women only houses . . . to living in lesbian only spaces', often in the country. 'For still others it can mean more intense involvement in women religions, witchcraft, spirituality, WICCA' (the magazine **WomanSpirit** covers these areas).

The best introduction to consciousness-changing for men that I know of is Part III of Warren Farrell, **The Liberated Man**; he also includes a chapter on joint men's and women's consciousness-changing groups. The most useful introduction to men's issues is Jack Nichols, **Men's Liberation**; he covers such topics as intellect ('the blind man's bluff'), playfulness ('recovering the missing ingredient'), competition ('winning isn't everything'), and dominance ('an impediment to awareness'). A number of 'men's liberation' magazines and gay men's magazines are published, e.g., **Gay Sunshine**.

If you want to get in touch with a men's or women's group in your home community, you might begin by getting hold of the local contact for the National Organization for Women or, in Canada, the Status of Women, or the people who put out your local feminist newspaper or magazine.

(B) Those of us who've wanted to break down our **egocentricity** have involved our selves in the spiritual movement. A good brief introduction to the spiritual scene is Theodore Roszak, **Unfinished Animal**. And there are some monthly magazines that can keep us up with issues — and current events — on the spiritual end of things: for example, **East West Journal**, **New Age Journal** and **New Directions**.

Nearly every major city now has a number of spiritual groups, and most of them will be kind enough to answer your questions and steer you to the group or groups that are most suited to your temperament and interests.

(C) Those of us who've wanted to break down our **scientific single vision** and get back in touch with the intuitive, emotional, feeling side of our selves have tended to join groups doing 'group therapy', or body therapy, or the 'new sports' (the activities make up what's often referred to as the 'human potential movement'). A good introduction to group therapy is William Schutz, **Joy** (1967); to body therapy, Alexander Lowen, **Bioenergetics** (1975); to the new sports, George Leonard, **The Ultimate Athlete**. An 'encyclopedic cookbook of human potential techniques' in all these fields is Howard Lewis and Harold Streitfeld, **Growth Games** (1971).

Most cities now have a number of consciousness-and-growth groups. If you can't find one that you like, or if you'd like to work more intensively away from your home, you can write away to any number of growth institutes; the best known are Esalen, in California, and Cold Mountain, in Canada.

(D) Some of us who've wanted to get rid of our **bureaucratic mentalities** have been dropping out of the work-world for a year or more, and living cheap and interesting lives on our savings. The Bible for these people has been Ernest Callenbach, **Living Poor With Style**. He covers everything — eating, getting around, dwelling, furnishing, clothing, staying fit, raising children, fun and games. . . .

(E) Others of us have managed to break down our bureaucratic mentalities — and also our **nationalism** — by getting involved in human-scale projects in our local communities. Nearly every community now has (or **should** have!) its own food co-op, parent-run daycare centre, co-op radio, alternative school (or simply: alternative educational arrangement), newspaper, bookstore, co-op restaurant . . . and most of these are always on the lookout for volunteer and-or part-time staff. Co-op Handbook Collective's **Food Co-op Handbook** is a very useful account of the problems that are involved in this kind of activity.

(F) Many of us have gotten over our **big city outlooks** by spending a year or more in the country, or in a communal situation, or in both. Two of the best magazines on country living are **The Mother Earth News** and **Natural Life**. Women should also see Sherry Thomas and Jeanne Tetrault, **Country Women: A Handbook for the New Farmer** (1976), a collection of dozens of articles (not to mention poetry and graphics) on 'how to negotiate a land purchase, dig a well, grow vegetables organically, build a fence and shed, deliver a goat, (etc.), all at the least possible expense and with minimum reliance on outside and professional help'.

The best information source on communal living is the bi-monthly magazine **Communities** which is edited — in part — by the very successful Twin Oaks community.

III. Breaking Out of Our Programming

Beginning to get free of the Prison is just that — a beginning. For most of us, breaking through one of the Prison's walls brings us up against the pain of realizing how badly we have been crippled as human beings — how difficult it is to be honest or spontaneous or real. It makes us conscious of old wounds and feelings of inadequacy. . . .

In the long run, though — if we hope really to transform society rather than get our selves more of the same — it is important for us to deal with the insights and fears that the Prison has protected us against. For until we are able to deal with these difficult understandings and fears, we will — most of us — continue to want to cling to the consolations of the Prison, no matter what our rhetoric might be, and no matter what our good intentions. (This is why so many 'political' people can work against sexism, say, or monolithic institutions, and still be into patriarchal attitudes or the bureaucratic mentality.)

In order to see the kind of programming we're up against — and what we can do about it — it helps to understand that, as many New Age people have recently pointed out, we have not one but three brains-in-one. National Aeronautics and Space Administration psychologist William Gevarter calls it the 'triune brain' and says that it consists of the 'reptilian', the 'old mammal' and the 'new mammal' brains.

The reptilian brain, says Gevarter, is associated with 'species-specific' behaviour — 'basic ways of acting associated with being human' — and is relatively unmalleable. It is not terribly important for our purposes. The old mammal brain contains one's emotional programming — 'the basic value system upon which one acts automatically'. The new mammal brain contains one's rational, 'mental', 'cognitive' programming.

Traditional 'political' people focus their attention exclusively on the new brain's programming. What they fail to realize is that all our responses to a situation are filtered through the old brain's programming as well as the new brain's, and unless we take steps to change the programming of the old brain — in other words, to change not just our intellectual selves, but our emotional selves — the old brain will continue to read even the most 'revolutionary' new programmes in the old way; to subvert them according to the fears and needs put into us by our old emotional programming.

The new brain programmes can be changed with new perceptions. Unfortunately, however, as we mature the old brain programmes become relatively permanent. And it is the very rare person, in Prison society, whose old brain isn't imprisoned in childhood. 'In the early years, the child builds in the old brain a basic value system and a basic way of looking at the world. New brain powers are relatively undeveloped so that dogma, rules, models, and ideology enter the old brain relatively uncritically'.

What beginning to break free of the Prison does is give us a sense of the depth and importance of our old brain programming. We begin to understand that the real key to healing self is, not just healing our selves on the level of new brain programming (ideas), but trying to change our old brain programming as well (emotions, psyche, spiritual crippling). Trying to **transform** our selves. . . .

According to Gevarter there are basically four ways that we can change our old brain programming: (1) defusing the emotional programming by removing the emotional 'pegs' that hold the programming in place; (2) adding to the emotional programming 'so that the net response is more favourable'; (3) removing the emotional programming from the 'feedback loop'; and (4) breaking up the normal response patterns to emotional stimuli.

Any of these ways can be effective; each of them appeals to somewhat different lifestyles and temperaments.

(1) **Defusing emotional programming.** Many of our new 'group therapies' can be of help here. For example, in **Primal therapy** the person tries to go back to the earliest incident that gave rise to a particular programme. This incident is relived with full emotional intensity. It is known as the original, or Primal, Pain, because pain is what we feel when we discover, as a child, that being our selves — being real — is unacceptible to our parents. 'The real feeling self', says Primal therapist Arthur Janov, 'is locked away with the original Pain; that is why (a person) must feel that Pain in order to liberate (him- or herself); feeling that Pain shatters the unreal self in the same way that denying the Pain created it'.

Our emotional programming is also responsible for much of our bodily tension. Therefore, much of the **body therapy** that goes on at human potential centres — rolfing, ta'i chi, acupressure massage and the like — can also serve to defuse our emotional programming. Stanley Keleman, director of the Centre for Energetic Studies in Berkeley, says, 'In coming to recognize how I hold myself, I begin to contact the feelings, thoughts, and memories that go along with my structure. I begin to experience the personal history of the bind in which I have bounded myself. And one way and another I make connection with the living body that I am'.

Finally, our emotional programming can be defused through **meditation**, which inactivates the new brain and lets our unresolved old brain patterns run themselves out. Lawrence LeShan's book **How to Meditate** (1974) is a good basic introduction to the various kinds of meditation.

The 'New Sports' movement can be seen as an attempt to 'defuse emotional programming' on a mass scale, and it can provide a good basic **experiential** introduction to **all** of the activities that I mention in this section.

According to psychologist Bob Kriegel (In **New Age Journal**, Aug. '77), the New Sports is an attempt to change the principles and philosophy of traditional sports from Prison-oriented values such as competition and vengeance to New Age values such as equal participation and spiritual awareness. This is happening in two ways. On the one hand, New Age coaches are trying to change the way in which some traditional sports are taught — 'the inner approach'. On the other hand, people are trying to develop new alternative models for participation — 'the outer approach'.

Inner. Tim Gallwey, author of **The Inner Game of Tennis**, says that our most formidable opponent is our selves — our own doubts, fears, and self-consciousness — our old emotional programming, in other words. To overcome this programming and develop our capacities, the 'Inner Game' focuses on developing nonjudgemental awareness, relaxed concentration, and awareness of self — or more specifically, of that part of self that learns naturally and performs effortlessly.

Outer. The 'New Physical Education' is trying to introduce, into the lower school grades, body movement and success-oriented activities designed to help young people develop a productive sense of their bodies and a positive self-image. The upper grades are introduced to sports they can participate in for the rest of their lives — sailing, skiing, tennis, backpacking. . . . The New Games Foundation (P.O. Box 7901, San Francisco 94120) has been putting on 'play festivals' in parks and recreation areas all over the U.S. These festivals tend to feature 'New Games' of every sort, some quite ancient, some made up on the spot . . . games that require a minimum of equipment and are designed to encourage creativity, spontaneity, and participation by young and old, 'skilled' and 'unskilled'. . . . Competition isn't necessarily **absent** from New Games, but it's definitely subordinate to cooperation.

(2) **Adding to the programming**. We can add to our emotional programming by learning to re-program our selves with appropriate phrases. Ken Keyes's Living Love Way is based primarily on learning to use such phrases; on learning to use the 'Twelve Pathways (to the Higher Consciousness Planes of Unconditional Love and Oneness)', a contemporary, practical condensation — in 12 phrases — of thousands of years of spiritual wisdom. Here, for example, is the third Pathway: 'I welcome the opportunity (even if painful) that my minute-to-minute experience offers me to become aware of the addictions I must reprogram to be liberated from my robot-like emotional patterns'. Instead of kicking the wall, repeat that to your self every time you fail to meet one of your 'security, sensation and power' needs — for example, the next time someone says they'd rather spend their time being somewhere else than being with you. Use those experiences for your consciousness-growth — that's the point. See what it gets you. . . .

The Cornucopia Institute holds workshops in the Living Love Way in major cities all over North America as well as at its centre in Kentucky (St. Mary, Ky. 40063). But you can learn to use the Living Love system entirely from Keyes's **Handbook to Higher Consciousness** and from some supplementary materials.

(3) **Removing the emotional programming from the feedback loop**. Transactional Analysis ('TA') is a kind of group therapy that teaches us to distinguish among our three 'inner voices': Parent, Adult and Child. The Parent is said to be stern and judgemental; the Adult, data-processing and prediction-making; and the Child, playful, spontaneous and creative.

The trouble with most encounters, according to TA, is that a person will speak to another as, say, one Adult to another ('How much is two plus two?'), but the response may be from the second person's Child to the first person's Parent ('I hate math!'). Or it may be from the second person's Parent to the first person's Child ('Can't you think about anything better than that?'). And so on. . . . This is called a 'crossed transaction' and it is said to make genuine communication (as distinct from banter, 'social conversation', put-downs and the like) virtually impossible. As TA therapist Claude Steiner puts it, 'Crossed transactions not only account for the interruption of communication but also are an essential part of games'.

In terms of the 'triune brain', it is clear that the Adult is a new brain function and that Parent and Child are old brain functions (i.e., Parent and Child embody our old emotional programming). Therefore, 'removing the emotional programming from the feedback loop' would mean learning to use our Adult whenever it seemed appropriate — for example, learning to speak out of our real wants and thoughts rather than out of the ones we're **supposed** to have (Parent). And it would mean learning to hook the other person's Adult whenever they started playing a social or psychological game that we didn't like.

The standard account bof TA therapy is Amy and Tom Harris's **I'm OK — You're OK** (1969); an extremely useful revision and extension of that book is Claude Steiner's **Scripts People Live**. There are many TA groups across North America now, and probably most of them are semi- or non-'professional' in the sense that the TA therapists — trained though they might be — lack their MD degrees or the **desire** to define themselves as 'professionals'. That puts TA therapy within the price range of just about everyone (same with Primal therapy, above).

(4) **Breaking up the normal response patterns**. We can overload the old brain with emotional stimuli and fatigue so that the normal response pattern is broken up, leaving the old brain much more responsive to new emotional programming. One healing method that makes good use of this technique (among other techniques) is Erhard Seminars Training, or simply 'est'.

The est Training ordinarily takes place on the Saturdays and Sundays of two consecutive weekends in a hotel conference room large enough to hold 250 participants. 'Each day's training lasts until the result intended for that day has been produced', says Werner Erhard. 'It starts at about 9:00 AM and can run until late that night or early the next morning; as it goes along, some people feel they have been deprived of some rest. Part of the training consists of trapping the mind in one position or another, so the trainer can't leave any hole unstopped; the training must let the mind exhaust all possible escape routes. Since it is exhaustive, it sometimes turns out to be exhausting.

'The real deprivation, however, is not a matter of sleep. It is in not being allowed to divert yourself when something powerful starts to come up. Ordinarily you light a cigarette, start a conversation, get up and walk around, or somehow make yourself busy when the person you are afraid is inside you begins to become even a little bit visible. These behaviours are all quite reasonable, and the true purpose behind them is to keep you from attending to the person you are afraid to attend to. And that keeps you from experiencing the person you really are'.

The est Training is available in most major cities for $300 (follow-up seminars for much less). An excellent introduction to est in all of its aspects is Luke Rhinehart's **Book of est**.

III. Voluntary Simplicity

As we begin to get free of the Prison — as we begin to heal our selves — we will naturally want to change our lives and lifestyles from thing-oriented to life-oriented; from status-oriented to personal growth-oriented. A number of New Age people have begun to do this already. They call their new lifestyle 'voluntary simplicity'.

'The essence of voluntary simplicity', say Duane Elgin and Arnold Mitchell (in Stanford Research Institute's most popular report ever), 'is living in a way that is outwardly simple and inwardly rich. This way of life embraces frugality of consumption, a strong sense of environmental urgency, a desire to return to living and working environments which are of a more human scale, and an intention to realize our higher human potential — both psychological and spiritual — in community with others'. In other words: voluntary simplicity is at least potentially an embodiment and expression of the New Age ethics . . . and of many New Age values.

Even the nonviolence ethic is an integral part of voluntary simplicity. Richard Gregg, nonviolent strategist and activist, says (in **Manas**, 4 & 11 Sept. '74), 'The concentration of much property in one person's possession creates resentment and envy or a sense of inferiority among others who do not have it. Such feelings, after they have accumulated long enough, become the motives which some day find release in acts of mob violence. Hence, the possession of much property becomes inconsistent with principles of non-violence'.

According to the Centre for Science in the Public Interest, voluntary simplicity means 'conserving material and human resources, be these food, fossil fuel, water, wildlife and community, or individual physical and psychological health'. Through simple living we 'open ourselves to a great variety of new experiences and values. We create a non-competitive atmosphere where people can reduce the tensions of modern life. . . . If we live at a slower pace, we have time to see the simple joys, especially the natural wonders around us'.

According to Ernest Callenbach, 'Penny-pinching is bad for the spirit', and voluntary simplicity is not a 'kind of trim-here and squeeze-there' approach to life. Instead, it 'recognizes that buying (with all the cost-consciousness and calculation it involves) is not the central question. The central question is **how to organize your life**. If you decide to organize it by your own standards and desires and needs, you will . . . come to know what your necessities really are. Obviously these will include food and shelter and clothes — possibly on a more modest scale than you tended to think. But they may also include music, or flowers or a southern-exposure window; privacy or an open-door policy; lots of heat or lots of fresh air . . . '.

According to Planetary Citizens (in **One Family**, Sept. '77), voluntary simplicity 'is the appropriate stance in the light of the lacks suffered by two-thirds of the human race. . . . Energy, materials, inventiveness, creativity and peoplepower can be freed in large amounts by voluntary simplicity, and can be reoriented toward raising the level of well-being and self-respect of Third World and Fourth World people. . . . At the same time, voluntary simplicity sets a model of creative self-reliance which may assist the "other worlds" in avoiding an unthinking adoption of the acquisition, competition, complication and consumerism models of Western society'.

It is important to understand what voluntary simplicity is **not**. It is not a back-to-the-land movement, though many people and eventually some communities may choose to lead a more agrarian existence. It is not limited to the counter-culture; by now probably most 'simple livers' would say they were not counter-cultural. It is not a passing fad — it is rooted too deeply in people's needs and in the emerging new ethics and values for that. Finally, it is the very **opposite** of poverty: poor people tend to **want** the material goods that they can't afford.

As an idea, voluntary simplicity is not new. 'Historically', say Elgin and Mitchell, 'voluntary simplicity has its roots in the legendary frugality and self-reliance of the Puritans' and the Quebecois fur traders and the **native** North Americans and in 'the teachings and social philosophy of a number of spiritual leaders such as Jesus and Gandhi'. What gives voluntary simplicity a uniquely modern aspect is the fact that it is no longer merely one way of choosing to live one's life; it is, rather, a rational and altogether **necessary** response (though by no means a sufficient response) to a number of serious social problems. Elgin and Mitchell list them: ' . . . the prospects of a chronic energy shortage; growing demands of the (insufficiently) developed nations for a more equitable share of the world's resources; the prospect that before we run out of resources on any absolute basis we may poison ourselves to death with environmental contaminants; a growing social malaise and purposelessness . . . '.

Some New Age people have begun to advocate voluntary simplicity for just that reason: that sooner or later we will almost certainly 'have to' live that way. This is an important point, but I am afraid it may be counter-productive if we use it as our **main** point. North Americans don't like to be told that they can't do what they're already doing, and their faith in technological solutions is boundless — largely because of the Prison and the (apparent) success of its monolithic institutions. This is changing somewhat, but even if North Americans were **perfectly** aware of the problems that we face, I think it would still be more effective to point to how much more satisfying a simple lifestyle might be, than to try to 'guilt' or frighten people into exactly the same behaviour. The simplicity must be voluntary, after all, if it is not to become grey and mean-spirited; and by stressing the positive aspects of voluntary simplicity we may be able to educate people out of the Prison and its institutions, rather than merely to the fact that North America is losing its power in the world.

No one is really sure how many North Americans are already living lives of voluntary simplicity. Elgin and Mitchell estimate that 2½ percent of the adult population — five million people (!) — are 'fully and wholeheartedly' living in voluntary simplicity with another 7½ percent or so living lives of 'partial voluntary simplicity'. However, Michael Phillips (in **CoEvolution Quarterly**, Summer '77) argues that these figures are about a hundred times too high. He defines voluntary simplicity as 'the rejection of "making a lot of money" as a personal goal', and he says, 'Almost no one **wants** to earn less next year than they earned this year. If a public opinion survey asked the question: "Would you like to make a lot of money?" you would not find 5,000,000 people saying "No" '. He concludes, 'I personally think the growth of (the) real simple living movement will parallel the spread of Eastern spiritual practices', and in this I think he is close to the mark: simple living is implicit in and a result, not of 'Eastern spiritual practices' **per se**, but of all our attempts to break free from the Prison.

IV. 80 Ways to Voluntary Simplicity

You don't have to join a group, lay out money, sign a petition, or anything else to begin living a life of voluntary simplicity. All you have to do is decide that you **want** to — and then begin **doing** the kinds of things that are listed below. (This list is meant to be suggestive, not exhaustive. If you want more information on any of these topics — or more suggestions! — you should refer back to my sources: Tom Bender, **Sharing Smaller Pies**; Ernest Callenbach, **Living Poor With Style**; Centre for Science in the Public Interest (CSPI), **99 Ways to a Simple Lifestyle**; Simple Living Collective, **Taking Charge**; and an excellent occasional newsletter, **Simple Living**.)

A. FIRST STEPS

1. **Re-Evaluate Your Priorities**. Lucy Anderson (in **Taking Charge**) suggests the following activity. Draw a circle (balloon) in the middle of a piece of paper. Put your name on it. Around this balloon, make a balloon for each of the activities that occupies your waking time each week (for example, job, family, friends, dance, women's group, exploring new ideas, television) — the size of each balloon should represent the amount of time you give to that activity. Then, draw a line from the centre balloon to each activity balloon. Make the thickness of the line represent 'the strength of your committment to that activity and the pleasure you receive from it'. What does your balloon chart tell you about your life?

2. **Play the Income Game**. Figure out how you could live on half your present income. One-fourth of your income. Don't say it can't be done, figure out how it **could** be done. Would you have to change your lifestyle in any way? Would you have to live by different values? Would the differences in lifestyle and values help you to meet your real priorities? Did you learn anything else from this game? (Try it again after reading through the list below.)

3. **TRY THINGS!** Tom Bender writes, 'Any proposal for changes can be met with a thousand reasons why it might not work. Most such questions can only be answered by trying it. One experiment is worth a thousand buts'.

B. FOOD

4. Consume Less Meat. Most North Americans eat more protein than their bodies need; a hang-over, perhaps, from the days when most of us were manual labourers. Worse, the amount of vegetable protein used in livestock feed **in North America** equals 90 percent of the **world's** protein deficit! For every pound of meat, we North Americans feed a cow from 14 to 21 pounds of protein from sources that could be used directly as food. And things are getting worse: North American per capita consumption of beef has **more than doubled since 1940.** But this doesn't have to be. There are many other sources of protein besides meat: dried milk, cheese, fish, eggs, nuts, brown rice, beans, peas. . . . The point is to eat them in their proper combinations, achieving 'protein complementarity', a kind of gastronomic synergy! See Ellen Ewald, **Recipes for a Small Planet** (1972). Also Anna Thomas, **The Vegetarian Epicure** (1972).

5. Eat Tofu. Often called bean curd, tofu is the best single source of protein: the cheapest, the most accessible (you can make it yourself), and potentially the tastiest. See Shurtleff and Aoyagi, **The Book of Tofu.**

6. Select Unprocessed Foods. White flour and white rice have been robbed of nutrients and fiber — and good taste! Many food additives are unsafe; nevertheless, since 1955 the number of additives in our food has doubled. And so on. Many cookbooks are now available that rely solely on natural healthgiving foods that are free of chemical preservatives, additives, pesticides, and artificial growing conditions; I suppose my favourite is Sharon Cadwallader and Judi Ohr, **Whole Earth Cook Book** (1972).

7. Avoid Non-Nutritious Food. Since 1940 per capita consumption of dairy products has declined 19 percent, fresh vegetables, 17 percent, fresh fruits, 44 percent. On the other hand, the pastry and fried snack industries have boomed. And soft drink sales are up by over 100 percent. If you're just plain getting tired of the 'usual' foods, chances are good that you're not preparing them in anything like the number of possible ways. You should certainly look into Sigrid Shepard's remarkable **Thursday Night Feast and Good Plain Meals Cookbook** ($12.95 from New Age Printing, Inc., East 9514 Montgomery, Spokane, Wash. 99206) — 800 natural food recipes from China, Japan, Indonesia, India and the Middle East, all using common, easy-to-obtain ingredients.

8. Reduce Intake of Refined Sugar. Refined sugar contains neither vitamins, nor minerals, nor protein, and is a chief cause of tooth decay, obesity and diabetes. Still and all — everyone loves sweets. So check out, e.g., Ruth Laughlin, **Natural Sweets and Treats** (1973).

9. Eat Wild Foods. Edible fruits, nuts, mushrooms, roots and greens can be found nearly everywhere! See, e.g., Bradford Angier, **Feasting Free on Wild Edibles** (1969).

10. Learn to Preserve Food. Canning, freezing, drying, etc. See Ruth Hertzberg et. al., **Putting Food By,** 2nd ed. (1975).

11. Conserve Nutritional Value of Food. Buy foods that are grown close to your area, that is, foods that are allowed to ripen on trees and vines, rather than in transit. Store foods properly. Don't overcook.

12. Bake Bread. Economical and satisfying. Bake it in quantity and freeze it. See Ed Brown's wonderful **Tassajara Bread Book** (1970).

13. Prepare Various Food Products at Home. Cereals, yoghurt, sprouts, party dips, peanut butter, salad dressings. . . . See esp. Cadwallader and Ohr, and Ewald (above).

14. **Drink Homemade Beverages**. Apple cider, fruit juices, applejack, natural teas, etc. See Shirley Ross, **Nature's Drinks** (1974). (Incidentally — in one year the average North American will consume about 35 gallons of soft drinks and 21 gallons of beer.)

15. **Question Pets and Pet Food**. North Americans spend about $2.75 billion a year on commercially-prepared pet food, which is equal to the dollar value of the food needs of nearly 40 percent of the world's poor. All domestic animals can be fed on table scraps supplemented with commercial dry cereals. Pets are, themselves, often the recipients of strokes that we are too shy or selfish or unimaginative to direct to other human beings.

16. **Shop Carefully**. For example: (a) Eat before you shop. If you don't, you'll end up buying more. (b) Never buy pre-sliced meats or cheese. The slicing and packaging can more than double the price. (c) Never buy canned baby food. Mash up regular people's food for babies. (d) Plan your shopping for a week. Make a list. The less often you go into a store, the less you'll spend. (e) Buy good food in small quantities rather than cheap food in large. A third of a pound of steak is better than a pound of fatty hamburger. (f) If you must eat meat — try organ meats. (g) Avoid canned vegetables. They're tasteless (actually, they taste of chemicals), and far less nutritious than fresh or frozen vegetables.

17. **Grow Your Own Food**. If you don't have a yard of your own, ask to use a friend's or neighbour's. Volunteer to share some of your produce in return. A good basic gardening book is Catharine Foster, **The Organic Gardener** (1972).

C. CLOTHING

18. **Get Some Perspective on Your Clothes Buying (I)**. Susan Lee (in **Taking Charge**) says, 'Make an inventory of the clothes you own. Consider how many pants, coats, shoes, socks, shirts, and suits you have. Which ones have you worn in the last year? In the last two years? Can you determine how they contribute to your well-being? Might your unused clothing be given, traded, or sold at low cost to others?'

19. **Get Some Perspective (II)**. Susan Lee would have us ask, 'What is my usual frame of mind when I set out to buy clothes? Do I go clothes shopping because I am not feeling good about myself and therefore need an ego boost? Do I shop when I am bored and need something to do? What else could I do to feel better or active, rather than buying clothes I may not really want?'

20. **Buy Used Clothes**. Fashion-conscious North Americans spend $70 billion on clothes each year. ('This is enough', says Susan Lee, 'to drape the Earth'.) Most of these clothes are thrown out sooner or later (usually sooner, when styles change), but some of them find their way into thrift stores, secondhand shops, and so on. If you pick out a second-hand store and frequent it occasionally, you should be able to meet your clothing needs for one-fourth or less what you might otherwise spend.

21. **Make Your Own Clothing**. Homemade clothing generally affords a better fit, wears longer, and costs less than factory-made clothing. Besides, sewing and knitting are meaningful activities that allow us to relax and develop a skill . . . and develop our self-reliance. Beyond a certain point they're even fun. For a clear and simple introduction to the simple art of clothes-making,

see Sharon Rosenberg and Joan Wiener, **The Illustrated, Hassle-Free, Make Your Own Clothes Book** (1969).

22. **Barter for Clothing**. Barter with friends who don't know how to sew. Barter sewing for baby-sitting and both parties will save money.

23. **Swap Clothing**. If you get tired of some of your clothing, get together with some friends and trade. You'll get a free new wardrobe and have a lot of fun besides.

24. **Mend and Reuse Clothing**. Conserve resources; avoid waste. If you don't want to wear mended clothes, mend them anyway and barter or swap for something else. At the very least, give them away.

25. **Do Not Wear Fur from Endangered Species**. Every year in North America, 13 million animals including beavers, lynx, otters, seals, wolves, foxes and raccoons are victims of a fur trade that caters to fashion. Many of these animals are caught in the steel-jaw trap, which not only tortures them 'needlessly' but also crushes — 'inadvertently' — literally millions of non-fur-bearing animals as well (which trappers refer to as 'trash': geese, ducks, song birds, eagles, owls, porcupines and the like). Spotted cats (including the tiger, leopard, jaguar, cheetah and ocelot) may soon be extinct because of our need to at least look like natural human beings.

26. **Sleep Without Pajamas**.

D. SHELTER ▮◀━━━━▶▮◀━━━━▶▮◀━━━━▶▮◀━━━━▶▮◀━━━━▶▮◀━━━━▶

27. **Insulate Properly**. Heating bills might go down by half.

28. **Investigate Solar Heating and Cooling Systems**.

29. **Paint Your Home**. Protects it from weathering. Will save you money in the not-so-long run.

30. **Decorate Your Home Simply**. 'Home decorations', says CSPI, 'are an expression of one's lifestyle. House plants and simple homemade creations . . . save money, resources, and energy over luxurious decoration'.

31. **Eliminate Unnecessary Appliances**. The average North American household has 29 electrical appliances — most of which are not labour-saving devices at all, but are wasteful and inefficient.

32. **Share Tools and Appliances With Others**. A block or a group of friends could arrange to share washers and dryers, power tools, lawn mowers, etc. Would save hundreds of dollars a year, provide many social opportunities. . . .

33. **Reuse Furniture**. Good quality used furniture is better than poor quality new, and can be bought for a fraction of the price of new at auctions, garage sales, thrift shops and the like.

34. **Repair Furniture**. It's easy.

35. **Make Furniture**. See William Schremp, **Designer Furniture Anyone Can Make** (1972).

36. **Consider Building Your Own Home**. Read and ponder: Ken Kern, **The Owner-Built Home: A How-to-do-it Book**, rev. ed. (1975); Ken Kern, Ted Kogon and Rob Thallon, **The Owner-Builder and The Code: Politics of Building Your Own Home**, 1976 ($5 from Owner-Builder Publns., P.O. Box 550, Oakhurst, Calif. 93664); and River, **Dwelling: On Making Your Own** (1974).

37. **Consider Living Co-operatively or Communally**.

E. SOLID WASTE ▶▮◀━━━━▶▮◀━━━━▶▮◀━━━━▶▮◀━━━━▶▮◀━━━━▶▮◀

38. **Avoid Disposable Paper Products**. Saves on trees and energy.

39. **Refrain from Buying Plastic-Wrapped Items**. In 1971 each of us bought

an average of 25 pounds of plastic packaging with our 'goods'. By 1980 industry officials espect this figure to triple! Plastic packaging litters the environment and **does not decompose**.

40. **Try to Avoid the Non-Returnable**. Forty billion throwaway bottles a year....

41. **Recycle Newspapers and Magazines**.

42. **Recycle Metal Cans**. Sixty-five billion metal cans a year....

43. **Make Food Scraps, Leaves, Weeds, Grass Clippings, Wood Chips, etc., Into Compost**. Most North Americans throw these things out — in green plastic bags!

44. **Avoid Aerosol Sprays**. They are harmful, expensive and wasteful, a major source of air pollution, a probable cause of lung cancer, and damaging to the skin.

45. **Don't Always Flush After Using the Toilet**. A family of four uses close to 90 gallons of fresh water a day for flushing toilets (at five gallons a flush).

46. **Investigate Flush-Less Toilets**. The flush toilet means that clean water is used to carry organic wastes to treatment plants. This wastes a great deal of water (see above); pollutes whole bodies of water; requires expensive, unreliable, and energy-intensive waste-treatment plants; and creates a dreadful 'sludge' that can't be properly disposed of. But non-water toilet systems are available! See, e.g., 'Goodbye to the Flush Toilet', $1 from **Rain** (Ap. '76).

F. TRANSPORTATION ═▶◀══════▶◀══════▶◀══════▶◀══════▶◀══════▶◀

47. **Avoid Unnecessary Auto Travel**. Most North Americans will drive their cars if their destination is more than **two blocks** away! (Several studies have found this to be true.)

48. **Share the Car**. Every day 64 million North American workers drive their cars to and from work. Of these, 44 million drive alone. If we got together with our friends and neighbours (or with people at work) and set up car pools, we could save hundreds of dollars each in commuting costs (gas, parking, repairs, etc.), do away with 'rush-hour traffic', and get a chance to talk with people.

49. **Ask Whether You Really Need an Automobile**. If you live within two miles or so of work, a bicycle — or a good brisk walk — might get you there just as well, and be better exercise and more fun. If you live father away from work, or if you like going on long trips, ask yourself whether public transportation might get you there just as well, and more cheaply and easily.

50. **Begin to Use Busses and Subways and Trains**. When many people complain about how bad public transportation is in their town, often what they're really saying is that they go stir-crazy if they have to spend some time waiting for a bus. They should ask themselves if they could spend this time in a happy or productive way — by thinking about things, by reading a magazine or book, by looking out calmly at the world. I strongly suspect that it is our inability to do this — to enjoy time rather than kill time — that causes us to rush everywhere in cars.

51. **Buy a Bicycle**. They're good exercise, they're fun, and they can carry almost anything.

52. **Walk More**. Prison-bound people resent walking, feel somehow victimized by it. Prison-free people love it.

G. HEALTH ▰▰▰▰▰▰▰▰▰▰

53. **Educate Yourself About Your Body.** To simplify our lives, we must know how to keep our bodies healthy and how to heal them once they get sick. We must take responsibility for healing our selves medically and view health workers as our assistants rather than our saviours. A number of self-help health books have recently been published; three that I consider essential are Mike Samuels and Hal Bennett, **The Well Body Book** (1973), which tells us how to treat the causes rather than the effects of our diseases; Naboru Muramoto, **Healing Ourselves** (1973), a good basic introduction to Eastern healing concepts; and Boston Women's Health Book Collective, **Our Bodies, Ourselves**, 2nd ed. (1976), subtitled 'A Book By and For Women'.

54. **Look For Alternative Health Clinics.** Many communities now have neighbourhood-based health centres. Often they operate on shoestring budgets with volunteer or 'para-professional' staff. But they tend to be very honest about what they can and cannot do; they tend to tell you exactly what is wrong with you and why — to treat you like an adult rather than a dependent; they're often controlled by the people who use and work in them; and they can save you a lot of money.

55. **Use Simple Personal Products.** We don't need to buy Ban Deodorant; we can mix one tablespoon alum and one cup water and come up with a 'product' that's just as effective. For Listerine Mouthwash we can substitute ½ teaspoon salt and one cup water (adding a couple of drops of peppermint oil extract for flavour). For Crest Toothpaste we can substitute baking soda. And so on. . . .

56. **Do Not Abuse Drugs.** Overall we spend $10 billion a year on drugs, mostly pills, whose purpose is to calm us down, stimulate us, put us to sleep. . . . In many cases these drugs are just substitutes (and poor ones at that) for getting in touch with our selves and learning to rest and relax.

57. **Stop Smoking Cigarettes.** The number of smokers is on the rise again. (A person who smokes half a pack a day surrenders, on the average, five and one-half years of life.)

58. **Do Not Abuse Alcohol.** Most North Americans drink alcohol to loosen up, to get rid of their inhibitions, to get free, for a fleeting time, of the Prison. North Americans spent about $24 billion on alcohol in 1974, or about $100 for every man, woman **and child**.

59. **Care For Teeth.** Most North Americans treat their teeth badly. By age 15, the average North American has had 11 decayed teeth. Buy Thomas McGuire's wonderful book **The Tooth Trip** (1972). Follow it like the wilderness guide that it is.

60. **Watch Weight.** Over one-half of the North American population weighs at least 10 percent more than the 'norm' for their particular age, sex and height! Nearly 30 percent of us weigh 20 percent more than the recommended weight. Most of these people are suffering from no more than overeating and lack of exercise. The best type of exercise — walking and jogging — requires no fuel energy, capital, maintenance, expense, or rigorous training.

H. FUN AND FULFILLMENT ▰▰▰▰▰▰▰▰

61. **Cut Down on Television.** Jerry Mander, in **Four Arguments for the Elimination of Television** (1978), says, 'People (are) seeing television images of Borneo forests, European ballets, varieties of family life, distant police ac-

tions, current events, or re-creations of historical crises, **and they (are) believing themselves to be experiencing these places, people and events**. Yet the television image of the Borneo forest or the news or historical event (is) surely not the experience of them. . . . It (is) only the experience of sitting in a darkened room, often alone, with the body totally stilled, even the eyes unmoving, . . . passively staring at flickering light' (emphasis added).

The average adult, in North America today, watches TV **for almost four hours a day**, according to Mander. (The average **set** is on for over **six** hours a day.) That's roughly half of the adult nonsleeping, nonworking time.

62. **Cut Down on Tourism**. 'People travel for many reasons, yet very few of those reasons can best be satisfied by travel. Entertainment, rest and "getting away" can all take place in our own home communities. Wise travel requires that we first minimize unnecessary travel by improving the places where we live and our relationship with the people with whom we live' (**Rain**, Ap. '76).

63. **Find Out About Free Events**. It's remarkable how many things go on in our communities that we could attend free, or for a very low cost. Check out the newspapers, especially the weekend newspapers, which often have listings of museums, special exhibitions, political meetings, lectures, free or low admission concerts, dances, court sessions, city council meetings; check out community and 'alternative' newspapers; check out bulletin boards, especially the ones in libraries and around universities and colleges (where most events, including movies and plays, are reasonably priced).

64. **Re-Discover Your Community**. Most communities have at least a couple of beautiful parks; tennis courts, baseball fields, etc., are often available; hanging out in different neighbourhoods is fascinating and educational.

65. **Cultivate Your Friendships**. Treat your friends well. Engage them in honest conversations and express your affections for them. Be open to new friendships and to many different kinds of relationships.

66. **Re-Claim Your Creativity**. 'An important part of simple living', say Lucy Anderson and Susan Lee (in **Taking Charge**), 'is an effort to reclaim ourselves and our creativity. . . . We want to make our own songs, dances, recipes, stories, crafts, ideas, humour; we want to fulfill our creative needs ourselves, and do so in ways that express our own set of values'.

67. **Give Creative Gifts**. 'Most of us', say Anderson and Lee, 'usually head for a store when we want to get a gift. . . . But how often do these purchased gifts make a statement that is genuinely personal, showing thoughtful consideration of the recipient's personality and interests, as well as being truly expressive of values we want to uphold? . . . Creative simplicity can inspire us to find or make meaningful gifts for those we care about' — gifts such as a jar of homemade preserves, a dragonfly wing, a poem, a song, a day of housecleaning by friends.

68. **Create Your Own Celebrations**. Rituals and celebrations don't need to be bought ready-made from the dominant culture; we can create our own. For example, on Easter day we could make a point of travelling to a beautiful spot with our friends, and read to each other — words of rebirth; or, for example, we could declare a day in early July 'Interdependence Day', a day to celebrate planetary consciousness (Planetary Citizens actually did this one year). Write away for the **Alternate Celebrations Catalogue**, 4th ed., 1978

($3.75 from Alternatives, 1924 E. 3rd St., Bloomington, Ind. 47401).

69. **Become Artistic.** You don't need to be a 'professional' to enjoy expressing your self artistically. The arts can, and should, be practiced for their own sake — and for your own sake! With little money, we can practice — and often become quite 'good' at — dancing and ballet, choral arts and singing, painting and sculpting, photography and drama, piano and guitar. . . . We can practice weaving, embroidering, batiking, appliqueing, knitting, quilting. We can make puppets, prints, collages, ceramics, toys. . . .

70. **Preserve a Place for Quiet.** Noise interferes with nearly all of our daily activities. The noise level in our cities is constantly rising (and government notions of 'acceptible' noise levels are correspondingly rising). Constant noise can threaten our sanity.

71. **Use Your Local Library.** For free books, magazines, films, talks and presentations.

72. **Camp and Backpack.** And don't take along every home comfort! See Colin Fletcher's wonderful book **The Complete Walker** (1974).

73. **Enjoy Participatory and Inexpensive Sports.** Watching sports on television is a way of escaping from the Prison by identifying — vicariously — with graceful, strong, and (seemingly) Prison-free human beings. Participating in expensive and energy-intensive sports like snowmobiling, motorboating, parachuting and race-car driving is a way of escaping from the Prison by merging with it totally. There are, however, some genuinely Prison-free alternatives that are participatory and cost little or nothing in either equipment, travel to site or fuel energy: tennis, outdoor swimming, basketball, soccer, baseball, fishing, skating, jogging, judo, gymnastics. . . . And see New Games Foundation, **The New Games Book** (1976), an illustrated compendium of games such as Tweezli-Whop, Catch the Dragon's Tail, Ooh-Ahh and Slaughter.

I. WORK

74. **Re-Evaluate Your Job (I).** Lucy Anderson suggests, 'Make a list of what you would like to do in your lifetime or write up your own **Who's Who** entry as if it were written about you at age 70. Be imaginative and complimentary. What do you really want to do? Please dream! . . . Having described what you want to do, examine what skills, abilities, and experiences you have or need to carry out your vision. . . . Assess each new skill according to the time and effort it involves. Research and discover the most resourceful ways to acquire the needed skills'. Ask yourself what relation your present job has to your real hopes for your self. To the skills and experiences you'll need to actualize those hopes.

75. **Re-Evaluate Your Job (II).** Do you really need a full-time job? Look over the ways to simple living, above, and ask your self: Am I spending too much on food? Are my clothing needs exaggerated? Could I do without my car? Could I fill my leisure time with inexpensive and rewarding things to do? If so, wouldn't I **rather** have time than money? And so on.

76. **Re-Evaluate Your Job (III).** Tom Bender asks, 'Is what you produce a luxury or does it fulfill a real need? Will what you do be affordable when we are less wealthy?' He advises, 'Move towards more useful and secure kinds of work'.

77. **Get Out of Debt.** The average North American — man, woman and

child — is over $500 in debt. There's nothing like 'credit' buying to keep a person working at a useless, boring and degrading job.

78. **Create or Invent Your Own Job.** Many communities need child-care centres, legal aid services, honest car repair services, tutors. . . .

79. **Consider Job Sharing.** Jobs that would ordinarily be filled by one person could be divided and shared by two people. Mark Zwick, a psychiatric social worker, says (in **Taking Charge**), 'Working half-time allows me as a husband to have more energy to plan and do things with my wife and children. . . . I can now think about community involvement with my wife, writing, and being involved in my children's education'.

80. **Consider Income Sharing.** 'Income sharing means equal distribution (or distribution according to need) of earnings within a family, an extended family, or an intentional community' (**Taking Charge**). In fact, income sharing could be practiced among **any** group of friends. Instead of **everyone** working **all** the time, everyone could take turns working — and pool the income. Everyone who wasn't working would be free to spend their time as they liked (New Agers would spend the bulk of their time in healing self and healing society). The point is to have something useful and compelling to **do**.

Chapter 21 — Healing Society

This chapter is about how New Age people are trying to heal or transform (at this point the words are synonymous) society.

A number of New Age people have argued that the process of social transformation should take place in three fairly distinct stages: (1) cultural change, (2) 'group work', and (3) political and institutional change. There is, however, an emerging consensus among many New Age people that would avoid all talk of stages and, more generally, all advice to others about what they 'should' do 'next'.

In this view, (a) the assumption that there can be one 'correct' scheme for healing society is an assumption that leads almost inevitably to authoritarian political parties — and authoritarian societies. Moreover, (b) North America is now so interconnected and interdependent that just about **anything we do that is in tune with the New Age ethics and political values** would help bring New Age society about.

If enough of us, a 'critical mass' of us, share in the New Age ethics and political values and are active in the areas that are most accessible to us or that 'feel right' to us when we've begun to meet our needs at self-development stages three through seven — then society will begin to move in a New Age direction. More rapidly than we might imagine.

People tend to 'burn out' (to get bored or depressed by working for social transformation) for either or both of these reasons: (1) they have not bothered to begin healing self; (2) they are engaging in the social transformation activities that they think they **should** be doing rather than the one(s) that come most naturally to **them**. However, it is rare that a person who begins to get in touch with him- or herself doesn't come to feel a deep inner need to help transform society in at least one of the ways in this chapter. And each of them can help to move society in a New Age direction.

I. Group Work

One of the ways that New Age people have been trying to heal or transform society has been by working in small or small-ish groups. Most New Age political thinkers feel that this is an essential part of the process of transforming society. Herb Kohl, educator and activist, says, 'No one can struggle alone with as much energy as is required to sustain something of value in this culture. . . . This is not a time for prophets but a time for action initiated and sustained by small groups of people'.

New Age people have been involving themselves in the work of at least eleven **kinds** of groups, depending on their temperaments, interests, and levels of commitment. (Groups whose addresses are not shown below are described more fully in Chap. 24, sect. III. And remember — nearly all of them are looking for volunteers!)

(1) **Caucuses** are being set up in factories, offices, professional organizations. Generally they consist of three or more factory workers or office workers or professionals who know and trust each other and spend part of their time trying to encourage fellow factory workers, etc., to think of themselves less as economic people, and more as self-developing persons.

Caucus members do this by trying to bring New Age perspectives to bear on immediate workplace issues and by trying to change office rules, union demands, professional standards, etc., in line with these perspectives. For example: a New Age factory caucus might emphasize such New Age 'basics' as: worker participation in management; bringing 'synergic principles' to bear on the workplace (see Chap. 13, sect. IV-3-4); the right to choose a 20- or 30-hour work week (leaving people free to work 40 hours if they wished); and a narrowing of the income gap among all those connected with the enterprise.

Caucus members usually do not expect their concerns to be adopted, or even taken very seriously — at first; but they often find that standing up for them can provide an 'opening wedge' for New Age ideas and energies.

Planetary Citizens suggests that we join existing institutions (which might include unions or professional organizations) **as a Planetary Citizen.** 'You should convey the idea that you are there to carry out your planetary citizenship responsibility by helping them, and you hope that your participation will also serve to strengthen the awareness of how their particular part of the picture fits into the whole'. They also suggest that we encourage unions, professional organizations and the like to set up 'study commissions' that will consider their 'global responsibilities'.

(2) **Alternative institutions** now include food co-ops, co-op stores, 'free schools', community radio and television stations, community and alternative newspapers, neighbourhood repair groups, health care clinics, print shops, credit unions, craft collectives. . . . In their structure and goals they are often

quite different from one another, but the important thing — what makes them 'alternative' institutions — is that they are based on many or all of the New Age ethics and political values.

Many alternative institutions begin in a similar way — and face similar problems. For example: the Bethesda Avenue Food Co-op, Bethesda, Maryland, began when people who were interested in food, economy and health began meeting regularly. Rounding up neighbours and acquaintances, this 'core of enthusiasts' discussed and decided on such things as: whether to be run as a co-op, non-profit corporation, or workers' collective; whether to obtain food by weekly prepaid orders (i.e. by everyone filling out forms every week) or by opening up a storefront; whether to use volunteer labour or paid labour; whether to hire 'professional management'; and whether to stock conventional packaged goods as well as natural foods (the larger question was whether or not to make a serious effort to appeal to the thing-oriented).

As these things were being decided, some future co-op workers began serving as volunteers in similar co-ops in other neighbourhoods. Many valuable lessons were learned. A board of directors was formed, composed half of salaried employees and half of volunteer workers. Anyone who paid a $100 membership fee (retrievable upon leaving) was a member of the co-op, and any member who volunteered three hours of work per month was entitled to vote. It was found that about $2000 was enough to stock a co-op store with 'the basics', and that low prices, high-quality produce, and excellent cheeses were more than enough to please the first customers who then spread the word and attracted more support and more membership fees . . . leading on to other pressing questions. For example: should we expand or divide? And should we give priority to consumer savings or to putting money in to community development?

Most alternative institutions are community-based, but some are regional, national, or even planetary in scope. The Centre for Studies in Food Self-Sufficiency (90 Main St., Burlington, Vt. 05401) is 'working toward a plan for increasing Vermont's self-sufficiency' (and has openings for 'research interns'). The Institute for Alternative Futures (1624 Crescent Place N.W., Washington, D.C. 20009), founded in 1977 'to explore Anticipatory Democracy', is exploring 'the concept of a college in Washington functioning as a shadow government, raising alternative policies'. Planetary Citizens hopes to convene — annually or periodically — the 'Planetary Elders', 'the people who have the insight into the human race, about where it is going, about what needs to be done. . . . When they speak on the nature of (our) dilemma, . . . the world will listen and statesmen will pay heed'.

(3) **Local chapters** of various New Age-oriented special interest groups — usually combining education and action — offer us many excellent opportunities to involve our selves in community problems and national issues.

A number of volunteers and staff people at Friends of the Earth, an environmental-action group, have recently reported on 'A Day in the Life' of FOE (**Not Man Apart**, July '77), and it looks something like this:

Bunny Gabel, a volunteer for New York FOE, writes, 'Since 1974 I've been FOE representative on the coalition against Westway (an interstate highway), studying the issues, talking to politicians, making calls, preparing testimony, speaking at meetings, ringing doorbells and baking cakes to raise money for the lawsuit against the interstate, passing out literature at street corners and block parties, and maintaining liaison with other groups fighting the interstate'.

Ann Roosevelt, a staff person for New England FOE, says, '(A number of people here) volunteer for at least one full day a week. . . . Nancy Shelmerdine works on wildlife issues, helps organize volunteers, and is trying to raise funds so we can set up an environmental intern programme. . . . Bob Elgin, a physicist and life member of FOE, . . . has testified on clean air and is working now on analysis of Carter's energy programme and various energy bills. Kerry Mackin is a professional photographer who teaches at night and often works during the day for FOE'. Carolyn Nelson, District of Columbia FOE: 'The afternoon is quieter, usually — a time to catch up on the chores you didn't get to in the morning. I leave at five because two children are waiting, but there are always people working on until who-knows-when'.

Friends of the Earth has branches in 60 cities and districts. The Sierra Club, another environmental group, has 49 chapters and 237 **local groups**. Movement for a New Society has about 40 local groups. Amnesty International has at least 113 'adoption groups' in the U.S. and Canada, and at least 16 'action groups'. . . .

Each adoption group, which consists of about 15 to 25 people, is assigned up to three 'prisoners of conscience' from countries of different political systems. 'Members write to the appropriate government, embassy, and prison officials to secure freedom for the prisoners. Members often write to the prisoners themselves and to their relatives to offer encouragement'. Action group members 'work on emergency cases requiring immediate attention, where torture or the threat of execution is involved'.

(4) **Support groups** are for those of us who are most committed to New Age values and who are most eager to propagate and live by them. They tend to arise — as Susanne Gowan et. al. point out — 'from already existing friendships, workplace ties, religious affiliations, etc., and range in size from about three to 12 individuals. They grow as cells grow, by division, and can proliferate rapidly when conditions are ripe'.

Support group members tend to live together (in communes, ashrams and the like), partly so they can 'act the New Age out in the present' by living simply, and partly so they can devote the bulk of their energies to the task of speeding up New Age evolution. But living together isn't really a defining aspect of support groups. The important point is that support group members are actively involved in helping to heal each other and helping to heal society.

Some support groups are made up of people who spend the bulk of their time and energy in New Age caucuses, alternative institutions, special-interest groups and so forth; other support groups have their own special projects. The Philadelphia Life Community — branch of the Movement for a New Society — consists of (a) 15 'autonomous household units' of 6-10 people each 'with diverse interests and collective commitments', and (b) 13 collectives working on a variety of concerns (feminist, nonviolence training, 'global justice', etc.). 'Each collective, while in constant communication with other work groups . . . , is responsible for its own life and concerns'. The household units and the work collectives **each** appear to function as support groups (MNS perfers the term 'teams'). Gowan et. al. note, 'The often criticized tendency in mass movements for a kind of mob hysteria to sweep people away is not likely in a movement made of teams. On the other hand, the positive movement feelings of joy and celebration of community can be captured by teams'.

Jim and Marge Craig would have support groups go through four distinct stages, as follows: (1) **the present** — talk about the experiences that each of you have found most rewarding . . . and least rewarding ('this open sharing . . . allows members to know each other at the deep level needed for a group to become a caring community'); (2) **the future** — list the experiences that each of you would like to have more of in the future, and come up with a list of social arrangements and practices that could maximize the wanted experiences, and minimize the unwanted ones; then build your vision of the future up out of this list; (3) **strategy** — develop the rough outlines of a 'strategy bridge' that leads from the present to your vision of the future; and develop one or two sub-goals that can help you cross that bridge; (4) **tactics** — figure out exactly what you'll have to do as a group, and what you might need in the way of resources, in order to reach your first sub-goal; and then agree to **do** your share of the tasks required to achieve the sub-goal.

(5) **Reach-out groups** (or branches of groups) are meant to serve other people with a minimum of red tape, simply and directly . . . 'just people helping people' is how reach-out workers like to put it.

An outstanding example of a reach-out group is PLENTY, founded on The Farm in 1974 because 'after three years The Farm was taking care of itself and was strong enough to reach out to help some other folks who were in worse shape'. (Farm members were making well under $1000 per person per year at the time, but they had already learned to be self-reliant and cooperative.) PLENTY went down to Guatemala when the earthquake struck in February, 1976, but unlike most of the rest of the relief crews from around the world, PLENTY stayed on after the emergency work was done.

Matthew writes (in **New Directions** no. 23), 'We fell in love with the Indians who had been up against it before the earthquake. We began to understand that we were in a position to help them learn some of the beneficial aspects of a (human-scale) technology that we were using with good results in America. . . . Since then we've sent down 37 more folks, two trucks, a school bus, . . . and tons of food, clothes, tools, medical supplies, and CB radios. We've helped rebuild a town in which 1200 of 1400 houses were destroyed and we've put up 12 schools in 12 different villages. . . .

'After we built the schools and the houses, CIDA (Canadian International Development Agency) told us there would be funds for more projects, and if we came up with some designs, they would see about supplying us with the materials for those projects. . . .

'One of the best things we've been able to do is work out a deal with the U.S. Immigration Service that allows some native Guatemalan Indians to come up here to The Farm and live with us for a while and . . . learn a skill or a trade that will be of benefit to him or her "back home". . . .

'When we go to CIDA or to anybody about helping us with our projects in Guatemala, it's with this thought in mind: we are with the Indian people. We understand their needs, and we will stay on the scene and help them connect. . . . It's no longer like we're swooping in like a silver eagle and dropping our gifts on an unknown land with a mysterious population; it's more like helping our cousins.

(6) **New Age education groups** (or group projects) try to propagate what I have called the New Age ethics and political values — in an almost infinite number of ways.

The National Centre for Appropriate Technology is soliciting proposals for slide projects, video tape projects, audio projects (cassette tapes) and film projects.

Movement for a New Society's 'Macro-Analysis Seminars' investigate (1) ecology, (2) foreign affairs, (3) domestic affairs, (4) 'visions of alternative orderings of society', and (5) how-to. 'The seminars last about 20 weeks, operate best with 10-12 participants, have a democratic group process, and provide a structure which helps groups develop their own creative social change programmes'.

Barbara Ann Teer's National Black Theatre (9 E. 125th St., Harlem, N.Y. 10035) — 50 young black artists — are trying to go beyond the narrow definition of Western theatre to create a 'Communication Station, Temple of Liberation, Centre of Re-Education, and a Theatre for a Black Nation'. ('Politics just reflects the culture', says Teer. 'We went to religion first, and discovered a creative process that can drastically change the total thrust of Western culture. Then we translated it into an art form that's in line with the spiritual age'.)

Planetary Citizens has launched a 'Planetary Citizenship Campaign' whose purpose is to educate people to their 'planetary responsibilities', first of all by registering them as 'planetary citizens' and urging them to carry — and use! — the Planetary Passport on their travels. They are also hoping to have a 'travelling show of audio-visual things, musicians, and follow-up rap-resource people, who would go around to different campuses, different communities and try to get people in touch with (New Age ideas and energies)'.

The Hunger Project (P.O. Box 789, San Francisco 94101) hopes to help 'create the context' for an end to hunger and starvation on the planet. Not by collecting money to send food to the hungry, but (a) by educating us to the fact that the way we **see** things causes us to **accept** hunger as a part of the condition in which we live our lives. And (b) by encouraging us to take responsibility for healing our selves, which is **how to transform** the way we see.

The Canada Project (Ste. 223, 1715 W. 11th Ave., Vancouver, B.C. V6J-2C2) is somewhat similar. It theorizes, 'If I am hungry, I am not fully able to meet the hungers of others'; and it suggests that our hungers may be physical **or** emotional **or** mental **or** spiritual. Its primary purpose will be to answer these questions: 'What are the hungers that Canada and Canadians have that prevent this country from being a solution to planetary hunger? What strategies are available or can be created to deal with these hungers? How can Canada be an embodiment of an answer for our world and not part of its problem?

'Tools of the Canada Project (will) be public presentations, multi-media, films, educational programmes for schools, art exhibits, music, lectures, seminars. . . . However, political, social and economic strategies could spin-off from this project if it does its grass-roots work skilfully and wisely'.

(7) **Groups that are explicitly and exclusively 'political' and that are New**

Age-identified or New Age-oriented are beginning to spring up here and there across the continent. For example:

In March, 1977, a group of locally prominent 'left-wing Democrats' and 'right-wing Republicans' joined together to form the Decentralist League of Vermont (care of Institute for Liberty and Community, Concord, Vt. 05824). Their first act was to hammer out a 'Statement of Principles' which — in their words — 'could unite both "Left" and "Right" decentralists against the "Managerial Centralists" '. The statement reads, in part: 'Decentralists share with "conservatives" a repugnance for unwarranted governmental interference in private life and community affairs. We share with "liberals" an aversion to the exploitation of human beings. . . . Decentralists thus favour a reversal of the trend toward all forms of centralized power, privileged status, and arbitrary barriers to individual growth and community self-determination'.

The League proposes to support such measures as: (1) 'removal of governmental barriers which discourage initiative and cooperative self-help'; (2) 'rebuilding of a viable and diverse agricultural base for the Vermont economy'; (3) 'use of technologies appropriate to local enterprise'; and (4) 'mediation of disputes rather than reliance on regulations and adversary proceedings'.

At the end of its statement the League says, 'This . . . programme implies a deemphasis of status, luxury, and pretense, and a new emphasis on justice, virtue, equality, spiritual values, and peace of mind'. And it says, 'It is . . . interesting to note that the statement seemingly rules out both large scale capitalist and socialist enterprise, while looking with favour on both small scale capitalist and socialist enterprises'.

In the summer of 1977, a number of people came together to form the California New Age Caucus (3725 Midvale Ave., Ste. 3, Los Angeles 90034). Daniel Maziarz, a spokesperson for the group, says, 'I think we have two unique contributions. One: we are advocating a comprehensive life-style. Two: we are organizing grass roots support for governmental policies that promote this life-style.

'New Age people have learned how to improve their lives by living in a way that is ecological, spiritual, personal, and at the same time economically sound. We like to call it "simple living and high thinking". Because this whole idea has worked so well for us, we feel it is the answer to other people's problems too'.

William Duryea, another spokesperson for the group, adds, 'Our strategy is grass-roots — down home, person-to-person communication. . . . We're going to go door to door and tell people about this, and pass out literature (initially an excellent brief newsletter, **The New Age Harmonist**), and organize a statewide network of people . . . '.

The Caucus has already worked out a (very tentative) 'Platform'. The platform attempts to outline 'some of the political positions the New Age community could support through the New Age Caucus'. Some of the 50-plus positions the platform supports are: (1) 'government-sponsored education programmes to promote natural living habits'; (2) 'a return to sound principals of organic farming'; (3) 're-establish(ment of) small business as the cornerstone of the country's economy'; (4) 'a complete restriction on the use of nuclear energy'; (5) 'the end of planned obsolescence'; (6) 'aid to foreign countries in the development of intermediate-appropriate technologies'; (7) 'pressuring the media to devote a significantly greater proportion of its time and space to showing humanity's and society's positive accomplishments, especially during news programmes'.

(8) **Groups that are trying to link personal-spiritual growth and political activism** are also beginning to appear now — harbinger of things to come.

Planetary Citizens and Movement for a New Society have already been mentioned. . . .

Self-Determination: A Personal-Political Network (P.O. Box 126, Santa Clara, Calif. 95052) is a group of Californians who are — in their own words — 'simultaneously committed to our evolving as persons and to humanizing politics and institutions. We want to gather together persons sharing this commitment — so we can enable each other to grow more powerful personally and more effective politically'.

Self-Determination was started in early 1975 by Calif. Assemblyman John Vasconcellos and others. Public sponsors now include at least six other Calif. Assemblypeople and Congresspeople — and a number of authors listed in sect. I above (Harman, Leonard, Rogers, Steiner). As distinct from Calif. Governor Jerry Brown, members of Self-Determination 'share a positive way of looking at ourselves as persons. We have a faithful vision of human . . . potential and what we can be-come. . . . We can be authentic and caring and cooperative. We can be open and honest with each other.

'And we share a way of looking at politics. We see that politics happens wherever any decision is made that affects other people. We — all persons — are political wherever we are. Thus, who we are is how politics is'.

At this point programmes include:

— a Network Exchange Programme 'to assist citizens in finding and working with others on projects of mutual benefit'.

— a Public Dialogue Programme to 'change the nature . . . of political dialogue by intruding into the public dialogue vital human considerations'. Political campaigns will be treated as 'opportunities for discussing vital human issues . . .'.

— a Skills Workshop Programme 'to bring to local communities workshops which fuse personal growth and interaction with political skills and processes'.

— publication of an excellent **Quarterly Journal** (sample copies free).

Renaissance Universal (2239 E. Colfax Ave., Denver, Colo. 80206) is 'a new association of concerned individuals from all fields dedicated to a world-wide intellectual and moral revolution integrating spiritual growth and social justice'. Renaissance Movement organizations are seeking to implement (and to further develop) a fascinating synthesis of tantrism, feminism, socialism, 'world order' theory, ecology theory, human potential theory, and — more and more — the economics of Henry George. (The 'irreducible core' of this synthesis is the social-spiritual philosophy of P. R. Sarkar, East Indian philosopher and founder of the Ananda Marga society.)

At this point programmes include: local study groups (and other 'RU Clubs'); an Institute 'integrating research, self (development), social development, and service functions'; and publication of a number of magazines.

(9) **Community and regional development groups** have an important role to play in the New Age. Because it's impossible for a community or a region to achieve any kind of political sovereignty without also — and **first** — achieving a considerable degree of economic self-sufficiency.

The Institute for Local Self-Reliance has done — and continues to do — pioneering work along these lines; work that suggests that economic self-sufficiency can be a real possibility. In their book **Neighbourhood Power**, Institute members David Morris and Karl Hess suggest that community activists might want to, for example,

a. make an inventory of community resources. Partly just to show how much wealth there is in the community — how much money, how many skills, etc. — and partly to show that more money is flowing **out** of the community (in taxes and fees) than is coming back in (in services and public welfare);

b. begin to build up alternative institutions;

c. begin to develop community- and household-based food sources;

d. begin to develop community- and household-based energy sources;

e. begin to develop community industry (begin small, they say, perhaps by contracting with the city or district to provide such services as police protection, fire protection, sewer maintenance and waste collecton . . . and then by using the savings to establish small manufacturing facilities);

f. create 'community sustaining funds' (a voluntary sales tax at cooperating community businesses?);

g. create community credit unions and development banks.

The Centre for Community Economic Development is an important advocate of what has come to be called Community Development Corporations (CDC's). The Centre states, 'A CDC is essentially a cooperative, set up in a neighbourhood to run economic and social service programmes for the community. Its main activity at the moment is operating business or profit-making-ventures for the community. . . . The CDC can be set up by civic groups and churches, by a (government agency), or by any group of individual residents of that community. It really merits the title of CDC, however, if any community member may join.

'Once it is established by law, it has the legal rights of any corporation, including the right of limited liability'.

A number of people in and around the Centre have begun to develop what Charles Hampden-Turner calls 'the strategy of social marketing'. Essentially, the strategy is to create a supplier-consumer alliance; in terms of this book, the alliance would be between those who were organized into CDC's and other community enterprises, and those who had begun to break free of the Prison, those who had begun to live by the New Age ethics and political values. CDC's and similar suppliers would invite such consumers 'to make socially, politically and ethically motivated purchases, based on accurate knowledge of what a CDC stood for and the social purposes which it was accomplishing'.

As more of us begin to break out of the Prison, the market for such products might grow quite large. In fact, if a New Age-oriented **five percent** of North American consumers is eventually willing and able to meet some of its needs through CDC's — then literally billions of dollars might pour in to businesses and industries that were run by and-or for our communities. CDC's wouldn't even have to begin by **manufacturing** goods, they could begin more simply (and cheaply) by using the 'social marketing' strategy to retail, **wholesale,** and **mail-order** supplies manufactured by others. . . .

The Future Associates (P.O. Box 912, Shawnee Mission, Kans. 66201) is 'now in the process of organizing resident-owned "not for profit" neighbourhood development associations throughout our market area' (Kansas City and environs). Neighbourhood associations are being organized on a block-by-block basis. Each block (of approx. 100 people) elects a 'block leader' to a 'board of leaders' which sets policy for the neighbourhood association. (But block leaders are to be 'elected by their neighbours as cooperative pace setters, not representatives'.) Eventually each neighbourhood association will assume direct control of its own affairs through an elected paid 'management team'. And neighbourhoods will cooperate in a 'regional association' which they would control. . . .

'The goals for this community wide effort are (1) to cut our cost of living, (2) to increase our property value, (3) to give everyone . . . an opportunity to become cooperative owners of some of the neighbourhood property and businesses, (4) to build a capital base and cash flow that will enable us to continue developing our neighbourhood as we see fit, (5) to create a spirit of community. . . . We are also organizing our neighbourhoods through their regional association so that they can compete effectively for the funds that are currently being spent on industrial, commercial and governmental construction projects. . . .

'The fact that our associations will be using proven techniques to gain effective control of our neighbourhoods, and that they will have the economic power and related political clout to do almost anything they want to do, should enable us to pioneer the development of a cooperative society made up of cooperative people who have learned to cooperate by doing it'.

(10) **Training communities** are being set up to help New Age-oriented activists learn how to translate their insights and understandings into effective political action.

The School of Living (P.O. Box 3233, York, Pa. 17402) offers 'workshops, seminars, apprenticeships and long term living opportunities' at various centres relating to such topics as 'New Age consciousness', decentralism, cooperation, 'intimate relationships', and nonviolence.

Movement for a New Society sponsors a nine-month training programme that 'seeks to provide participants with the knowledge, skills, confidence and sensitivity necessary for effective change agents'. Through workshops, seminars, participation in community (communal) living, and involvement in the 'field', people are helped to explore what MNS considers to be 'essential elements' of self-and-social transformation, including: personal growth, spiritual growth, interpersonal skills; analysis, vision, strategy; consciousness-changing (how-to); subsistence living (how-to); group dynamics; 'organizing and technical skills'; nonviolent action; and the new culture.

Planetary Citizens hopes to have summer workshops that 'will deal both with the outer preparation — concerning knowledge, practical use of skills and efficiency in problem areas, and also with the process of inner awareness and development of consciousness appropriate to becoming a fully functioning human (and planetary) being'.

(11) **Networking**, says **Cascade Magazine** (Sept. '77), is 'the process of bringing people together to cooperatively change their communities, their environment, or their self-perceptions'. New Age networking is the process of bringing people together on behalf of some or all of the New Age ethics and political values.

(a) **Paper networks**. .Magazines like **The Mother Earth News**, catalogues like the **Rainbook**, special-interest newsletters like **Growing Without Schooling**, and regional newsletters like **Cascade**, all help put people and groups and ideas in touch with each other.

Cascade: Journal of the Northwest (P.O. Box 1492, Eugene, Ore. 97401), started in 1977, is already, in my opinion, an almost ideal model for a New Age regional networking magazine. Regular contents include: a cover story on a topic of regional interest (community economic development; forestry management); 'news from the region', covering good ideas in periodicals and publications from the region **and** developments in groups and community organizations around the Northwest, organized under 20 topics including ethnic cultures, economics, food, spirit, and women's and men's liberation; reviews of books and recordings produced in the Northwest, 'or of special note'; and readers' comments on subjects of regional interest (e.g., 'ecotopian succession'). Subscriptions are free to Northwesterners (people and groups) who are 'involved in community change activities', $10 a year to everyone else.

(b) **Networks of persons**. Steve Johnson (in **Rainbook**) reports that 'Conferences, meetings and workshops have created networks . . . of people with common ground, or reasons to know each other'. Particularly successful in this regard have been the Alternative Agricultural Conference (1974, Washington State), the Toward Tomorrow Faire (1976, Massachusetts), and Habitat Forum and the World Symposium on Humanity (both 1976, both Vancouver, B.C.).

(c) **Networks of groups**. Many of the groups mentioned above have begun to share their views through newsletter exchanges and visitations. The National Centre for Appropriate Technology is trying to put thousands of community groups in touch with each other 'so they can share common problems, resources, and technical expertise to begin developing workable solutions toward the goal of community self-reliance'.

Many New Age people think (or feel or hope) that it is only a matter of time before New Age-oriented alternative institutions, support groups, special-interest groups, and the rest, will begin to come together. At first in order to pool resources and ideas, share a common office of information and a common publication, co-sponsor regional travellers and an annual Celebration of Wholeness. And then —.

II. Intentional Communities

Some of us have chosen to leave our cities and towns and come together in 'intentional communities' that are more expressive of the New Age ethics and values. Traditional Marxists and liberals often accuse these people of 'copping out', and copping out from traditional Marxism and liberalism they may very well be doing. But there are a number of reasons why intentional communities are an important and even an essential part of the New Age strategy for social transformation.

For one thing, their existence suggests — to millions of people who might never join an intentional community themselves — the fact that **there are other ways of doing things**. As Theodore Roszak puts it, 'Nothing — no amount of argument or research — will take the place of such living proof'.

Some intentional communities are able to demonstrate the viability of new kinds of **structural** arrangements. For example: in Oregon, a new town is being built with no cars (!) — a 'do-it-ourselves village for 2000-2500 people with individually owned homes on commonly owned land clustered in a natural setting. . . . Community economy is to be based on small businesses with broad markets outside the community' (for more information write: Cerro Gordo Community, P.O. Box 569, Cottage Grove, Ore. 97424). Other intentional communities are able to demonstrate the viability of new kinds of **social-emotional** arrangements. And to David Spangler, the Findhorn community, in particular, has been able to demonstrate the viability of New Age **consciousness**, the viability of what I would call the trans-material worldview. The fact that it is potentially more **useful** and potentially more productive of **fulfillment and joy** than the old materialist worldview. (Findhorn has many differrent programmes for visitors and it states, 'All that is done at Findhorn is ultimately intended to demonstrate the power, the beauty, the abundance and the freedom of a life that is lived in harmony and oneness with God within the individual and within all things'.)

Intentional communities are a kind of **laboratory for New Age activists** as well as a kind of display-window for the rest of us. Rosabeth Moss Kanter, sociologist and communard, points out that the intentional community is a great place for learning about 'the possibilities for new forms of social organization and the practical limitations of these new forms'. Intentional communities confront almost 'every known problem of social organization . . . and almost every social-psychological issue'. They are a way of trying aspects of the New Age out in the present . . . trying them on for size.

To Stephen Gaskin, intentional communities provide a space — the necessary ground — where New Age people can begin working out a different lifestyle. In The Farm's brochure he states, 'We're trying to settle on a standard of living that would be fair if everybody in the world lived that way — not grim, but graceful and fun and full of love and friendship and being happy living together — a level that everybody in the world could make it on with the existing resources'.

Some intentional communities are organizing themselves **as alternative institutions**. The Cooperative College Community will eventually 'constitute an economically cooperative village of academics, artists, artisans and craftspeople that is minimally dependent on the economy of the larger society. . . . Our self-sufficiency will allow the community to operate a small, liberal-arts college that does not require its students to furnish their professors with a material living' (for more information write: Cooperative College Community, P.O. Box 299, Cambridge, Mass. 02138).

Finally, many New Age people would say that intentional communities are useful because of **their effect on the people involved**. Vince, of the Twin Oaks community, feels that the presence of many of (what I've been calling) the New Age ethics and values is a factor 'leading to healthy, responsive people'. Ananda Cooperative Village believes that intentional communities are particularly well suited to helping us in our spiritual growth . . . and operates a lovely Meditation Retreat for residents and non-. According to David Spangler, 'Findhorn allows us as individuals to bring the different levels of our being into a meaningful whole' — to meet and merge our material, emotional, mental and spiritual needs (self-development stages 1-2, 2-5, 6 and 7, respectively).

There are over 750 known intentional communities in North America today — and many of them are looking for new members (see the **Directory of Intentional Communities**, published annually by **Communities** Magazine; 1978 edition, $2). A couple of the best-known are:

Ananda Cooperative Village, 900 Alleghany Star Route, Nevada City, Calif. 95959; 110 members; 'still accepting members who are attuned to our way of life'; visitors arrange in advance.

Founded by Swami Kriyananda, disciple of Yogananda, who 'presently resides in the community as the spiritual leader. . . .

'Ananda is organized as a village, with the land held in common. Individuals and families each have their own private homes and support themselves through the various industries located within the community. Businesses are privately owned and operated and residents work for small salaries'. Industries include macrame, natural foods, flour mills, forest management. . . . Spiritual schools for children include a certified boarding high school.

Another Place, Rt. 123, Greenville, N.H. 03048; needs new members; visitors arrange in advance.

'Another Place is a community, a conference centre, a place to live and grow. . . . We function by consensus, share equal salaries, love each other a lot, help each other grow and learn, and we sing and dance and celebrate life.

'A major part of our energy goes into organizing conferences and festivals. . . . Through these gatherings we are developing a New England network of people working for personal and social transformation'.

Deep Run Farm, R.D. 7, Box 388-A, York, Pa. 17402; 19 members; visitors arrange in advance.

'The administrative headquarters of the School of Living is at Deep Run (see sect. I-10 above; & publishes **Green Revolution**). We also put a lot of our energy into Deep Run School, an ungraded, sliding-scale-tuition school stressing nonviolent values; arts and crafts . . . ; and organic living and gardening.

'Political actions, particularly the struggle against nuclear armaments and power, are important to us. . . . We must each learn and train ourselves and others to work, play and love in a non-violent, cooperative and human manner where 'ism's' no longer exist. . . .

'Wednesday night swimming and Thursday night meetings, and every night holding hands in a silent thanks before meals, and special parties on birthdays and at the Solstices and Equinoxes help to keep us busy and happy'.

The Farm, RFD 1, P.O. Box 197, Summertown, Tenn. 38483; 900 members; needs new members; visitors welcome.

Spiritual community founded and led by Stephen Gaskin. 'We're complete vegetarians, growing most of the food we eat. We're also delivering our babies at home. We have our own school, bank, motor pool, construction company, . . . public utilities, medical clinic and ambulance service. . . . We hold all property in common and share what we have according to need'.

Integrity, P.O. Box 9, 100 Mile House, B.C. J0K-2E0; visitors write in advance.

'We number about 110 here in our 10 acre community and operate some 15 businesses in the village of 100 Mile House, employing a number of townsfolk and holding considerable responsibility in the operation of the village. . . . We don't shy away from "earthly" duties, but rather assume responsibility in many ways, exercising many facets of creative ability, providing a balance point between what may be seen as "spiritual" and "earthly" considerations. In fact they are all one. . . .

'We adhere to no particular dogma, creeds, rules or regulations and find in a humble and open hearted way that there is a solid, true basis for presence on Earth'.

Twin Oaks Community, Rt. 4, Box 169, Louisa, Va. 23093; 85 members; needs new members; visitors arrange in advance.

'Together we are engaged in an experiment, an attempt to build a social system based on cooperation, egalitarianism (economic as well as political), non-violence, and interpersonal openness. . . . We are a diverse group. . . . And our approaches to designing our culture reflect this diversity. . . . Ours is a continual struggle to restructure our lives along lines that feel right to all of us. . . . We are interested in growing to at least 300 members'.

Twin Oaks sponsors an important and well-attended conference on community each July.

III. Electoral Politics

In Chap. 19 I argued that electoral politics is not **the** way to New Age social transformation. But it can be **a** way — it can get us **part** of the way there. It can be **a** way when it involves working for candidates or reforms that (1) are based on and communicate to others at least some of the New Age ethics and political values, and (2) involve an extension of popular and local control (as distinct from bureaucratic and-or centralized control). In other words: New Age-type electoral activity should be conducted on behalf of candidates and proposals that can **advance us toward** New Age society. It should **not** be conducted on behalf of candidates or proposals that might serve to reinforce the Prison or to strengthen monolithic institutions.

Often this will cause New Age political people to disagree sharply with traditional 'left-wing' candidates and proposals. For example: compulsory government-run automobile insurance, a favourite left-wing proposal, does tend to save drivers money. But for that very reason, it tends to **reinforce our reliance on the private automobile**. Wherever it's been tried it's tended to **increase** the number of two-car families; **increase** the 'need' for highways and wide(r) streets; **perpetuate** our love affair with speed; and **discourage** our thinking about alternatives to the private automobile. There are many other similar instances in which short-term economic savings involve long-term social losses, and New Age people must have the courage of their convictions and point this out to people.

New Age political proposals do not, generally speaking, seek to require the state to do things **for** us; characteristic New Age proposals attempt to obtain the tools and opportunities and training for people to do-for-themselves. When federal funding is required, the reason is partly and always to help us create a population that would be ultimately less dependent on federal funding. (A 'public works' programme would have the **opposite** effect.) When proposals involve changes in the school system (as in proposals 8-10 below), one purpose is to help us create a population that would be ultimately less dependent on schools as monolithic institutions. And so on. . . .

The following 12 proposals are intended to serve as **examples** of the **kinds** of political proposals that manage to meet the criteria for New Age electoral politics above (further New Age ethics and values; preserve or extend popular-local control). New Age people who are drawn to electoral political work should not hesitate to work for candidates who espouse these or similar proposals (and see also sect. I-7 above); New Age people who feel that electoral work is largely irrelevant should make it a point to at least vote for candidates who espouse such proposals.

If a growing number of North Americans begin to register their support for such proposals, then it isn't far-fetched to imagine that New Age groups will begin to want to enter the political arena. Groups that have banded together as envisaged at the end of sect. I might begin to recruit candidates for political office on New Age-oriented platforms, just like the Green Party is doing in France. And with possibly one great advantage over the Greens. We wouldn't be basing our appeal on ecology-and-appropriate-technology (alone) or simple living (alone) or feminism (alone) or spirituality-and-self-development (alone) but on **all** the New Age issues . . . **together**.

If the New Age movement **becomes** a movement that can hang together — if it doesn't get caught up in pseudo-socialist, they're-doing-it-to-us type rhetoric; if it doesn't get caught up in my-emphasis-is-more-important-than-your-emphasis type rhetoric — well, then I think anything is possible.

(1) **Live lightly.** New Age people have proposed basically five solutions to the problems of unemployment and underemployment: (1) provide full employment for all; (2) induce employers and unions to make the 20-hour work week an option for people; (3) induce employers and unions to permit job sharing; (4) provide free or easy access to land and tools; and (5) provide a 'guaranteed subsistence income' **to all those who were willing to remove**

themselves from the 'job economy'.

I believe that the first of these solutions would almost certainly do more harm than good. I also believe that solutions (2) through (5) are **absolutely necessary and urgent**. (My sources for what follows include especially Warren Johnson, 'The Guaranteed Income as an Environmental Measure', in Daly, ed.; and Robert Theobald, **Beyond Despair**, Chap. 3.)

My first objection to the full employment economy is that it would reinforce and perpetuate many Prison-bound attitudes. For example, the notion that a person doesn't deserve to eat unless he or she works at a job ('no jobee-no eatee'). Or the notion that unless people are forced to hold jobs the work won't get done. (Tests have shown that most people would **not** stop working if they were able to receive a subsistence income — though some of them would choose to work at different things.) Or the notion that the best way to get people to work is by depriving them (of a livelihood) if they don't. (In Chap. 8 we saw that the basic needs of people have to be met before we can expect them to act lovingly and intelligently!)

My second objection is best expressed by economist Robert Theobald: 'The long-run results of . . . a public employment programme are not difficult to imagine. In a year (Congress or Parliament) would ask for a report on the programme. The analysis would show that many people came to work irregularly, that many of the projects were less than useful and far from successful. (Congress or Parliament) would then tighten up the rules. . . . (And) further crackdowns would be inevitable, because people caught in a system they can neither understand or control (i.e. the 'public employees' — M.S.) are almost always irresponsible. The result over time could easily be described in terms of an old condition: "slavery"'.

Finally, a tremendous amount of state initiative, intervention and control would be needed, first of all to provide the jobs, second of all to administer them, and third of all to deal with the unanticipated consequences of the jobs on other sectors of the economy and in society. Theobald writes, 'The degree of control demanded by (full employment) is actually not feasible, because the greater the degree of control of any system, the greater the unanticipated secondary consequences'. The full employment economy would seem to require a fully planned economy for its successful functioning (which may be why many socialists tend to favour this solution). But that would be highly inefficient and objectionable in its own right (see Chap. 17, sect. V).

Solutions (2) through (5) would encourage many of us to take our selves off of the production-and-consumption treadmill. Solutions (2) through (4) would require us to learn to live more simply. And (5) would have many other advantages as well. For example:

a. It (would) (could) do away with the hated and demeaning welfare system;

b. It would virtually force employers to pay adequate wages for unpleasant jobs;

c. It would almost certainly foster a movement away from the biggest cities and back to the rural areas, where living is simpler and cheaper (already surveys tell of large numbers of North Americans who would like to return to small towns and rural areas if they felt that they could);

d. It would encourage the re-establishment of community (with low incomes there would be a real need for community cooperation and community provision of services and facilities);

e. Jobs vacated by workers would become available to all those people who really **wanted** to find paid full-time employment (it might be possible to raise the subsistence income level until a sufficient number of jobs were available);

f. A guaranteed subsistence income 'would encourage labour-intensive activity rather than the resource and energy intensive activities now encouraged. . . . Would-be (craftspeople) could quit their jobs and become working artisans . . .' (Johnson);

g. A guaranteed subsistence income would encourage us to vary our lives and lifestyles. Adoption of a guaranteed income 'would not have to be permanent, but could be an interlude in one's working career, before college or after, or an encouragement to leave a dull, dead-end job and train for a more satisfying one' (Johnson);

h. Today, those at the 'top' of society are responsible for determining what needs to be done — a full-employment economy would, in fact, augment their power. But with a guaranteed subsistence income, we would 'move toward a situation in which people felt that it was their **own** responsibility to determine what needs to be done' (Theobald).

Take, for example, child-care centres. Today the traditional left is demanding that the government establish child-care centres **for** us. But if we were able to choose to obtain a guaranteed subsistence income we might feel challenged to create child-care facilities our selves, ones we could design and run as we pleased.

That is the real point: a guaranteed subsistence income would **expand our opportunities for healing society**. It would mean that we wouldn't have to work for large, bureaucratic, federal agencies if we wanted to do some good. It would mean that college graduates, ghetto dwellers, or anyone else could apply their energies to the task of social healing in their **own way** and without having to **ask**.

(2) **Tax on energy.** 'If energy were taxed as it left the ground', says Bruce Hannon of the Energy Research Group of the University of Illinois (in **Technology Review**, Mar.-Ap. '77), 'then the effects would filter through the economy and appear as increases in the cost of consumer goods and services. Naturally, the price of the most energy-intensive of these goods and services would increase the most. Consumers should respond by shifting their spending from higher to lower energy-intensive products' — in other words, by demanding goods that were produced primarily by hand or by solar energy. Consumers might also respond by becoming more interested in voluntary simplicity. . . .

'The tax should gradually increase, relative to the unit costs of labour and capital, until a unit of fossil fuel costs as much as its renewable replacement'.

Hannon advises that the tax be returned as a reduction in personal income tax, 'thereby offsetting its inflationary effects', or that it be used to subsidize energy-conserving changes in industries and households.

(3) **Minimum and maximum levels on income.** Plato felt that the richest citizens should be four times as wealthy as the poorest. 'For the sake of political consensus', says Herman Daly, 'let us propose that the richest be allowed

to (make) 20 times as much as the poorest . . . , with progressive taxation levied within the limits. Below the lower limit the tax rate becomes negative (one way of providing us with the 'guaranteed subsistence income' above — M.S.). Above the upper limit the tax rate becomes 100 percent. In other words, if the lower limit were $2400 a year, the upper limit would be $48,000.

Maximum income limits 'would remove many of the incentives to monopoly', says Daly. 'Why conspire to corner markets, fix prices, etc., if you cannot keep the loot?' At the same time, the upper limit can be seen as a kind of defence of private property. As Daly explains it, the purpose of private property is to protect us against exploitation. But it can only serve this purpose if the inequality of income is kept within some 'tolerable limits'. Otherwise private property tends to become 'an instrument of exploitation rather than a guarantee against it'.

Most important of all, perhaps, the maximum limit on income would serve as a bulwark against inflation, since it would force us to finally decide **who should make more** than another — university lecturers vs. garbagemen and so forth (for more on this point see Chap. 18, sect. O).

(4) **Sharing our wealth.** North America has six percent of the world's population — but nearly 35 percent of the world's material wealth. How can anyone want this to continue?

Russian dissident Andrei Sakharov has proposed a 20 percent tax on the national income of all industrial countries as a 'basis for solving the problem of world poverty'. A more politically acceptable measure (and a less 'heroically' motivated one) might be to commit an increasing proportion of our gross continental product to New Age-oriented international groupings — say, an additional 0.05 percent a year — **until the percentage of our material wealth begins to approximate the percentage of our population.**

(5) **Loans for industrial cooperatives.** Joseph Blasi, contact person for the Institute for Cooperative Community (see sect. II above), is coordinating a task force 'which will soon complete legislation establishing federal guidelines for loans to worker and worker-community groups for the purchase and operation of industrial plants (in cases of planned shutdowns) as cooperative ventures'. This legislation deserves our support — and it is an opening wedge.

(6) **Encourage the small farm; encourage farming as a way of life (rather than as a 'good investment').** 'Radicals' are elated over the recent farm strike in the U.S. and the farm strikers' demand for 100 percent parity pricing. However, as National Land for People director George Ballus puts it, 'If your main aim is to keep the small farmer on the land, it would have the opposite effect'. With a sharp increase in farm prices, land prices would also rise sharply as farmer-speculators and outside investors bid among themselves for land . . . until even at parity prices, most farm income would be absorbed in land value. (The same thing happened after the sharp rise in farm prices during 1973-74. Many farmers used their extra income to expand by buying more acreage — by buying out other farmers. The sudden demand for farmland bid the price up sharply, making it harder to farm profitably on the inflated land. Also, bigger machinery was purchased by these farmers . . . pushing the price of machinery up too.)

Brian Livingston, writing in **Cascade** (Feb.-Mar. '78), says, 'The farm strikers' demand for parity pricing would do nothing to alter the basic causes of the agricultural crisis, and instead would add fuel to the flames of inflation and economic hardship. . . . Those farmers who need help most would benefit most from parity income (as distinct from parity pricing — M.S.). . . . In the long run, nothing will help the farmers' plight unless a lid can be placed on the speculative pricing of supplies and land values'.

Livingston suggests five measures whose purpose is to encourage the **small** farm . . . measures that manage to summarize succinctly what many New Age-oriented people have been saying all along:

a. Enact a progressive property tax which allows small and modest-sized land holdings to be taxed at lower rates than larger farms (as advocated by Thomas Jefferson!);

b. Eliminate the favoured treatment which capital gains receive in the federal income tax laws (would discourage land speculation);

c. Eliminate depreciation and investment credits which subsidize investment in new and high-priced machinery (the machinery requires larger tracts of land);

d. Limit the total amount of government payments any producer can receive (minimizes incentive to invest in more land);

e. Forbid investment in farmland by non-farmers, absentee investors, and non-family corporations (their investment in farmland drives prices artificially high).

Livingston concludes, 'Many farmers who own land won't be excited about these proposals. . . . But the present crisis calls for a re-evaluation of our attitudes toward land and the role of rural producers'.

(7) **Children's bill of rights**. John Holt, the educator, has proposed that the 'rights, privileges, duties, responsibilities of adult citizens be made **available** to any young person, of whatever age, who wants to make use of them'. These might include — in Holt's words:

a. The right to the full and equal protection of the law;

b. The right to vote, and to take full part in political affairs;

c. The right to work for money and to own and use, spend or save, the money they earn;

d. The right to own, buy, and sell property, to borrow money, establish credit, sign contracts, etc;

e. The right to control and direct their own learning, that is, to decide what they want to learn, and when, where, how, how much, how fast, and with what help they want to learn it;

f. The right to travel and to live away from home without parents' permission;

g. The right to receive from the state whatever minimum income it may guarantee to adult citizens;

h. The right to seek and choose guardians other than one's own parents and to be legally dependent on them;

i. The right to choose to live as a fully legally and financially responsible citizen.

(8) **Oppose sex-role training in school**. Two steps can and should be taken immediately. First, consciousness-changing classes should be made

available at different times throughout the school years, with the specific intention of undoing sex-role training for both sexes. The model would be androgyny and not masculinity or femininity. And, second, school books should be changed so that they no longer reinforce sex roles.

(9) **Combat the diminished self in school.** Many of the new therapies lend themselves to classroom instruction; est's Werner Erhard has even said that he would 'like to give est up to the environment' and specifically to the educational system. Therefore, at least one year of instruction in the various consciousness-and-growth therapies should be made available — say, a month-long introduction to what they're all about, and then an eight-month-long 'intensive' in one or more of them.

(10) **Begin training in nonviolent defence in school.** Until North Americans are able to defend themselves nonviolently (and confident that they can do so), nuclear disarmament — let alone genuine disarmament — will remain an unrealistic goal. Therefore, the theory and practice of civilian and-or territorial defence (see Chap. 14, sect. 11) should be taught in school, with the same seriousness and for the same **reasons** that we now teach civics.

(11) **Step up funding for appropriate and solar technologies.** Another way that federal (and state and provincial and local!) monies can be spent to help **decentralize** power and make our institutions **less** monolithic. U.S. federal expenditures for nuclear development were $5.25 billion in 1975, compared to $0.07 billion for solar.

(12) **Self-determination.** Canada and the U.S. should declare (a) their intention to permit community-districts and regions to opt for full sovereignty (by majority vote); and (b) their willingness to (re-)negotiate the status of community-districts and regions **within** the larger nation ('sovereignty-association').

IV. Nonviolent Action

Some New Age people have begun to use nonviolent action as a tool that can help in bringing the New Age about — a tool that can help us in our work against our monolithic institutions and also, at the same time, help us learn to be more self-reliant and more cooperative. Refusing to cooperate with draft boards, blocking the entrances to nuclear power-plants, boycotting South African wines or neighbourhood Safeways — all can be what Jim Douglass calls 'symbols of invitations' to people, 'living statements' that invite people 'to realize their own power, if they would only do likewise and act in concert'.

Nonviolence has often been presented as a turn-the-other-cheek, we-can-endure-longer-than-you-can-hate kind of philosophy. But as Julius Lester points out, 'The opposite of violence is not its absence — nonviolence. The very word commands one **not** to do something. But it does not say what one should do'.

To Gandhi, nonviolence was an aspect of **satyagraha** which he himself defined as 'the Force which is born of Truth and Love' and which is often translated, more simply, as 'soul-force'. Following Gandhi's lead, most nonviolent activists have defined nonviolent action in positive terms: as action that seeks to actualize Truth and Love (however that might be defined). Most New Age political people would say that Truth and Love are embodied by what I have called the New Age ethics and political values; therefore, most New Age political people would say that nonviolent action is action that attempts to actualize the New Age ethics and political values — nonviolently.

Some New Age people believe that nonviolent action is never coercive. But most believe that nonviolence can and **should** sometimes contain an element of coercion — non-cooperation, boycott, strike. The difference, as Joan Bondurant points out, is that in violent coercion 'deliberate injury is inflicted upon the opponent', whereas in nonviolent coercion injury indirectly results — 'withholding of services or profits (or rent) may cause a very real discomfiture to the opponent, . . . but compared with physical destruction . . . the contrast is significant'.

Some New Age people would include the concept of 'armed self-defence' under the category of non-violent coercion. The rationale is as follows: nonviolence means doing no harm to others **or to self**, and failure to defend one's self from physical violence — by any means necessary — is a kind of self-abuse. Julius Lester says, sometimes physical violence 'is one's only defence, . . . the only way in which one can insure (one's) physical survival and that of others. In that instance, and, only in that instance, is physical violence permissible'. However, it is possible to argue that the willingness to use physical violence almost **always** leads to more suffering, overall, than the refusal to use physical cal violence — particularly among organized groups; see, e.g., Sharp. The question of whether or not 'armed self-defence' is (a) consistent with the New Age ethics and political values, and (b) the most effective defence strategy, may turn out to be an extremely important one for New Age activists.

In many ways, nonviolent action is an almost ideal tool for New Age activists.

Richard Gregg, Gene Sharp, and many other nonviolent strategists and activisists have emphasized that nonviolent action is a way of healing **self**. It encourages us to end our submissiveness by getting us to stand up to people and groups that might have seemed 'superior' before (Gregg feels that this may be the single most important contribution that nonviolent action can make). It is, or should be, motivated by love — and it tends to encourage a vulnerability that can only be sustained by love for others (Gregg). It increases our sense of self-respect (Sharp) and it gives us esteem in the eyes of significant others (Gregg). It breaks the psychological link between masculinity and violence by establishing new group standards in which the willingness to suffer, and despite or even because of this suffering to **become and remain whole**, is the highest expression of so-called manly courage (psychologist Jerome Frank, in Sharp). It encourages us to be more enthusiastic and less cynical (Sharp). And it increases — through the power of example — our willingness to defy authority, our ability to break out of what Milgram called (in Chap. 3, sect. IV) our 'agentic state of mind'.

Erik Erikson, Harvard psychologist, compares nonviolent action to psychotherapy and finds many interesting parallels; for instance, that in both movements the practitioners learn to be nonviolent to themselves as well as to others. Chogyam Trungpa, Tibetan Buddhist, draws a distinction between aggressive and truthful action. He says that Christ chasing the money lenders out of the temple is an example of truthful action, 'because he saw the precision of the situation without watching himself or trying to be heroic'. And he adds: 'We need action like that'.

Unlike some political activity, nonviolent action does not try to make other people feel guilty or evil or that they have nothing to contribute to the solution of the problem at hand. It does try to point out to others that they're on the wrong course — in some cases it even tries to prevent others from carrying out their wrongdoing — but as Erikson says, it simply couldn't work if its practitioners lost all respect for their opponents.

Nonviolent action is, in fact, an almost perfectly **synergic** form of conflict resolution. Leroy Pelton, who is a social psychologist as well as a nonviolence strategist, says, 'Nonviolent action does not aim for victory over the adversary. Conflict is not taken as a game in which there is a winner and a loser and in which we attempt to "beat" the other party. On the contrary, the nonviolent activist strives to avoid this game mentality. What is sought is a resolution of the conflict at a higher level of understanding and satisfaction (for both parties) than perhaps either party possessed before the conflict resolution. The resolution that emerges is ideally a new Gestalt, or structure, in which both parties are somewhat transformed'. Richard Gregg says much the same thing: 'The aim of the nonviolent resister is not to injure, or to crush and humiliate (his or her) opponent, or to "break (his or her) will", as in a violent fight. The aim is to . . . change (the opponent's) understanding and his sense of values so that he will join wholeheartedly with the resister in seeking a settlement truly amicable and truly satisfying to both sides, . . . a settlement that will implement the new desires and full energies of both parties'.

New Age political people are less interested in obtaining behaviour change alone than in attitude or value change — change on the third level of analysis. All too often, as Gregg points out, behaviour change alone rests on the 'suppression or repression of the energy of the wishes or will of the defeated party, and this is certain to result in waste, friction and trouble sooner or later'. In order to obtain attitude and value change along with behaviour change, one should, as Pelton notes, 'apply the minimum pressure necessary. . . . Nonviolence perhaps represents the minimum pressure necessary'. Even nonviolent coercion is capable of producing attitude and value change if the nonviolent activist 'seeks to offset the psychological resistance engendered by noncooperation with simultaneous friendly, sympathetic, trusting, and helping gestures. . . . (These) may generate attractions to offset the resistance'.

The larger point, in any case, is that an enduring peace cannot rest upon behaviour change alone: cannot rest upon grudgingly given concessions or upon violent force. Gregg concludes, 'Peace imposed by violence is not psychological peace but a suppressed conflict. . . . The outer condition is not a true re-flection of the inner condition. But in peace secured by true nonviolent resis-tance there is no longer any inner conflict; a new channel is found, in which both the formerly conflicting energies are at work in the same direction and in harmony'. And he adds, 'The nonviolent (activist), by using longer psycho-logical leverages, may have to move more slowly sometimes, but the work is more effectively done and tends to be more permanent'.

For a New Age activist, nonviolent action is more effective in another way too: if violence centralizes, **nonviolence decentralizes**. For one thing, nonvio-lent groups wouldn't have to be dependent on a Central Committee for weap-ons or money. Their tactics would require few or no weapons, little or no money, and lots of sensitivity to local nuances and needs. For another thing, a successful violent revolution tends to vest great powers of violence in the top-down state . . . as we've seen; and that tends to make us feel **helpless** against it forever after. But nonviolent action is different — as Sharp suggests, the more that we engage in it, the more potent a tactic it becomes in our hands. . . . and the more **willing and able we are to use it** when it suits us.

In what is probably the single most influential book among radicals, **The Wretched of the Earth**, Algerian psychiatrist Frantz Fanon argues that revo-lutionary violence is necessary and desirable because it serves a therapeutic function for the oppressed. In North America, however, where most of us are 'oppressed' above all because of the Prison and its institutions, it would seem more therapeutic for us to assert our strength in a way that was not Prison-bound — in a way that was oriented to life rather than death. Nonviolent ac-tion would depend on our doing just that.

A number of nonviolent action groups have started up in the 1970's — and many of them are oriented to New Age ideas and energies.

The Greenpeace Foundation has sailed ships into U.S. and French nuclear test zone areas, and, more recently, Greenpeace members have been position-ing themselves between seals and whales and those who would kill them — saving thousands of animals in all, and at least as importantly, focussing world attention on **what we are capable of doing** to other living beings. Focus-sing world attention on our Prison-bound behaviour.

The Clamshell Alliance is a loose coalition of anti-nuclear organizations from the New England area. Many of the Clamshell's actions have focussed on the nuclear reactor construction site at Seabrook, New Hampshire — one nonviolent 'occupation' there in April, 1977 led to the arrest of over 1400 per-sons. . . . But what has really begun to catch people's eye about Clamshell is less 'dramatic':

(1) **Beyond protest (I)**. Harvey Wasserman, one of the organizers of the Al-liance, wrote (in **The Progressive**, Sept. '77), 'The actions (at Seabrook) would be occupations, not demonstrations. . . . The tactic of mass occupation, although untried (in North America), seemed to be our last resort. Nobody was winning any legal interventions, and there was no prospect of govern-mental action. We were not merely protesting nuclear construction — we were trying to stop it. Our actions would not be for show; if we failed, it would

be because we lacked numbers, not intent, and next time we would be back with more people'.

(2) **Beyond protest (II)**. Susan Hoak, a Clamshell Alliance activist, writes (in **Communities** no. 28), 'The Seabrook statement was not simply and exclusively "No Nukes". This time the "protestors" were demonstrating alternative directions in **everything they did** — from the very **way** they said what they said and organized what they did, down to the renewable energy sources they proposed to replace nuclear power'.

(3) **Women**. Hoak writes, 'The contributions women made were extremely crucial, and what to a large extent made this action different from demonstrations in the '60's. . . . Women dealt with the media, they were medics, marshals, they facilitated huge, tense meetings, organized support functions, and handled legal proceedings. When women do something, they tend more often than men to want to look at the **way** it's being done, in terms of what it **feels** like (as well as what the results are) to all involved. Much of the community-building that happened at Seabrook was a result of a great deal of woman energy'.

(4) **Participatory decentralization (affinity groups)**. Hoak: 'The Seabrook occupation was a mass action organized in such a way that individuals did not get lost in the crowd. Everyone who occupied went through a nonviolence preparation session beforehand and then joined an "affinity group" of eight to 15 people. The affinity group members stayed together throughout the action. . . . When decisions had to be made during the action, the (affinity group's spokesperson) would relay the consensus of the affinity group to a representative group of all the affinities . . . '.

(5) **Community (I)**. Hoak: 'Some baffled journalists attempted to describe what they saw as "military efficiency" and "discipline". . . . But what they did not understand they were seeing was the force of . . . a group of people committed — not only to a cause — but to each other, to communication with "opponents", and to a sense of community evolving out of conflict. . . . (A) sense of community created not only through common experience, but through shared feelings, needs, humour — the caring for each other that makes us open to both appreciating our strengths and giving support through our weaknesses . . . '.

(6) **Community (II)**. 'In reiterating its adherence to nonviolence as a tactic for June (1978)', says Rob Okun, a Clamshell organizer (in **New Age Journal**, Feb. '78), 'the Clamshell added a new requirement: Future occupiers must put in a week of door-to-door canvassing in their own communities or in New Hampshire before they will be permitted to take part in the occupation'. In the same article, Sharon Tracy, another Clamshell organizer, explains, 'We have to build a movement that's based upon more than occupations. By having people go door-to-door, talking about nuclear power, alternative energy, and why they are occupying **before** the action, they will have a clear understanding of what they are about to do, and so will the fellow citizens they talk to'.

Chapter 22 — Celebration of Wholeness: Beyond Hope and Despair

In the last three chapters I tried to suggest a way out of Prison society — a way that would be democratic and evolutionary and based on New Age ethics and values. But if it isn't possible for there to be an evolutionary transformation of society until a significant number of us have at least begun to heal self and society — then what hope does it have, really? And therefore what hope do **we** have? What is there that can keep us from despair?

Psychologists tell us that we're born with hope, and when we lose it we become corrupt and harden our hearts. The only apparent alternative to hope is despair, and I believe it is to ward off this despair that liberals continue to fool themselves about the nature of Prison society, and Marxists continue to dream of violent revolution in North America, and academic intellectuals like L. S. Stavrianos continue to believe that the Third World will show us the way. Those of us who have begun to heal our selves should know that we need to get to a point that is beyond hope and despair . . . that transcends either, and by doing so, allows us to see things clearly enough to be able to possibly **survive** as ethical and compassionate and vulnerable persons.

In order to survive with integrity we must begin with the fact that we are Prisoners. But we must never allow our selves to believe that we are only Prisoners — a mistake that the trans-material worldview can help us avoid. In order to survive with integrity in a world that seems bent on self-destruction and in which we seem to be our own best jailers, we have got to learn an important lesson from Eastern philosophy: we have got to learn to be **in** the world, but not **of** it. We have got to learn to do things for our own reasons, to measure our selves by our own standards, to live by the ethics and values that emerge effortlessly from the process of healing our selves.

One of the consolations of the liberal and Marxist philosophies is that their practitioners sometimes get to 'act like heroes'. New Age politics sees that the descent of the Prison isn't an event but a condition of daily life, and in these kind of circumstances the old kind of heroism is dead — as dead as Patty Hearst's friends. Storming the Pentagon or shooting some corporation executive won't help to end the culture of things and of death (and **will** help to glorify it). New Age politics sees that we need to develop a new concept of heroism — one that recognizes that in North America, the struggle to evolve in a New Age direction, as individuals and as a culture, may be more valuable than trying to inspire Prison-bound people to fight for more **things**.

(Robert Lifton sees heroism in the person who 'out of courage, refuses violence'. Robert Theobald sees heroism in the act of taking personal responsibility for one's life and one's immediate situation. Kate Millett sees heroism in women's courage to make themselves personally vulnerable. And Jane Roberts sees heroism in daring to 'fully be' — and daring to allow 'doing' to emerge as a 'natural characteristic' from fully being, wherever that might lead. . . .)

A number of leading academics and activists have decided that trying to heal our selves at this late date can only be seen as narcissism or self-indulgence. (Curiously, trying to get psychiatrists to do the healing **for** us is still considered legitimate.) What these people tend to forget is that social action that is not based on a firm sense of self can only be based on guilt or rage — and guilt or rage does not allow us to see clearly; renders us, in fact, extremely susceptible to manipulation by demagogues.

Moreover: by trying to work for a traditional revolution we would not be 'giving up the struggle'. As we saw in the previous three chapters, we **would** be struggling — nonviolently — against the Prison and its institutions, which are more responsibile for the sterility of our lives (and our society) than 'human nature' or 'capitalism'. But even if we can't do any more than embark on the stage of self healing, even if we can't get a strong group together, or if all our group efforts fail to heal society, we would still be learning to preserve our worth as human beings. And that is an essential part of the political process today. For without life-oriented people — without people who have reached self-development stages six or seven, or are definitely on their way there — there can be no New Age evolution. And only New Age evolution can take us off of the production-consumption continuum and out of the Prison.

Prison society celebrates material growth, speed, power, revenge; New Age evolution celebrates wholeness.

To David Spangler, wholeness means nourishing one's self fully — physically, emotionally, psychologically and spiritually.

To Herb Kohl, wholeness 'means being conscious of the different components of one's existence; means keeping social and historical awareness present along with personal and psychological need and insight; means attempting to bind together the internal and external, physical and spiritual, conscious and unconscious, cultural and personal, communal and individual aspects of one's life no matter what pain or conflict is involved. This last means breaking away from the dichotomized life that is one characteristic of the "Western" way of living. Wholeness also means utilizing what one knows about the self and the world instead of filing away whatever knowledge might lead to conflict and change'.

In terms of this book, wholeness means meeting one's needs on all seven stages (or: levels) of self-development. And it means learning to be at home in all four states of consciousness — learning to use the trans-material worldview rather than the materialist or the non-material worldviews. And it means learning to live by the ethics and political values that emerge effortlessly from out of the trans-material worldview.

Along with wholeness, New Age evolution celebrates life-as-a-learning-experience. Ken Keyes advises us to use 'every uncomfortable emotion' as an opportunity for consciousness growth. He says, 'Everything and everyone around you is your teacher. If your washing machine won't work, (imagine that) you are being checked out on your ability to peacefully accept the unacceptible. . . . If someone does something that "hurts your ego", you will grow fastest if you consciously regard him or her as your teacher who is enabling you to discover which addictions you will have to reprogram'. He concludes, 'Your moment-to-moment stream of consciousness becomes interesting and real when you experience everything as a step in your growth toward higher consciousness'.

Experiencing life as a learning situation is **very different** from coming to see society as one big schoolhouse — the approach that is being taken in, e.g., China and Cuba. John Holt says that the schoolhouse society would be a place 'in which one group of people did things to another group of people, without their consent, because still another group thought this would be good for them. . . . A global schoolhouse would be a world, which we seem to be moving toward, in which one group of people would have the right through our entire lives to subject the rest of us to various sorts of tests, and if we did not measure up, to require us to submit to various kinds of treatment, i.e., education, therapy, etc., until we did'. He adds, 'A worse nightmare is hard to imagine'.

New Age politics is based on the assumption that, as E.F. Schumacher puts it, 'Nothing is worth having in this sphere unless it comes from the **inside** of you'. Schumacher draws an essential political point from this assumption: 'I believe that it is everyone's personal task to try and demonstrate in some way, by word or deed, what (he or she) considers to be true, adequate, right, etc., and not look over (his or her) shoulder whether people follow (his or her) example or believe what (he or she) says'. If people then start ridiculing you, or criticizing you, 'you say, "Yes, thank you very much. I hear what you say". You just carry on'.

Schumacher adds, 'It is not so easy to maintain this sturdy attitude. In India they call it "karma yoga": you just do what you consider right, and you don't bother your head with whether you are successful or not, because if you don't do what you consider is right, you're wasting your life!'

Beyond hope and despair, then, there is something absolutely essential to do, and that is to live. To live with simplicity and intensity, gentleness and generosity, so that the idea of a freely self-developing humanity does not die, no matter how comfortable or 'happy' or obedient the mass of the people may become.

Part VIII — Appendix

Chapter 23 — Clearing the Ground: A New Age Critique of Marxism

In North America, the old liberal belief system is on the verge of collapse. Goodbye, says Garry Wills at the end of his bittersweet swan song, **Nixon Agonistes**, to all our old beliefs: that the system rewards us fairly; that there is a 'free enterprise' system; that our problems are traceable to 'bad men'; and so on. (Maybe these beliefs were never really believable, says sociologist Robert Bellah, but now they're not even useful as myths.) And just as important, the liberals have begun to admit that they're — well, not wrong — but at their wit's end. For example, the respected liberal columnist, Anthony Lewis, recently conceded in the **New York Times** that no social or economic programme 'known to us now' can solve the problems of crime and violence in New York City.

You'd think that the collapse of the liberal mythology would clear the ground for a new awakening: for vigorous new analyses to be made, goals proposed, strategies debated. But, no. With the exception of the work done by the people I've referred to in this book (and their like), there are **no** new analyses, goals or strategies afoot in North America today. Instead, most of those who are searching for so-called radical solutions to our social problems have been charging bravely into the 19th century and coming up with one or another variety of — Marxism.

Why is this? Why is it that, in an era that is absolutely unique in world history, our 'political' people seem to lack the ability or even the will to think for themselves in new ways? One reason, I believe, has to do with the **kind** of appeal that Marxism has for those of us who want to think differently — an appeal that's partly intellectual, but is also psychological, even (fraudulently) religious; and that owes a great deal to the ability of the Marxists themselves to make us feel guilty — to 'blackmail' us, morally and emotionally, by means of various specious arguments. This chapter will examine Marxism's psycho-spiritual appeal, guilt-inducing arguments, and dishonest political practices, each in turn; and then, I think, we'll be in a better position to understand why the ideas of Marxism, enumerated and criticized in sects. IV and V of this chapter, are far less persuasive than we might expect, given the capital-i Idea of Marxism which seems so persuasive to so many.

Before I begin, though, I should add this: there is a difference between criticizing Marxism as an ideology and saying that there's **nothing to** Marxism.

New Age politics borrows from Marxism — and it borrows from many other political (and social and spiritual) movements and traditions. . . .

I. Psychocultural and Religious Appeal

(1) Liberalism is collapsing, the times are desperate — and Marxism is the only coherent alternative to liberalism, at the present time. (The only coherent alternative: that's an important point. A lot of intellectuals seem to need a political philosophy that might or might not speak to their experience of the world, but is above all intellectually coherent and 'complete'.)

(2) We've lost our cultural bearings, our morality, our ethics, our values. In this context, it's very difficult to say, all right, we're going to have to create another culture, another value system. Many of us are going to be tempted to 'escape from freedom', as Erich Fromm put it (somewhat self-righteously) many years ago, and lay our burdens down at the feet of some authoritarian ideology.

(3) In high school, Marxism was forbidden fruit, like sex; and when we learned, usually on our own or at a good university, that Marx had things to say that weren't dreamed of in liberal philosophy — well, was it really all that surprising that some of us chose to go all the way with him?

(4) It's scary to propose a new vision — you might stumble and fall (if you're a professional, one bad fall and you're out). As Robin Morgan, the feminist writer, puts it in a recent interview (Sojourner, July-Aug. '77), 'It is mortal peril — stepping off the edge into someplace that has never existed before. There are no maps for that place. All the self-preservatory tendencies are to run back and say Marx! Hegel! Or, Give me a Capitalist! Give me Religion! Give me Anything! (That's) why at a certain point you backslide into a sudden renaissance of socialist feminism. It's the same with women's spirituality settling for religion . . .'.

(5) In North America, intellectuals tend to lack all conviction. Marx radiated conviction; so much so that he became a kind of role-model for thousands of would-be intellectuals.

(6) Marxism is the only academically 'respectable' alternative to liberalism. It is difficult to master, impressive to espouse, and has a 140-year-old intellectual tradition behind it. Radical-liberal professors tend to present it as the only 'serious' alternative to liberalism . . . and as the only possible alternative to liberalism.

(7) Marxism's very lack of respectability among the 'bourgeoisie' only serves to increase its respectability in 'radical' circles.

(8) In a society that's overwhelmingly smug and self-satisfied, what could be more engaging than a philosophy that promises us combat, struggle, dedication, zeal, self-sacrifice — ultimately, the barricades — and ultimately, inevitably, sweet, sweet Victory? To a people that feels only half alive, what could be more satisfying than that?

(9) As a philosophy that purports to speak for the poor, Marxism contains a powerful appeal to our underlying sense of guilt — for not being poor, or for not being poor enough. I've observed that we can be 'guilted' into just about anything by Marxists, once we've begun to accept their premises.

(10) Marxism is extremely hostile to the spiritual and religious states of consciousness. Denies that they exist. Is so adamant about it that you begin to wonder whether Marxism isn't a kind of substitute religion. Consider the following (from Henry Mayo, Introduction to Marxist Theory):

1. Use of religious language in Marxism (e.g., Marx and Engels first considered calling the Communist Manifesto the Communist Catechism);

2. Use of the works of Marx and Engels to settle arguments and justify

policies — just like some devout people use the Bible or the Koran;

3. 'May be regarded as a revelation, a gospel of deliverance to the poor';

4. The proletariat — 'a kind of Chosen people, who alone will possess the New Jerusalem';

5. After the revolution will come the Great Judgement — the dictatorship of the proletariat — to separate the proletarian sheep from the bourgeois goats;

6. Beyond the struggle lies — the millennium;

7. Eden before the Fall: the stage of primitive communism;

8. The Communist Party as a church hierarchy or priestly caste;

9. The Party has its saints and martyrs (whom it venerates) and its evil ones (whom it expels);

10. One function of the Party: to preserve the 'doctrinal purity' of Marxism;

11. The same belief in inevitability, the same belief in ultimate victory — guaranteed by the 'eternal laws' of history and the universe;

12. The same claim to universally valid truths.

II. Blackmail and Manipulation

Some of the arguments that Marxists use to justify their claims are highly illegitimate. Some of them amount to a kind of blackmail — an 'if you don't agree with us we'll write you out of the human race' kind of a thing. Others are meant to manipulate us into agreeing with them.

A. Blackmail

(1) **'The socialist is the political'.** Often Marxists will imply that only socialism is 'political', that is, politically serious, politically worthy of consideration. They'll say that a book or a person is 'very political', 'quite political', or 'political', depending on how close he or she or it comes to their brand of Marxism. If an idea is non-liberal but non-Marxist, it's often called, not 'wrong' — that would be to take it too seriously — but 'non-political' (or, worse, 'poetry'). This virtual identification of 'socialist' with 'political' has been a powerful factor in discouraging many of us from working out a new political philosophy.

(2) **'Socialism and the high ideals of humanity are identical'.** Marxists often imply that socialism is, and has been, the only true carrier of such ideals as fraternity, cooperation and equality. However, as Soviet dissident Igor Shafarovich points out (in Solzhenitsyn, ed.), fraternity, cooperation, equality, etc., go all the way back to Plato (who was an idealist — the very opposite of a Marxian materialist); were first propagated in schools of philosophy and narrow **mystical** circles; later penetrated to the Gnostic sects; were introduced into various heretical religious movements in the Middle Ages; and began to adopt the trappings of the western European enlightenment only in the 18th century. Fraternity, cooperation, equality, etc., are essentially the ideals of dissident **spiritual** groupings.

(3) **'Marxian socialism represents the historical aspirations of the working class'** (or the poor, or the minorities, etc.). This is a variant of (2) above and can be answered as follows. Marxian socialism is **one possible way** of expressing those aspirations. It is not the only way; it has not been the only way in the past — or even, in North America, the dominant way; and it may not be the most productive way in the future (read Chaps. 1-22 above and judge for yourself!).

B. Manipulation

(1) Marxists will often try to get us to come around to their position by telling us **that they agree** with our ideas. They might even mention these ideas in

their discussion groups, pay lip service to them in front of audiences, and so on. Only, the ideas will have been subtly changed. You might not even notice it at first — indeed, when couched in Marxist rhetoric your ideas might sound stronger than ever — but what's actually happened is that your ideas have been stripped of their unique power and force so that they can conform to the essentials of the Marxian analysis which simply can't change if Marxism is to remain . . . Marxism.

Consider what's happened to those forces in the feminist movement that have allied themselves with Marxian socialism. As Allison Platt, an editor of the Boston women's newspaper, **Sojourner**, expresses it (Dec. '76), these feminists seem to have forgotten that women aren't ' "just another oppressed class" which must join all the other oppressed groups (the male left, presumably) to overthrow the White Man'. Some of them even believe that 'freedom for women can only come . . . after we kill the imperialist pigs'. Real radical feminism, according to Platt, 'is more than and different from' the struggles of other oppressed groups; it implies an entirely different analysis of society. Moreover, 'I have always believed that violence only breeds more violence, and I will never be convinced that this belief serves only to keep me oppressed'.

(2) If you refuse to be blackmailed or co-opted, you may then be earnestly **patronized** by Marxists. They'll try to convince you that you're coming along, that with a little more reading of Marx you might make it, that you've got a good head on your shoulders, etc. And if you suffer from a lack of self-esteem, or from a lack of faith in your own efforts, or from a lack of support from your friends — then their blandishments might swing you over to their side.

Allison Platt saw through all this right away. 'The hardest part to endure', she says, 'is the subtle (and sometimes not-so-subtle) condescension. (Marxist) feminists assume that their viewpoint represents absolute truth, and presume to define everyone else according to this assumption. I have been told innumerable times that reformism (i.e., anything not strictly revolutionary) is just the first step along the ultimate path to revolution. Such put-downs remind me alarmingly of the way parents put down children with such phrases as "You'll understand when you're older, dear" '.

(3) Finally, if you refuse to be blackmailed **or** co-opted **or** patronized into line, you'll almost surely be **written off** by Marxists as: bourgeois, intellectual, capitalist, reformist, liberal, elitist, proto-fascist, or what-have-you. But don't let those terms bother you; all they really mean is that it doesn't look like you'll ever be a Marxist. (Specifically, 'elitist' means that you don't agree with Marx or Mao. And 'proto-fascist' means that you don't agree with Lenin.) Remember that this kind of name-calling reflects more on the name-callers than on you, shows them to be as self-righteous and as hostile to diversity as are those they wish to replace. And **use** your freedom from the 'revolutionaries' to help us work out the politics that we desperately need now

III. Marxism in Practice

As human beings, Marxists are neither better nor worse than the rest of us (in fact, as we've seen, they're probably more religiously motivated than most). But I believe that Marxist theory — its priorities, its goals, its so-called 'scientific' validity — induces and even requires us to act in ways that are arrogant and self-righteous; to allow little room for personal, let alone spiritual growth; and to engage in various forms of intellectual betrayal.

᠅᠅᠅᠅᠅ A. Tendencies to Arrogance and Self-Righteousness ᠅᠅᠅᠅᠅

These traits are necessary and inevitable features of all Marxisms, and therefore of all Marxists to the extent that they're being 'political'. It's what happens whenever **any** ideology proclaims itself to be the one 'correct' way to world 'development'; proclaims itself to represent the one true 'science' of society; preaches a doctrine of 'us-against-them' and 'they're doing it to us' as a way of stirring up tensions and hatreds; has as its goal the setting up of a dictatorship; and is willing to use violence to attain that goal (or any goal).

Historically these traits have led to the fact of the Soviet 'labour' camps — 70 million victims, according to Solzhenitsyn; to the fact that between five and 10 million Chinese have been slaughtered **since** the revolution of 1949 (Berger, **Pyramids**); to the fact that up to 1.4 million Cambodians have been slaughtered by the new, 'revolutionary' Cambodian government which feels it has the right to create what it calls the 'new man', initially by eliminating all those whose class backgrounds might stand in their way (Jean Lacouture, **New York Review of Books**, 31 Mar. & 26 May '77).

Closer to home, Marxist arrogance and self-righteousness can be seen — can be previewed — in their pet phrase, 'If you're not part of the solution you're part of the problem'; in the emphasis Marxist groups place on doctrinal purity (an emphasis that's led to the flourishing of literally dozens of Marxist sects — and an incredible amount of bitterness among them); and in the brusque and humourless manner with which the Marxist 'heavies' deliver their explanations, try to 'enlighten' us on all points, drag out their favourite quotations from Father Karl or Father Leon as if to settle the issue. (Platt remembers how one young revolutionary, bothered by all her questions, 'stopped and regarded me with an unbelieving and suspicious look, and then said: "I thought you were **with** us" '.)

Perhaps most disturbing of all, Marxist arrogance and self-righteousness can be seen in the bland insistence that the camps, the dictatorships, the unfreedoms, and the killings that have taken place as a result of all the other Marxist revolutions, wouldn't happen **this** time around. There's an almost congenital inability to hold Marxian socialism accountable — even in part — for its failures (as distinct of course from its successes). Marxian socialism is defined as: what is ideal, and then when a socialist project or government turns out to be less than ideal the Marxists turn around and say: but that's not socialism! For example: Leszek Kolakowski, the Polish Marxist, once wrote an article whose first part, 'What Socialism Is Not', is a virtual history of socialism everywhere. The next and last part is titled 'What Socialism Is' and it consists of one sentence: 'Socialism is a good thing'. Similarly, Samir Amin, a much more tough-minded Marxist, states categorically (in **Accumulation on a World Scale**, 1974) that socialism 'cannot exist unless it is superior to capitalism in every way'.

ᛒᛒᛒᛒᛒᛒᛒᛒᛒᛒᛒᛒB. **Tendency to Ignore Personal Change**ᛒᛒᛒᛒᛒᛒᛒᛒᛒᛒᛒᛒ

Marxism stresses the importance of economic as distinct from psychocultural factors; so much so that psychocultural factors are said to be ultimately a reflection of the economic. It isn't surprising then that individual Marxists tend to put the bulk of their time and energies into the 'social struggle' — saving the so-called personal stuff until After the Revolution. It's not that they care for their own selves less than New Agers **or that they care for others more**. It's that their politics (like every other politics) has a certain strategy and certain priorities, which they must follow.

To everyone's cost. In Russia, for example, Wilhelm Reich tells us that after the revolution young Marxists threw themselves so passionately into their organizing activities that they spent virtually no time working out their lives together in their communal quarters; let alone enjoying themselves.

People's self-understandings and sense of themselves actually **withered** in the early stages of the Revolution, and that, according to Reich, was one reason why it was able to turn so repressive.

Our Marxists haven't learned much. Theodore Roszak recently observed that there's no more shelter for the person in Marxist movements than in the societies they're meant to overthrow; an observation that's only reinforced by the accusations such as 'narcissistic' and 'self-indulgent' and (lately) 'psychobabble' that Marxists like to hurl at all aspects of the consciousness-and-growth movement. Jerry Rubin recalls that the 1960's 'vision of the model human being was a totally committed person fighting against oppression, willing to sacrifice his life and freedom for the people'. But if the 1960's taught us anything, he says, it's that 'people out of touch with their bodies and souls cannot make positive change'.

ᎧᎧᎧᎧᎧᎧ C. **Intellectual Betrayal: Refusal to Acknowledge 'What Is'** ᎧᎧᎧᎧᎧᎧ

The Marxist conviction that they 'have the answer' (a conviction that comes, remember, not from personal pride, but from the ideology itself) induces them to ignore certain facts that might throw a dangerous doubt on their certainty. (If the facts can't be ignored, still, they can always be played down or covered up or misrepresented.)

The press in the Marxist countries makes no pretense: it never tells the 'whole truth'. In fact, it denies that there can even be such a thing, ignoring — or pretending to ignore — the obvious distinction between complete objectivity, which is impossible, and many-sidedness, balance, which is **essential** to the life of the mind.

Henri Levy, born in 1948, publisher and spokesperson for many of the young French revolutionaries-circa-1968 who are currently engaged in criticizing Marxism as a 'necessary first step' in the creation of a new politics, has drawn up an impressive list of instances in which French Marxists have **deliberately concealed** an important part of the truth — thereby betraying the people to and for whom they were speaking. For example, he points to the refusal by the leading French radical intellectuals to reveal the conditions in the prison-camp system in Russia. Their rationale (according to Sartre, who was one of them): the 'workers of Billancourt' (a suburb of Paris) would have thereby lost all hope.

All hope in Marxism maybe. But now that there's a **better** Marxist state, China, the truth can now come out. About Russia.

It isn't hard to find similar — and very recent — instances of intellectual betrayal by Marxists on our own continent. I'll confine myself to two:

(1) In mid-1976, Jean Lacouture, the anti-war journalist and democratic socialist, revealed that between 200,000 and 300,000 Vietnamese were being forcibly detained, for unlimited time periods, in 're-education camps'. Never, he wrote, in any revolution, 'have we had such proof of so many detainees'.

In December, 1976 an appeal to the government of Vietnam was made public at a press conference in New York. In the appeal, the signers — 105 in all (including a number of the authors listed in Chap. 24, below) — identified themselves as having been 'actively engaged in opposition to the war' and added, 'our criticisms . . . cannot be separated from our friendship'. They went on to ask about reports, like Lacouture's, of 'grievous and systematic violations of human rights by your government'.

I was impressed by the tentative tone of the appeal (it admitted the possibility of being wrong-headed) and by the fact that it was careful to note that many other governments, 'including our own', were lax in the area of human rights. One might have expected that the vast majority of the well-known activists from the 1960's would have signed the appeal. Instead, just the opposite happened. Not **one** of the former national officers from SDS signed; no one from SNCC or the Black Panthers signed; no one from the Chicago Seven signed. The vast majority of the 'radicals' were actively hostile.

In February, 1977 Nat Hentoff wrote an article on the appeal for the **Village Voice**, and some of the responses he collected from the 'radicals' are almost perfect illustrations of what I mean by 'intellectual betrayal', by the playing down or even complete refusal to acknowledge 'what is':

— 'It's a rotten, sneaky way of undermining our efforts to get Vietnam into the United Nations'.

— 'I'm convinced more people are unjustly imprisoned in **this** country than in Vietnam'.

— 'I wish we could all give him (Jim Forest, organizer of the appeal) a rest in any re-education camp of his choice'.

— 'Many of the "detainees" are held for only a few months'.

— 'In Vietnamese, "reeducation camps" are really called "study-practice sessions" '.

— 'Conditions in the re-education camps are the same for instructors as they are for detainees'.

— 'The government of Vietnam is socialist and has to mobilize all souls, each and every one, to get on with rapidly overcoming poverty and inequality by socialist means. (Therefore,) the state must deal with those who are dragging their feet'.

(2) During the first part of the 20th century, most North American Marxists felt that **Russia** was the place where socialism was aborning, and so — like the French left — they never really told us the whole truth about Russia. Possibly most of them needed to believe in the 'Russian experiment' so much that they couldn't have seen more than a part of the truth if they'd tried.

Today the players have changed, but the game's still the same. Today's Marxists like to point to **China** as the country that's 'putting socialism to work'. And in the process they're leaving out — ignoring or repressing — certain crucial facts. Worse, they're being joined, this time, by hordes of radical-liberals who have a deep need to find something — anything — to believe in, and who lack the will to work out a coherent alternative to Marxian socialism. In their travelogues these radical-liberals aren't just telling us about China, they're writing morality pieces about the way they think North America should go.

The following passages represent a very small sampling of what the Marxists **don't** tell us about China. With two exceptions, they come from three very recent accounts of China by people who've been there and who've managed to retain their critical faculties: Simon Leys (**Dissent**, Fall '76), Edward Luttwak (**Commentary**, Dec. '76), and Orville Schell (**The New Yorker**, 7 & 14 Mar. '77, & **Rain** Magazine's **Rainbook**). Leys and Schell could be considered democratic socialists, Luttwak is a neo-conservative.

a. **Facts**

— 'The cheapest suit of clothing for little boys is a mini-uniform complete with toy rifle' (Luttwak).

— Very little of the ecological consciousness that I had hoped to find. Pollution in many manufacturing centres is as bad as in the West and growing daily worse. People recycle and reuse things because they can't afford to waste them (Schell).

— 'A man is usually deferred to in his own house by his wife, and she normally does all the cooking, washing, and cleaning' (Schell).

— 'Every time a Maoist speaks of the miracle of modern China, I remember that the "incurable" lesbian in that country is summarily executed' (Lucia

Valeska in **Quest**, a socialist-feminist quarterly, Fall '75).

— About 100 death sentences were reported in various provincial cities during the first half of 1977. 'Among those sentenced to death was a 24-year-old man reportedly accused of founding a political movement called the "China revolutionary party", of listening to foreign radio broadcasts and of attempting to reach the Soviet border'; another 'was accused of keeping a "revisionist" diary and of writing "counter-revolutionary" poems and slogans' (**Matchbox**, Amnesty International quarterly, Summer '77).

— 'Most Chinese children who are asked what they want to do when they become adults reply, "Whatever the Party wants, I will do", or, "I want to serve the people" ' (Schell).

— People seem to have no desire ever to be alone (Schell).

— 'The object of conversation usually is not achieving free give-and-take but providing the other person with a chance to reeducate (him- or herself) to the "correct line" ' (Schell).

— The 1954 constitution protected 'the inviolability of private correspondence between citizens; free choice of domicile; freedom to change residence; freedom to engage in scientific research, literary and artistic creation, and other cultural activities'. In the 1975 constitution, all 'disappeared without a trace'. But 'most important of all, a new article was added allowing the Public Security (the political police) to make arrests without (prior) authorization . . . — in other words, the arbitrary power of the police has been enshrined in the constitution' (Leys).

b. **Conclusions**

— The Chinese are plunging full speed into an industrial society — albeit on their own terms (Schell).

— 'The Maoist regime has not liberated the individual; it has merely substituted the all-encompassing authority of party or state for that of the earlier family and village collectivity — which was limited, after all, if only territorially' (Leys).

— 'In essence, it is a new departure in the totalitarian experience, a system of **positive** instead of negative control. In the Soviet Union one can do anything, except for the very long list of forbidden things. In China there is no forbidden list at all. Instead, all activity is forbidden except for that which is specifically permitted and promoted by the party' (Luttwak).

IV. Marxism in Theory

As soon as we begin to criticize Marxist theory we end up in the quicksand: there are at least 20 competing and often contradictory varieties of Marxism. Marx contradicted himself at least as much as you might expect, given that he was writing more or less steadily for 40 years; Marx, Engels, Lenin, Stalin, Mao all diverge on various important points; and the various recent interpretations and 're-interpretations' of Marx and Marxism are even more contradictory, ranging all the way from Michael Harrington's 'democratic' Marx who sounds awfully much like a Catholic social democrat from St. Louis, to Bernardine Dohrn's Marx, the Che Guevara of the British Museum.

This isn't the place to go into what Marx really meant most of the time. Nor do I think that this is one of the most pressing questions that a person interested in self and social transformation at the tail end of the 20th century should be asking him- or herself. So, I'm going to confine myself to two observations. First, all of the current interpretations or re-interpretations of Marx and his followers appear to me to be, above all, attempts by the authors to sneak their **own** politics in under the (supposedly) formidable guise of being the 'one, true' Marxism. What I find objectionable in this is mostly the intellectual cowardice: surely our leading so-called radical thinkers should have enough confidence in their own ideas to defend them **as** their own and take **full responsibility** for them. Second, re-reading the original texts convinces me that you **can** find in Marx pretty much what you want to find, like a Rorschach test or like the Bible. . . . So I think it's legitimate to look at Marx's **personal** life to provide the ultimate answer to the insistent question, how authoritarian was he?

When we look at his personal life we find that only 'where he could dominate', as in the family circle or with Engels, was he gentle or kind; but that 'Most people who met him found him irritating, condescending and arrogant', and those who disagreed with him — even his fellow communists — could expect not only to be bitterly attacked for their 'incorrect' views but to have their **motives** questioned (Mayo). According to Lewis Mumford, 'He worshipped power as much as he hated greed: he had an inner need to dominate every group he became part of, and would unhesitatingly wreck it when it threatened to escape his control'.

But, enough of this. . . .

The following ideas are, in my opinion, basic to Marxism. If they change, Marxism becomes that much less **Marxist**.

(1) **Capitalism is the enemy**. Capitalism, say the Marxists, is the root of our problems, and being radical means: going to the root. Therefore, . . .

Throughout this book I argue that capitalism (as we know it today) and also socialism (as we know it today) can more usefully be seen as **symptoms** of our problems: of the Prison and its institutions (Parts I & II). I argue that if we're able to break out of the Prison (i.e., begin to change our consciousness) and convert our monolithic institutions to 'biolithic' ones, then capitalism would or at least could be humane. (Same with socialism.)

(2) **Economic determinism**. The economic structure of society is said to be the 'real foundation' of society and is responsible for the political 'superstructure' and also for people's consciousness. Some Marxists try to trace everything back to the 'powers of production' but more sophisticated Marxists tend to argue that the economic structure is determining only 'ultimately' or 'on the whole' or 'in the final analysis' — whatever that means.

I believe that the whole material-conditions-versus-social-consciousness debate is a chicken-and-egg problem — strictly speaking, there can be no 'ultimate' answer. And short of 'ultimately', society is determined by everything in it and by everything people think about it. (Twentieth-century physics as well as Eastern philosophy bear me out in this: as Fritjof Capra, the physicist, summarizes them, 'everything in the universe is connected to everything else and no part of it is fundamental'.)

Still, a political activist will want to take a clear-cut stand with regard to 'ultimately' because of the political (strategic) importance of the issue. If material conditions are said to be 'ultimately' determining then there's a strong inducement for people to define themselves primarily as **victims**. It was important to get people to think of themselves as victims in the 19th century because many if not most of them felt that they were (and-or God was) totally responsible for their lives and that nothing could or should be done to ease their pain. However, today the situation is very different. In North America today people have given up much too much of their power and responsibility to their monolithic institutions, including the top-down state; nearly everyone feels victimized and nearly everyone wants their institutions to 'give' them more. A pair of black Marxists said it: in North America today, the Marxist assumption that we're **not** ultimately responsible leads to dependency and parasitism, not to social change (see James and Grace Lee

Boggs, **Revolution and Evolution in the Twentieth Century,** 1974).

For me (and for New Age politics as I understand it), the lesson is clear. Before society can change at its core, we are going to have to be willing to assume a lot more personal responsibility for our selves, our communities, and the planet as a whole. If consciousness (rather than material conditions) is said to be 'ultimately' determining then there's a strong inducement for people to define themselves primarily as **responsible** creatures rather than primarily as victims (not **totally** responsible — the emerging new trans-material worldview would see to that; see Chap. 11, sect. VI).

Throughout this book I've argued that **consciousness** is 'ultimately' determining. That's my perspective. It isn't 'right' or 'wrong' — there is no 'ultimate' answer. But it's a valid answer, as valid as the Marxists', and it's a lot more useful to us in North America today.

(3) **Materialist worldview.** The metaphysical basis for Marxism **and** liberalism **and** anarchism. . . . It's criticized at length in Chap. 11 along with its (symbiotic) opposite, the non-material worldview; and a more relevant and sophisticated worldview, the 'trans-material' worldview, is proposed.

(4) **Dialectical analysis.** According to Marxists, the dialectic is a 'true description' of nature, and also of history; and it expresses the 'iron laws' of nature and history, as follows: (1) the gradual accumulation of small changes leads, over time, to a sudden qualitative change (revolution!); (2) every thing or event is a unity ('thesis'); then contradictions appear which negate the thesis, and these accumulate to become the 'antithesis'; (3) the contradictions continue to accumulate until there's a transition — a sudden leap — to a new equilibrium, a new unity. And then the process begins again.

We can see why the Marxists would want to treat the dialectic as an 'iron law': it appears to 'prove' that revolution is inevitable. But apart from the fact that it appears to give a kind of scientific (actually — blush — metaphysical) validity to the Marxists' belief that the end, of capitalism, is at hand, it is difficult for me to see why anyone should take the dialectic to be more than what it really is: a special case of logic, useful in describing some historical events and processes, less useful in others, and useless or misleading in most.

Then again, it's not so difficult. Remembering my own early infatuation with the dialectic, I can report that it was my need to believe in the ultimate **rightness** and **goodness** of what I was doing that caused me to think of the dialectic as an 'iron law' rather than as a special case.

In some cases the dialectic can be positively harmful. It should always be used with extreme caution, since it's so clearly an expression of the dualistic consciousness that's fostered by the Prison (if we want to think dialectically we have to forever be dividing things up and polarizing them). Consider too that the dialectic can be used to 'prove' almost anything. Lysenko used it to 'prove' his now discredited theory of genetics. Engels used it to 'disprove' immortality, and I can use it to 'prove' immortality: life is the thesis, death the antithesis and immortality the synthesis. Dennis Forsythe, a black sociologist, tells us (in Ladner, ed.) that Marx welcomed the British conquest of India, feeling that it was India's 'historic' mission to carry out — in Marx's words — 'the annihilation of old Asiatic society and the laying of the material foundations of Western society in Asia'. Similarly, Engels regarded the conquest of Algeria by the French as a working out of the dialectic — as (in Engels's words) 'an important and fortunate act for the progress of civilization'.

My point — to repeat — is not that the dialectic is always wrong, but that it is a special case in logic, applicable to some ideas and events and processes, but more often not. 'Neither in ideas nor in nature is it true that opposites always generate a synthesis', says Mayo. 'In the realm of ideas, sometimes a number of conflicting theories may be discarded as wholly false'. Boulding says that the dialectical pattern 'is too simple; history always refuses to fit into intellectual strait jackets. Its cyclical movements are never particularly neat; systems are not usually succeeded by their opposites; change is sometimes regular and slow, sometimes cyclical and violent; chance plays an important part at critical moments; history sometimes does and sometimes does not repeat itself; and so on'. Mumford reminds us that 'there are many modes of change, other than dialectic opposition: maturation, mimesis, mutual aid are all as effective as the struggle between opposing classes'.

New Age people have been making use of a number of alternative ways of thinking about things — alternatives that can be used in place of or along with dialectics:

a. **Tri-level analysis.** See Chap. 5.

b. **'Intuition and imagination'.** Robert Pirsig's alternative to dialectics, in **Zen and the Art of Motorcycle Maintenance**.

'Meditate deeply', says Swami Kriyananda, 'and when you feel very peaceful, very calm, pose alternatives and see which feels harmonious in the heart and which doesn't'.

c. **'Integral Thinking'.** A refusal to make polarizing distinctions — an insistence on remaining open to the opposites without and within. 'If either side is preferred at the expense of the other, the result is death', says Andre Carpenter of the Human Dancing Company (in **Communities** no. 17).

Mad Bear Anderson, a medicine man from the Tuscarora tribe, Iroquois Nation, tells us (in Boyd) that it is 'a mistake to think of any group or person as an opponent, because when you do, that's what the group or person will become. It's more useful to think of every other person as another **you**. . . . If you have a sense of opposition — that is, if you have contempt for others — you're in a perfect position to receive their contempt . . . '. There are many opposites within us, says Jungian analyst June Singer, they've been there all along, and they'd 'coexist in harmony if only we did not drive a wedge between them' and project one opposite out **onto** the 'other', the 'enemy'.

d. **The cosmic dance.** According to Fritjof Capra, 20th-century physics asserts that the world can no longer be seen as completely causal and determinate (as in 19th-century science). Rather, 20th-century physics shows that the world is engaged in endless activity — is engaged in 'a continual cosmic dance of energy' — and that the 'cosmic dance' is almost infinitely varied and complex. There are no 'iron laws' that can be attached to it, and if we want to understand it we have to make use of a number of different analytic frameworks.

(5) **Economic theory of class.** Marxists claim that it's useful for us to think of people in terms of their 'relationship to the means of production' and-or in terms of economic 'class' generally (bourgeois, proletariat). In Chap. 10 I argue that, in North America today, economic class analysis tends to be misleading, and I make a case for the usefulness of 'psychocultural' class analysis (life-, thing-, and death-oriented classes).

(6) **Class struggle.** According to this theory, all of history is the history of class struggles. Moreover, class struggle is how the dialectic chooses to work itself out in history; therefore, class struggle is inevitable, and also inevitably 'progressive' and good.

But as social philosopher Jacques Ellul points out at some length (in **Autopsy**, Part I), **most** social conflict and **most** major 'turning points' in history can only be inadequately understood in terms of the class struggle theory ('turning points' are emphasized by neo-Marxists). The Spartacus rebellion, yes; the American revolution, very partially; the conquests of Alexander or the struggle of Papacy versus Empire, no. Mumford points out that the voluntary renunciation of their feudal rights by the French aristocracy did more to transform French society than the most vicious 'struggles' of the French revolution — his point being that class understanding and class cooperation have also played a constructive role in history and that without them society might be 'thrown back into barbarism' (certainly it could never be healed).

It is difficult to explain the events in postwar North America according to the doctrine of the economic class struggle. It is fairly clear, at least to me, that the current struggles are over worldviews and values (see Part IV of this book). Ellul makes the case that value conflict has been at least as much of a factor in history as class conflict; he also points out that, 'The loss of values suddenly renders intolerable a social or economic situation that was otherwise bearable. The social and economic factors are the pretext and not the basis; they are the cause only in so far as there is no longer any reason to go on living and what made life bearable has disappeared'.

As for the notion that the class struggle is inevitable — once the dialectic is assigned a more limited role (no. 4 above) the class struggle is no longer theoretically 'inevitable' (since class struggle is how the dialectic is said to work itself out in history). Eugen Loebl, once one of Dubcek's top economists and now a refugee in North America, adds that in practice the notion of class struggle is a **self-fulfilling prophecy**, that with it we create ('we are induced to create') the conflict that we say we see. About the Soviet Union and Czechoslovakia he says, 'The believers in this concept, of whom I was one, actually fostered the most militant, ruthless, and inhumane class struggle known in history. We even turned peasants and small shopkeepers into a "class enemy" by persecuting them and their children'. Let his conclusion stand as a warning: 'The way we categorize influences the way we act'.

(7) **False consciousness.** People who disagree with Marxists don't just 'think differently' and they're not just 'wrong'. They are said to be suffering from 'false consciousness'. Their understanding of reality is **deficient** and needs to be remedied — by persuasion if possible, by coercion if necessary (as in Vietnam and China).

I find the notion of false consciousness to be morally offensive and politically extremely dangerous. It implies what sociologist Peter Berger calls 'the hierarchical view of consciousness. There is something medieval about this . . . — the mind of God is at one end, that of the dumb animals on the other, and in between are we humans, carefully stratified in terms of proximity to either pole'. For a Marxist, only 'revolutionary' consciousness can raise the proletariat to the level of humanity. And revolutionary consciousness has to be **brought** by someone else, someone who is, by definition, more human already.

With the concept of false consciousness, says Berger, 'the intellectual identified with the "vanguard" lays claim to a cognitively privileged status: (He or she) and only (he or she) has reality by the shortest possible hair. This cognitive superiority, which allows (him or her) to designate other people's consciousness as false, is (by that very fact) a human superiority: The cognitively superior individual is, by virtue of (his or her) consciousness, at a higher level of freedom, and thus of humanity'.

Clearly, this is the assumption that gives Marxist parties the notion that they have the right to herd literally millions of people, i.e. 'the' people, whom they claim to respect so much, into 're-education' camps for unlimited time periods.

Berger's conclusion: 'Put simply, no one is "more conscious" than anyone else; different people are conscious of different things. . . . No one is in a position to "raise" anyone else. . . . All of us are moving around on the same level, trying to make sense of the universe and doing our best to cope with the necessities of living'.

Most political activists would agree that people should have the right to participate in the decisions that are made about their lives. New Age people go further and say that people should have the right to participate in the **therories** that are made and that define-describe the **reality within which** the decisions are made. All known political ism's are loathe to relinquish **this** right. Still, as Berger says, 'It is a very limited notion of participation to let an elite define a situation in complete disregard of the ways in which this situation is **already defined** by those who live in it — and then to allow the latter a voice in the decisions made on the basis of the preordained definition. A more meaningful notion of participation will include a voice in the definitions of the situation that underlie this or that decision-making option'.

If all of us were encouraged to contribute our own definitions to the situation, then the material **and** the spiritual **and** the religious **and** the mythic states of consciousness (which are differently important for different people) would each make some definite contribution to the way we see our world — and to the priorities we set for self and society.

(8) **Dictatorship of the proletariat**. According to Marx and Engels (and to 'humanist' Marxists generally), the 'dictatorship of the proletariat', the dictatorship of the popular majority over the 'bourgeois' minority, would last only a short time — only until the bourgeoisie was stripped of its power and of its ability to make a counter-revolution. And **within** the dictatorship, among the 'proletariat', there would be a great deal of genuine democracy.

Marx and Engels prided themselves on their tough-mindedness, but the assumptions they made about the 'dictatorship of the proletariat' can only be regarded as sentimental nonsense whose consequences in the real world are as disastrous as they are predictable.

1. 'Any dictatorship must have its hierarchy' (Loebl). Therefore the leadership of the proletariat, that is, the Marxist party, becomes the source of authoritarian rule.

2. Any dictatorship needs to stifle all genuine democracy as a matter of sheer survival.

3. Inevitably — since dictatorships are loathe to give up their power — they've tended to claim that the bourgeoisie has managed to **maintain or even increase** its power after the Revolution (**vide** Stalin and Mao). (They've also redefined 'bourgeois' to mean: anyone who disagrees with the existence of the dictatorship.) This does two things: (a) it provides justification for the continuation of the dictatorship, and (b) it provides justification for the **strenthening** of the dictatorship.

4. To a large extent, defining the bourgeoisie as the enemy is a self-fulfilling prophecy.

5. It is only a short step from the position that a proletarian dictatorship is necessary 'to the argument that a government on behalf of the proletariat, serving their "real" interests, can hardly be called a dictatorship at all' (Mayo).

Counter-productive as the idea of a 'dictatorship of the proletariat' may be, the problem that the Marxists are speaking to is very real. Though they lack the political honesty to put it in these terms, it is: how can we change society deeply if we don't have a 51 percent majority?

In North America, I believe that any committed person pulls more weight politically than the weight of sheer numbers. If a 'critical mass' of 10-20 percent of us were actively engaged in self-and-social healing (on the basis of the New Age ethics and political values), then society would definitely change in a New Age direction (see Chap. 19, sect. IV).

(9) **Economic theory of imperialism**. Imperialism 'refers to any relationship of effective domination or control, political or economic, direct or indirect, of one nation over another' (Benjamin Cohen, political scientist, in **The Question of Imperialism**). According to Marxism, (1) economics is the 'taproot' of imperialism, and (2) imperialism is a 'final stage' or at least a necessary part of capitalism (not, however, of socialism).

A number of writers have pointed out that there are three likely sources of imperialism: (1) our values, perceived needs, wants and prejudices, selfishness and aggressiveness; (2) political factors ('national security', national prestige, the nation-state system itself); (3) economic factors. New Age politics believes that imperialism owes its existence primarily to (1), and that (2) is generally more causative than (3).

In Part I of this book I argue that imperialism, like racism, environmental degradation and the like, is primarily rooted in a complex of cultural attitudes that I call the 'Six-Sided Prison' and that can be traced back hundreds or even thousands of years before 'capitalism'. (In his massive study of foreign policy, Franz Schurmann concludes that imperialism is a **popular** phenomenon and has been supported by 'the people' even over and against the efforts of at least some corporate and bureaucratic interests.)

Many New Age writers have emphasized that the state has been the determining factor, has had the final say, with regard to imperialism (as compared to the corporations). Cohen argues that 'traders and investors' have more often been used as the instruments of diplomacy than the reverse. His conclusion: 'Imperialistic behaviour is a perfectly rational strategy of foreign policy . . . (a) response to the uncertainty surrounding the survival of the nation'. In this view, it's the nation state system itself that's largely at cause — a view shared by Boulding who sees imperialism as an 'essential part of the dynamic of national defence — wherever a "defence vacuum" exists in the world, some armed power may be expected to occupy it'.

Richard Barnet, political economist, argues that the state continues to be primarily responsible for imperialism in the era of the multinational corporation: 'The (MNC) has certain crucial advantages. . . . Yet the nation still holds the strongest cards'. Seymour Melman, political economist, argues that many of our biggest corporations have become overly dependent on state subsidies, contracts, tax favours, etc., and have thus become more or less docile servants of the state — at home and abroad.

What of the contributing argument, that imperialism is a 'final stage' or, at least, a necessary part of capitalism? Boulding reminds us that 'imperialism is a much older institution that capitalism, and states with all kinds of economic systems have been imperialistic, both states with planned economies (ancient Egypt, modern Russia) and states with capitalistic ones'. Barnet tells us that 'A society dedicated to growth will make the same demands on resources whether it is capitalist or socialist. . . . If the price for ending imperialist policies is to cut wasteful consumption, then the solution must be more radical than socialism as it has been preached'. Barrington Moore looks at each of the leading primarily economic explanations for capitalist imperialism (need for raw materials, need for extra profits, need for new outlets for investment) and finds each of them wanting. He notes that, for example, most non-capitalist governments have been more than willing to trade with us; and that there's no evidence to show that individual corporations have had difficulty finding profitable ways to re-invest. He also says that Marxism has never been able to prove that economic institutions are **unchangeable** under capitalism; a point made also by Barnet, Cohen and Melman. What each of these writers emphasizes is, in Moore's words, 'the absence of a demand for change — not the impossibility of change'. Which brings us back to my first point. . . .

(10) **Labour theory of value.** This theory — the central one in Marxist economics — doesn't quite go so far as to say that the price or value of goods is determined by the labour that goes into those goods. What it does say is that every good that's produced in society, as well as the output of society as a whole, can be regarded as the outcome of what Boulding calls 'a series of acts of labour'. Everything else, capital, technical knowledge, etc., can be regarded as 'raw material' that depends on labour to give it substance and shape. Therefore — and this is the point of the theory — the 'proletariat' is obviously being deprived of a share of its rightful income.

The problem with this theory can be seen if, as Boulding suggests, we stand it on its head. Suppose labour is seen as a raw material like iron or coal that doesn't and can't produce anything of value until it's been organized by a clever entrepreneur. Then we get an 'entrepreneurial theory of value' that holds that the organizer of labour is responsible for the production of all the goods of a society (but isn't allowed to enjoy the fruits of his or her entrepreneurship because of all those **unions**).

My point isn't that the entrepreneurial theory is the 'correct' one (though logically speaking it's no less correct than the labour theory). My point is that neither labour nor entrepreneurship, acting alone, is **sufficient** to produce commodities. (Economist Walter Weisskopf has suggested that Marx may have exaggerated the value of labour in general, and of industrial labour in particular, because labour represented and still represents the **male principle** to the Prison-bound consciousness; service and leisure, the female principle.)

Then there's the fact that the kind and the quality of the **institutions** in a society — legal, social, spiritual — definitely affects the course of economic development, and so is part of the productive process too. And then there are the **values and attitudes** that are prominent in society; for as economist Harvey Leibenstein points out, it isn't really labour **time** that's crucial for production, it's the amount of directed effort. And directed effort involves motives and choices on the part of those directing their efforts (and motives and choices are intimately bound up with values and attitudes).

Because of all this I'd like to propose, as the New Age alternative to the labour theory of value, the **synergic theory of value.** It says that the goods that are produced in a society as well as the output of the society as a whole, can be regarded as the outcome of a complex and 'synergic' (see Chap. 15, sect. II) mixture of such factors as labour time, entrepreneurial skills, organizational efficiencies, institutional elements, and values and attitudes.

(11) **Exploitation — or negative symbiosis?** Exploitation is a technical term in Marxist economics, but Marxists often use it more generally to mean that people are being taken advantage of, that people are being hurt. As a descriptive term exploitation has some merit, but I balk at the implication that the harm is all being done to us by a 'them'. Therefore, I'd like to steal a term from ecology and propose that we're living in a state of **negative symbiosis** with our society.

In a symbiotic relationship, both parties come to need each other. If they come to need each other's strengths, the relationship is often called positively symbiotic. If, however, they come to feed off (and reinforce) each other's weaknesses, the relationship is often called negatively symbiotic.

Parts I-III of this book are about how and why our needs and those of the society have become negatively symbiotic. They argue that we are, by nature, self-defining and self-developing, but that the descent of the Prison within us has made us much more interested in self-aggrandizement than in self-development. And so we've created 'monolithic institutions' that make it almost impossible for us to meet our needs for love and esteem and self-actualization and Self-realization, but that **do** make it possible for us to meet the needs that are generated by our Prison-bound personalities — for romance, for power, and most of all, for a seemingly endless supply of goods and services (literally, 10 times as many goods and services as we need to meet our physiological and security needs).

Inevitably, as time went on we became more and more dependent on our monolithic institutions, until our Prison-bound personalities and our monolithic institutions began to reinforce and perpetuate each other in a classic case of negative symbiosis.

Where does this leave us? Liberals who think of themselves as part of a 'social contract' are able to feel warm and secure . . . and justified in their use and abuse of others. Marxists who think of themselves as 'exploited' are able to feel self-righteous and vengeful . . . and have a cover for their envy (of precisely what they claim to want to destroy). But those of us who understand that we're living in a state of negative symbiosis with our society can take no comfort in the fact. We can only take comfort in our efforts to change our monolithic institutions — and to change our selves.

V. Alienation: The Last Refuge of the Neo-Marxist

Many of us are initially drawn to Marxism because of the concept of alienation. It at least appears to speak to the heart of the modern predicament: we **know** we're alienated; who among us doesn't feel it in their bones? At the same time, there are some Marxists (called neo-Marxists) who've given up most of the traditional Marxist beliefs and who've made the concept of alienation the cornerstone of their philosophy.

In this section I'm going to show that the concept of alienation goes back long before Marx; that what he meant by alienation is far too narrow to explain our predicament (so narrow that it **contributes** to our alienation); and that he misled us badly by blaming alienation on 'capitalism'. Then I'm going to describe three crucial dimensions of alienation that Marxism understates or misses: political, self and spiritual alienation.

A. History of the term

To the Romans 'alienation' meant separation from the body in the mystery rites (and they heartily disapproved!). To the early Christians it meant the separation of people from God. Grotius introduced the term into political philosophy in the 17th century — he took it to mean the transference of authority over one's self to another person or to government. Beginning in the early 19th century, Kierkegaard and other philosophers analyzed the various forms of alienation that we suffer from as individuals. Marx **narrowed** the meaning of the term; and he traced its **cause** to the world of work.

B. What Marx meant by alienation

Marx identified four **kinds** of alienation, as follows: alienation of the worker from the process of his or her work; alienation of the worker from the product of his or her work; alienation of the worker from his or her fellows; and alienation of the worker from him- or her self. Also, Marx traced the **root** of alienation to 'capitalism' — to the fact that the worker didn't control his or her work place and-or own the things that he or she produced.

It is important that in all four instances Marx was speaking of the alienation of the **worker**. As David Herlihy puts it (in Frank Johnson, ed., **Alienation**, 1973), 'Marx was not concerned with individual alienation, self-alienation (individuals who believed themselves isolated from their society) but rather with social alienation'. Indeed, Marxists tend to regard individual, self-alienation as a sign of 'bourgeois individualism' and-or as a sign of 'social decadence'.

ᴕᴕᴕᴕᴕᴕᴕᴕᴕᴕᴕᴕᴕᴕ C. Critique of the Marxist concept ᴕᴕᴕᴕᴕᴕᴕᴕᴕᴕᴕᴕᴕᴕ

Marx was right about one thing: boring, meaningless work over which the worker has no control, **does** alienate the worker in the ways he described. But Marx was wrong to limit his use of the concept in the way that he did. By doing so he managed to keep many political activists — not just Marxists — from taking seriously some of the other key aspects of alienation: the political aspects (Grotius), the self aspects (Kierkegaard) and the spiritual aspects (early Christians). And to the extent that it diverts us from consideration of these other types of alienation Marx's concept itself serves to 'alienate' us from a true understanding of our selves and our society.

Marx was also wrong to trace the source of alienation, even worker alienation, to capitalism. Worker alienation doesn't appear to vary significantly according to whether a company is publicly, privately or worker-owned, or according to whether a country calls itself socialist or capitalist. Roderic Gorney, the psychiatrist, reports on one extensive study, done in Yugoslavia, that demonstrates conclusively that 'membership in workers' councils made no significant difference in the degree of alienation or job satisfaction' — this in a socialist country! To find out what the true reasons are for worker alienation — for alienation as Marx defined it — we need to look, not to orthodox Marxists, but (ironically) to the kinds of people whose work makes up the emerging New Age politics.

Among these people, David Dickson, an appropriate technologist, suggests that worker alienation is primarily a result of the kinds of **machines and technologies** that are used by a society; and especially whether these are (a) human scale, and (b) easily or fully understood by the workers who use them. Charles Hampden-Turner, political economist and psychologist, suggests that the key question is whether or not the workers' product has a **social purpose** that the workers can understand and identify with. Frederick Thayer, a political scientist, suggests that worker alienation is a function of **hierarchy** at the workplace: the more hierarchy, the more alienation . . . period. And Gorney suggests that we'll always be alienated from work 'so long as (we are) forced to work by scarcity and the necessity to make a living' (another good reason for granting us access to the 'guaranteed subsistence income' that I advocate in Chap. 21, sect. III-1).

ᴕᴕᴕᴕᴕᴕᴕᴕᴕᴕᴕᴕᴕᴕ D. Deeper forms of alienation ᴕᴕᴕᴕᴕᴕᴕᴕᴕᴕᴕᴕᴕᴕ

In North America, in the latter part of the 20th century, the kinds of alienation that Marx consciously **downplayed or ignored** in his formulations — political, self and spiritual alienation — run at least as deep as worker alienation; and point the way to the kinds of political changes that are needed.

(1) **Political alienation.** By political I mean two things. First, the fact that we've allowed our selves to become more and more dependent on the top-down state (on exactly the kind of centralized state that was envisaged in Marxist philosophy). Second, the fact that we've abdicated far too much of our personal responsibility to our other monolithic institutions (see Chap. 7).

In order to end our political alienation (as defined above), we need to stop defining our selves primarily as producers and consumers of goods — as 'economic people'. Because with this self-definition we might very well continue to prefer a comfortable, 'plastic' unfreedom to the challenges and responsibilities of true, decentralized democracy. But **before** we can begin to re-define our selves we need to get in touch with our selves at a very deep place. And that brings us up against the other two alienations that are searing us today.

(2) **Self alienation**. On the one hand, we experience a natural desire, a **hunger** for closeness and affection; on the other hand, we find it almost impossible to achieve this closeness, get this affection (except in tantalizing bits and flashes). Because we've never been taught to cultivate our selves. Because we've been taught that to do so is 'self-indulgent navel gazing' — in men, even a little 'queer'. But as Anais Nin puts it, 'If we did not spend some time in creating our selves in depth and power, with what were we going to relate to others? . . . How could we love, how could we give, how could we trust, how could we share what we didn't have to give?'

Carl Rogers, a psychotherapist, has focused on our tendency to alienate our selves from our experience of our selves. The fact that our needs for closeness, affection, esteem, etc., are frustrated, makes us feel less than worthy as human beings; and in response (and out of self-protection) we learn to 'perceive our experience selectively', that is, to make sure that negative experiences are either 'perceived . . . distortedly as if in accord with the conditions of worth' or are 'in part or whole, denied to awareness'. According to Rogers, this is a **natural** tendency that may begin as early as infancy; and if it's ignored it will remain 'the basic estrangement' in people.

Abraham Maslow, a psychologist, points out that we're cut off from our 'primary thought patterns': from our original and creative and playful thoughts. At home and at school especially, we're taught that 'revery, poetry and play' need to be suppressed because 'reality' is harsh and demands 'a purposeful and pragmatic striving'. (In other words: we're systematically cut off from the 'mythic state of consciousness'.)

(3) **Spiritual alienation**. Marxist theory may pretty much ignore political and self alienation (as defined above), but it's positively joyous about the existence of spiritual alienation, about the fact of our estrangement from what we shyly call 'life's mysteries'. Bourgeois twaddle, the opiate of the people, say the Marxists, all in unison.

Nikolai Berdyaev, the Russian 'personalist' philosopher who fled after the Revolution, had a different position. The bourgeois, he said, **is the person who's banished all mystery from life**. And Theodore Roszak is even clearer. 'The spiritual void in our lives', he says, ' . . . is the prime political fact of our time. It is the secret of our discontent'.

What is this 'spiritual void'? Lawrence Blair puts it well when he says, 'We are aware of only a fraction of the spectrum of nature in which we have our being. . . . It is generations now since we were close to the immediate symbolism of poetry, the cyclical pulse of birth and death. . . . We cannot see the seasonal movement of the lichen across the continent, as did the Red Indians. . . . We of the cities scarcely gaze up at the night sky any more, and when we do, what we see is flat, pinpricked like a board — not coiling with suns through deep dimensions of time . . . '. Michael Worth, of the Findhorn community, adds (in **Onearth** no. 1), 'Most of us can't see one another's auras any more. . . We've blinded our selves to the beings of the Nature Kingdoms, and to their needs. . . . In fact, most of human consciousness has become so material and form-oriented that there might as well be no life beyond what is directly perceived by the physical senses'.

The spiritual void can't be filled unless and until we learn to get in touch with the spiritual and religious states of consciousness (see Chap. 11, sects. III-IV). Until we do the void will continue to be felt — and we'll continue to search for a 'fix' on the material plane: continue to indulge our selves in overconsumption; continue to live vicariously through the television tube and the lives of our 'stars'; continue to engage our selves in mindless mass movements (Roszak) and in dreams of violent revolution, dreams of revenge for what it is we've lost.

Chapter 24 — New Age Books, New Age Periodicals, New Age Groups

I. 200 New Age Books

This doesn't pretend to be a list of the 200 'best' or 'most important' New Age books (who could choose?) — it is a list of the 200 books, articles and cassette tapes that I relied on most while writing **New Age Politics**. Nearly three-fifths of them have been published (or recorded) since 1974.

(1) Roberto Assagioli, **Psychosynthesis: A Manual of Principles and Techniques** (Viking, trans. 1965). Personal growth and spiritual development, and their interconnections. Also **Act of Will** (1971).

(2) Elizabeth Bardwell, **More Is Less: The Case Study of a City that May Be Growing Too Big for its Citizens' Good**, 2nd ed. (Madison, Wisc., 1974). Argues against big cities on economic, political, socio-cultural grounds. Available for $2.25 from The Capital Community Citizens, 114 No. Carroll St., Madison.

(3) Richard Barnet, **Roots of War: The Men and Institutions Behind U.S. Foreign Policy** (Penguin, 1972). 'The corporations continue to exercise the dominant **influence** . . . but the **power** keeps passing to the state'.

(4) Richard Barnet and Ronald Muller, **Global Reach: The Power of the Multinational Corporations** (Simon and Schuster, 1974). Critique of the MNC's from an 'antigrowth, anticonsumption, antihierarchy' perspective.

(5) Robert Bellah, **The Broken Covenant: American Civil Religion in Time of Trial** (Seabury, 1975). Sociologist calls for a 're-awakening' of religious state of consciousness.

(6) Daryl Bem, **Beliefs, Attitudes, and Human Affairs** (Brooks-Cole, 1970). Tri-level analysis of consciousness. Advertising less persuasive than we think.

(7) Tom Bender, **Environmental Design Primer: A Book of Meditations on Ecological Consciousness** (Schocken, 1973). Written from out of all four states of consciousness.

(8) Tom Bender, **Sharing Smaller Pies** (Portland, Ore., 1975). New Age values; appropriate technology; what is to be done. Available for $2 from **Rain** (sect. II below).

(9) Nikolai Berdyaev, **Slavery and Freedom** (Scribner's, 1944). Early personalist. Argues against Marxists, liberals from a 'trans-material' perspective.

(10) Peter Berger, Brigitte Berger and Hansfried Kellner, **The Homeless Mind: Modernization and Consciousness** (Vintage, 1973). Material state of consciousness the 'modernizing ideology' that Marxists, liberals share.

(11) Peter Berger, **Pyramids of Sacrifice: Political Ethics and Social Change** (Anchor, 1975). Questions Marxist and liberal development strategies;

questions concept of false consciousness.

(12) Wendell Berry, **A Continuous Harmony: Essays Cultural and Agricultural** (Harvest, 1972). On: poetry; community; regionalism; (need for) reawakening of personal responsibility, personal life; more.

(13) Black Elk (as told through John Neihardt), **Black Elk Speaks: Being the Life Story of a Holy Man of the Oglala Sioux** (Pocket, 1932). Trans-material worldview in action.

(14) Lawrence Blair, **Rhythms of Vision: The Changing Patterns of Belief** (Warner, 1976). Spiritual and mythic states of consciousness — an anatomy.

(15) Joan Bondurant, **Conquest of Violence: The Gandhian Philosophy of Conflict**, rev. ed. (Univ. of California Press, 1965). Good, 'tough-minded' introduction. With implications for our time and place.

(16) Kenneth Boulding, **The Organizational Revolution: A Study in the Ethics of Economic Organization**, 2nd ed. (Quadrangle, 1968). Searching critique of bureaucracy; bureaucratic mentality; nation-state system....

(17) Doug Boyd, **Rolling Thunder** (Delta, 1974). About an American Indian medicine man; about a practical, down-to-earth spirituality.

(18) Fernand Braudel, **The Mediterranean and the Mediterranean World in the Age of Philip II**, 2 vols., rev. 2nd ed. (Harper & Row, trans. 1974). Outstanding example of 'tri-level analysis'. See also J. H. Hexter, 'Fernand Braudel and the **Monde Braudellien** . . . ', **Journal of Modern History**, vol. 44 (Dec. 1972), pp. 447-539.

(19) Scott Burns, **Home, Inc.**, paperback as **The Household Economy: Its Shape, Origins, and Future** (Beacon, 1975). The 'household economy' — and how and why it's 'overtaking the corporate economy'....

(20) Ernest Callenbach, **Ecotopia** (Bantam, 1975). Novel about Wash., Ore., and northern Calif. after they've separated from the U.S. and evolved a society based on appropriate technology and ecological consciousness.

(21) Ernest Callenbach, **Living Poor With Style** (Bantam, 1972). Simple living — 600 pages worth....

(22) Fritjof Capra, **The Tao of Physics: An Exploration of the Parallels Between Modern Physics and Eastern Mysticism** (Shambhala, 1975). Shows that the material state of consciousness needs to be re-defined, expanded.

(23) Carlos Castaneda, **Journey to Ixtlan: The Lessons of Don Juan** (Pocket, 1972). Vivid description of non-material states of consciousness and of positive 'master'-student relationship.

(24) Centre for Science in the Public Interest, **99 Ways to a Simple Lifestyle** (Anchor, 1976). Very basic book on simple living. Meant to appeal to the thing-oriented.

(25) Benjamin Cohen, **The Question of Imperialism: The Political Economy of Dominance and Dependence** (Basic, 1973). State's role dominant, corporations' secondary; people's values the really determining factor.

(26) James and Marge Craig, **Synergic Power: Beyond Domination and Permissiveness** (Berkeley: ProActive Press, 1974). New Age approach to power. Available for $3.95 from Synergic Power Centre (III below).

(27) Harold Cruse, **The Crisis of the Negro Intellectual** (Morrow, 1967). Advocates an alternative to Marxism based on **ethnic-group** consciousness and **psycho-cultural** analysis.

(28) Herman Daly, ed., **Toward a Steady-State Economy** (W.H. Freeman, 1972). New Age economics. See esp. Daly (all), Johnson ('The Guaranteed Income as an Environmental Measure'), and Weisskopf ('Economic Growth Versus Existential Balance').

(29) Mary Daly, **Beyond God the Father: Toward a Philosophy of Women's Liberation** (Beacon, 1973). Feminist spirituality and its social and political implications.

(30) Elizabeth Gould Davis, **The First Sex** (Penguin, 1971). History of women's experience from the matriarchies to the present.

(31) Sebastian de Grazia, **Of Time, Work, and Leisure** (Anchor, 1962). Makes the case for a 'leisure economy' and a leisure society.

(32) Vine Deloria, Jr., **God Is Red** (Dell, 1973). We have more to learn from North American Indian spirituality than from Christianity.

(33) David Dickson, **The Politics of Alternative Technology** (Universe, 1974). Good introduction to biolithic ('utopian') technology and its implications; good critique of monolithic technology.

(34) Calvert Dodge, ed., **A Nation Without Prisons: Alternatives to Incarceration** (Lexington, Mass.: Lexington Books, 1975). See esp. Chaps. 2 ('Toward a New Criminology') and 5 ('Community Alternatives to Incarceration').

(35) James Douglass, **Resistance and Contemplation: The Way of Liberation; The Yin and Yang of the Non-Violent Life** (Doubleday, 1972). Spiritual growth and non-violent activism, and their interconnections.

(36) Constantinos Doxiadis, **Anthropopolis: City for Human Development** (Norton, 1974). Critique of the modern city. Presents an alternative whose purpose would be to foster our personal growth.

(37) Rene Dubos, **A God Within** (Scribner's, 1972). 'Perceptual and conceptual' environments, conservation vs. stewardship, etc. Very wise book.

(38) Andrea Dworkin, **Woman Hating** (Dutton, 1974). Radical feminism; pagan spirituality; androgyny.

(39) Richard Easterlin, 'Does Money Buy Happiness?', **The Public Interest**, no. 30 (Winter 1973), pp. 3-10. Beyond the hard-core poverty level, the answer is no.

(40) Anne Ehrlich and Paul Ehrlich, **Population, Resources, Environment: Issues in Human Ecology**, 2nd ed. (W.H. Freeman, 1972). Good basic introduction.

(41) Duane Elgin and Arnold Mitchell, 'Voluntary Simplicity', **CoEvolution Quarterly**, no. 14 (Summer 1977), pp. 4-19. Who, what, when, where, why. Stanford Research Institute's most popular report ever.

(42) Jacques Ellul, **Autopsy of Revolution** (Knopf, trans. 1971). 'We have no legacy to fall back on; everything must be initiated'.

(43) Jacques Ellul, **The Political Illusion** (Vintage, trans. 1967). There's more to politics than — conventional politics. Values must be transformed; technique, dethroned; the state, decentralized.

(44) Joe Falk, **Cooperative Community Development: A Blueprint for Our Future** (Shawnee Mission, Kans., 1975). New Age community organizing: how-to. Available for $2.95 from The Future Associates, P.O. Box 912, Shawnee Mission, Kans. 66201.

(45) Richard Falk, **A Study of Future Worlds** (Free Press, 1975). Argues for a 'planetary guidance system' based on specific New Age political values.

(46) Warren Farrell, **The Liberated Man; Beyond Masculinity: Freeing Men and Their Relationships with Women** (Bantam, 1974). Written especially for thing-oriented males. Excellent section on consciousness-changing groups (how-to).

(47) Marc Fasteau, **The Male Machine** (Dell, 1974). Another good basic introduction to men's liberation and its implications.

(48) Hassan Fathy, **Architecture for the Poor** (Univ. of Chicago Press, 1973). Critique of monolithic housing policy. Presents a biolithic alternative that was actually tried (in Egypt).

(49) Shulamith Firestone, **The Dialectic of Sex: The Case for Feminist Revolution** (Bantam, 1970). Patriarchal attitudes came before capitalism, racism.

(50) Edgar Friedenberg, **The Disposal of Liberty and Other Industrial Wastes** (Anchor, 1975). Critique of monolithic institutions; cultural conflict (now) underlies class conflict; more....

(51) John Friedmann, **Retracking America: A Theory of Transactive Planning** (Anchor, 1973). Task oriented working groups; working group assemblies; networks of assemblies.

(52) Erich Fromm, **The Anatomy of Human Destructiveness** (Fawcett, 1973). Intellectual-theoretical basis for my life-, thing- and death-orientations.

(53) Erich Fromm, **To Have or To Be?** (Harper & Row, 1976). Along with life-death, the basic distinction between Prison and New Age society. Makes use of many untranslated German New Agers' writings.

(54) Buckminster Fuller, **Utopia or Oblivion: The Prospects for Humanity** (Bantam, 1969). Good general introduction to his thought. See also Alden Hatch, **Buckminster Fuller: At Home in the Universe** (1974).

(55) Stephen Gaskin, ... **This Season's People: A Book of Spiritual Teachings** (Summertown, Tenn., 1976). By founder and spiritual leader of The Farm. Available for $2.95 from The Book Publishing Co., Summertown, Tenn. 38483. See also 'The Plowboy Papers', **The Mother Earth News**, no. 45, pp. 8-20.

(56) William Gevarter, 'The Human Brain and Its Programming', in **Loving**, no. 1 (1976), pp. 42-46. The 'triune' brain — and how it can be re-programmed by the consciousness-and-growth movement. Available for $1 from Cornucopia Institute (St. Mary, Ky. 40063).

(57) Robert Ghelardi, **Economics, Society and Culture: God, Money and the New Capitalism** (Dell, 1976). Essays — literally, steps — toward a new analysis that would link the far left and far right.

(58) Allen Ginsberg, **The Fall of America; poems of these states 1966-1971** (City Lights, 1972). Successful integration of political, spiritual, Hebraic and poetic consciousnesses (i.e. of all four states of consciousness).

(59) Erving Goffman, **The Presentation of Self in Everyday Life** (Anchor, 1959). The social role as a monolithic institution.

(60) Roderic Gorney, **The Human Agenda** (Bantam, 1972). 800-page re-examination of evolution, love, work, play, values, racism.

(61) Alvin Gouldner, **For Sociology: Renewal and Critique in Sociology Today** (Basic, 1973), Parts I and III. Role of the New Age intellectual. Objectivity as the search for wholeness (as distinct from power-and-control).

(62) Susanne Gowan, George Lakey, William Moyer and Richard Taylor, **Moving Toward a New Society** (Philadelphia, 1976). Analysis, goals and strategy of Movement for a New Society (as of 1976) — available for $4 from MNS (III below).

(63) Richard Gregg, **The Power of Nonviolence**, rev. ed. (Schocken, 1959). New Age approach to non-violent action.

(64) Charles Hampden-Turner, **From Poverty to Dignity: A Strategy for Poor Americans** (Anchor, 1974). Chaps. 4-8 on (promise of) Community Development Corporations.

(65) Charles Hampden-Turner, **Sane Asylum** (San Francisco Book Co., 1976). John Maher and the Delancey Street Foundation — a residential community of ex-felons that stresses personal responsibility, personal growth, **and** social and political action.

(66) Willis Harman, **An Incomplete Guide to the Future** (San Francisco Book Co., 1976). Tri-level analysis. Trans-material worldview. Personal

growth as a society's 'central project'. More. . . .

(67) Paul Hawken, **The Magic of Findhorn** (Bantam, 1975). Excellent introduction to the Findhorn community: garden, people, vision, promise.

(68) Carlton Hayes, **Nationalism: A Religion** (Macmillan, 1960). Thorough
critique of nationalism and the nation-state.

(68) Fred Hirsch, **Social Limits to Growth** (Harvard Univ. Press, 1976). Material goods vs. 'positional goods' (those that depend on the fact that
they're owned by a **few**).

(70) Shere Hite, 'Toward a New Female Sexuality', in ibid., **The Hite Report:
A Nationwide Study of Female Sexuality** (Dell, 1976), pp. 525-70. New
Age sexuality. Alternatives to the 'stroke economy'.

(71) John Holt, **Escape from Childhood: The Needs and Rights of Children**
(Ballantine, 1974). Young people should be able to make use of the
rights and responsibilities of adult citizens . . . if they want to.

(72) John Holt, **Instead of Education: Ways to Help People Do Things Better**
(Delta, 1976). Excellent critique of monolithic education — many biolithic alternatives suggested.

(73) William Howton, **Functionaries** (Quadrangle, 1969). New Age-oriented
critique of bureaucracies and the bureaucratic mentality.

(74) The Hunger Project, 'An Idea Whose Time Has Come: The End of Starvation Within 20 Years', booklet (San Francisco, 1978). A consciousness-and-growth approach. Available for $1.50 from The Hunger Pro-
ject, P.O. Box 789, San Francisco 94101.

(75) Ivan Illich, **Deschooling Society** (Harrow, 1971). Critique of monolithic
education; alternatives. Revised and deepened by Illich, 'The Alternative to Schooling', **Saturday Review**, vol. 54 (19 June 1971), pp. 44-48.

(76) Ivan Illich, **Energy and Equity** (London: Calder & Boyars, 1974). Great
critique of monolithic transport — many alternatives suggested.

(77) Ivan Illich, **Medical Nemesis** (Bantam, 1975). Critique of monolithic
healing — some alternatives suggested.

(78) Ivan Illich, **Tools for Conviviality** (Perennial, 1973). General critique of
monolithic institutions ('radical monopolies'); biolithic institutions en-
visioned; evolutionary political strategy proposed.

(79) Arthur Janov, **The Primal Scream; Primal Therapy: The Cure for Neu-
rosis** (Dell, 1970). Good introduction to the subject — and to the origins
of the stroke economy.

(80) Rosabeth Kanter, ed., **Communes: Creating and Managing the Collective Life** (Harper & Row, 1973). Compleat introduction to the problems — and promise — of communal living (decision-making, work,
relationships, child-rearing, etc.).

(81) George Katona, **Psychological Economics** (Elsevier, 1975). Interesting
attempt to combine the disciplines of psychology and economics.

(82) Stanley Keleman, **Your Body Speaks Its Mind: The Bio-Energetic Way to
Greater Emotional and Sexual Satisfaction** (Pocket, 1975). 'You are
your body'. Personal, social and spiritual implications.

(83) Ken Keyes, Jr., **Handbook to Higher Consciousness: The Science of Hap-
piness**, 5th ed. (Berkeley: Living Love Centre, 1976). The 'Living Love
Way' to happiness and higher consciousness. Available for $2.95 from
Cornucopia Institute (St. Mary, Ky. 40063).

(84) Donald Keys, **The United Nations and Planetary Consciousness** (New
York, 1977). Planetary consciousness and the real world. Available for
$2 from Planetary Citizens (III below).

(85) Anne Koedt, Ellen Levine and Anita Rapone, eds., **Radical Feminism**
(Quadrangle, 1973). Basic, 'radical' feminism (as distinct from Marx-

ist feminism). Includes Joreen, 'Tyranny of Structurelessness'; Koedt, 'Politics of the Ego'; Kreps, 'Radical Feminism 1'.

(86) Herbert Kohl, **Half the House** (Bantam, 1974). Personal survival, personal growth, and working for social change in small groups (how-to).

(87) Lawrence Kohlberg, 'Development of Moral Character and Moral Ideology', in Martin Hoffman and Lois Hoffman, eds., **Review of Child Development Research**, vol. I (Russell Sage, 1964), pp. 383-431. The stages of moral development.

(88) Leopold Kohr, **Development Without Aid: The Translucent Society** (Llandybie, Wales: Christopher Davies, 1973). Takes the argument for 'self-sufficient localism' to an unnecessary, and not altogether unconvincing extreme. Also **Breakdown of Nations**, 'Small Is Beautiful' applied to the nation-state.

(89) Joel Kovel, **White Racism: A Psychohistory** (Vintage, 1970). Racism is traceable to psychocultural factors (the Prison).

(90) Joel Kramer, **The Passionate Mind: A Manual for Living Creatively with One's Self** (Milbrae, Calif., 1974). Critique of the monolithic mind; instruction in how to develop the biolithic mind. Available for $3.95 from Celestial Arts, 231 Adrian Rd., Milbrae 94030.

(91) Bonnie Kreps:
(A) 'Compulsive Heterosexuals', **Homemaker's** (Mar. 1978), pp. 90-98.
(B) 'Mother-Daughter', **Miss Chatelaine** (May 1977), pp. 91, 94.
(C) 'Roll Over, Play Dead: Just How "Dead" Is the Women's Movement?', **Homemaker's** (Sept. 1977), pp. 100-12.
New Age feminism. (Canadian periodicals.)

(92) J. Krishnamurti, **The First and Last Freedom** (Harper & Row, 1954). Good introduction to the range and 'radical' nature of his thought.

(93) Swami Kriyananda, **Crises in Modern Thought, Vol. I: The Crisis of Reason** (Nevada City, Calif., 1972). Critique of monolithic institutions; reinterpretation of evolution; meditation as a source of New Age values; more. Available for $4.45 from Ananda Publications, 900 Alleghany Star Route, Nevada City 95959.

(94) Elisabeth Kubler-Ross:
(A) 'Death Does Not Exist', **CoEvolution Quarterly**, no. 14 (Summer 1977), pp. 100-07.
(B) 'Out of the Body: A New Age Interview with Elisabeth Kubler-Ross', by Peggy Taylor and Rick Ingrasci, **New Age Journal** (Nov. 1977), 39-43.
The spiritual state of consciousness — how it can help us love life (and accept bodily death).

(95) Joyce Ladner, ed., **The Death of White Sociology** (Vintage, 1973). Black sociologists indict liberal and — often enough — Marxist social science. See esp. essays by Forsythe and Scott.

(96) Ervin Laszlo, **A Strategy for the Future: The Systems Approach to World Order** (Braziller, 1974). Advocates a planetary guidance system (based largely on synergic power) rather than a nation-state writ large.

(97) Harvey Leibenstein, **Beyond Economic Man: A New Foundation for Microeconomics** (Harvard Univ. Press, 1976). Begins with 'decision-making individuals' (their motives) rather than with the firm.

(98) E. E. LeMasters, **Blue-Collar Aristocrats: Life-Styles at a Working-Class Tavern** (Univ. of Wisconsin Press, 1975). Deceptively simple study of blue-collar trade unionists by a sociologist who has no ideological axe to grind.

(99) George Leonard, **The Transformation: A Guide to the Inevitable Changes in Humankind** (Delta, 1972). Well-written overview of New

Age insights and understandings from a human potential perspective.

(100) George Leonard, **The Ultimate Athlete: Re-visioning Sports, Physical Education, and the Body** (Avon, 1975). Sports as a path to personal enlightenment and transformation.

(101) Lawrence LeShan, **Alternate Realities: The Search for the Full Human Being** (Ballantine, 1976). Four 'alternate realities' that are, essentially, my four 'states of consciousness'.

(102) Doris Lessing, **The Golden Notebook** (Ballantine, 1962). Novel; shows that a life based on love, friendship, creative activity and political awareness can be rich and rewarding.

(103) Julius Lester, **All Is Well** (Morrow, 1976). Autobiography — the black movement in the 1960's and Lester's own growth through Marxism to a spiritually-aware, 'third-level' politics.

(104) Robert Jay Lifton, **Home From the War; Vietnam Veterans: Neither Victims nor Executioners** (Simon and Schuster, 1973). New Age alternative to 'thought reform' (brainwashing): confrontation of self; reordering of personal and social priorities; renewal of self and society.

(105) John Lilly, **The Centre of the Cyclone: An Autobiography of Inner Space** (Bantam, 1971). 'This is the story of my personal search of some 56 years for meaning in life as we know it'. Includes conceptualization of system taught by Oscar Ichazo, Arica Institute.

(106) George Lodge, **The New American Ideology** (Knopf, 1975). Capitalism is not the enemy. North American values must be re-interpreted from a New Age perspective — not changed. New Age critique of Galbraith.

(107) Eugen Loebl, **Humanomics: How We Can Make the Economy Serve Us — Not Destroy Us** (Random House, 1976). Ideas for a non-liberal, non-Marxist economics. By one of Dubcek's top economists (once). . . .

(108) Amory Lovins, 'Energy Strategy: The Road Not Taken?', **Foreign Affairs**, vol. 55 (Oct. 1976), pp. 65-96. Excellent brief introduction to the 'soft' energy strategy (solar, plus voluntary simplicity); excellent brief critique of the 'hard'.

(109) Ferdinand Lundberg, **The Rich and the Super-Rich: A Study in the Power of Money Today** (Bantam, 1968). The kind of behaviour that makes people rich in North America today. The fact that most of us envy and even imitate this behaviour, in our smaller ways.

(110) Eleanor Maccoby and Carol Jacklin, **The Psychology of Sex Differences** (Stanford Univ. Press, 1975). Survey of studies of sex differences. Finds that women are not 'naturally' passive, irrational, etc.

(111) Michael Maccoby, 'Emotional Attitudes and Political Choices', **Politics and Society**, vol. 2 (Winter 1972), pp. 209-39. 'Quantitative' approach to Fromm's life- and death-orientations. Questionnaire, data, interpretation.

(112) Joan McIntyre, ed. (for Project Jonah), **Mind in the Waters: A Book to Celebrate the Consciousness of Whales and Dolphins** (Scribner's, 1974). Moving introduction to the subject.

(113) Abraham Maslow, **The Farther Reaches of Human Nature** (Viking, 1971). Posthumous essays. Pioneering concern with self-transcendence, spiritual development.

(114) Abraham Maslow, **Motivation and Personality**, 2nd ed. (Harper & Row, 1970). Systematic presentation of his stages of self-development.

(115) Henry Mayo, **Introduction to Marxist Theory** (Oxford Univ. Press, 1960). Devastating critique of Marxism from a liberal perspective that doesn't often get in the way. See also sections in (16), (128), (132).

(116) John Mbiti, **An Introduction to African Religion** (London: Heinemann,

1975). Trans-material worldview on the African continent.

(117) Margaret Mead, **World Enough: Rethinking the Future** (Little, Brown, 1975). Sense of social justice isn't enough; it's counter-productive to identify indiscriminately with the oppressed; we tend to see life as (literally) man-made; more. . . .

(118) Seymour Melman, **The Permanent War Economy: American Capitalism in Decline** (Touchstone, 1974). 'The new state-controlled economy, whose unique features include maximization of costs and (maximization) of government subsidies . . . '.

(119) Men face themselves:

(A) Jack Litewka, 'The Socialized Penis', **Liberation** (March 1974), pp. 16-25.

(B) Leonard Schein, 'An Introduction to Male Psychology, Consciousness, and Liberation', paper (Vancouver, B.C., 1975). Available free from The Non-Sexist Psychology Assn., 2211 Parker St., Vancouver V5L-2L8.

(C) John Stoltenberg on men's liberation: **WIN** Magazine (11 July 1974), pp. 12-14; **WIN** (20 March 1975), pp. 6-9.

(120) Mihajlo Mesarovic and Eduard Pestel, **Mankind at the Turning Point: The Second Report to the Club of Rome** (Signet, 1974). More sophisticated computer projections than earlier 'Limits to Growth' study — same general conclusions.

(121) Stanley Milgram, **Obedience to Authority: An Experimental View** (Harper & Row, 1974). Description and interpretation of the famous Yale experiments. Main conclusions: need for assumption of personal responsibility; need for non-authoritarian social settings.

(122) Jean Miller, **Toward a New Psychology of Women** (Beacon, 1976). Women's psychological strengths. Self-development, 'affiliation' and personal power as 'mutually reinforcing attributes'. Power redefined.

(123) Kate Millett, **Sexual Politics** (Avon, 1970). Chap. 2 still an outstanding treatment of patriarchal structures and attitudes. See **Flying** (1974), autobiographical, for her alternative(s) to patriarchal attitudes. . . .

(124) Marcia Millman and Rosabeth Kanter, eds., **Another Voice: Feminist Perspectives on Social Life and Social Science** (Anchor, 1975). Many alternatives to liberal and Marxist approaches. See esp. essays by Hochschild and McCormack.

(125) Ezra Mishan, **The Costs of Economic Growth** (Praeger, 1967). Growth generates 'bads' as well as goods. We need to start taking 'social costs' into account. . . .

(126) Edgar Mitchell (and John White, ed.), **Psychic Exploration: A Challenge for Science** (Capricorn, 1974). Covers the whole spectrum of psychic research and its political and philosophical implications.

(127) Stephen Monsma, **The Unraveling of America** (Downers Grove, Ill.: InterVarsity Press, 1974). Critique of all ism's 'from the point of view of "evangelical Christianity" '.

(128) Barrington Moore, Jr., **Reflections on the Causes of Human Misery and upon Certain Proposals to Eliminate Them** (Beacon, 1972). Critique — by a 'radical' — of much of what passes for radicalism today. Argues that future movements must seek to combine the achievements of 'liberalism' and 'revolutionary radicalism'.

(129) Arthur Morgan, **The Community of the Future and the Future of Community** (Yellow Springs, Ohio, 1957). On the need for community and for community self-sufficiency; on the characteristics of a 'good community'; on the 'spirit of community'. Available for $2.20 from Community Service, Inc., P.O. Box 243, Yellow Springs.

(130) David Morris and Karl Hess, **Neighbourhood Power: The New Localism** (Beacon, 1975). Need for: local self-reliance; New Age community organizing; 'intercommunalism'.

(131) Lewis Mumford, **The City in History: Its Origins, Its Transformations, and Its Prospects** (Harbinger, 1961). The over-large city has often been with us.

(132) Lewis Mumford, **The Condition of Man** (Harvest, 1944). Attempts to work out a kind of North American personalism that builds on Whitman's **Democratic Vistas**, Ruskin's economics, the concept of 'social synergy', etc.

(133) Lewis Mumford, **The Myth of the Machine**:
    Vol. I, Technics and Human Development (Harvest, 1967)
    Vol. II, The Pentagon of Power (Harvest, 1970)
    Origins and development of the Prison and its institutions. Prison-free attitudes; 'biotechnic' institutions. More. . . .

(134) Gunnar Myrdal, **The Challenge of World Poverty: A World Anti-Poverty Programme in Outline** (Vintage, 1970). Much more important than our aid to the IDC's 'are the needed social and economic reforms within these countries themselves'.

(135) Ruben Nelson, **The Illusions of Urban Man** (Ottawa, Ont.: Ministry of State for Urban Affairs, 1976). Our society and our lives 'are not convincing' — and our problems are deeper than we imagine. . . .

(136) Jack Nichols, **Men's Liberation: A New Definition of Masculinity** (Penguin, 1975). Good introduction — from a resoundingly New Age perspective.

(137) Mike Nickerson, **BAKAVI: Change the World I Want to Stay On** (Ottawa, Ont.: All About Us, 1977). Strategy for cultural evolution based on the principles of (a) ecology, (b) voluntary simplicity, (c) appropriate technology. Available for $3.95 from The Bakavi Foundation, P.O. Box 2011, Stn. D, Ottawa.

(138) Anais Nin, **The Diary of Anais Nin, Vol. Two, 1934-1939** (Harvest, 1967). Foray into the world of friendship, creative activity, self-development, political awareness.

(139) Will Noffke and Michael Toms (interviewers), 'Politics and Consciousness', four hour cassette tape (1975). Ron Dellums, Eugene McCarthy, Michael Rossman, Jerry Rubin, John Vasconcellos, others. Available for $15.50 from New Directions Tapes, 267 States St., San Francisco 94114.

(140) Michael Novak, **The Experience of Nothingness** (Colophon, 1970). Behind our frenetic activity: collapse of our values, fear of the nothingness we (think we) see.

(141) Robert Ornstein, **The Psychology of Consciousness** (Penguin, 1972). Left and right sides of the brain: differences; implications; need to integrate.

(142) Joseph Pearce, **The Magical Child: Rediscovering Nature's Plan for Our Children** (Dutton, 1975). New Age developmental psychology.

(143) Leroy Pelton, **The Psychology of Nonviolence** (Pergamon, 1974). Psycho-cultural arguments for non-violence — and for 'reconciliation' rather than 'victory'.

(144) Michael Phillips (with Salli Rasberry et. al.), **The Seven Laws of Money** (Random House, 1974). New Age business — principles, practices, practical benefits for self and society.

(145) Marge Piercy, **Small Changes** (Fawcett, 1974). Feminist novel. Personal awareness and growth ('small changes') as a source of political change . . . as a **precondition for** political change.

(146) Robert Pirsig, **Zen and the Art of Motorcycle Maintenance: An Inquiry into Values** (Bantam, 1974). Philosophical adventure story. Concept of 'Quality'; need for intuition, imagination; critique of dialectics.

(147) The Editors of **Rain** (Lane deMoll, ed.), **Rainbook: Resources for Appropriate Technology** (Schocken, 1977). Hundreds, no, thousands of publications and organizations, succinctly described and arranged by topic: A.T., place, economics, community building, communications, transportation, shelter, agriculture, health, energy. . . .

(148) Ram Dass (with Stephen Levine), **Grist for the Mill** (Santa Cruz, Calif., 1976). Book of spiritual teachings. 'Every experience you have is grist for the mill of awakening'. Available for $3.95 from Unity Press, 113 New St., Santa Cruz.

(149) Charles Reich, **The Sorcerer of Bolinas Reef** (Bantam, 1976). Autobiography by a man who, many lifetimes ago, wrote **The Greening of America**, and is now a gay activist and advocate of new age politics.

(150) Luke Rhinehart, **The Book of est** (Holt, Rinehart and Winston, 1976). Fictional account of Erhard Seminars Training — and of the 'monolithic mind' transformed.

(151) Adrienne Rich, **Of Woman Born: Motherhood as Experience and Institution** (Bantam, 1976). Patriarchy rooted in men's fear of women — not in economics. Concept of 'transformative power'. We must begin to 'think through the body'. More. . . .

(152) Tom Robbins, **Even Cowgirls Get the Blues** (Bantam, 1976). New Age novel. Politics; spirituality; love of life. Also **Another Roadside Attraction** (1971).

(153) Adam Roberts, **Nations in Arms: The Theory and Practice of Territorial Defence** (London: Chatto & Windus, 1976). One New Age alternative to nuclear **and** nonviolent defence.

(154) Jane Roberts, **The Nature of Personal Reality: A Seth Book** (Prentice-Hall, 1974). 'You choose your own experiences' (including your sex, parents, etc.) — a starting point for viewing reality.

(155) Carl Rogers, **On Becoming a Person: A Therapist's View of Psycho-Therapy** (Houghton Mifflin, 1961). 'From fixity to changingness, from rigid structure to flow'.

(156) Michael Rossman, **On Learning and Social Change** (Vintage, 1972). Critique of industrial society by a radical Taoist.

(157) Theodore Roszak, **Unfinished Animal: The Aquarian Frontier and the Evolution of Consciousness** (Colophon, 1975). Good broad overview of the spiritual and human potential movements. Their social and political relevance. The dangers ahead.

(158) Theodore Roszak, **Where the Wasteland Ends: Politics and Transcendence in Postindustrial Society** (Anchor, 1972). Critique of urban-industrial society — and urban-industrial consciousness — from a neo-personalist perspective.

(159) Jerry Rubin, **Growing (Up) at Thirty-seven** (Warner, 1976). Why he's no longer a 1960's radical. His experiences in the consciousness-and-growth movement. 'Revolution as an evolutionary process'.

(160) John Ruskin, **'Unto This Last': Four Essays on the First Principles of Political Economy** (London: Smith, Elder and Co., 1862). 'There is no wealth but life', etc. Gandhi's favourite economist.

(161) Mark Satin, **Big Plans**, published as **Confessions of a Young Exile** (Toronto: Gage, 1976). Desperately honest novel about 'the 1960's'.

(162) E. F. Schumacher:
  (A) 'Changing Knowledge to Wisdom: An Interview with E. F. Schumacher', by Sherman Goldman and Bill Tara, **East West Jour-**

nal (Nov. 1976), pp. 14-18.
- (B) 'On Inflation', **Rain** (Nov. 1975), pp. 14-15.
- (C) 'Technology and Political Change', **Rain** (Dec. 1976 & Jan. 1977), both pp. 8-10.

Beyond capitalist and socialist platitudes, priorities.

(163) E. F. Schumacher, **Small Is Beautiful: A Study of Economics as if People Mattered** (Perennial, 1973). All about appropriate technology. Call for a 'Buddhist economics' appropriate to a society of A.T. plus voluntary simplicity. Call for a return to the 'traditional wisdom'.

(164) Franz Schurmann, 'Arcana of Empire', Part I of **The Logic of World Power** (Pantheon, 1974). Government has become more powerful than business, 'ideology' more powerful than corporate-bureaucratic 'interests'.

(165) Bob Schwartz (interviewed by Sam Keen), 'American Business Needs You! An Interview with Bob Schwartz', **New Age Journal** (Mar. 1976), pp. 16-25. The New Age entrepreneur. Schwartz is director of The School for Entrepreneurs (III-2 below).

(166) Gene Sharp, **The Politics of Nonviolent Action** (Porter Sargent, 1973). 1000-page study of nonviolent action: history, theory, practice. Nonviolence as the most **effective** military strategy.

(167) William Shurtleff and Akiko Aoyagi, **The Book of Tofu: Food for Mankind** (Kanagawa-Ken, Japan: Autumn Press, 1975). Every genuine political movement has a cookbook; this one is ours.

(168) The Simple Living Collective — American Friends Service Committee, **Taking Charge: Achieving Personal and Political Change Through Simple Living** (Bantam, 1977). Some useful essays.

(169) June Singer, **Androgyny: Toward a New Theory of Sexuality** (Anchor, 1976). 'Androgyny as (a) guiding principle of the new age'.

(170) Philip Slater, **Earthwalk** (Anchor, 1974). Our egocentricity; our fear of community; our 'mechanical-mindedness'.

(171) Huston Smith, **Forgotten Truth: The Primordial Tradition** (Colophon, 1976). The trans-material worldview. . . .

(172) Gary Snyder, **Turtle Island** (New Directions, 1974). New Age poetry. See also Peter Chowka (interviewer), 'The Original Mind of Gary Snyder', **East West Journal** (June & July 1977).

(173) Paolo Soleri, **The Bridge Between Matter and Spirit Is Matter Becoming Spirit: The Arcology of Paolo Soleri** (Anchor, 1973). Evolutionary theory behind Soleri's 'cities in the image of people'.

(174) Alexander Solzhenitsyn and Igor Shafarevich, eds., **From Under the Rubble** (Bantam, 1975). Political statement of the spiritual wing of the Soviet dissident movement.

(175) David Spangler:
- (A) 'Economics as a Way of the Spirit', cassette tape (1976). Available for $6.75 from Findhorn Foundation (III below).
- (B) 'From Strategy to Wholeness . . . The Meaning of Community', **Yoga Journal** (Mar.-Ap. 1977), pp. 4-5.
- (C) 'Identity in Action: The Power of Knowing Who You Are', **New Age Journal** (Feb. 1975), pp. 36-39.

The politics of the spirit.

(176) David Spangler, **Revelation: The Birth of a New Age**, 2nd ed. (San Francisco, 1976). New Age spirituality — Christian mystical tradition. Basic text at Findhorn. Available for $4.95 from The Rainbow Bridge, 3548 22nd St., San Francisco 94114.

(177) L. S. Stavrianos, **The Promise of the Coming Dark Age** (W.H. Freeman, 1976). Kind of a left wing version of **New Age Politics**. Something's

missing. And see Walter Laqueur's critique in **Commentary**, vol. 62 (Feb. 1977), pp. 43-45.

(178) Claude Steiner, **Scripts People Live** (Bantam, 1974). Transactional analysis . . . explained and expanded. The stroke economy.

(179) Grace Stuart, **Narcissus: A Psychological Study of Self-Love** (Macmillan, 1955). Critique of egocentricity (reflects not self-love but self-hate).

(180) Merlin Stone, **When God Was a Woman** (Dial, 1976). On the matriarchies, and on matriarchal attitudes.

(181) Patricia Sun, World Symposium on Humanity cassette tapes (1976). 'I . . . (create) an opportunity for people to experience who they are, really to experience their own power . . . '. Available for $5 each from The Humanity Foundation, 1962 W. 4th Ave., Vancouver, B.C.

(182) Charles Tart, 'Science, States of Consciousness, and Spiritual Experiences: The Need for State-Specific Sciences', in ibid., ed., **Transpersonal Psychologies** (Colophon, 1975), pp. 9-58. Our first 'multiple-vision' science.

(183) Charles Tart, **States of Consciousness** (Dutton, 1975). Theoretical basis for trans-material worldview.

(184) Robert Thamm, 'Toward a Family of the Future', Part One of ibid., **Beyond Marriage and the Nuclear Family** (Canfield, 1975). Summarizes communitarian critique of monogamy, marriage, the nuclear family. Biolithic alternatives proposed.

(185) Frederick Thayer, **An End to Hierarchy! An End to Competition!: Organizing the Politics and Economics of Survival** (New Viewpoints, 1973). Hierarchy and competition — not 'capitalism', etc. — the problem. Non-hierarchical, synergic, face-to-face groups the solution.

(186) Robert Theobald, **Beyond Despair: Directions for America's Third Century** (New Republic, 1976). Need for value change, networking, 'win-win' model, etc. Important critique of job economy.

(187) Robert Theobald, **Habit and Habitat** (Prentice-Hall, 1972). New Age political economy. 'Sapiential authority'; 'systemic thinking'; more. See also **Teg's 1994** (1972), 'communications-era' novel by Theobald and Jeanne Scott.

(188) William Irwin Thompson, **Evil and World Order** (Colophon, 1976). Technology a culture not a tool; need to confront self; etc.

(189) William Irwin Thompson, **Passages About Earth: An Exploration of the New Planetary Culture** (Perennial, 1974). The emerging new worldview. Portraits of some New Age thinkers, activists. See also **At the Edge of History** (1971).

(190) Jan Tinbergen, coord., **Reshaping the International Order: A Report to the Club of Rome** (Dutton, 1976). Devastating factual summary of planetary inequities; 'post-ideological' solutions proposed.

(191) Alvin Toffler, **The Eco-Spasm Report** (Bantam, 1975). Need for 'service economy'; need for 'anticipatory democracy'.

(192) Chogyam Trungpa, **Cutting Through Spiritual Materialism** (Shambhala, 1973). Tibetan Buddhist approach to personal and spiritual growth.

(193) Peter van Dresser, **Development on a Human Scale: Potentials for Ecologically Guided Growth in Northern New Mexico** (Praeger, 1973). Good introduction to 'watershed politics' (regionalization).

(194) Jaroslav Vanek, **The Participatory Economy: An Evolutionary Hypothesis and a Strategy for Development** (Cornell Univ. Press, 1971). Workers' self-management as the basis for a 'new major economic system'.

(195) Mitch Walker:
- (A) 'Visionary Love: The Magickal Gay Spirit-Power', **Gay Sunshine**, no. 31 (Winter 1977), pp. 18-22.
- (B) 'Becoming Gay Shamanism: More Visionary Love', paper (San Francisco, 1977).

Introduction to gay men's spirituality. Argues gay consciousness has an important contribution to make to the New Age, and vice-versa. Both essays together, $2.40 plus postage from Mitch Walker care of **Gay Sunshine** (II below).

(196) Barbara Ward, **The Home of Man** (Norton, 1976). Critique of monolithic housing policy; need for human-scale community. Need for ecology ethic, 'new economic order', etc. Many practical suggestions.

(197) Frank Waters (with Oswald White Bear Fredericks), **Book of the Hopi** (Ballantine, 1963). Spiritual and ecological consciousness. Hopi as practitioners of New Age ethics and values.

(198) Alan Watts, **Beyond Theology** (Vintage, 1964). What the Judeo-Christian tradition can learn from Eastern philosophy and from the 'ecological view of (people)'.

(199) Walter Weisskopf, **The Psychology of Economics** (Univ. of Chicago Press, 1955). Psycho-cultural history of economic theory.

(200) H. B. Wilson, **Democracy and the Work Place** (Montreal: Black Rose, 1974). Workers' self-management — an evolutionary perspective.

II. 25 New Age Periodicals

This isn't meant to be a 'complete' list (because I've listed **Natural Life** doesn't necessarily mean that I think it's better than **Harrowsmith**, etc.), but it is meant to be representative. I find it interesting that, of the 31 periodicals that are actually listed here, 10 of them have their editorial offices in California (five in New England, five in New York-Pennsylvania, four in the Pacific Northwest); 18 of them have female editors or co-editors; and only two of them are printed on glossy paper.

(1) **Akwesasne Notes** (five times a year; Mohawk Nation via Rooseveltown, N.Y. 13683; subs by donation or request; single issues 50 cents);
Many Smokes (quarterly; Bear Tribe Medicine Society, P.O. Box 9167, Spokane, Wash. 99209; $2 a year, $3.50 in Canada; single issues 50 cents).
Akwesasne covers native North American events from a number of different perspectives — from the conventionally 'radical' to the New Age as I've described it in this book. Areas of special interest include: political movements and spirituality (and their interconnections), ecology, alternative technology, self-sufficiency. **Many Smokes** is mimeographed, more personal. Devotes more space to spiritual subjects and does not lack a spiritual politics.

(2) **Alternative Sources of Energy** (bi-monthly; Route 2 Box 90-A, Milaca, Minn. 56353; $10 a year, $12 in Canada; single issues $1.75).
'For people concerned with the development of alternative (mostly energy) technologies for a decentralized society. . . . The purpose of A.S.E. is to provide a communications network . . . ; to foster mutual aid in the development of skills: and to encourage experiments in individual and cooperative management of goods and services'.

(3) **Brain-Mind Bulletin** (bi-weekly; P.O. Box 42211, Los Angeles 90042; $15 a year; back issues 75 cents, minimum order two).
Covers research discoveries, new theories and practical applications (all in

field of brain-mind research); news of conferences and workshops; books and journals; important trends. Very clearly and interestingly written.

(4) **Co-Evolution Quarterly** (P.O. Box 428, Sausalito, Calif. 94965; $8 a year, single issues $2.50).

The closest thing the New Age has to an intellectual journal. Long historical articles — and Robert Crumb cartoons; excellent balanced features on, e.g., voluntary simplicity and watershed politics — but then again, one issue featured a long debate, mostly pro, on space colonies, and another a virtuoso performance by Herman Kahn. Everyone likes and dislikes many things in C-E Q, that's one reason why it's an essential New Age magazine.

(5) **Communities** (bi-monthly; P.O. Box 426, Louisa, Va. 23093; $6 a year, $7.50 in Canada; single issues $1.25).

'Journal of Cooperative Living'. Especially for people involved in communal living and-or cooperative ventures of all sorts. Most issues have a major theme (government, sex, planning, spirituality); regular features include Reach ('places, events and people to connect with') and Grapevine ('new projects beginning, notes from all over').

(6) **East West Journal** (monthly; P.O. Box 305, Dover, N.J. 07801; editorial offices near Boston; $10 a year, $12 in Canada; single issues $1).

'Common Sense for Modern Times'. One of the magazines on North American spiritual community and its social, cultural, political, etc. ramifications. Areas of special interest include organic and macrobiotic alternatives.

(7) **(Rodale's) Environment Action Bulletin** (bi-weekly; 33 E. Minor St., Emmaus, Pa. 18049; $6 a year);

Organic Gardening and Farming (monthly; same address; $7.85 a year, $8.85 in Canada; single issues 75 cents).

E.A.B. carries news briefs and articles on topics of concern to environmentalists and small farmers. Very clearly and concisely written. O.G.F. is full of practical information, news and reviews, tips, resources.

(8) **The Feminist Art Journal** (quarterly; 41 Montgomery Place, Brooklyn, N.Y. 11215; $7 a year, single copies $2).

Gives a good picture of the new feminist sensibility. Focus is on (women's) painting and sculpture with occasional additional articles on (women's) films, music, literature, drama, etc.

(9) **Gay Sunshine** (several times a year; P.O. Box 40397, San Francisco 94140; $10 for 12 issues, $15 in Canada; single issues $1).

Gives a good picture of the new gay men's sensibility. Literature and poetry; politics and social theory; book reviews and (excellent long) interviews. Can help non-gay men be more aware of their experience as men and as human beings.

(10) **Green Revolution** (monthly; P.O. Box 3233, York, Pa. 17402; $8 a year, $9.50 in Canada; single issues $1).

'A Voice for Decentralization'. Grounded in the decentralist, humanistic philosophy of Ralph Borsodi. Areas of special interest include land trusts, personal relations and the cooperative movement.

(11) **Growing Without Schooling** (occasional; 308 Boylston St., Boston, Mass. 02116; $10 for six issues).

Editor John Holt writes (in issue no. 1), 'This . . . newsletter (is) about ways in which people, young or old, can learn and do things, acquire skills, and find interesting and useful work, without having to go through the process of schooling. . . . Much of what is in it, we hope, will come from its readers . . . '.

(12) **Humanizing City Life** (bi-monthly; P.O. Box 303, Worthington, Ohio 43085; $8.50 a year, single copies $2).

Good general articles on people and groups working (in) (for) (with) community, self-reliance, health, economics, solar energy, children, etc. New sections feature information on various kinds of resources, a place for information exchange, and a section about tools for simple living.

(13) **Journal of Transpersonal Psychology** (twice yearly; P.O. Box 4437, Stanford, Calif. 94305; $10 a year, $7.50 for students).

Concerned with self-actualization, self-transcendence, spiritual paths, the theories and practice of meditation, 'individual and species-wide synergy', etc. At least 11 authors listed in sect. I have published in the **Journal**.

(14) **Manas** (weekly; P.O. Box 32112, El Sereno Stn., Los Angeles 90032; $10 a year, $7.50 if poor; sample copies free).

Every genuine political movement has a journal of philosophy and practical psychology; this one is ours. It is an excellent review of New Age literature and ideas in many fields, and it is written 'in as direct and simple a manner as its editors and contributors can write'.

(15) **The Mother Earth News** (bi-monthly: P.O. Box 70, Hendersonville, N.C. 28739; $10 a year, single copies $2);

Natural Life (monthly; P.O. Box 640, Jarvis, Ont. N0A-1J0; $8 a year, $6 in Canada; single issues $1.50).

Mother's masthead: 'More than a magazine . . . a way of life'. Focus is on small scale farming and rural living, emphasis is always and everywhere on the practical, the concrete. Some of my favourite regular features: 'The Plowboy Interview' (long and searching) and 'Positions and Situations' which is 'designed to help would-be back-to-the-landers get in touch with folks already out there'. **Natural Life** is kind of like **Mother** was when it first started, un-'professional' and unassuming.

(16) **New Age Journal** (monthly; P.O. Box 4921, Manchester, N.H. 03105; editorial offices near Boston; $9 a year, single issues $1.50).

Focus is on the spiritual, human potential, environmental and nonviolent-action movements — and on the effect(s) that these movements are having on North American life. Written in a bright and accessible style — more than any magazine I know, gives me the sense that the New Age is here now. Issues tend to have a focus (e.g., body-mind; love and relationships; death; birth; play!; solar energy) plus many regular features.

(17) **New Directions** (monthly; 1962 W. 4th Ave., Vancouver, B.C.; $10 a year, single issues $1).

Excellent coverage of spiritual and spiritually-oriented people and ideas and events. Published by the organizers of the World Symposium on Humanity 1976 and 1979. . . .

(18) **Planet-Drum** (occasional 'bundles' and newsletters; P.O. Box 31251, San Francisco 94131; $10 a year brings all available back issues; 'please send whatever you can' for single issues).

Localization and regionalization (watershed politics). The bundles (of articles) are physically beautiful — designed to make you feel like an individual. Recent bundles have focussed on indigenous cultures. The newsletters are meant to 'introduce correspondents to each other, share mail and track on signals of local-planet transformation'.

(19) **Plexus** (monthly; 2600 Dwight Way, Rm. 209, Berkeley, Calif. 94704; $5 a year, $7 in Canada; single issues 45 cents);

Sojourner (monthly; 143 Albany St., Cambridge, Mass. 02139; $4 a year, single issues 35 cents).

To the best of my knowledge, there are no specifically New Age feminist newspapers. But there are a number of feminist papers that bring many different perspectives to bear on issues, and among them are **Plexus** ('Bay Area Women's Newspaper') and **Sojourner** ('A New England Women's Journal of News, Opinions, and the Arts'). Both are regionally oriented, both cover issues of national importance and both carry good book reviews.

(20) **Rain** (monthly; 2270 N.W. Irving, Portland, Ore. 97210; $10 a year, $5 if 'living lightly' — income under $5,000; single issues $1);

Tranet (quarterly; P.O. Box 567, Rangeley, Maine 04970; $15 a year).

Rain — 'Journal of Appropriate Technology'. A couple of feature articles in each issue, some rather technical, others that explore the ecological and philosophical implications of A.T. Current information on projects, people, groups, events. Many brief book and booklet reviews. **Tranet** describes itself as 'a newsletter-directory **of**, **by** and **for** those . . . who are actively developing appropriate-alternative technologies'. Features an ongoing 'directory of A.T. centres' in special fields of A.T. and a review of A.T. news and publications.

(21) **Renaissance Universal Journal** (quarterly; 2239 E. Colfax Ave., Denver, Colo. 80206; $6 a year, $7 in Canada).

'Dedicated to fostering a renaissance of the human spirit in every aspect of our planetary culture'. Reprints articles and speeches and excerpts from books by (usually) well-known New Age thinkers; some original material as well.

(22) **Seriatim** (quarterly; 122 Carmel, El Cerrito, Calif. 94530; $9 a year in 'Ecotopia' — Wash., Ore., northern Calif. — $12 elsewhere; sample copies $2.50).

A journal about 'Ecotopia', where 'an environmentally-attuned, stable-state society is emerging. **Seriatim** aims to document and foster the growth of that society'. Regular sections now include: shelters, transport, forestry, A.T.

(23) **Simple Living** (several times a year; 514 Bryant St., Palo Alto, Calif. 94302; subscriptions $3 or whatever you can afford, $5 or whatever in Canada; subscriptions last for an unspecified time period).

Well-written, well-thought-out newsletter that focusses on different aspects of simple living (recent issues: barter, bicycle transport, human scale, roots, needs). Articles tend to combine personal experience, intellectual understanding.

(24) **WomanSpirit** (quarterly; P.O. Box 263, Wolf Creek, Ore. 97497; $6 a year, $7 in Canada; single issues $2).

Feminist spirituality — pagan, not Eastern. One of the editors writes, 'For us, (feminist spirituality) is a **radical** search for NEW ways to live together on this planet'.

(25) **Yoga Journal** (bi-monthly; 2054 University Ave., Berkeley, Calif. 94704; $7.50 a year, $9.50 in Canada; single issues $1.50).

Focus goes beyond 'yoga practices' narrowly defined to include: holistic health, nutrition, psychic phenomena, spiritual communities; the meeting of east and west; and the social and political implications of same.

III. 25 New Age Groups

Again, this isn't meant to be a 'complete' list but I think it's fairly representative. It is **not** meant to suggest that Erhard Seminars Training is 'better' than Arica (which I haven't listed), Greenpeace more 'effective' than the Jonah Project, and so on . . . and on and on. None of the groups asked to be listed here — none of them were even consulted (same with the periodicals above). If you write the smaller ones for more information, you should enclose a dollar if you can (they're always short of funds).

(1) **Amnesty International** (U.S.national section, 2112 Broadway, New York 10023; Canadian section, 2101 Algonquin Ave., Ottawa, Ont. K2A-1T1).

International League for Human Rights (777 United Nations Plaza, Ste. 6-F, New York 10017).

AI is a worldwide movement working on behalf of Prisoners of Conscience; see Chap. 21, sect. I-3. ILHR helped organize the appeal to the Government of Vietnam to release prisoners held solely for political or religious beliefs; see Chap. 23, sect. III-C. AI is a mass membership organization with 'adoption groups' in dozens of North American cities; ILHR works more exclusively 'from within'. Each has been careful to document abuses of human rights on both the left and right.

(2) **Briarpatch Network** (330 Ellis St., San Francisco 94102)

School for Entrepreneurs (Tarrytown House, East Sunnyside Lane, Tarrytown, N.Y. 10591)

The Briarpatch is a network of hundreds of New Age businesspeople around the Bay Area; the School for Entrepreneurs offers an intensive two-weekend course for the New Age entrepreneur. See Chap. 17, sect. III. The **Briarpatch Review** is an excellent quarterly journal of 'right livelihood' business practices and philosophy ($5 a year, $7 in Canada, single issues $1.25).

(3) **Centre for Community Economic Development** (639 Massachusetts Ave., Ste. 316, Cambridge, Mass. 02139).

An independent research and policy development group working to promote the concept of community-based economic development. Provides community groups with general information on the concept, advice on how to get started, and help in planning for economic development. Publishes a bimonthly newsletter ($5 a year, 'free to community groups').

(4) **Centre for Science in the Public Interest** (1757 S St., N.W., Washington, D.C. 20009).

Collects and disseminates information and initiates action on energy and the environment, health and nutrition. Some long-term goals: local energy self-sufficiency (solar energy), simple living. Founded in 1971, staff already includes 20 full-time employees and dozens of volunteers and 'student interns'. Publishes three regular newsletters.

(5) **Clamshell Alliance** (62 Congress Ave., Portsmouth, N.H. 03801).

Loose coalition of anti-nuclear organizations from the New England area; see Chap. 21, sect. IV. At least 14 other Alliances have sprung up in its wake, including the Potomac Alliance, in D.C.; the Great Plains Alliance, in the Midwest; and the Abalone Alliance, in California. Publishes **Clamshell Alliance News** (bi-monthly; 'please send a few dollars to cover printing costs') — covers anti-nuclear news and actions across North America.

(6) **Erhard Seminars Training** (765 California St., San Francisco 94108);

Actualizations (3632 Sacramento St., San Francisco 94118).

'Est' — a 60-hour experience whose purpose 'is to transform your ability to experience living so that . . . the need to prove or display well-being is replaced by the experience of well-being'; see Chap. 20, sect. II-4. Actualizations — a 3½ day experience that 'is really a lesson in relationship. . . . We get an education to be competent at all things in life except how to relate. . . . The world would work if everybody who was with someone at this moment were relating to one another passionately, freely, with a sense of having touched each other's essence . . . '.

(7) **Esalen Institute** (Big Sur, Calif. 93920);

Cold Mountain Institute (Granville Island, B.C. V6H-3M5).

Esalen conducts workshops in personal and spiritual growth; body awareness; gestalt; 'conscious childbirth'; psychosynthesis; massage; self-healing; more. . . . Cold Mountain is a Canadian version of same — 'an educational centre dedicated to the learning and development of the whole person in the context of the society in which (he or she) lives'.

(8) **Farallones Institute** (15290 Coleman Valley Rd., Occidental, Calif. 95465).

A small independent association of scientists, designers and technicians who are carrying out research and education in appropriate technology (especially in the areas of food, shelter and energy).

(9) **Findhorn Community** (The Park, Forres IV36-OTZ, Scotland).

The Findhorn community (pop. 265) is 'pioneering a new consciousness through planetary service. . . . We see our basic purpose as the bringing into existence "a new heaven and a new earth", where spiritual ideals are manifested in daily life. . . . With the establishment of Cluny Hill College we have expanded into a new age centre of education and culture with an ongoing programme of workshops and conferences.

'Findhorn is primarily a working community. The exploration of spiritual principles is directly related to work programmes. All who come add their time and energy to community tasks that need to be done'.

Publishes an excellent occasional magazine, **Onearth** ($5 an issue).

(10) **Friends of the Earth** (124 Spear St., San Francisco 94105).

An environmental-action group. Publishes conservation literature; lobbies substantially in Congress and state capitals; has branches and staff reps in 60 cities and areas across the U.S. (see Chap. 21, sect. I-3). Publishes an excellent newspaper, **Not Man Apart** (semi-monthly; $10 a year). Five of the authors listed in sect. I, above, are on the FOE Board of Directors or Advisory Council.

(11) **Greenpeace Foundation** (2108 W. 4th Ave., Vancouver, B.C. V6J-1M5).

Dedicated to direct action solutions to such problems as nuclear weapons testing, proliferation of nuclear reactors and the destruction of whales and seals (see Chap. 21, sect. IV). 'Our ultimate goal . . . is to help bring about that basic change in thinking known as "planetary consciousness" '.

(12) **Institute for Humanistic and Transpersonal Education** (P.O. Box 575, Amherst, Mass. 01002).

Offers an off-campus MA degree in 'humanistic-transpersonal education' (see Chap. 14, sect. III); conducts professional training workshops; consults with school systems. 'Functions as a clearinghouse for the dissemination of ideas, people, consultants, books, conferences, projects and developments in the field of consciousness and education' — is developing a 'Transpersonal Education Network'. Publishes **Wholistic Education: The Journal of Humanistic and Transpersonal Education** ($12 a year, $8 for students).

(13) **Institute for Liberty and Community** (Concord, Vt. 05824).

A nonprofit research and educational group with principal interests in: preservation of individual liberty; restoration of small-scale community; 'changing distributions of wealth, income, and land ownership'; 'restoring and strengthening genuine private property ownership'. Six of the authors listed in sect. I, above, are on the ILC advisory council.

(14) **Institute for Local Self-Reliance** (1717 18th St., N.W., Washington, D.C. 20009).

Advocates self-reliant humanly-scaled cooperative communities. Provides technical assistance to communities and community groups in its areas of expertise: waste recycling, community-controlled banking and credit, solar technologies, rooftop hydroponics, self-help housing, etc. Publishes **Self-Reliance** (bi-monthly; $6 a year, $7.50 in Canada; sample copy 50 cents).

(15) **Lorian Associates** (229 Mead's Mtn. Rd., Woodstock, N.Y. 12498; in Canada, Apt. 808, 88 Bernard Ave., Toronto, Ont. M5R-1R7).

'A non-profit, educational corporation exploring the related phenomena of human identity, its growth, its potentials and its divinity; synergy and co-creativity; spiritual transformation; communication and community; new insights into reality; new perspectives on humanity's role in the universe; new

consciousness; societal change — in short, Lorian explores and works to foster the emergence of an understanding of planetary culture and the birth of a
New Age'. David Spangler involved. Publishes an occasional newsletter.

(16) **Movement for a New Society** (care of Network Service Collective, 4722
Baltimore Ave., Philadelphia, Pa. 19143; for New England and Canada,
R.F.D. 2, St. Johnsbury, Vt. 05819).

'Widespread network of small groups working nonviolently for fundamental social change'. Also working to develop an original overall analysis of society, vision of the future and strategy for change. Most MNS analyses hold
'capitalism' partly but not entirely to blame for our troubles; some MNS visions avoid words like 'socialism' feeling we need something more (or different) than that. Some MNS people feel quite close to the ideas in this book;
others, much less so. MNS publishes a seasonal newsletter, **dandelion** ($2.50 a
year); see also Gowan et. al. (sect. I above), & see Chap. 21, sect. I (passim).

(17) **Naropa Institute** (1111 Pearl St., Boulder, Colo. 80302).

'Inspired by a buddhist approach to education — one that combines meditation with intellectual and artistic study'. Classes combine eastern and western traditions of dance, poetry, theatre, visual arts, psychology, philosophy,
science. Most classes summer only; some degree programmes available.
1977 faculty included Capra, Ginsberg, Hampden-Turner, Trungpa (founder
and President); 1977 enrollment, 1500.

(18) **National Centre for Appropriate Technology** (P.O. Box 3838, Butte,
Mont. 59701).

Goals: to develop A.T. solutions to energy and energy-related problems experienced by low-income communities; to expand A.T. solutions 'which address all aspects of the ecosystem and the political economy'; to promote social, economic and technical self-reliance and self-determination on the part
of low-income communities; to generate an awareness of alternatives
through A.T. Hopes to establish regional centres 'which undertake work
tailored to the unique characteristics of each biological region'. Funded by
the U.S. Community Services Admin. Publishes two quarterly newsletters.

(19) **New Alchemy Institute** (P.O. Box 432, Woods Hole, Mass. 02543; also
based in P.E.I., Canada).

'A small, international organization dedicated to research and education on
behalf of humanity and the planet. . . . Our major task is the development of
ecologically derived forms of energy, agriculture, aquaculture, housing and
landscapes that will encourage a repopulation and revitalization of the
countryside'. Publishes an annual **Journal**.

(20) **New Age Feminism** (care of Anne Ironside, Ste. 1, 1144 Robson St.,
Vancouver, B.C.).

'An exploration of feminism and its relationship to New Age consciousness'.
Seminars and discussion groups.

(21) **Planetary Citizens** (777 United Nations Plaza, New York 10017).

Planetary Citizens people share a 'global view' (or 'post-ideological politics') that goes 'beyond social, religious and political beliefs' and looks awfully much like what I've been calling New Age politics. Planetary Citizens tries
to get people to understand that we're all citizens, 'not only of our countries,
but also of planet earth'; and it sponsors workshops, gatherings, etc. that can
help us 'improve the quality of life' — material, emotional, psychological and
spiritual life. For some specific programmes, see Chap. 21, sect. I (passim).
Publishes a slim but valuable newsletter, **One Family** (quarterly; $5 a year).
Eleven of the authors listed in sect. I, above, are on the Board of Directors or
Advisory Council.

(22) **Sierra Club** (530 Bush St., San Francisco 94108).

Members work in hundreds of Club committees on urgent campaigns to save threatened areas, wildlife and resources; and to make the environment of the cities 'more fit' for people. 'A local and worldwide outing programme helps you see what needs to be conserved and lets you explore, enjoy, and learn how to properly use what has been conserved . . . '. Publishes **Sierra Club Bulletin** (monthly; $8 a year, single copies $1).

(23) **Synergic Power Centre** (1190 Miller Ave., Berkeley, Calif. 94708).

Dedicated to empowering individuals and groups with Synergic Power — 'power to generate creative cooperation', as distinct from power to destroy enemies (see Chap. 15, sect. II). The Centre researches how it is that some people 'gain the cooperation of others' and it trains people in the use(s) of Synergic Power. Publications include James and Marguerite Craig, **Synergic Power** (sect. I above), and Marge Craig et. al., **Power from Within: A Workbook to Guide Women in Discovering their Power and Expressing it in Creative, Caring Ways** ($3).

(24) **Zen Centre** (300 Page St., San Francisco 94102).

Buddhist awareness 'includes knowing our mind, feelings, emotions, and conditions of our physical existence', and Zen Centre practice is designed to foster that awareness in us. Many regular activities (and 'everyone is invited to participate'); basic instruction in zazen every Saturday at no charge; lecture every Saturday at 10 a.m. Publishes a fine magazine, **Wind Bell** (two or three times a year; $4 for three issues).

(25) **Zero Population Growth** (1346 Connecticut Ave., N.W., Washington, D.C. 20036).

A mass membership organization — many local chapters. Would stabilize, then gradually reduce, U.S. population by voluntary means (by, e.g., 'promoting expanded role opportunities for women'). Advocates 'national improvement rather than national growth'. Lobbying, publicizing, educating, organizing, etc. Four authors listed in sect. I, above, are on the Board of Sponsors.

This book is about the new politics that is arising out of the ideas of the feminist, men's liberation, spiritual, human-potential, environmental, appropriate-technology, simple-living, and nonviolent-action movements of the 1970's (and out of the ideas of social scientists and others who share these concerns)

MARK SATIN has written two other books: a novel, **Big Plans**, published as **Confessions of a Young Exile** (Toronto: Gage, 1976) and the **Manual for Draft-Age Immigrants to Canada** (Toronto: Anansi, 1968), which sold 100,000 copies in eight editions. He has been a good liberal (Mississippi, VISTA), a good Marxist (president of an SDS chapter, director of the Toronto Anti-Draft Programme), and a good student (Sidney Smith fellow, University of Toronto graduate school). Currently he is involved with many of the movements whose ideas he has written about here — and he is travelling around North America giving talks and workshops on New Age politics.